css *Alabama*

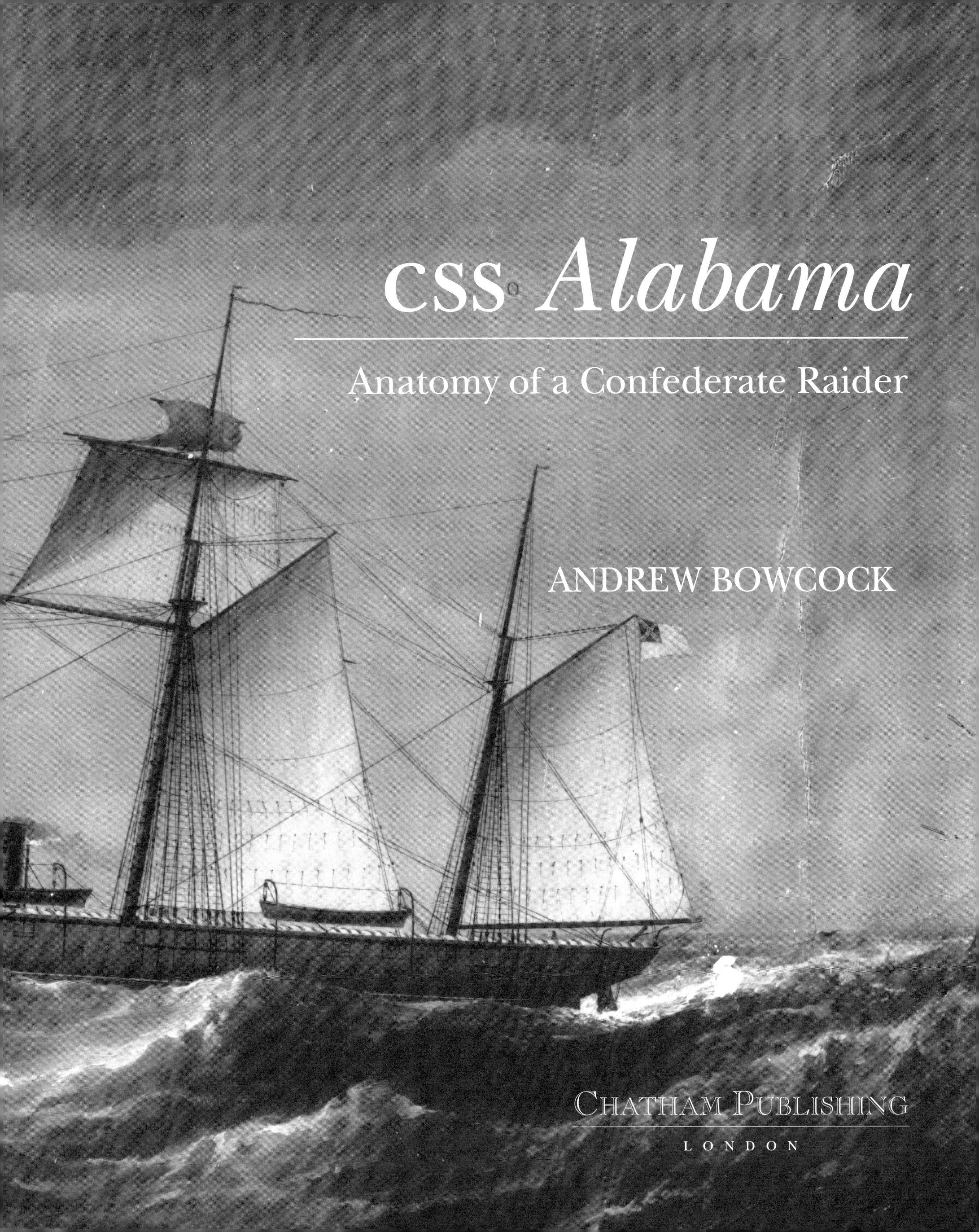

css *Alabama*

Anatomy of a Confederate Raider

ANDREW BOWCOCK

CHATHAM PUBLISHING

LONDON

Frontispiece: CSS *Alabama* off Cape Town, by Samuel Walters. (*Courtesy Williamson Art Gallery and Museum, Birkenhead, Wirral*)

Copyright © Andrew Bowcock 2002

First published in Great Britain in 2002
by Chatham Publishing,
99 High Street, Rochester, Kent ME1 1LX

Distributed by Gerald Duckworth & Co Ltd,
61 Frith Street, London W1D 3JL

British Library Cataloguing in Publication Data
A catalogue record for this book is available from the British Library

ISBN 1 86176 189 9

All rights reserved. No part of this publication may be reproduced or transmitted in any form or by any means, electronic or mechanical, including photocopying, recording, or any information storage and retrieval system, without either prior permission in writing from the publisher or a licence permitting restricted copying. The right of Andrew Bowcock to be identified as the author of this work has been asserted by him in accordance with the Copyright, Designs and Patents Act 1988.

Designed and typeset by Tony Hart, Isle of Wight
Printed and bound in Great Britain by
Bookcraft (Bath) Ltd

Contents

Foreword   6

Introduction   8

ORIGINAL DOCUMENTS AND PLANS   14
The Proposed Ship   14
The Ship as Built   28
In Service   44

VISUAL EVIDENCE   48
Photographs   48
Paintings   57
Models   60

DRAWINGS   66

Hull and Decks   66
Hull   66
Upper Deck   77
Lower Deck   81
Below lower deck   83

Sails and Rigging   83
General   83
Masts and yards   85
Sails and rigging   90
Flags   94

Armament   104
Guns   104
Ammunition & stores   132
Operating a Pivot gun   134
Firing a Broadside gun   136

Machinery   139
Engine   139
Boilers & funnel   176
Propeller   178
Miscellaneous. Pumps, valves etc   179
Speed   180

Appendices   182
1 Iron-work Capabilities of Liverpool   182
2 Speed and Power   186
3 Propeller   186
4 Powder   187
5 Masts, Sails and Sail Areas   188
6 Hull Form   189

Index   191

Foreword

IN 1988 the CSS *Alabama* Project was launched with the intention of building a replica of the ship for display in Birkenhead. This project went through several changes before eventually being abandoned after a few years. I had been working on these plans and decided to continue the work myself. The first task was to collect as much original information as possible, on the principle that you cannot build a replica without knowing exactly what the original looked like. The first part of this book therefore contains what I would hope to be copies of all the remaining original documents and plans describing the ship. The second part consists of a reconstruction of the ship, as she was in service, based upon the original information collected, and details of contemporary ships built by Lairds, if available.

This work has been concerned only with the ship herself, and her career has not been considered in any detail unless it provided information to help in the reconstruction.

Acknowledgements

The original documents, plans and illustrations are provided courtesy of the following:

DOCUMENTS

Contract, Specification & Maguire's report – Mariners' Museum, Newport News, Va.
Copy Specification, First Cost Accounts and Boilers – Cammell Laird Shipbuilders Ltd, now in the Wirral Archives.
Estimate of Building Costs, Dimensions and Particulars of Ships & the Book of Elements – Williamson Art Gallery and Museum, Birkenhead, Wirral.
Newspaper description – US National Archives, Washington, DC.

PLANS

US National Archives, Washington, DC.
W S Hoole Special Collections Library, The University of Alabama.
Cammell Laird Shipbuilders Ltd – now in the Wirral Archives.
National Museums & Galleries on Merseyside (Merseyside Maritime Museum).

PHOTOGRAPHS OR PRINTS

As noted, anything not acknowledged is part of the author's collection.

Over the last ten years many people and institutions have helped me with information and details, and all their help was much appreciated. In addition to the institutions listed above there were also Jim Bacon, John Taylor, Jerry Williams, Harry Hignett, A S Davidson, Antonia Macarthur, Stephen Kinnaman, Kevin Foster, Harry Cannell, Birkenhead Central Library, Liverpool Central Library, Old Dartmouth Historical Society Whaling Museum, Cape Archives and George Eastman House.

There has been an exchange of information with the people diving on the wreck, particularly Max Guérout and the Association CSS *Alabama*, and Gordon Watts and the CSS *Alabama* Association.

Andrew Bowcock
Newcastle, 2001

People & companies mentioned in the text

Charles Francis **ADAMS** was the American ambassador to London at the time of the Civil War. The son of John Quincy Adams, the sixth president of the United States, he was born in 1807. He was unsuccessful in stopping the *Alabama* from sailing, but he did stop the *Alexandra* (built by W C Miller) and the Laird rams. He was subsequently a member of the tribunal regarding the '*Alabama* Claims' in Geneva in 1871.

James Dunwoody **BULLOCH** was the Confederate Naval agent in Europe. Born in Georgia in 1823, at 16 he became a midshipman in the US Navy. He resigned from the Navy in 1853 after having commanded government mail steamers. At the outbreak of the Civil War he was in New Orleans in command of the steamer *Bienville* which he returned to New York, before taking up service with the Confederate government. He was sent almost immediately to England to buy arms and ships, and the record of his work is in his book *The Secret Service of the Confederate States in Europe*. Bulloch stayed in Liverpool after the war, and died there in 1901. His half-sister was the mother of President Theodore Roosevelt.

General Sir John **BURGOYNE** was Inspector-General of Fortifications when he visited the Laird shipyard in April 1862. He was accompanied by a number of people, including the Mayor of Liverpool, and as well as visiting the yard they went on board the ships *Scotia* and HMS *Majestic*. His only son, Captain Hugh Burgoyne VC, was lost in HMS *Captain* in 1870, which was built by Lairds (yard number 346).

A E BYRNE & Co. were listed in trade directories as a firm of general merchants of 8 Tower Buildings in Liverpool. It appears that there were two Byrnes, Andrew and Thomas, and that one of them formerly did business in New Orleans. They were paid a commission equivalent to 1 per cent of the contract price of the *Alabama* by Lairds but it is not clear why. It may be that they introduced Bulloch to Lairds after his arrival in Liverpool. The services of one of the Byrnes was used by Bulloch to purchase a ship, the *Fingal*, to run the blockade. The company was also paid commission by Lairds for three other vessels, two of which were the Laird rams. The third ship was called the *Azemia* (yard number 303) launched in February 1864, which apparently had no connection with the Confederates as it was lost during a cyclone in Calcutta, India on 5 October 1864.

A Quaker lawyer, Thomas Haines **DUDLEY** was the US consul in Liverpool, and had his office at 69 Tower Buildings. His main task was to gather evidence regarding Confederate activities, and he used spies and informers to do this (including Maguire). He was unsuccessful regarding the *Florida* and the *Alabama*, but did provide evidence which stopped other ships such as the *Alexandra* and the Laird rams leaving. After the war Dudley remained in Liverpool assisting with the *Alabama* Claims before returning to legal practice in the US in 1872.

FAWCETT, PRESTON & Co. is an engineering firm that can trace its origins back to 1758, but there have been a number of changes of name over the years. In 1829, the company built the first iron steamship on the Mersey, and also large numbers of marine steam engines and guns. The foundry was in York Street in Liverpool. In 1935 the company moved to new premises on the Wirral side of the Mersey, and are still in existence today (2001) as Fawcett Christie Hydraulics Ltd.

FRASER, TRENHOLM & Co. were financial agents of the Confederate government with offices at 10 Rumford Place, Liverpool (where Bulloch also had his office). The resident partner was Charles K Prioleau who had a town house at 19 Abercromby Square, Liverpool.

The company that became **JOHN LAIRD** Sons & Co. was started in 1825 by John's father William, to make boilers. They built their first iron ship, a barge, in 1829, which was launched about a month after the iron steamship built by Fawcett, Preston & Co. At about the time the *Alabama* was ordered John Laird retired from the company, leaving it in the hands of his sons William, Henry and John, when the company name became Laird Brothers. The company was taken over in 1903 by Charles Cammell when the name became Cammell Laird. John Laird became the first Member of Parliament for Birkenhead in 1861 and represented the town until his death in 1874. The company survived various name changes and owners before closing in 1993. However, part of the yard and the name were taken over by a firm specialising in ship repair. Unfortunately this company went into receivership in April 2001, and at the time of writing the future is uncertain. The part of the yard that contains Number 4 Dock is separate from the company and has been refurbished as an apprentice training centre called the Laird Foundation.

Mathew **MAGUIRE** was a private detective employed by Thomas Dudley. He reported on the building of the *Alabama* and other ships allegedly for the Confederates.

Stephen **MALLORY** was Secretary of the Confederate Navy. He was responsible for ordering ships and equipment from Britain.

Lord John **RUSSELL** was the Foreign Secretary, in the government of Lord Palmerston, during the period of the war. He had previously been Prime Minister from 1846-52 and would succeed Lord Palmerston for a short period after the latter's death in 1865. As Foreign Secretary Russell was the one who dealt with Adams and the question of ships built in the country.

Raphael **SEMMES** commanded the *Alabama* throughout her two-year career. He was born in 1809 and appointed a midshipman in the US Navy in 1826. He studied law and was admitted to the bar in 1834, later serving in the war with Mexico. He was in the service of the Lighthouse Board when the Civil War broke out. Resigning his commission he received the same rank, Commander, in the Confederate Navy. He was given command of a packet, the *Sumter*, which was converted into a cruiser in New Orleans. Running the blockade out of New Orleans Semmes cruised the Caribbean and South America capturing Federal ships. A voyage across the Atlantic resulted in the *Sumter* getting blockaded in Gibraltar, and then laid up and sold. Semmes and most of his officers left Gibraltar for London and then went to Nassau ready to run the blockade into the South. However, while in Nassau Semmes received orders to return to England and take command of the *Alabama*. He arrived in Liverpool just after the *Alabama* had sailed from the Mersey. Semmes and Bulloch sailed on 13 August 1862 on the *Bahama* to join with the *Alabama* off the Azores. After the battle with the *Kearsarge* in 1864 Semmes returned to the Confederacy and was promoted to Rear-Admiral in charge of the James River fleet. After the end of the Civil War he returned to Mobile where he practised law until his death there in 1877.

UNITS OF MEASUREMENT

The units of measurement used in this book are the Imperial system, and are as follows:

One ton = 2240 pounds (lbs)

One hundredweight (cwt) = 112lbs with 20 cwt to the ton.

In the Cost Accounts some weights are given in terms of t c q – which is tons, hundredweights, quarters, pounds, where 'quarters' is a quarter of a hundredweight or 28lbs.

The monetary units are pounds, shillings and pence, where there are 20 shillings of 12 pence each to the pound (£).

Introduction

AT THE beginning of the American Civil War the Confederate States lacked warlike stores and equipment, and did not have the industrial base to manufacture them. Their solution was to send agents abroad to Europe to purchase what was required, such as guns, ammunition and ships. There were virtually no ships of sufficient size and strength to form a navy, even though there were officers available who had resigned from the US Navy.

Stephen Mallory had been appointed Secretary of the Navy and on 26 April 1861 he reported: 'I propose to adopt a class of vessels hitherto unknown to naval services. . . . Vessels built exclusively for ocean speed, at a low cost, with a battery of one or two accurate guns of long range, with an ability to keep the sea upon a long cruise and to engage or to avoid an enemy at will.'[1] Among the men selected to go to Europe to procure supplies was James Dunwoody Bulloch, who was given orders (dated 9 May 1861) by Mallory to purchase or build ships for the Navy. Bulloch had been in the US Navy but at the outbreak of the Civil War he was in command of a merchant steamer which he returned to her owners in New York before going South. Travelling via Canada, Bulloch arrived in Liverpool on 4 June. His first job on arrival was to contact the financial agents of the Confederate Government, Fraser, Trenholm and Company at their offices at 10, Rumford Place. Following a meeting in London with the two Confederate Commissioners, Yancey and Mann, Bulloch started to buy the stores and ammunition required, and he quickly ordered two ships to be built. He also took legal advice about the Foreign Enlistment Act from a solicitor, F S Hull. This Act forbade either of the two American belligerents to equip, furnish, fit out or arm any vessel within the realm. Legal opinion was there was no problem in building a ship as long as it had no armament aboard in British waters. If the armament was then added outside British waters, it was not a violation of the Act.

The ships were to act against the commerce of the North. For this task the ships would have to fulfil specific criteria. They would have to be good sailing vessels, as most of their time would be spent under sail. The steam engines of the day were fairly inefficient and burnt a lot of coal each day. The *Alabama*, for example, carried coal for less than twenty days steaming, even with all the bunkers full. A propeller that could be hoisted clear of the water when not needed helped to improve the sailing performance. The hull would be built of wood so that it would be possible for the crew to carry out any necessary repairs without the help of a dockyard. This would not be possible if the hull was of iron, and there was also the serious problem of fouling with an iron hull (a problem which is still important today).

Bulloch first contracted with the Liverpool firm of Fawcett, Preston & Co. for a ship which was eventually named *Florida*. The hull was built by William C Miller and Sons at Toxteth Dock in Liverpool and Fawcett, Preston built the engine. His second contact was with the Lairds at the Birkenhead Iron Works in Birkenhead. At a second visit a few days later he asked if they would be willing to draw up the specification, do the necessary calculations, prepare the drawings and make a model for a second vessel. This was the ship known in the yard as Number 290, and later known to the rest of the world as the *Alabama*. All the ships built in the yard were given a number, the series starting with the first iron steamship at Number 1 in 1833, subsequent ships being given consecutive numbers. It is not clear who exactly designed the *Alabama* but the work appears to have been done by the company, with Bulloch approving the finished model and specification. The first money on the account of the Confederate Navy reached England on 27 July 1861.[2] At this time the *Florida* was partly in frame and the contract was finalised with Lairds and signed on 1 August 1861.

The first thing in building a ship is to lay the keel, and the *Alabama*'s keel was laid on the slip at the extreme southern end of the yard. At this time the yard was being extended on the southern side by leasing land from the Corporation of Liverpool. It was on this new land that the *Alabama* was built under cover of a shed (see Appendix 1). While the ship was being built the pair of engines was being constructed in the engine shop. Once the keel had been laid the next step was to erect the stem and stern posts and then the frames, starting at midships and working towards the bow and stern. It took several attempts to get a suitable piece of timber for the stern post, the single piece eventually used costing £100.[3] Each of these large items (frames etc.) was built up of pieces of wood joined together by dowels or copper bolts. These bolts were driven through a hole that had been drilled slightly smaller than their diameter and then riveted over washers at each end. Some of these bolts could be up to 6ft long where they passed through the deadwood at the bow or stern. The various parts of the frames are illustrated in the drawings. The external faces of the frames were then faired as appropriate. Internally the frames were faired by means of battens, then the diagonal iron riders are let into them. The garboard strake (planking next to the keel), the wales and the shelves for the upper and lower decks then followed to hold the shape rigidly. By March 1862 Bulloch recorded 'Her comely frame had

---

1 ORN II, 2 p51. See p46 for abbreviations used in references.

2 B I, p68.

3 B I, p226.

4 B I, p225.

5 *Journal of Commerce*, 12 January 1924.

INTRODUCTION

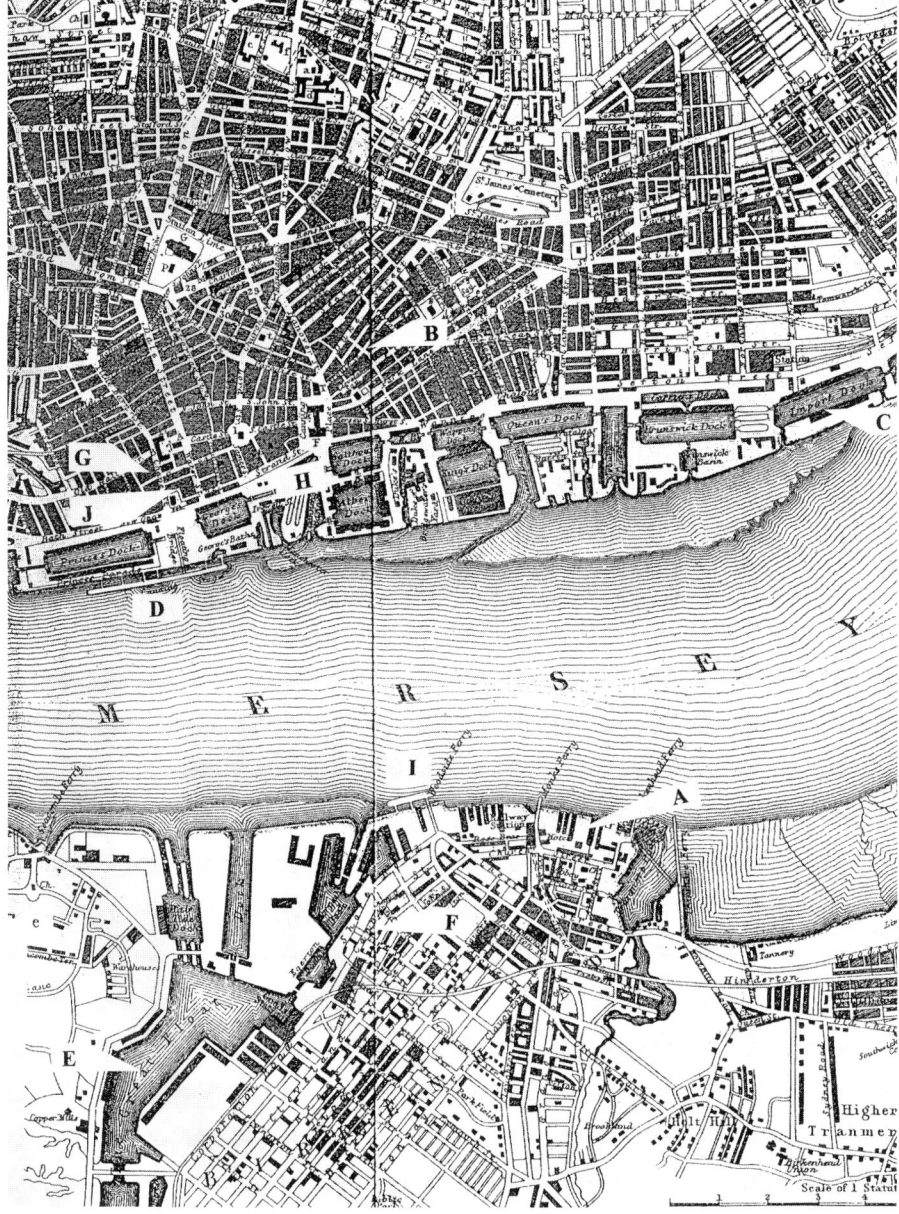

Liverpool and Birkenhead
A Birkenhead Iron Works
B Fawcett, Preston & Co.
C Toxteth Dock (W C Miller, builder of *Florida*)
D Liverpool landing stage
E Great Float, Birkenhead
F Canning Street
G Fraser, Trenholm & Co. (and Bulloch's office)
H Canning Dock (moored off 28 July)
I Woodside ferry landing
J American Consul, Thomas Dudley

been covered in by the binding grip of the outside planking, which had developed the graceful curves of her counter and the delicate wave-lines of her bow; but, nevertheless, I was disappointed to find that she was hardly up to specified time'.[4] The *Florida*, having been launched at the beginning of December under the name *Oreto*, sailed out of the river on 22 March 1862 heading for Nassau. Overall she was a slightly smaller ship than the *Alabama* and took less time to build and fit out.

On 3 April 1862 there was a visit by General Burgoyne, the Inspector General of Fortifications, to the Mersey which included the yard. The visit is reported, at varying lengths, by the different local papers and best description of the yard being in the *Liverpool Journal* of Saturday 5 April. According to the newspaper the engine shop had recently been extended to 170ft long by 60ft wide. Number 3 Dock was being widened and deepened so that the *Agincourt*, Number 291, an iron screw steam frigate for the Royal Navy, could be built in it under cover of a new iron roof. The newspaper also listed the ships being built in the yard, including the following:

Under a wooden shed there is being built for the Spanish Government a wood screw steam frigate of about 1,100 tons builder's measurement, to be fitted with engines of 300 horse-power, nominal.

The fiction of a Spanish connection was continued when the ship, still known as 290, was ready to be launched on 14 May. High tide that day was at 11:19am, and it was usual to launch about half an hour before this time. The ship was christened *Enrica* by a lady who Bulloch would not name in his book, and whose name is still not known, as far as I am aware. However, when all the shores had been removed the *Enrica* refused to move, so the foreman told the men on the forecastle head to dance and the ship glided down the ways and was successfully launched.[5] According to Maguire, Bulloch's wife and several other ladies were watching from the office windows, though generally people were kept out of the yard. The river by the shipyard was very wide so there was no need to restrain the movement of the ship when afloat by any means such as drag chains. So when she was clear of the slipway the *Enrica* was towed by two tugs to the entrance to Number 4 graving dock where she was warped in and placed under the 50-ton crane.

The process of installing the engine and boilers started immediately, the boilers being weighed before being fitted. The larger and heavier parts of the engines were lowered by the crane through the engine-room skylight on the upper deck, and then through the hatch underneath in the lower deck. There was no other way of getting the boilers in other than by removing the iron deck beams for both the upper and lower decks. The beams would be replaced afterwards and the iron coal bunkers then built. The funnel and its elevating mechanism would also be installed at this point. Within a few days the boilers were in, and in just over two weeks they had been filled and steam was raised, allowing the first trial of the engine, with the ship still in Number 4 Dock. Felt and lagging was added to the pipes and cylinders, and on 9 June there was the second trial of the engines, also in the dock. The weight of

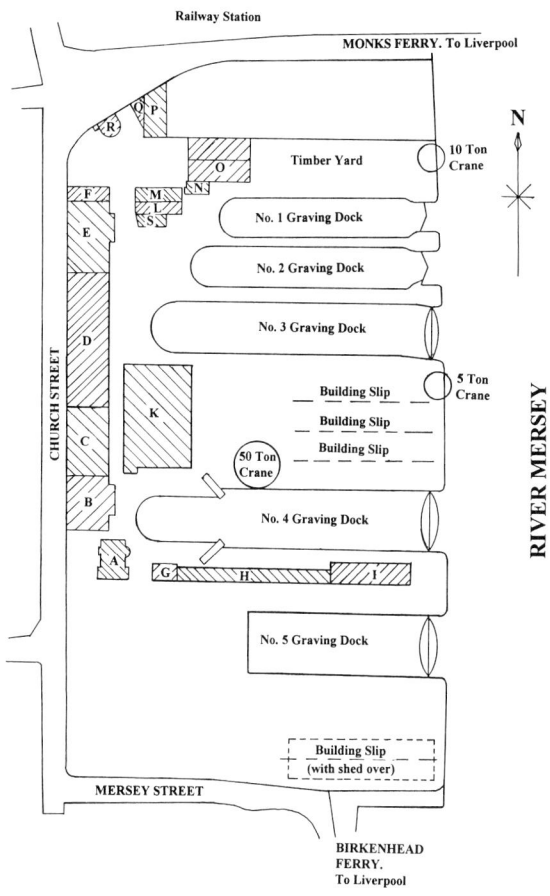

Birkenhead Iron Works - 1861

A	Office and general entrance	E & F	1st floor: Joiners' shops
B	Engineers' fitting and erecting shops		2nd floor: Mould loft for laying off vessels
	Ground floor: Erecting shop and large engineering tools	G & H	Engine house and smiths shops
	1st floor: Fitting shop and light engineering tools	I	Shed for carpenters, mast making etc
	2nd floor: Pattern and millwrights' shop	K	Shed for erecting boilers
C	Ground floor: Boilers for yard engines	L	Steam drying stove
		M	Fireproof store rooms and paint shop
	1st floor: Boiler shop	N	Engine and boiler for saw mill
	2nd floor: Rigging loft	O	Steam saw mill
D	Ground floor: Smiths' shop	P	Dining room for men and reading room above
	1st floor: Joiner shops and timber store	Q	Gatekeeper's house
E	Ground floor: Furnaces for bending ships frames and smithy	R	Ticket office and entrance for workmen
		S	Shed for angle iron fitting
F	Ground floor: Store room		

6 *Liverpool Telegraph & Shipping Gazette*, 14 July 1862.

7 ORN II, 2 p379.

8 B I, p286.

9 *Beneath the Stainless Banner*, p204

10 ORN I, 7 p629.

11 ORN I, 1 p414.

the water in the boilers was found by reading the draughts of the ship (from the marks carved on the stem and stern) firstly with the boilers empty. The displacement of the ship could then be read from a set of hydrostatic curves. The boilers were then filled with water and the draughts read for a second time and the corresponding new displacement found. The weight of the water in the boilers is simply the difference between the two displacements. On 12 June the ship left Number 4 Dock for the first trial of the engines under way, running out to the Formby Light Ship and some time during the day using the Indicators to find the indicated horse power. There were a number of observers on board, including Bulloch.

During this time the US consul, Thomas Dudley, was trying to stop the ship, using reports from his private detective Maguire. At the same time Bulloch was busy finalising details of two other ships to be built by Lairds. These ships, Yard Numbers 294 and 295, were to be ironclad steamships, fitted with guns in revolving turrets, quite different to the *Florida* and the *Alabama*. The ships are usually known as the 'Laird Rams' and were ordered on 1 July 1862 for delivery at the end of March and May 1863 respectively.

After this trial it appears that the *Alabama* went back into the yard for further work, including bending the sails. Probably on 12 July she moved from the yard into the Great Float in the Birkenhead Docks.[6] Whether this was done under her own power or by tugs is not clear. Apart from the engines and boilers, the rest of the ship needed to be fitted out. The cabins were apparently furnished by Mr Blair of Paradise Street in Liverpool, the fittings and furniture being selected by Bulloch.[7] The magazines were fitted out and the powder canisters made by Messrs Sidderley & Co. were installed. The powder was manufactured and put into cartridges by Messrs Curtiss and Harvey.[8] The amount of powder in the cartridges would depend on the gun they were to be used with, and the canisters they were stored in were marked accordingly.

Work continued on the ship in the Great Float and stores were put on board, such as food and coal. Items such as the china would have been ordered and delivered to the ship. According to Kell there were four sets of crockery on board each of the design shown (page 12), the difference being in the colour: gold for the captain, blue for the wardroom, green for the steerage and brown for the crew.[9]

Bulloch had already appointed a captain to take care of preparations regarding getting the ship to sea such as engaging the crew. This was Mathew Butcher who had previously been on ships of the Cunard line and was engaged to take the ship from British waters to the place where she could safely receive her armament. In October 1861 Bulloch had been aboard the *Fingal* on a voyage to Bermuda (loaded with guns and ammunition) when the ship had to put into a bay at Praya on the island of Terceira in the Azores. He realised the potential of that place as a rendezvous for a cruiser to fit out with her armament, and this was where the *Alabama* would be sent.

Around 18 July Fawcett Preston were reported to have sent some fifty boxes of cannon and shells to London by rail.[10] These would have been loaded on board the *Agrippina*, a barque of around 400 tons which had been purchased a month or so before. A suitable ship was required that would attract no attention but be able to carry heavy weights to supply the *Alabama* when she was at sea. The *Agrippina* was entered as sailing from London to Demerara so that the various stores could be forwarded to her without creating suspicion. (Unsuccessfully as it appears, because the *Agrippina* was mentioned in a dispatch from the American consul, but not in connection with the *Alabama*.)

Bulloch received information (from a source he does not name) on Saturday 26 July that it was not safe for the *Alabama* to remain in Birkenhead. The expectation was that the ship would be seized for violation of the Foreign Enlistment Act. Another trial voyage was agreed immediately with Lairds, to take place out of the river. Bulloch then warned Butcher to complete the stores, take on extra coal and a few more crew ready to leave the dock on Monday for this trial, and that the ship would not return. The same day (Saturday) Maguire reported that he met some of the seamen coming down Canning St. from the ship, playing 'Dixie's Land' [*sic*], on a fife, concertina and a cornopean (or cornet) and they all took the 4:30 Woodside boat for Liverpool. They still kept playing 'Dixie's Land' on board the ferry boat.

On the night of Monday 28 July the *Alabama* left the Birkenhead Docks and moored in the River Mersey abreast the Canning Dock. The following morning (the 29th) she sailed about 9am, partially dressed with flags, with a number of guests aboard for the trial trip. There were also men from the builders – riggers and engineers – to provide help if required. The ship spent some time running between the Bell Buoy and the North West lightship taking Indicator diagrams and measuring the speed. At about 3pm Bulloch explained that he wanted to keep the ship out all night and that the guests would be taken off by the tender, the steam tug *Hercules*. When the guests and Bulloch had left the *Alabama* she then proceeded to Moelfre Bay to anchor and await Bulloch the next day. The USS *Tuscarora* was in Southampton having some necessary repairs done when the captain received a dispatch from Mr Adams (the American Ambassador in London) at 4:30pm saying 'The vessel is steaming out of the Mersey'.[11]

The next morning (the 30th) Bulloch joined the *Hercules* at the Woodside landing stage and took on board a number of additional crewmen. Just before they sailed he was given a telegram from a friend in Southampton to say that the *Tuscarora* had sailed and was believed to be heading for Queenstown (southern Ireland). The *Hercules* took the Rock Channel on leaving the Mersey (because it was a shorter distance) and joined the *Alabama* that afternoon in Moelfre Bay. Most men eventually signed on, the tug leaving about midnight to return to Liverpool. At about 2:30am the next day (31 July) the *Alabama* got under way and headed north around the north coast of Ireland. Bulloch and the pilot went ashore off the Giant's Causeway at about 6pm, leaving the *Alabama* continuing around the north coast of Ireland and then out into the Atlantic.

Local papers reported that the *Alabama* had sailed. For example the *Liverpool Telegraph & Shipping Gazette* reported on Wednesday 30 July that No. 290 (s-s) Captain Butcher had sailed on the 29th on a 'Trial-trip'. A few days later the *Liverpool Chronicle* of 2 August 1862, under the heading Sailed from Liverpool had:

No. 290 (ss) – July 29 Nassau (supposed).

By then it was obvious that the *Alabama* was not going to return to Liverpool. The destination of Nassau was probably assumed because that was where the *Florida* sailed when she left – *The Albion* on 4 August described the *Alabama* as 'sister to *Oreto*'.

At this time Captain Raphael Semmes was on board the ship *Bahama* returning to Liverpool from Nassau. He had been there waiting to run the blockade into the South, after leaving his

Alabama Trials
12 June. From the yard to the Formby Lightship, returning to the yard.
29 July. Moored in the river, having left the Great Float the previous day. Ran between the Bell Buoy and the NW Lightship. Sailed to Moelfre that evening.

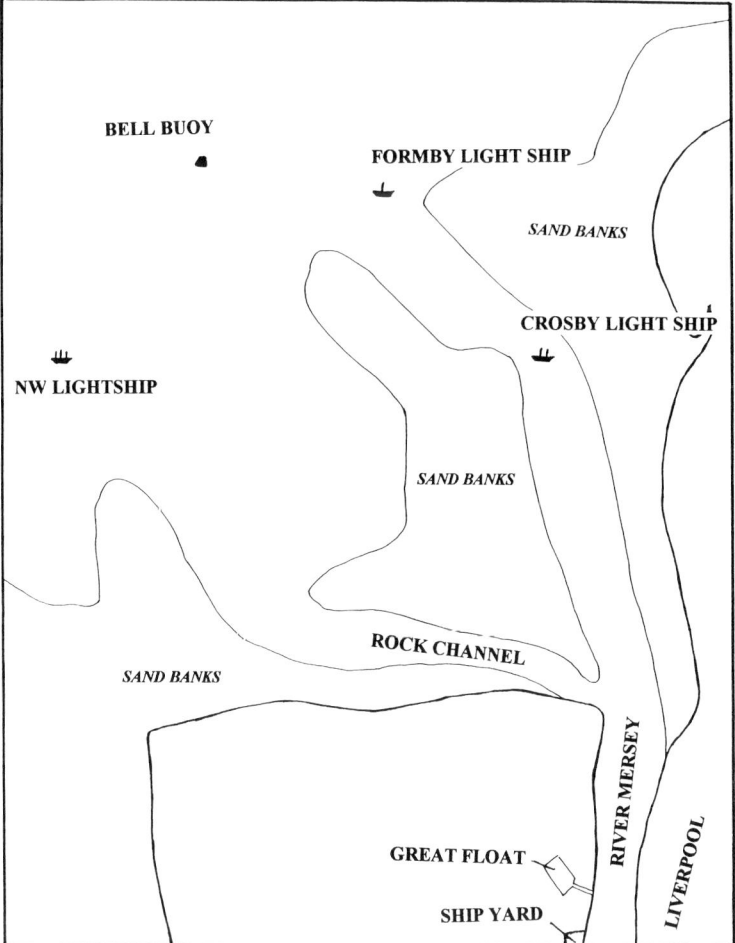

A plate recovered from the wreck of the ship on 18 June 2001. The decoration is brown, implying it is one for the crew. Plates with both blue and green decoration have been recovered but they have additional decoration around the anchor. All the plates are marked with the Davenport stamp, for the Davenport pottery of Longport, Stoke-on-Trent.

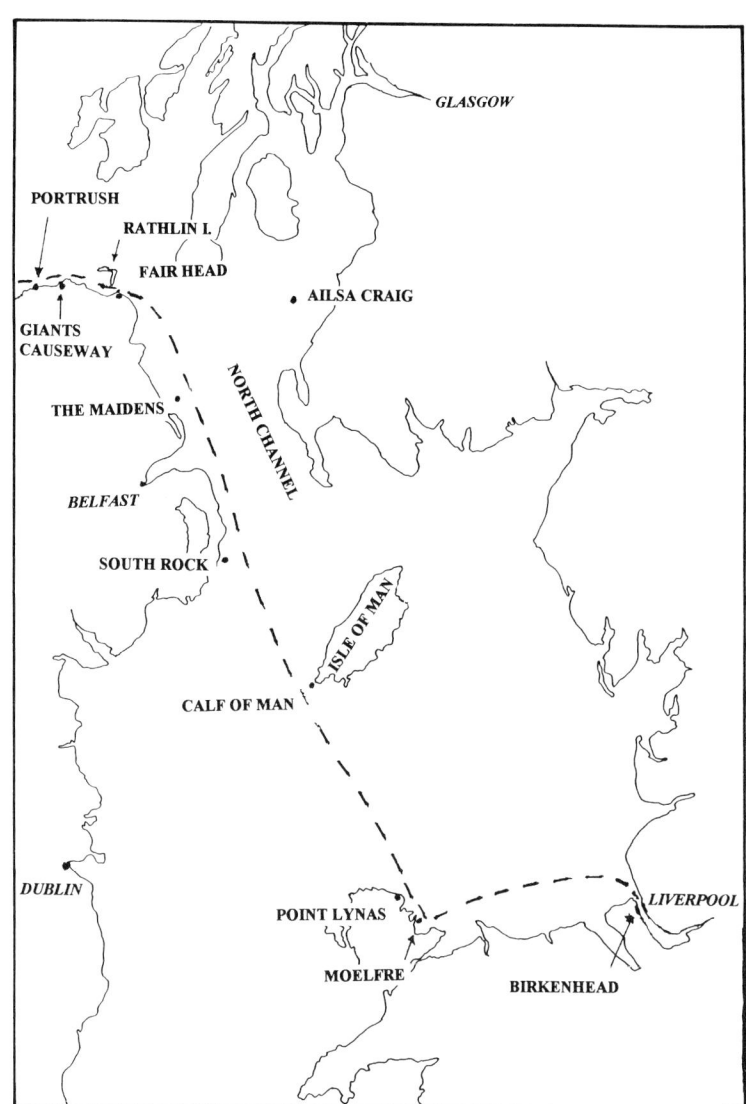

Alabama Departure from Birkenhead
28 July. Leaves the Great Float and moors in the river.
29 July. Trial trip, then departs for Moelfre, anchoring there.
31 July. Departs from Moelfre and sails around the north coast of Ireland into the Atlantic.

previous ship, the *Sumter*, in Gibraltar. While in Nassau he had been appointed to command the *Alabama* and was returning to Liverpool, arriving on 5 August and the ship going straight into Bramley-Moore dock. Bulloch, Semmes and his officers sailed from Liverpool on board the *Bahama* on 13 August along with two additional guns and stores to meet the *Alabama* off Praya.

The *Alabama* arrived off Praya on 9 August after a voyage through heavy gales which had caused some damage. The ship anchored and was then placed in quarantine for three days. It was not until the 18th that the *Agrippina* arrived from London (having cleared outwards on 28 July) with six guns and stores. She was hauled alongside the *Alabama* the next day and the guns and a lot of the stores and purser's slops were transferred. On the 20th the *Bahama* arrived from Liverpool with two additional guns (32pdrs) and Semmes and his officers. Because of the sea conditions all three ships moved round the island to the western side which made it safer for the ships to lie alongside. That night Semmes relieved Butcher of his command and moved his baggage into the cabin which was to be his home for the next two years. For the following few days work went on transferring stores, guns and coal on to the *Alabama* from the other two ships. At times the ships steamed out beyond the three-mile limit of national waters. The carpenter and the gunner were engaged in putting down the sweeps for the pivot guns, the plans for which had been handed to Bulloch a few days before the *Bahama* sailed from the Mersey.[12]

By Sunday 24 August 1862 all the armament was on board and in place, the coal bunkers were full, the stores were unpacked and the ship had been cleaned of the dirt and coal dust that had collected. The ship steamed away from the shore and Semmes summoned all hands aft so that they could hear him read out the commission appointing him a Captain in the Confederate States Navy. The ship was still flying the British flag at that point and when Semmes finished reading a bow gun was fired. The ensign and pennant of a man-of-war were then broken out, the British flag lowered, and the names 290 and *Enrica* were replaced by the *Alabama*. The next thing was to recruit a crew from the men who had come out from Liverpool on the *Alabama* and *Bahama* and after a speech from Semmes eighty of the men signed on.

That night Bulloch returned to the *Bahama* and left the *Alabama* on the start of a cruise which would last nearly two years. During this cruise the *Alabama* captured sixty-five ships, burning or sinking fifty-five and releasing the remainder on ransom bond. The total value of all these ships was estimated to be $5,176,164. On 11 January 1863 the ship was approaching Galveston when Federal warships were seen bombarding the city, which had only just been retaken by the Confederates. When the *Alabama* was spotted one Federal warship steamed towards her. This was the USS *Hatteras* which, after being drawn far enough away from the main fleet, was

12 SM p407.

sunk by the *Alabama* in a battle lasting just 13 minutes (the wreck of this ship has recently been found).

After commissioning the *Alabama* sailed the Atlantic Ocean before heading through the Indian Ocean to Singapore and then back to the Atlantic before heading for the French port of Cherbourg for repairs and drydocking. While at Cherbourg, awaiting permission to drydock, the USS *Kearsarge* appeared, having sailed from the Dutch port of Flushing. Semmes challenged the captain of the *Kearsarge*, and sailed from Cherbourg on 19 June 1864 for a battle which lasted just over an hour and resulted in the sinking of the *Alabama*. The wreck of the ship was found by a French navy minehunter in 1984 and identified by means of objects recovered by divers. The work on the wreck is directed by a joint French and American Scientific Committee with the French Association CSS *Alabama* and now the American CSS *Alabama* Association of Mobile, Alabama is in charge of the diving.

The Captain of the *Alabama*

The choice of who was to command the *Alabama* when complete went through several names before Raphael Semmes finally joined the ship off the Azores.

Letter from Mallory to Bulloch, 30 November 1861: 'So soon as either of the vessels under contract in England shall be completed and delivered you will adopt such measures as you may deem best to equip and arm her as a war vessel, to be called the *Manassas*– and, having obtained a crew and all things necessary for an extended cruise, you will leave England in command and proceed against the enemy in whatever quarter of the ocean circumstances may then indicate.' (ORN II, 2 p114)

Letter from Stephen Mallory to James North, dated 11 January 1862: 'Captain Bulloch will take command of the first ship [*Florida*] that shall be finished, and the entire completion of which is looked for next month; and you will receive orders to command the other vessel, whose completion is looked for in May.' (ORN II, 2 p128)

Bulloch to Mallory 13 January 1862 following delay in getting the *Fingal* to sea from Savannah: 'I therefore request that you will so far modify your instructions of 30 November, as to direct me to assume command of the second ship.' (ORN II, 2 p130)

Mallory to Bulloch 20 January 1862: '–you express a preference for the command of the second ship to be built in England, and you will therefore regard the department's instructions of the 30th of November so modified as to authorize you to assume command of either ship.' (ORN II, 2 p133)

Mallory to Bulloch 30 April 1862: 'I write to Commander Semmes by this conveyance, instructing him to take command of the largest of the two vessels built by you and to transfer his officers and crew to her, if he shall not be able to put the *Sumter* in seaworthy condition; I write also to Lieutenant North to take command of the other vessel.' (ORN II, 2 p187)

Mallory to Bulloch 3 May 1862: 'I have instructed Commander Semmes to transfer his command to the second vessel constructed under your direction.' (ORN II, 2 p190)

Mallory to Bulloch 29 May 1862: 'In my letters to Commander North I directed to take command of this vessel, or of the second one, and I trust he has made his arrangements to do so, as in my instructions to Commander Semmes I have authorized him, if he deems it practicable, to transfer his officers and crew to the second vessel, which may be called the *Alabama*.' (ORN II, 2 p205)

North to Bulloch 26 June 1862: 'I am now ready to assume the command of the vessel' (ORN II, 2 p209)

Bulloch to North 27 June 1862: 'I hereby formally and officially transfer to you the command of the ship built by me here.' (ORN II, 2 p209)

Bulloch to North 8 July 1862 '–and I therefore revoke my letter of transfer–' (ORN II, 2 p213)

Mallory to Bulloch 12 July 1862: 'Captain Semmes returns to England to assume the command of the *Alabama*.' (ORN II, 2 p.215)

There appears to have been some confusion with North over which vessel he was to command. The time delay in getting orders from Mallory to the appropriate person may have contributed to this.

A mass of items stuck together which was recovered from the wreck of the *Alabama* on 19 June 2001. The largest item visible is a nozzle for a fire hose about 45in long (the end is out of the picture). Resting on top of it, with the open end towards the camera, is part of a leather fire hose. There is a second piece of hose (not clearly visible), with copper rivets, above it. Other objects in the mass include a piece of flat glass and the top of a glass bottle.

Original documents and plans

THERE IS still a lot of original information available about the *Alabama* but it tends to be spread about in different museums or archives. Since the time of the American Civil War there have been hundreds of books wholly or partly about the ship but most of these are concerned with her career or are biographies or autobiographies of her crew. This books is concerned with the construction and outfitting of the ship and there is very little information in most of these works which provides much detail.

The life of the ship falls into three separate categories:

1. The proposed ship
2. The ship as built
3. In service

Any significant changes will occur during the building of the ship as things are modified as necessary. Most major items will not change throughout the life of a ship but there will be many small changes during this time, particularly when in service. Information is available for each of these periods as given below and some of the changes that occurred are given. The excavation of the wreck is outside the scope of this work, though a few of the items recovered are described.

The proposed ship

The basic information to build the ship is contained in the Contract and Specification. A set of plans will accompany the

Profile and upper deck (scale = 1:192)

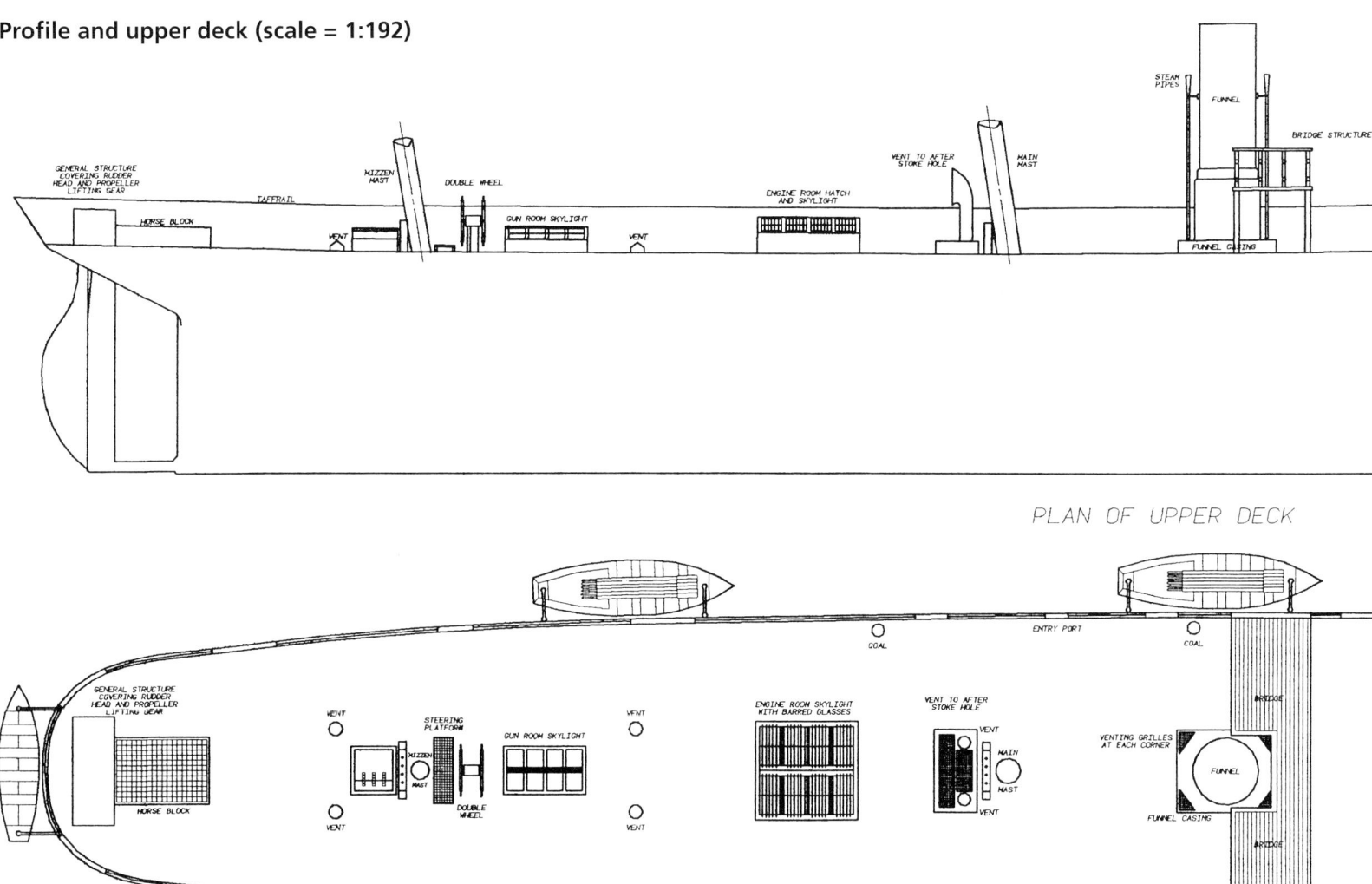

THE PROPOSED SHIP

Specification and in this case there was also a model to show what the ship would be like. The models of the ship are discussed on pages 60-3. Bulloch's original copy of the Contract and Specification is in the Mariners' Museum, and is here reproduced in full. The Specification covers the size of the scantlings of the timber as well as details of the engines and boilers and the spare parts that were to be supplied with them. The two documents were signed by Bulloch and William Laird representing the builders John Laird Sons and Company. There would be a second copy held by the company, but the whereabouts of this are unknown.

Parts of the contract and specifications are also in one of the books in the Cammell Laird archives. All the original contracts were kept in separate packets or envelopes by the company but unfortunately the one for the *Alabama* is not amongst those relatively few which have survived. However, parts of the contract were copied into a book and amongst details of over 150 vessels are those for No. 290, which later became the *Alabama*. This information is reproduced and labelled 'Copy Specification' and is essentially an abbreviated form of the main Contract and Specification. It also contains some additional details regarding suppliers of some of the smaller items of equipment, such as the hammocks and mess utensils.

Three original plans survive and are in the US National Archives. These plans are:

Profile of Inboard Works
Plan of Lower Deck
Sail plan, Masts and Spars

There are also copies of these plans and two additional ones at the University of Alabama. In 1957 William Stanley Hoole of the University of Alabama visited Liverpool and obtained tracings of the original plans and copies of the contract and specifications. These plans were retraced and then reduced to half size for inclusion in the book *CSS Alabama Builder, Captain and Plans* by Summersell which was published in 1985.

The five plans in the book are:

Plan of Lower Deck
Profile of Inboard Works
Sail Plan, Masts and Spars
Profile
Plan of Upper Deck

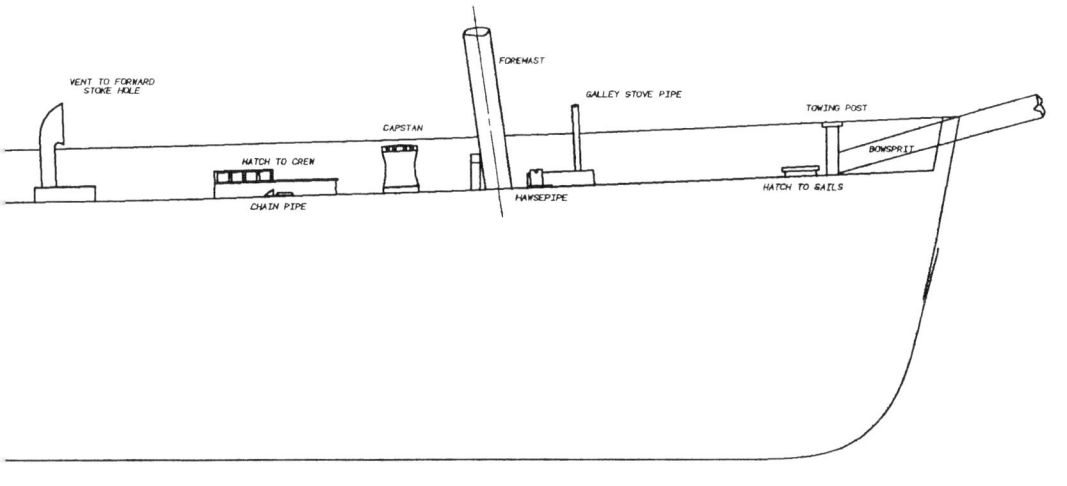

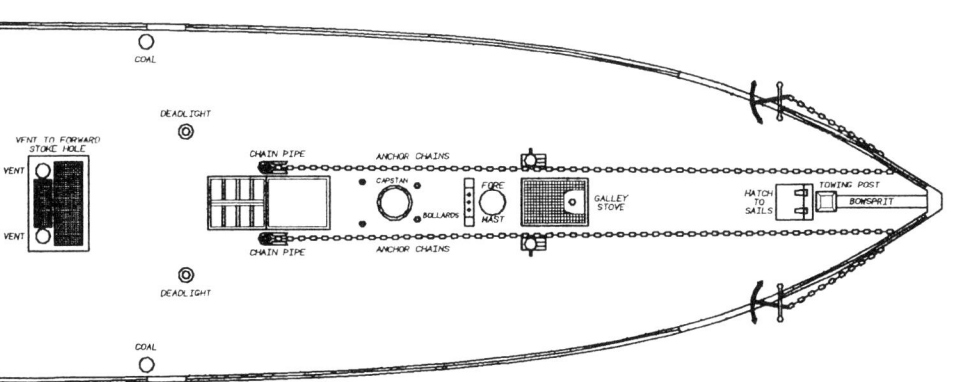

The first three plans are the same as those at the National Archives, but have been redrawn and reduced from the originals, and therefore are not as clear. The last two plans listed do not appear to be available from any other source. I have redrawn four of these plans, and only the Sail plan has not been redrawn. The Profile of Inboard Works is the most detailed plan and so has been used as a basis for all four. Because the frame spacing (the 'room and space', sometimes called the 'timber and space') is known from the Specification it is possible to check if the paper plan has been distorted in any way over the years or as a result of being copied. Every fourth frame is marked on this plan and so the spacing should be 9ft amidships (room and space 2ft 3in) and 9ft 4in fore and aft (room and space 2ft 4in). However, when measuring the spacing on the plan they are all the same at 9ft, there being no increase towards the bow or stern. It is possible that the drawing was done ignoring the change in frame spacing, or

Inboard profile and lower deck (scale = 1:192)

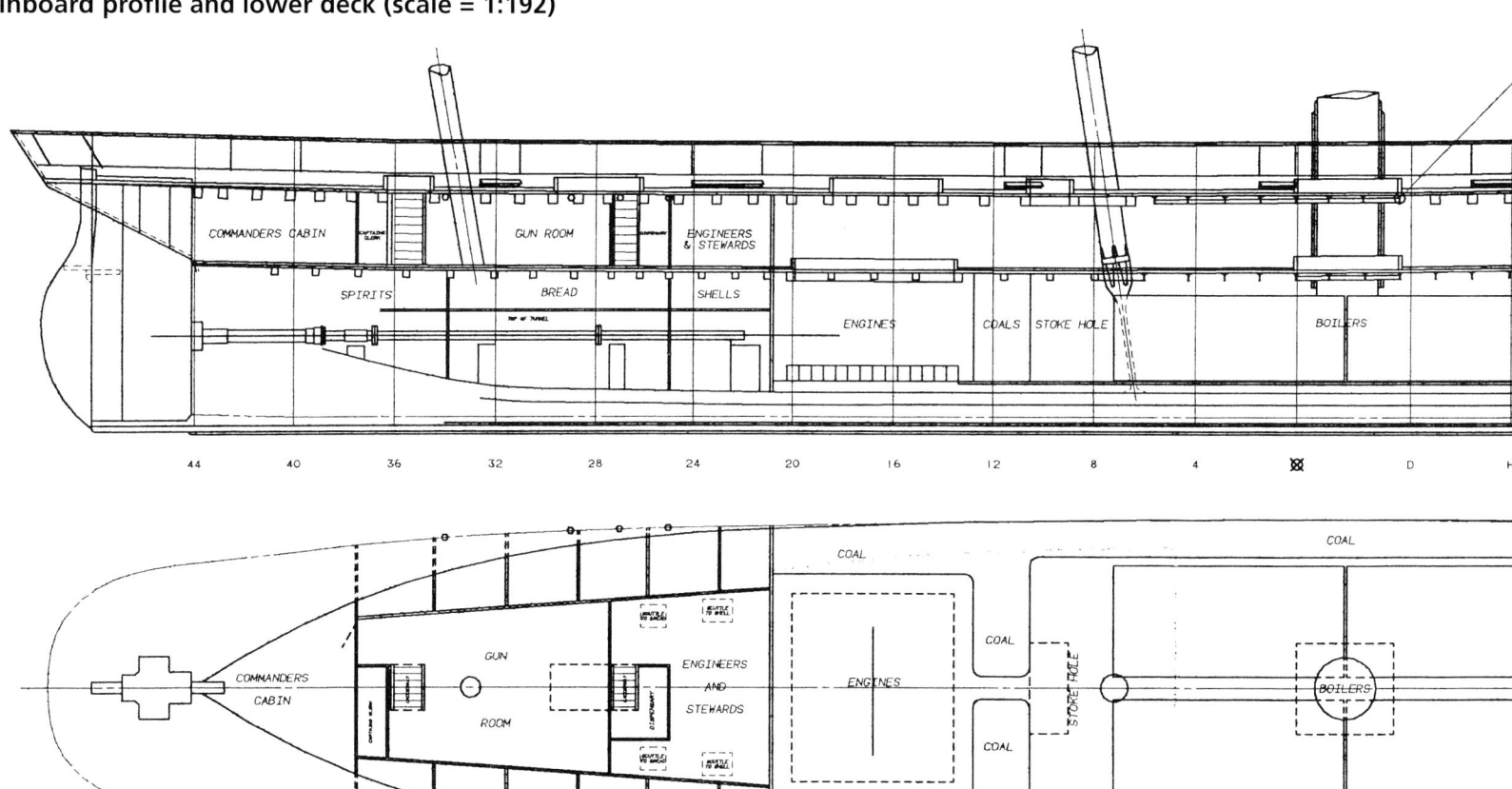

it could be that the frame spacing was changed to be the same throughout the length of the ship and the fact not recorded. In view of this plan (which is dated October 1861) it has been decided to ignore the Specification (which is dated 1 August 1861) and use a frame spacing of 2ft 3in throughout the length of the ship.

The other three plans were redrawn but making sure that everything lined up in all the views, which was not always the case, particularly with regard to the two copied plans. The labelling has been retained, except where it is known to be wrong. For example, on the Upper Deck the riding bitts were originally labelled as hawsepipes.

The Sail Plan as proposed has not been redrawn, and the original has been reduced in size to fit the page. The table of spars has been listed separately for convenience.

SPECIFICATION & CONTRACT

The most accessible copy of the contract and specification for the ship is in the book *CSS Alabama Builder, Captain, and Plans* by Summersell, published by the University of Alabama Press in 1985. The plans, contract and specification are copies of those held in the University of Alabama Library Special Collections. How they arrived at the library is described by Summersell in the Preface to the book.

The plans were obtained through a most unusual set of circumstances. Whilst in England in 1957 William Stanley Hoole, then Director of Libraries at The University of Alabama, visited the Liverpool offices of Hill, Dickinson Company, successor to John Laird Sons and Company, the shipbuilding firm that constructed the CSS *Alabama*. It was discovered that the firm possessed the original blueprints for the vessel, as well as the original contract between the Laird Company and James D Bulloch, who served as agent of the Confederate States government. Hoole obtained a photostatic copy of the contract and specifications, and he commissioned the preparation of a tracing of the blueprint. These are now housed in the William Stanley Hoole Special Collections Library at The University of Alabama. Subsequently, the original documents were either discarded or destroyed by the Hill, Dickinson Company.

Hill, Dickinson Company is a firm of Liverpool solicitors, and could not be considered as the successors to John Laird Sons and Company, even though they were solicitors to that company. John Laird Sons and Company continued, through various name changes and amalgamations, finally becoming Cammell Laird Shipbuilders, before closing in 1993.

I had noticed a few minor typographical errors in the printed

THE PROPOSED SHIP

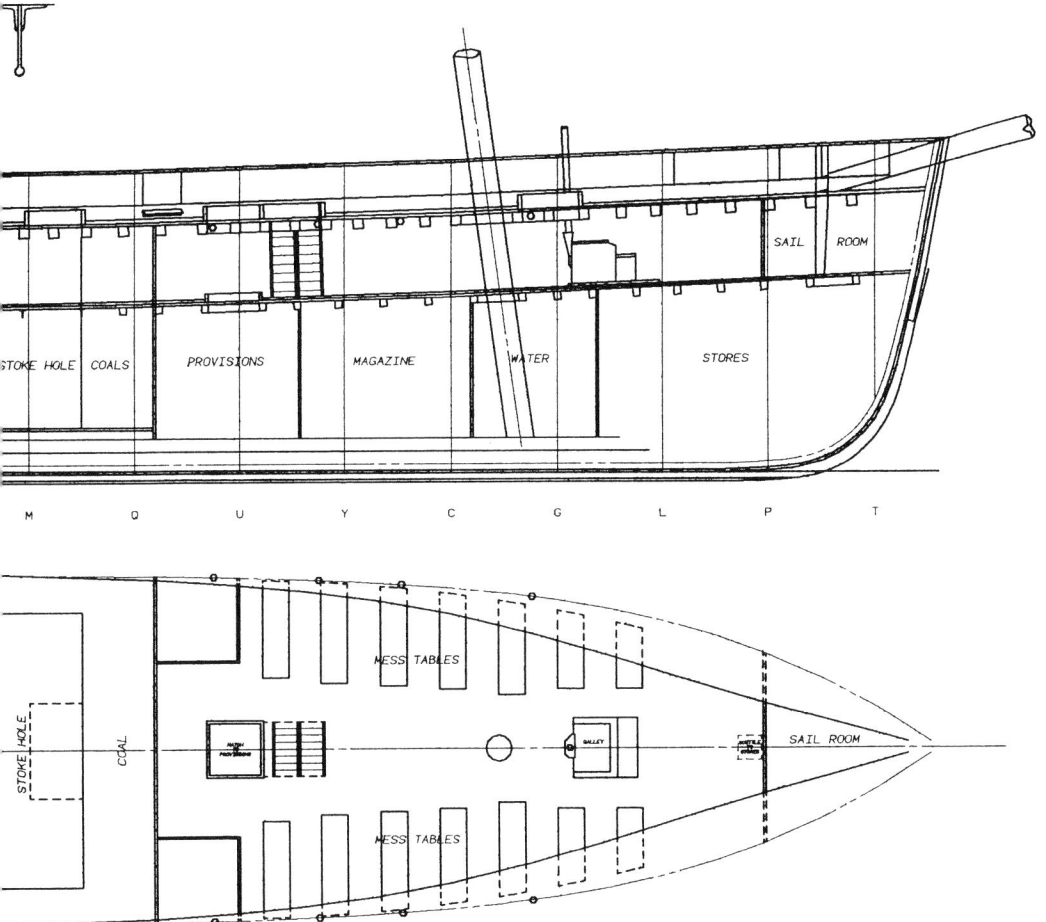

version of the contract and specification which appears in Summersell's book and for my own convenience decided to retype the specification, correcting the errors. There is a second copy of the contract and specification, in manuscript form, at the Mariners' Museum (which I believe was presented along with the model by relatives of Bulloch in about 1985). In comparing the Summersell copy with the one in the Mariners' Museum I found that some of the details in the latter were in a different order. It turned out that by transposing two of the pages in the Mariners' Museum copy I got the same as in Summersell's book. On checking, it was Summersell's copy that was wrong, and with the pages in the correct order the description of the structure was easier to follow, the implication being that at some time the pages of the copy at the University of Alabama had been confused and it had not been noticed. To check on this I asked a friend if I could borrow his copy of the photocopy of the University of Alabama specification to compare the two. There were probably only two original copies of the contract and specification produced, one each for the owner and the builder, and both would obviously be identical (it being assumed initially that the owner's was in the Mariners' Museum and the builder's at Hill, Dickinson). The two original copies of the specification could have been written by the same person in exactly the same format and page layout, only the signatures of Laird and Bulloch would vary slightly in position. Comparing the same part of the first page of the specification showed that the marks and words crossed out are exactly the same. The fifth page shows an ink blot in exactly the same place on each copy.

Therefore, based on similar marks elsewhere on the two copies it would appear that the contract and specification that Hoole saw and copied in Liverpool in 1957 is the one that is now in the Mariners' Museum. At that point it appeared that somehow the copy of the contract and specification had travelled from Liverpool to the Mariners' Museum between 1957 and 1985. However, two subsequent events muddied the waters.

Firstly I bought a copy of the book *Four Years in the Confederate Navy* by William Stanley Hoole, published by the University of Georgia Press, 1964. In the Preface to this book Hoole describes a visit to Cammell Lairds in January 1957; '... perusing old records – among them the manuscript contract for building the *Alabama* and a set of her original specifications complete to the last bolt and rivet...'. There is no mention of the plans of the ship, a visit to Hill Dickinson, nor of getting copies of the plans and contract and specification. However, he does mention a visit to Fawcett Preston (the next day) and getting a photostatic copy of the page referring to the engines of the CSS *Florida*.

The second thing was that I found that The University of North Carolina at Chapel Hill also have a photocopy of the contract and specification in their Southern Historical Collection. On obtaining a copy it is exactly the same as the other two. The marks, especially the ink mark on page five, are identical. However, the most interesting thing is the provenance that came with the copy of the pages. This states that: 'This photocopy was a gift... in September 1955... the original manuscript is owned by one of the Roosevelts, and that the photocopies were obtained via The Confederate Research Club of Portsmouth, England.'

It now seems certain that the photocopies of the contract and specification held by the University of Alabama and the University of North Carolina were both from the original manuscript copy which is currently in the Mariners' Museum. This manuscript version would appear to be Bulloch's original copy, however the Mariners' Museum does not have the plans that accompanied it.

The following questions are raised by this conclusion:

1. Where did Hoole get his copy of the contract and specification from?

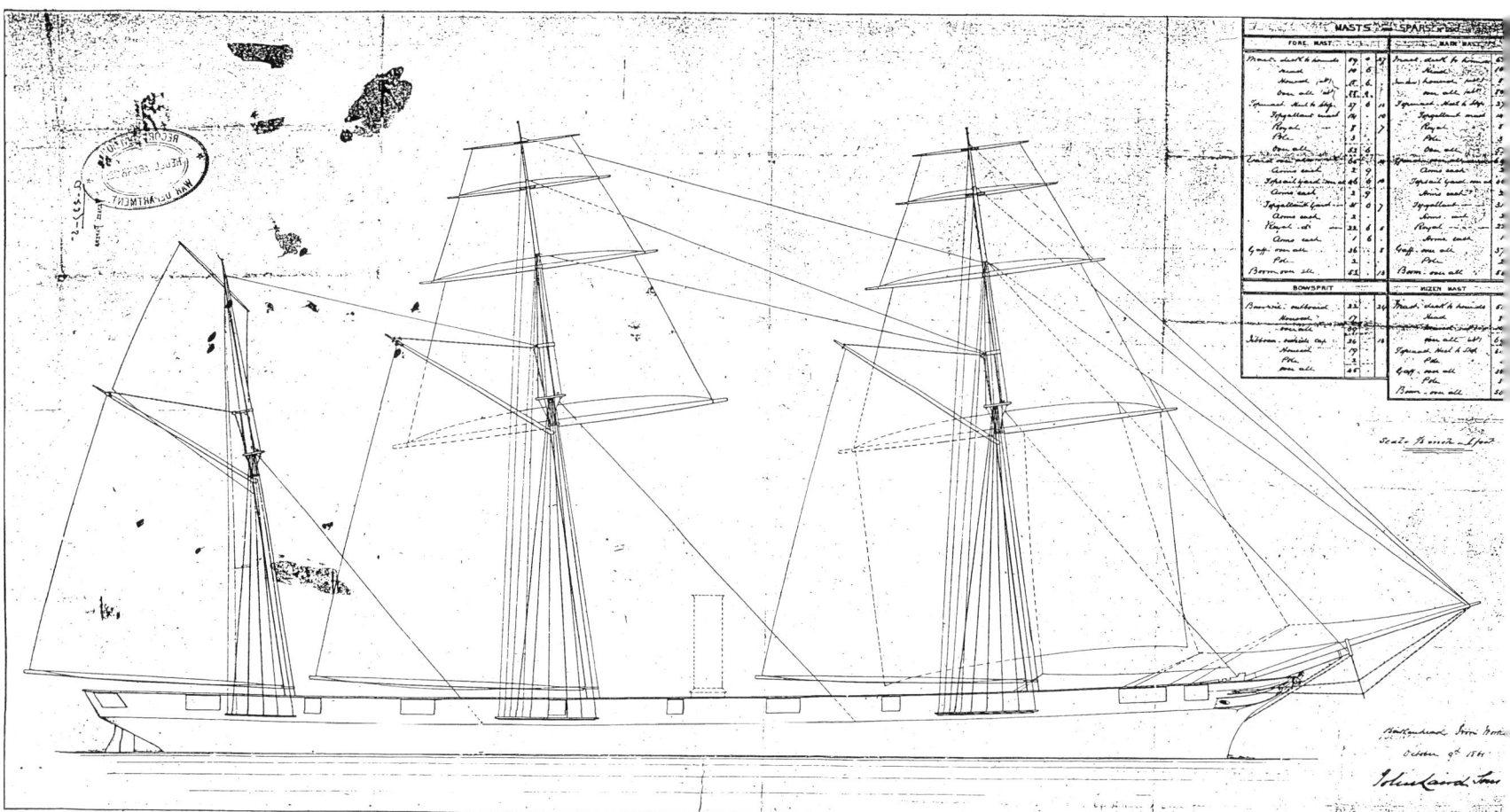

CSS *Alabama*, Sheet 3: 'Masts and Spars, 1861'. (Cartographic Record). Vessel Papers; War Department Collection of Confederate Records, Record Group 109. National Archives, College Park, Maryland. (scale = 1:384)

2. What happened to the plans that he got copies of? Were they Bulloch's copies?
3. What happened to the original documents and plans that were the shipbuilders copies?

As well as the original Contract, Specification and Plans of the *Alabama* there were extra copies made for various people. Captain James H North asked for copies and Bulloch replied on 18 May 1862, 'When you asked me for copies of my contracts with plans, etc., I did not suppose you wished them for any immediate purpose but simply to file away, and I have not made haste to complete them. I have, however, requested the draftsman at Lairds to prepare drawings from the original plans, which, of course, will take some time. The contracts are very minute and cover so many sheets that it will take some days to copy' (ORN II, 2 p192).

In a letter dated 11 August 1862 Bulloch wrote to Mallory, 'I have furnished Lieutenant [George T] Sinclair with minute drawings and specifications and the identical contract under which the *Alabama* was built' (ORN II, 2 p238).

It would also appear that copies of the drawings were sent to the Confederate States because the following was part of the evidence of the *Alabama* Arbitration of 1872; 'The drawings found among the archives of the insurgents signed by the Messrs. Laird, as early as the 9th October, 1861, copies of which are part of the documents and evidence filed by the United States with their Counter-Case, show conclusively that she never was intended for anything else than a vessel of war' (p59 of North America No. 12 (1872) Argument of the United States delivered to the Tribunal of Arbitration at Geneva, June 15, 1872).

It would therefore seem that there were at least three additional copies of the documents and plans made. As copies of the original it is unlikely that they would show any additional information.

CONTRACT
(Original at Mariners' Museum)

Articles of Agreement made the First day of August One thousand eight hundred and sixty one Between William Laird the Younger of Birkenhead in the County of Chester Shipbuilder on behalf of himself and his several Copartners in trade carrying on business in the name of John Laird Sons and Company of the one part and James Dunwoody Bulloch of the other part, Whereas it has lately been agreed between the said parties hereto that the said William Laird the Younger and his said Copartners shall build launch and complete for the said party hereto of the other part a Wooden Screw Steam Vessel of the dimensions and particulars hereinafter mentioned for the sum of Forty seven thousand five hundred pounds and upon the terms hereinafter expressed   Now these presents Witness that in consideration of the several payments to be made by the party hereto of the other part in pursuance of the covenant in that behalf hereinafter contained they the said William Laird the Younger and his said Copartners do hereby for themselves their heirs executors and administrators Covenant with the said party hereto of the other part his executors administrators and assigns in the manner following that is to say   That the said William Laird the Younger and his said Copartners their executors or administrators will at their own costs and charges build rig and complete for the said party hereto of the other part with the best materials and of the best description which can be obtained and with every requisite ready for Sea and in accordance with the Specifications hereto annexed and signed by the parties hereto A Good staunch and substantial Wooden Screw Steam Ship or Vessel   And also that the said Vessel shall at the costs expenses and risk of the said William Laird the Younger and his said Copartners their executors or administrators be launched and safely delivered afloat and uninjured in the River Mersey so completed as aforesaid into the hands of the party hereto of the other part or his Agent authorised in writing on or before the First day of June next ensuing the date hereof or sooner if possible   And that the said William Laird the Younger and his said Copartners on or before such last named day will deliver to the said party hereto of the other part his executors administrators or assigns the Builders Certificate of the said Vessel wherein the said last named party or his nominee or nominees shall be declared to be the first purchasers of the said Vessel   And further that from the day of the date hereof until the said Vessel shall be delivered uninjured as aforesaid they the said William Laird the Younger and his said Copartners their executors or administrators will from time to time keep the said Vessel insured against fire to such an amount as the said party hereto of the other part shall for the time being have paid on account of the price of the said Vessel in the Office of the Royal Insurance Company Liverpool or in such other Office as may be agreed upon for the benefit of the said party hereto of the other part and that the said William Laird the Younger and his said Copartners shall pay all such premiums duties and other monies (if any) as shall become payable in order to keep the said Vessel so insured   and that in default thereof it shall be lawful but not obligatory for the said party hereto of the other part his executors administrators or assigns to insure the said Vessel in manner aforesaid in his or their own name or names but at the cost of the said William Laird the Younger and his said Copartners their executors or administrators and that the premiums of such Insurances and all other costs of and attending the same and the recovery of the sums insured shall be deducted from the monies hereinafter mentioned to be paid to the said William Laird the Younger and his said Copartners and that in case the same premiums and costs shall not be so deducted the said William Laird the Younger and his said Copartners their executors or administrators shall upon demand pay the same to the said party hereto of the other part his executors administrators or assigns   And that the said William Laird the Younger and his said Copartners their executors or administrators shall replace any and every defective or bad material or work of any description in the Engines Boilers Machinery and appurtenances of the said Vessel that may become apparent within six months after such delivery as aforesaid and which shall be proved by the said party hereto of the other part to have existed at the time of such delivery without charge to the party hereto of the other part his executors administrators or assigns   And that at all times during the building launching and completing of the said Ship hereinbefore agreed to be built such person or persons as the said party hereto of the other part his executors administrators or assigns shall from time to time appoint for that purpose on his or their part shall be allowed to come in upon and about the said Vessel and every part thereof to superintend direct and view the materials and workmanship and state of progress of the same   And these presents further Witness that in consideration of the premises the said party hereto of the other part doth hereby for himself his heirs executors and administrators covenant with the said William Laird the Younger and his said Copartners their executors administrators and assigns that he the said party hereto of the other part will pay to the said William Laird the Younger and his said Copartners their executors or administrators as the price of the said Ship so to be built launched fitted and completed as aforesaid the sum of Forty seven thousand five hundred pounds by five equal instalments or payments such payments to be made as follows that is to say One equal fifth part of said Sum on the execution of these presents–One other equal fifth part thereof when the Frame of said Ship shall be up–One other equal fifth part thereof when the upper and lower deck shelves are in place, Beams in, Keelson in place, Garboard Strakes fitted and bolted, and Bends dumped on–One other equal fifth part thereof when the Ship is launched–and the remaining equal fifth part thereof when the same shall be satisfactorily tried and on delivery by the said William Laird the Younger and his said Copartners their executors or administrators of the said Builders Certificate stating the said party hereto of the other part or his nominee to be the first purchaser of the said Ship and delivery of the said Ship uninjured into the possession of the said party hereto of the other part or his authorized agent duly appointed to receive the same   And it is hereby covenanted and agreed by and between the parties hereto that if at any time during the building and completing of the said Vessel the said party hereto of the other part should direct any alteration or addition to be made in the building and constructing of the said Ship the same shall be made by the said William Laird the Younger and his said Copartners their executors or administrators upon the amount thereof being first agreed to by the parties hereto   And further that if either of the said parties hereto their executors or administrators shall in the building and constructing of the said Vessel consider that any modifications of or deviations from the said Specification will be desirable, it is hereby agreed that any such modifications or deviations shall be made by the said William Laird the Younger and his Copartners but without any extra charge to the said party hereto of the other part   It being hereby declared and agreed by and between the parties hereto that no such modifications or deviations shall in any manner injuriously affect the general intention and design of the said Specification nor the efficiency of the said Vessel when completed   Provided always and it is hereby further agreed that any ommissions which may occur in the said Specifications shall be supplied and made good by the said William Laird the Younger and his said Copartners their executors or administrators without any extra charge in the same manner as if the same had formed part of the original Specifications   And it is further agreed that such damage as shall happen to the said Ship from fire or otherwise previously to her being delivered to the said party hereto of the other part or his agent as aforesaid shall be forthwith made good by the said William Laird the Younger and his said Copartners their executors or administrators and any monies recovered from the said Insurance Office or Offices shall be applied in payment of the expense thereof   And further that the said Vessel to be built as aforesaid shall during the building and completion thereof and until the same shall be launched and delivered as aforesaid stand chargeable and charged with and be a security to the party hereto of the other part his executors administrators and assigns for all such sums of money as he or they shall in the meantime have advanced or paid to the said William Laird the Younger and his said Copartners their executors or administrators in pursuance of these presents to the intent that the said party hereto of the other part his executors administrators and assigns and the said Vessel shall and may be thereby protected from and indemnified against the debts contracts or engagements or otherwise affected by any act of the said William Laird the Younger and his said Copartners their executors or administrators   And it is hereby expressly covenanted and agreed by and between the parties hereto that if during and until the construction equipment and delivery of the said Vessel as aforesaid any dispute shall arise between the parties hereto their respective executors or administrators out of or relating to the said Vessel her building equipment and delivery or the terms and construction of these presents the same shall within thirty days after request in writing by either of the parties in difference be referred to two indifferent persons one to be named by the said William Laird the Younger and his said Copartners their executors or administrators and the other by the party hereto of the other part his executors or administrators   And in default of either party naming an Arbitrator within thirty days then the Arbitrator to be named by the other party shall have power to appoint the second Arbitrator and the two Arbitrators to be named in either of the manners aforesaid shall before proceeding in the reference appoint a third Arbitrator   And if such two Arbitrators shall neglect to appoint a third for one month after their own appointment such third Arbitrator shall be named by Her Majesty's Attorney General or Solicitor General for the time being on the application of either party   And the award of any two such Arbitrators shall be conclusive if given under their hands within thirty days and the disputing parties shall enter into such Bonds and Agreements of Arbitration and with such clauses therein as are usual and proper in such instruments and any submission or reference to Arbitration under or by virtue of these presents may be made a rule of any of her Majesty's Courts at Westminster according to the statute in that behalf if any such Court shall so please and either party shall be at liberty to apply to the said Court for that purpose and to instruct Counsel to consent thereto for the other party.   In Witness whereof the said parties to these presents have hereunto set their hands the day and year first above written.

William Laird Jr
James D Bulloch

Signed by the Parties
in the Presence of
John Green
Book keeper
Birkenhead

SPECIFICATION
(Original in the Mariners' Museum)

Specification of a Screw Steam Vessel and her Machinery referred to in the Contract attached hereto

Dimensions		
	Length	210ft
	Beam Extreme	32ft
	Depth	17ft 3in
	Tonnage	$1023^{827}/_{940}$ Tons
	Estimated draught of Water when complete without Coals or Stores	Aft 12 ft / Ford 10 ft
	Estimated draught of Water with Stores Water & Coals for 10 days easy Steaming Say 250 to 300 Tons	15 ft
	Estimated Speed when in fair trim	12 knots

The Hull	and Machinery to be built in general accordance with the Plans & Specification. Everything both as to materials fastenings and workmanship to be of the best quality.	
The Rig	To be that of a Barque as shewn on Plan – long lower masts and good square sails. The Masts Spars and Rigging to be properly proportioned and fitted.	
The Outfit	of Sails, Ropes, Shipchandlery, Anchors, Cables, Boats Hawsers Warps &c to be generally the same in quantity and quality as usually known by the term of "East India Outfit" which is in fact a double suit of Sails (except Studding Sails and Skysails) and other stores in proportion so that the Ship is ready for a long voyage	
General Conditions	The Specification and Plans now prepared shew <u>generally</u> the class of Vessel and Machinery intended – but as many things cannot be drawn on the plans or named in the Specification it is understood that the Contract includes the entire completion of the Ship for Sea as usual for Vessels of this class.	
Payments	⅕th On Contracting ⅕th On Frame being up ⅕th When the upper and lower deck Shelves are in place, Beams in, Keelson in place Garboard Strakes fitted and bolted and Bends dumped on ⅕th When the Vessel is launched ⅕th When satisfactorily tried	

Scantlings

Keel *Elm Eng. except the foremost and after piece which are to be English Oak*	Sided in Midships " Forward " Aft Moulded To have Six ⅞" Copper Bolts in each Scarph Lip Bolts to be ½" diameter	14 inches 11 " 11 " 16 "
Keelson *Teak or Greenheart*	Sided in Midships " Forward & Aft Moulded Bolted with Copper Bolts 1⅛" and 1¼" diameter	14 inches 11 " 15 "
Stem *English Oak*	Sided at the Head " " " Fore foot Moulded as per draught	14 inches 11 "
Apron *English Oak*	Sided as the Stem	
Stern Post *English or African Oak*	Sided at the Head " " Upper Pintle " " Heel	15 inches 13 " 11 "
Fore Post *English Oak*	Sided at the Head " " " Heel	14 inches 11½ "
Room & Space	Amidships Forward & Aft	2ft 3in 2ft 4in
Cross Pieces *English Oak*	Sided in Midships " Forward & Aft Moulded at the Cutting down " " the Head	10 @ 11 inches 9 @ 10 " 13 inches 10 "
Half Floors *English Oak*	Sided in midships " Forward & Aft Moulded at the Head	10 @ 11 inches 9 @ 10 " 9 "
First Futtocks *English Oak*	Sided in Midships " Forward & Aft Moulded at the Head	8 @ 9 inches 8 " 8½ "
Second Futtocks *English Oak*	Sided in Midships " Forward & Aft Moulded at the Head	7 @ 8 inches 7 " 7½ " "
Third Futtocks *English Oak*	Sided in Midships " Forward & Aft Moulded at the Head	7 inches 6½ " 7 "
	Larch or Mahogany may be used in upper part of the Frame except in Wake of Channels, Ports &c where the timbers are to be of Oak	
Fourth Futtock & Top Timbers	Sided Moulded at Planksheer " " Rail	7 inches 6 " 5 "
Rough Tree Timbers	Sided at Planksheer " " Rail Moulded at Planksheer " " Rail	6 inches 5 " 6 " 4½ "
Port Timbers and those in Wake of Channels *English Oak*	Sided	8 inches
Garboard *English or American Elm*	and Thick Strakes next the Keel to be of Elm 6 in thick and bolted with ⅞" Copper bolts	

Bottom Plank	Thick	3½ inches
	To be of Larch or Pitch Pine from the Garboard to the turn of the Bilge, between this and the Wales English Oak or Teak or Mahogany or Greenheart. The fore and after hoods to be of English Oak in all cases. To be copper fastened.	
Wales	Thick	5 inches
English Oak or Teak or Greenheart	The whole of the outside Plank above the height of the Lower deck beams to be fastened with ¾" copper through bolts	
Planking of Topside	Thick	Tapering from 2 to 3 inches
Oak Teak or Mahogany		
Rough Tree Rail	Broad	8 inches
	Thick	4 "
Oak or teak		
Limber strakes	Thick	4 inches
Oak or Greenheart		
Bands at Floorheads	Thick	4 inches
English Oak or Greenheart		
Diagonal Truss Pieces	Broad	10 inches
	Thick	4 "
English Oak	To be fastened with a ¾" Copper bolt in each Timber	
Iron Diagonal Riders	Broad	4 inches
	Thick	⅝ "
	To be fastened alternately with ¾" Copper Bolts and ¾" Galvanized Iron	
Lower Deck Shelf	Deep	8 inches
	Broad amidships	12 "
Teak or African or English Oak or Mahogany	" fore and aft	10 "
	To be fastened with ⅞" Copper bolts	
Lower Deck Beams	Sided	7 inches
	Moulded at Middle	7 "
Dantzic fir except in wake of Mast Bitts, Engine Room Bulkheads &c which are to be of Oak or Teak – over Engine room of iron	" " Ends	6½ "
	To round	4 "
Iron Knees	Weighing about 3 qrs bolted in the throat with ⅞" Bolts, and in the Beam and Side Arms with ¾" Bolts	
Lower Deck Waterway	Broad	10 inches
	Thick	6 "
Oak or Teak or Mahogany	Fastened with ¾" Copper through bolts and ¾" Tie bolts through each beam	
Lower Deck Flat	Thick	2½ inches
Dantzic fir properly seasoned	Fastened with mixed metal nails	
Upper Deck Clamps	To be worked in Six Strakes 5" thick tapering to 4" at the Lower edge	
Oak or Teak		
Upper Deck Shelf	Deep	11 inches
	Broad amidships	13 "
Teak or Mahogany	" forward & aft	11 "
	Fastened with 1" Copper bolts	
Upper Deck Beams	Sided	10 inches
	Moulded in the middle	9½ "
Dantzic fir or Mahogany except those under the Pivot guns and at the masts, riding bitts &c which are to be of Oak or Teak	" at the ends	9 "
	To round	6 "
Iron Knees to Upper Deck	To weigh not less than 1 cwt – throat bolts 1" diameter – those in the beam & side arms ⅞"	
Upper Deck Flat	Thick	3½ inches
Dantzic fir properly seasoned	Except those Strakes over which the trucks of the Pivot Guns will pass and those in a line with the working of the chain cables which are to be of Oak	
Waterway & Planksheer	Thick	8 inches
Teak or Mahogany	Fastened with ¾" Copper through Bolts and a ⅞" up and down Tie bolt in each beam	
Engine Room Bulkheads	Thick	3 inches
Teak or Dantzic Oak		
Ekings	Sided	8½ inches
English Oak		

THE PROPOSED SHIP

Riding Bitts *African Oak or Greenheart*	Square at the head " " " heel	14 inches 10 "
Standards *English Oak*	Sided	9 inches
Coamings & Head Ledges *Teak or Oak*	Thick Above the beam Except those round the Propeller well and the Engine Room Ladderways	5 inches 16 "
Catheads *English Oak*	Sided Deep Supporters to be fastened with ¾" Copper bolts	10½ inches 9 "
Channels *Teak or Mahogany*	Thick Tapering to	4 inches 3½ "
Chain Plates	Main and Fore Mizen	2" x 1⅛" 1½" x 1"
Rudder *English Oak*	Main Piece	16" diameter at head 14" " at Upper Pintle
Pintles & Braces	To be four in number disposed of as shewn on the drawing and fitted on the late Captain Lihon's plan, one set of spare Pins to be supplied by the Contractor	
Tillers	To have an Iron Tiller and efficient Steering Gear	
Circular Scuttles	To be 6" diameter disposed of as shewn on the profile	
Bitts	To be fitted at each Mast if required with all necessary blocks Pins &c	
Blocks Cleats &c	All necessary Blocks, Belaying Cleats and Pin racks to be fitted	
Bowsprit	Whatever Security may be requisite for either iron or wood Bowsprit	
Boat Davits	To have Iron davits on each side and one pair at the Stern as shewn upon the drawings to be completed	
Iron Coaling & Ventilating Scuttles	To be fitted as shewn on the Plan	
Warping Blocks	To be fitted complete with scores & rollers	

Pillars	All necessary Pillars whether of Iron or Wood to be fitted
Carlings *of Oak*	Middle Line and other Carlings requisite for Gun Pivots &c to be fitted
Ring Bolts	To fit all necessary Ring Eye & Stopper Bolts
Ports	To be arranged as shewn upon the drawing and fitted with all requisite Sills, Port Holes &c as may be directed by the Overseer hung with metal hinges if required
Shot Racks	Iron Shot Racks to be fitted round the hatches and at such parts of the Deck as may be required
Magazine Bulkheads	To build Magazine and Light Room with lining and all racks complete as described upon the drawings: Bulkheads to be of Teak or Oak 3 inches thick
Shell Rooms *of Dantzic fir*	To build three shell rooms with all racks complete as is usual in H.M. Service and as described upon the drawings
Ladders	To fit Ladders where and of the description shewn upon the drawings
Galley	To fit the cant, Lead & Tin the Beams and copper the flat complete
Chain Lockers	To be built complete of Oak
Store Rooms &c *Dantzic Fir*	To build Store Sail & Bread Rooms complete with all Bulkheads
Cabins	To be fitted according to the Plans
Lockers &c	Lockers and all conveniences for berthing the crew to be fitted as shewn on the drawings
Metal Castings	for connecting the Knee and afterpost – to be provided and fitted by the Contractor agreeably to a sketch which will be furnished
Water Closets	abaft and conveniences for Seamen forward to be fitted as shewn upon the drawings
Iron Tanks	The Iron tanks forward and aft for the protection of the Magazine and Shell Room
Capstan & Riding Bitts	on Brown & Harfield's Patent
General Fastenings	The Outside planking to be fastened down with mixed metal bolt nails and copper through bolts – the bolts to be at the butts and at about every 5 feet – ¾" diameter – All through bolts to be

	driven and clenched upon Rings – The Metal dumps to be of sufficient length to be ¼ more in the timber than in the plank – The whole of the fastenings to be executed as is usual in H.M. service
Caulking	The Vessel to be caulked with the same number of threads of Oakum and Spunyarn as is used in H.M. Service
Painting	To be payed within and without board with three coats of Paint. The Cabins to be grained or painted with such color as the overseer may direct

Witness	William Laird Jr
John Green	James D Bulloch

Specification of a Pair of Marine Steam Engines with Screw Propeller of 300 HP

Dimensions &c	No. of Cylinders	2
	Diam of "	56 ins
	Stroke Not less than	27 "
	No. of Revolutions per Minute	65
	Power by English Admiralty Rule	300 HP

The Engines to be direct acting horizontal condensing Engines having the Cylinders on one side of the Crank Shaft, & the condenser, Pumps &c on the other

The Slide Valves to be fitted with rings on the back to relieve the pressure
Air Pump valves to be of India rubber with brass seals and guards
Discharge valves at ships side to be of Brass
Air pumps to be horizontal, double acting
Feed & Bilge pumps, horizontal, single acting with solid plunger & India rubber valves
Hand pump, single acting, of suitable size
Donkey Engine Pump, double acting, of suitable size

Bed plates with main bearings & guides, Cylinders Pistons, Cylinder Covers, Slide Valves & Valve casings, Condensers & covers, Eccentric Wheels Balance weights, Plummer blocks for Screw Shafting, safety & Stop Valve Boxes, all to be of Cast Iron

The Shafts, Piston rods, Connecting rods & other working parts to be of wrought iron

All Bearings to be of Brass, & if required to be lined with Patent Metal

Screw Propeller & lifting frame, to be of Brass, & fitted on the same plan as adopted in H.M. Service

The Propeller Shaft Bearings to be lined with Lignum Vitae Strips

Boilers

The Boilers to be tubular, 4 in number, having the tubes across the Boiler at the back of the Furnaces, with a combustion chamber between the Bridge & the Tube plate on the plan adopted for Boilers We are now making for Government

The thickness of the Boiler plates to be as follows
Bottoms of Shells & Furnaces, & lower parts of Fronts, to be $7/16$" – Uptakes ½" – Tube Plates ⅝"
All other parts of ⅜"

Each boiler to have 3 furnaces, each about 2 ft 9 in wide with a length of Fire Bar of about 6 ft 6 ins

Tubes	The Tubes to be of Brass	
	The length of the Tubes	about 5 ft 9 in
	" diameter " "	2½ in
Funnel	The Funnel to be made to lower (if possible, below the level of the Rail)	

List of Tools & Spare Articles for Marine Engines (with Screw Propeller) of 300 HP

Engineer's Tools

Brushes for Boiler tubes	60
Drifts, Short & long	6
Fire Irons (assorted)	18
Mandrills	6
Scrapers circular & forked	15 each
A complete set of Spanners & wrenches to fit all parts of the Engines	
Stocks, Taps & Dies from ¼" to 1¼"	1 set

Spare Gear

Air Pump rod	1
Bars, Furnace	½ set
Bearers for 1 Furnace	1 set
Boiler plates	6 cwt
Bolts & Nuts for Engines properly assorted	120
Brasses for Hoisting Frame	1 set
Collars for Brass Thrust	2 "
Cylinder Cover of each kind	1
Eccentric Ring (if of Brass) of every size	1
Ferrules for Boiler Tubes	150

Piston & Rod, with Brasses, caps & bolts complete	1
Plummer Block Brasses for Propeller Shafting	1 pair
Propeller Blades	1 "
Rod, connecting, with cap bolts & brasses complete	1
Rod, Feed Pump	1
" Bilge Pump	1
" Slide	1
Springs for each Piston	1 set
Springs for other parts of Engines for 1 Engine	1 set
Tubes, Boiler	30
" Glass for Boilers	8
Valves of Vulcanized India Rubber for each Engine	2 sets
Washers, Iron, of various sizes	1 Gross
White Metal	1½ cwt

Witness	William Laird Jr
John Green	James D Bulloch

COPY SPECIFICATION FROM LAIRD BOOK
(Original now in Wirral Archives)

No. 290   James Dunwoody Bulloch
Wooden Screw Steamer *Enrica*

Launched & docked in No 4 Dock   14 May 1862
Sailed   29 July   "

Contracting Parties	James Dunwoody Bulloch Esq and John Laird Sons & Company
Date of Contract	1st August 1861
Price	£47,500
Payment	⅕ (£9,500) on execution of Contract
"   9,500 when the Frame is up
"   9,500 when the upper and lower Deck shelves are in places – Beams in – Keelson in place – Garboard strakes fitted & bolted – and bends dumped on
"   9,500 when Vessel Launched
"   9,500 when satisfactorily tried and delivered afloat uninjured in the River Mersey with the Builder's Certificate
———
£47,500

	To build rig & complete the Vessel with the best materials, and of the best description which can be obtained, and with every requisite ready for Sea, and in accordance with the Specifications annexed to the Contract
Fire Insurance	Until Vessel delivered Contractors to keep the same Insured against fire in the office of the Royal Insurance Co. Liverpool, or in such other office as may be agreed upon, for the benefit of the Owner, to the amount of the Instalments paid by him
Any damage by fire or otherwise previously to delivery to be made good by the Contractors, and any monies recovered from the Insurance Office to be applied in the expence thereof
Guarantee	Contractors to replace any and every defective or bad material or work of any description in the Engines Boilers Machinery & appurtenances of the Vessel, that may become apparent within 6 months after delivery, and which shall be proved by the Owner to have existed at the time of delivery, without charge
Inspection	Any person or persons appointed by the Owner for that purpose, shall be allowed to come aboard the Vessel to superintend direct and view the materials and workmanship, and state of progress of the same
Alterations or Additions	If the Owner shall direct any alteration or addition to be made in building and constructing the Vessel, the same shall be made by the Contractors, upon the amount thereof being first agreed to by the Parties
Modifications or Deviations	If either party shall consider that any modifications of, or deviations from, the Specifications will be desirable, such modifications or deviations shall be made by the Contractors but without any extra charge to the Owner.
It being agreed that no such modifications or deviations shall in any manner injuriously affect the general intention and design of the Specifications, nor the efficiency of the Vessel when completed
Omissions	Omissions which may occur in the Specifications to be supplied and made good by the Contractors without any extra charge, in

	the same manner as if the same had formed part of the original Specifications
Security to Owner	Until launched and delivered to Owner, the Vessel to be a Security to him for all monies he shall pay to the Contractors in the mean time
Disputes	To be referred to Arbitrators to be mutually appointed
Completion & Delivery	On or before 1st June 1862, or sooner if possible

Specification of Vessel

Dimensions	Length	210 feet
	Beam extreme	32 "
	Depth	17 ft 3 ins
	Tonnage	1023^{827}/$_{940}$ Tons

Net Customs Measurement 288 ^{50}/$_{100}$

Draft	Estimated Draft of Water when complete without Coals or Stores } Aft 12ft Ford. 10ft
	Estimated Draft with Stores Water & Coals for 10 days easy steaming, say 250 - 300 Tons } 15 ft
Speed	Estimated Speed when in fair Trim 12 knots
Hull & Machinery	to be built in general accordance with the Plans & Specification. Every thing both as to Materials, fastenings & workmanship to be of the best quality
Rig	To be that of a Barque, as shown on the Plan Long lower masts, and good square sails The Masts, Spars & Rigging to be properly proportioned & fitted
Outfit	of Sails, Ropes, Shipchandlery, Anchors, Cables, Boats, Hawsers, Warps &c, to be generally the same in quantity & quality as usually known by the term of East India Outfit, which is, in fact, a double suit of Sails (except Studding Sails & Skysails), and other Stores in proportion, so that the ship is ready for a long voyage
General Conditions	The Specification & Plans now prepared, shew generally the class of Vessel and Machinery intended, but as many things cannot be drawn on the Plans or named in the Specification, it is understood that the Contract includes the entire completion of the ship for Sea as usual for Vessels of this class

Specification of Engines with screw Propeller

Dimensions &c	No. of Cylinders	2
	Diameter of "	56 ins
	Stroke not less than	27 ins
	No. of Revolutions per Minute	68
	Power by English Admiralty Rule	300 HP

Direct acting, horizontal, condensing Engines having the Cylinders on one side of the crank shaft, and the Condenser, Pumps &c on the other.

Shafts Piston rods, connecting rods and other working parts to be of wrought iron

All Bearings to be of Brass, and if required to be lined with Patent Metal

Screw Propeller & Lifting Frame to be of Brass, & fitted on same plan as adopted in H.M. service

Propeller Shaft Bearings to be lined with lignum vitae strips

Boilers

The Boilers to be Tubular, 4 in No., having the Tubes across the Boiler at the back of the Furnaces with a combustion chamber between the Bridge & the Tube Plates, on plan adopted for Boilers we are now making for Government

Thickness of Boiler Plates;
Bottom of Shells & Furnaces & lower parts of fronts ^{7}/$_{16}$"
Uptakes ½"   Tube Plates ⅝"
All other parts ⅜"

Furnaces	Each Boiler to have 3 furnaces, each about 2 ft 9 in wide, with a length of fire Bar of about 6 ft 6 in
Tubes	To be of Brass
	Length of Tubes — about 5 ft 9 in
	Diameter — 2½ in
Funnel	To be made to lower (if possible below the level of Rail)

Engineer's Tools

Brushes for Boiler tubes	60
Drifts, Short & long	6
Fire Irons (assorted)	18
Mandrills	6
Scrapers circular & forked	15 each
A complete set of Spanners & winches [?wrenches] to fit all parts of the Engines	
Stocks, Taps & Dies from ¼" to 1¼"	1 set

Spare Gear – (included in Contract price)

Air Pump rod	1
Bars, Furnace	½ set
Bearers for 1 Furnace	1 set
Boiler plates	6 cwt
Bolts & Nuts (properly assorted) for Engines	120
Brasses for Hoisting Frame	1 set
Collars for Brass Thrust	2
Cylinder Cover of each kind	1
Eccentric Rod (if of Brass) of every size	1
Ferrules for Boiler Tubes	150
Piston & Rod, with Brasses caps & bolts complete	1
Plummer Block Brasses for Propeller Shafting	1 pair
Propeller Blades	1 "
Rod, connecting, with cap bolts & brasses complete	1
Rod, Feed Pump	1
" Bilge Pump	1
" Slide	1
Springs for each Piston	1 set
Springs for other parts of Engine, for 1 Engine	1 set
Tubes, Boiler	30
" Glass for Boilers	8
Valves of Vulcanized India Rubber for each Engine	2 sets
Washers, Iron, of various sizes	1 Gross
White Metal	1½ cwt

Extras

Hammocks Beds Blankets }	ordered from	J Wrenn & Co
Mess Utensils	"	Foster & Son
Canister in Magazine	"	Siddeby & Co
Handing Buckets	"	J Boulton
Additional Steering gear –		fitted below deck
Provisions		Ewing & Co
Additional Nautical Instruments		Frodsham & Keen
2 Chronometers		"
Extra Storm Sail		Callan & Co
Sundry Ensyns?? nations		Phillip

Masts and Spars No. 290   Original Sail Plan

		Fore Mast			Main Mast		
		Ft.	*in.*	*Dia.*	*Ft.*	*in.*	*Dia.*
Mast	Deck to Hounds	59	0	27	62	0	27
	Head	10	6		10	6	
	Housed (abt)	18	6		8	0	
	Over All (abt)	88	0		80	6	
Topmast	Heel to Stop	27	6	13	27	6	13
	Topgallant Mast	14	0	10	14	0	10
	Royal	8	0	7	8	0	7
	Pole	3	0		3	0	
	Overall	52	6		52	6	
Yard	overall	65	0	14	65	0	14
	Arms each	2	9		2	9	
Topsail Yard	overall	46	6	10	46	6	10
	Arms each	2	9		2	9	
Topgallant Yard	overall	31	0	7	31	0	7
	Arms each	2	0		2	0	
Royal Yard	overall	22	6	5	22	6	5
	Arms each	1	6		1	6	
Gaff	overall	36	0	8	37	0	8
	Pole	2	0		2	0	
Boom	overall	52		13	53		13

Mizen Mast

		Ft.	in.	Dia.
Mast	Deck to Hounds	51	0	23
	Head	8	6	
	Housed (abt)	10	0	
	Over All (abt)	69	6	
Topmast	Heel to Stop	34	0	9½
	Pole	3	0	
Gaff	overall	35	0	7½
	Pole	3	0	
Boom	overall	50	0	12

Bowsprit

		Ft.	in.	Dia.
Bowsprit	outboard	22	0	24
	Housed	17	0	
	Overall	39	0	
Jibboom	outside cap	24	0	13
	housed	19	0	
	Pole	2	0	
	Overall	45	0	

The ship as built

Details of the ship as built (as she sailed from the Mersey) are given in various books that are now in the Cammell Laird Archive or the Williamson Art Gallery. Information on costs during building are given in First Cost Accounts and Estimate of Building Cost, both of which also include the weights of some of the items fitted – for example the copper sheathing was over 8½ tons. Unfortunately in some places the writing has faded or is difficult to read. In such cases the words or figures are replaced by question marks, or are preceded by a question mark. Both books give the time in man-days for some of the different trades. Where the figures exist they have been taken from these two books and are shown in the table.

Alabama Construction Times
Based on First Cost Accounts & Estimate of Building Costs
(only known figures given)

	Days		Days
Hull		Rigging	
Woodwork		Smiths	124
Carpenters	14,052	Riggers	272
Joiners	1885		1368½
Laborers	4378	**Cabins**	
Painters	523	Woodwork	
Ironwork		Joiners	920
Smiths	2879	Carpenters	4
Boilermakers	10	Painters	162
Machinery	59	Ironwork	
Fitters	90	Smiths	19
Coppering Bottom			1105
Carpenters	204	**Outfit**	
	24,080	Smiths	345
Masts & Spars		Machinery	46
Woodwork		Boilermakers	256
Carpenters	277	Painters	1½
Painters	11	Laborers	45
Ironwork		Carpenters	?59
Smiths	551	Fitters	29
Machinery	8½		781½
Laborers	95	TOTAL 27,335 days	
Lightning Conductors			
Carpenters	30		

The sum of these man-days worked is 27,335. The total will be higher than this because for some jobs only the costs are given, without any indication of time taken, possibly because they were subcontracted out. Work done by tradesmen on equipment bought in is similarly an unknown quantity. The engine side of the works operated separately from the shipbuilding side and there are no records of the work and time involved in constructing the engine (or any other engine of that period).

The Book of Elements contains the final dimensions of the ship, displacement, tonnage, sail area etc. for most of the ships built by the company. The entry for the *Alabama* has been extracted.

Pages from Dimensions and Particulars of Vessels, Book 1 contain details of draughts and displacements and some trial results. The details included in these books (there are six altogether) vary from ship to ship with *Alabama*'s entries being fairly typical. For the *Alabama* the actual weights are compared with the estimated ones for major items such as hull, boilers and engines. Also included is a copy of the particulars of the ship sent to the French naval architect Dupuy de Lôme.

The boiler book is no longer in the company archive but photocopies of four pages referring to the *Alabama* were made before it went missing. These pages give a drawing of the boilers and details of the number and size of the tubes. Also included are copies of indicator diagrams for the engines for two trial trips, one of which was on 29 July, the day the ship sailed from the Mersey. The diagram for 12 June 1862 is unfortunately very faint and has therefore had to be redrawn to the best of the available information. The diagram for the second trial is much clearer and easily read. From the different handwriting and way the diagram has been divided up it would appear that the calculations were done by two different people. The second trial has the engine number – 70 – written on it, and both have the name *Alabama* on.

The only two plans of the *Alabama* still in the Cammell Laird archive are actually copies of the originals (the whereabouts of which are unknown). In 1919 a copy was made of a sail plan held by Roy Laird which shows the ship as built and is slightly different to the one in the US National Archives. The differences are detailed and compared in Appendix 5, but the most significant one is that some masts are longer on the (later) Laird plan. The increases in length in the lower masts is 15in or 18in and the topmast and topgallant masts by 6in. A table giving these new spar sizes is given (page 37).

Possibly about the same time a copy was made of the plan of the engines. Some of the plan is in colour to show different parts (and is not easy to understand with everything shown on the three views), but unfortunately it shows only the engines and very little surrounding structure. This plan is reproduced, with an explanation of the various parts, in the section on Machinery (pages 139 to 181).

Most of the armament was from the Liverpool company Fawcett Preston and a lot of their plans of the guns survive. These for the *Alabama* have been redrawn, and missing ones reconstructed, and are included in the relevant section (pages 104 to 138). Parts of the upper deck are shown in the plans giving the position of the sweeps for the pivot guns. The original of this drawing was given to Bulloch on 8 August 1862, five days before he sailed with Semmes to meet the *Alabama* off the Azores. The hatches and companionways shown are presumably given just to show the clearance dur-

THE SHIP AS BUILT

ing pivoting the guns. These plans do give information as regards the size and spacing of various hatchways.

A private investigator called Maguire was employed by the American consul in Liverpool, Thomas H Dudley, to spy on the ship during building. Towards the end of this period he got aboard the ship and a description of the interior is included among manuscript pages of his reports at the Mariners' Museum. These reports are reproduced in full, and as well as covering the building of the ship has reports from men who served on the ship and returned home before the end of the cruise.

The American consul was collecting information to prove that the *Alabama* was a ship of war and he reported to the American ambassador in London, Charles Francis Adams. There was a lot of correspondence between Adams and the British Foreign Secretary, Earl Russell, over the ship. The letters were published in 1863 in *North America* No. 3 (1863), 'Correspondence respecting the "*ALABAMA*"'. The details contained in the letters are essentially the same as in Maguire's reports, and have not been reproduced.

COST

The cost of the *Alabama* as fitted for sea was given as:

Hull, complete with all equipment	£47,500
of which Machinery was £15,900	
Guns	£2,500
Magazine tanks	£616
Ordnance stores	£500
Small arms	£600
Total	£51,716

The builders made a profit on the contract of £453/16/10 (less than 1 per cent).

WEIGHT BREAKDOWN

Estimate based on Dimension & Particulars Book of the finished ship.

When she sailed from Birkenhead docks 28 July 1862 displacement was 1421 tons

This consisted of

HULL	Hull	655
	Chain & anchors	21
	Masts, spars, sails, outfit, etc	59
Total		735
MACHINERY		
	Engine	102
	Boilers	67
	Boiler water	51
	Propeller, shafting etc	20
	Spare gear, bunkers etc	10
Total		250
Total HULL & MACHINERY		985
Coal	in bunkers	285
	on deck	61
		346
Therefore water, stores, crew etc		90
Grand total (as sailed from Birkenhead)		1421
Armament (added later) about		50

FIRST COST ACCOUNTS

Alabama
No 290   Wooden Screw Steamer
213' 8" x 31' 2" x 18' = 1044 Tons BM   NR 288 Tons

Hull & Woodwork

Timber & Sawing		11,946/ 1/ 9
Cr. Ass P. Timber generally defective		357/ 3/ –
		11,588/18/ 9
Copper Rods, Dumps & Rings 20 -10-0-3	2178/ 5/ 5	
Comp. Nails Oakum, Bolts & sundries	388/ 6/ 9	
2 Kingston Valves	39/ –/ 4	2,605/12/ 6
Carried Forward		14,194/11/ 3

Brought Forward		14,194/11/ 3	

Wages

	ds 3864/6/-	ds 494/16/3		
Carpenters 14052 @ 5/6	Joiners 1885 @ 5/3		4359/ 2/ 3	
	893/16/10	106/15/7		
Laborers 4378 @ 4/1	Painters 523 @ 4/1		1000/12/ 5	
Turning, Planning Dks. Scrpg. Whitewashing &c			49/12/ –	5,409/ 6/ 8
				19,603/17/11

Ironwork

Smithwork Chain &c	48 - 6 - 2 - 16	580/12/ 4	
Castings &c	2 - 6 - 1 - 16		30/ 6/10
Galvanizing			8/ 9/ 9

Time

	ds 587/15/11	ds 2/2/6		
Smiths &c	2879 @ 4/1	B.Makers 10 @ 4/3	589/18/ 5	
	ds 29/10/-	ds 20/5/-		
Machinery	59 @ 10/- Fitters	90 @ 4/1	49/15/ –	1,226/ 5/ 9
Tradesmens Accounts				960/12/ 8
				2,219/15/ –

Coppering Bottom

Copper & Composition Nails 9 - 12 - 3 - 13		943/19/ 3	
Brown sheathing paper		5/19/ 7	949/19/ 3
Carpenters 204 days @ 6/-			61/ 4/ –
			1,011/ 3/ 3

Masts & Spars

Timber, Sawing & Sundries			341/10/11	
	83/2/-	2/15/-		
Carpenters 277 ds @ 6/-	Painters 11 ds @ 5/-		85/17/ –	
	6/10/-	1/15/-		
Riggers Painting	Leathering Gaffs		8/ 5/ –	435/12/11
<u>Ironwork</u> Mountings &c 2 - 19 - 0 - 18			44 / 7/ 5	
	112/9/11	4/5/-		
Smiths 551 ds @ 4/1 Machinery 8½ ds @ 10/-			<u>116/14/11</u>	161/ 2/ 4
Tradesmens Accounts			47/ 8/ –	
Laborers & Riggers Shipping				<u>20/12/11</u>	664/16/ 2

<u>Lightning Conductors</u>

Copper strips, Screws & vanes		36/14/ 6
Carpenters 30 days @ 6/-		9/ –/ –	45/14/ 6

Carried Forward 23,525/ 6/10

Brought Forward			23,525/ 6/10
Rigging			
Blocks, Dead Eyes, Sheer Poles &c			
Chain &c 2 - 11 - 3 - 3	40/14/ 1		
Smiths 124 ds @ 4/1	25/ 6/ 4	66/ -/ 5	
Tradesmens Accounts		632/18/ 8	
Riggers Rigging 272 ds	65/18/ 6	764/17/ 7	
Cabins			
Timber & Sawing & Sundries	395/11/ 8		
241/10/- 1/4/-			
Joiners 920 ds @ 5/3 Carpenters 4 ds @ 6/-	242/14/ –		
21/5/- 4/6/10			
French Polishing W.Washing Magazine	25/11/10		
40/10/- 1/17/-			
Painters 162 @ 5/- Deck cleaning	42/ 7/ –	706/ 4/ 6	
Cabins "			
Ironwork 0 - 4 - 2 - 0	2/14 / –		
Time Smiths Men 19 ds @ 4/1	3/17/ 7		
Galvanising Rods &c	–/18/ 2	7/ 9/ 9	
Tradesmens Accounts		267/ 8/ 4	
			981/ 2/ 7
Outfit			
Smithwork Chain &c 6 - 0 - 0 - 20	73/ 4/ 4		
d 70/8/9 23/ –/ –			
Smiths 345 @ 4/1 Machinery 46 d @ 10/-	93/ 8/ 9		
Galvanizing (J Hamilton Jun.)	1/19/ 4	168/12/ 5	
4 Water & 4 Oil Tanks & Fittings		94/ 8/ 6	
Paint & Painting, Boats Buckets &c		17/ 15/ 5	
Tradesmens Accounts		2245/19/ 6	
Riggers Bending Sails &c	4/11/ 6		
9/3/9 16/4/6			
Shipping Anchor &c ?Fittg stg gear	25/ 8/ 3	29/19/ 9	
Fresh Water Condenser complete		115/ 7/11	
			2672/ 3/ 6
Sundries		347/16/ 2	
475/0/0 150/0/0			
Commission (A E Byrne & Co) G D Rates	625/ –/ –		
Use of Launch Logs Gas &c	150/ –/ –	775/ –/ -	1122/16/ 2
Incidental Expenses on Iron 63 Tons@ £4		252/ –/ –	
" on Carptrs & Joiners Wages 37½% on £4772/10/ –		1790/ –/ –	2042/ –/ –
No. 70 Engines of 300 HP by Laird Bros. Spare Gear included			15,900/ –/ –
			£ 47,028/ 6/ 8

ESTIMATE OF BUILDING COSTS

No. 290 Gunboat S S *Alabama*

213¾ x 31¾ x 18 = 1044 BM   Keel laid July 1861

<u>Hull & Woodwork</u>

E Oak &c 56837 cft Gro		10,485/ 8/ 9		
Sawing 893/10/11 Pine Moulds &c 209/19/1		<u>1,103/10/ –</u>		
			11,588/18/ 9	
Copper Rods (Invcd. 11 d/oz)		1,582/ 5/ –		
Compo dumps & rings (" 11½ @ 1/1)		<u>596/ –/ 5</u>		
			2,178/ 5/ 5	
Nails, oakum &c		267/ 1/ 5		
Paint &c 96/4/9 Bolts fr Ribd 18/17/1		115/ 1/10		
5 Kingston Valves		39/ –/ 4		
			421/ 3/ 7	
Carpenters (Mould &c 271) 14052 @ 5/6		3864/ 6/ –		
Joiners (" 302) 1885 @ 5/3		494/16/ 3		
Labourers 4378 Painters 523 = 4901		1000/12/ 5		
Turning,16/12/- Planing 20/5/- ????????		<u>49/12/ –</u>	5,409/ 6/ 8	
				19,597/14/ 5

                                t   c   q

Iron Beams, straps bolts &c 48 - 6 - 2 - 16		580/12/ 4		
Castings (@ 11/6) 2 - 6 - 1 - 16		30/ 6/10		
Galvanizing		8/ 9/ 9		
Smiths 2879 587/15/11, B.M 10 2/2/6		589/18/ 5		
Machy 59 29/10/ – Fitters 90 20/5/-		49/15/ –		
			1,259/ 2/ 4	
Brass (rudr & sternfit. £277) 489/15/3 ⎫		520/ 8/ 3		
sidelts. 30/13/- ⎭				
Pumps & plumbing 240/12/3 Capstan 166/5/-		406/17/ 3		
polishing		4/ 8/ 4		
Carving, glazing & sundries		28/18/10	960/12/ 8	
				2,219/15/ –
Coppering bottom Sheets 8 - 13 - 2 - 24 10½		846/ 5/ 2		
Compo. nails (& paper 5/19/7) 0 - 19 - 0 - 17		103/14/ 1		
Carpenters 204 @ 6/-		<u>61/ 4/ –</u>		
			1,011/ 3/ 3	

<u>Masts & Spars.</u> Timber (spare 26)	324/13/ 8			
Paint, Leather nails &c	<u>16/17/ 3</u>	341/10/11		
Carpenters 277 83/2/- Painting &c		94/ 2/ –	435/12/11	

Mountings & tops 2 - 19 - 0 - 18		44/ 7/ 5		
Smiths 551 112/9/11 Machy. 8½ 4/ 5/ –		116/14/11		
Brass 32/12/- sheavg. &c		47/ 8/ –		
Labourers 95 19/7/11, Riggers 25/-		20/12/11	229/ 3/ 3	

                                        Carried Forward   23,057/15/11

	Brought Forward			23,057/15/11
Lightning Conductors (copr. 1/5 ?)		36/14/ 6		
Carpenters 30 days @ 6/-		9/ -/ -	45/14/ 6	
				710/10/ 8

                 t c q

Rigging. Blocks, sheaves &c 0 - 19 - 2 - 23		11/16/ 5		
Chain 1 - 12 - 0 - 10		28/17/ 8		
Smiths 124		25/ 6/ 4	66/ -/ 5	
	24/ 2/ 4			
Cordage (4T @ 36/6 & M 1T @ 33/-)	232/ 5/ 5	256/ 7/ 9		
Wire do. 221/3/11 Webg. 36/1/4		257/ 5/ 3		
Blocks &c 134/0/8 clip hks canvas &c 9/7/4		134/ 8/ -		
Riggers bendg sails 4/11/ 6		70/10/ -	703/ 8/ 8	24/ 2/ 4
				769/ 9/ 1

Cabins. Rods &c 0 - 4 - 2 - 0	3/12/ 2		
Smiths 19 days	3/17/ 7	7/ 9/ 9	
Timber 321/17/8 Paint & Sundries 73/14/ -	395/11/ 8		
4 1/4/-			
Joiners 920 241/10/- Painters 162 40/10/-	283/ 4/ -		
Polishing (???) 21/5/- Whitewashing 6/3/10	27/ 8/10	706/ 4/ 6	
Upholstery 155/8/-, Brass & tin, closets &c, lamps &c	267/ 8/ 4		
			981/ 2/ 7

Outfit

Galvanizing	1/19/ 4		
Outfit Davits & fittings 4 - 13- 2 - 21 ⎫	73/ 4/ 4		
Steering gear &c 1 - 6 - 1 - 27 ⎭			
Smiths 345 70/8/9 Machiy 46 23/-/-	93/ 8/ 9	168/12/ 5	
4 Water (& 4 Oil Tanks 3¾) 2 - 12- 3 - 1	31/13/ 1		
Blrmakers 256 54/8/- Paintrs 1½ 7/6	54/15/ 6		
Moulds, paint, coprpipes &c	7/19/11	94/ 8/ 6	

Anchors & cables 348/6/- Sails 661/0/10 ⎫	3/ 3/ -	flathr?	
242/-/8 ⎭	1,271/13/ 6		
Awnings, covers &c 20/6/-			
5 Boats 208/17/8 Hooks 10/10/-	219/17/ 8		
Cordage 42/0/3 Comps. &c 69/3/-	111/ 3/ 3		
25/7/6			
5 Hawsers (33/- & 36/6) 49/14/5 Coopr stores	75/ 1/11		
Cookg Range 57/9/8 Hose 39/19/8	97/ 9/ 4		
6/6/9	6/6 / 9		
Steerg Gear 89/5/10 Paint oil pitch &c 37/14/10	127/ -/ 8		
Shipchandlery & sundries	103/14/ 9		
Eplate, linen, Eware & glass	230/18/ 8	2245/19/ 6	

                                      Carried Forward   25,543/ -/ 7

Brought Forward			25,543/ –/ 7
Paint for Boats &c 7/7/11, Paintrs 10/7/6		17/15/ 5	
Labs do. 45 9/3/9, Carps ????? 59 16/ 4/ 6		25/ 8/ 3	
FW Condenser £35, Tanks &c 72/4			
Cocks 24/8/4 & 5/18/-		68/18/ 8	
Boiler 39/11/3 Fitters 29 6/18/-		46/ 9/ 3	
			2667/12/ –
<u>Sundries</u>			
Tallow &c Launch	8/14/ 4		
Tughire 64/14/6 Bt. hire 16/16/- Pilotage 8/14/-	90/ 4/ 6		
Riggers 24/14/- Nightkeepers 15/3/6	39/17/ 6		
Launch logs &c 156/10/4	168/ 6/ 6	168/ 6 / 6	
Paintg 15/15/- Sundries 18/6/6	<u>22/ 5/ 4</u>	161/ 1/ 8	
£100			
Insurance Buildg & Trials		168/ 8/ –	
Graving dock rates		150/ –/ –	168/ 6/ 6
			479/ 9/ 8
			28,605/ 3/ 2
Incidental Expenses 63 Tons		252/ –/ –	
" on Carps & Joiners 37½% on £4772/10/-		1790/ –/ –	2042/ –/ –
Carried Forward			
			30,647/ 3/ 2
No. 70 Engines 300 HP & Spare Gear			<u>15900/ –/ –</u>
			46,547/ 3/ 2
			24 2 4
Commission			475/ –/ –
			47,022/ 3/ 2
			24 2 4
			47,046/ 3/ 2

NOTE. Some words have faded or are difficult to read and so have been replaced by question marks.

BOOK OF ELEMENTS NO. 290 SCREW STEAMER *ALABAMA*

Length	Between Perpendiculars	213' 8"
	On Load Water Line	201' 8"
Breadth	Extreme	32' 0"
	Moulded	31' 2"
	For Tonnage	31.75
Depth	In Hold	18' 0"
	at Side	19' 9"

Note: Depth in Hold is given from top of Limber strake to top of Beam

Tonnage	BM		1044^{24}/$_{94}$
	Customs Measurement		288.5
		- Gross	682.31
Load Draught	from bottom of Keel	- Forward	15'
of Water		- Aft	15'
	from bottom of Rabbet	- Forward	14'
		- Aft	14'
Load Displacement			1438
Area of	Sails		14661
	Midship Section		362.2
	Load Water Line		5185.3

THE SHIP AS BUILT

Midship Section abaft Middle of Load Water Line		2.4
Centre of Gravity - Displacement	abaft Middle of LWL	3.667
	below LWL	5.48
	Load Water Line abaft Middle of LWL	5.287
	Midship Section - below LWL	5.85
Immersion per Inch on Load Water Line		12.35
Centre of Effort of Sail-	before Middle of LWL	17.4
	above LWL	51.3
Moment of Sails above LWL		748356
Ratio to Cir. Par.	Breadth to Length of LWL	6.306
	Breadth to Depth from LWL	0.4374
Metacentre - Height above Centre of Gravity of Displacement		7.33
Area of Rudder		48.6
Area of Plane of Lateral Resistance		2985
Square Foot of Ditto to one Foot of Rudder		61.4
Expanded Surface to Gunwale		11163
Girth of Midship Section		60
Ditto Multiplied by Length		12828
Ratio of Ditto to Expanded Surface		0.8702
Date of Launch	May 14, 1862	

ALABAMA: EXTRACTS FROM DIMENSIONS AND PARTICULARS OF VESSELS

Book 1

No. 290   May 14th 1862

Launching draught	Forward	8' 9"
	Aft	10' 7"
	Mean draught	9' 8"

Displacement at do.   690 tons

Weights on board

Chain   18¼
Anchor   2¾   } 35
Screw shafting and gear about 14 tons

Weight of Hull   655 tons

May 17th   Before lowering in the Masts, with the Boilers in and all the heavy weights of engine

Draught Forward 9' 5"
"   Aft   12' 0¾"   } Mean draught 10' 8⅞"

Displacement at do.   832 tons

May 31st   Steam up, all boilers full and 8 tons of Coal in

Draught Forward 10' 8½"
"   Aft   12' 10½"   } Mean draught 11' 9½"

Displacement at do.   978 tons

Draught	Displacement			
12 ft	1007 tons	Say armament	50 tons	
13 ft	1149	Stores	50	1438
14 ft	1294	Coal	300	-978
15 ft	1438		400	460

June 12th 1862

With 85 tons of coal, 10 tons Bread on board, Boilers empty

Draught Forward 11' 3"
"   Aft   12' 11"   } Mean draught 12' 1"

<u>1st Trial Trip underweigh</u>   Displacement at do.   1016 tons

Draught with boilers filled, 85 tons coal, and 10 tons bread

Draught Forward 11' 8¾"
"   Aft   13' 1¾"   } Mean draught 12' 5"

Displacement at do.   1067 tons

Displacement with boilers full   1067 tons
"   with boilers empty   <u>1016</u>
Weight of water in boilers   51 tons

The first trial of Engines was made in No 4 Dock on 31st May when they were kept working for 2 or 3 hours at a speed of about 40 revolutions – Every worked well & all bearings cool –

2nd Trial in Dock on Monday 9th June after having felted & lagged Pipes, Cylinders &c worked for 2 or 3 hours up to about 53 or 54 revolutions Every thing satisfactory –

1st Trial underweigh on June 12th for particulars see other book (*note book not available*).

Memorandum as to weight as compared with original <u>Estimate</u>

		Estimated	*actual* Real
Weight of Hull	{ with outfit including anchors, chains, masts, spars, sails, ropes &c }	750	735

*Hull when Launched   655 tons
Outfit as above   <u>80</u>
                              735

Weight of Machinery with water	275	250
(*including Bunkers & 9 tons spare gear)		
Coal		300
Armament		50
Stores		50
		1425

This was to be carried on 15 ft

Draft of water when first tried with 85 tons coal } 12' 5"   1067 tons
10 ton bread all outfit complete &c

or equal total weight of ship & machinery complete } 972
with water in boiler but without coal or stores

Displacement on 15 ft	1440 tons	
Weight of hull &c	972	
	468 for coals - store armament	
or say coal	285 in Bunkers	
Provisions	50	
Armament	50	
	385 = 83 tons for extra stores &c	

the Vessel was undocked from B.head on Monday 28th July her draft was

ford.	15' 3"	
aft	14' 6"	mean 14' 10½"
Displacement	1421 tons	

<u>Weight on board</u>

Coal in Bunkers	285
On deck	61
	346 tons

Water Tanks all full,
an extra amount of Stores &c,
provisions, spare spars, gear &c
but no armament or warlike stores

Actual Displacement			1421 tons
Weight of Hull & machinery	972		
Known weight Coal &c	346		
	1318	1318	
Leaves for weight of stores &c on board		103 tons	

4th August 1862

NO. 290 *ALABAMA*: PARTICULARS SENT BY MR LAIRD TO M. DUPUY DE LÔME 8 JANY 1863

	ft	ins
Length between Perpendiculars	213	8
Breadth extreme	32	-
Depth in hold	18	-
Draught of Water loaded	15	-

Tonnage   O M   1030 Tons

Engines   Nominal HP 300

Indicated HP 3 or 4 times depending on the grade of expansion used

Speed under Steam about   13 knots

This Vessel was built of wood sheathed with copper – of the best materials and workmanship same as in Vessels built for Her Majesty's Navy.

The Engines are on the direct Acting Horizontal principle, were also made by Messrs. Laird Bros. and are of the same description as Engines made by them for the Admiralty.

BOOK 2
(Part of table giving details for 14 vessels)

No. 290 *Alabama*

Length on LWL	201.8
Load Displacement	1438
Area of Mid Sec	362.2
Areas of Sails in ft.	14970.5
Position of centre of effort of all	
plain sail before middle of LWL	17.4

BOOK 4
(Part of table giving details for 9 vessels)

No. 290

Length between perps	213' 8"
Length on LWL	201.8
Breadth extreme	32
Depth – moulded	19.9
Draft ford. bottom of keel	15
" aft	15
Displacement	1438
Area of section	362.2
Area of Plain Sail	14661
Area per ton	10.2

THE SHIP AS BUILT

Area per foot of Section	40.47
Depth of Keel	12"
Centre of Effort before mid of LWL	17.4
Centre of Effort above LWL	51.3

BOILER SPEC

No. 79 Boiler for 290 Ship "*Alabama*"

Working pressure 20 lbs per sq inch

Nom H.P. of Engine   300

4 Boilers   1 Funnel (Telescopic)

No. of Furnaces	12
Width "	2' 9"
Length " Fire Bars	6' 6"
Fire Grate area	Total 214 sq ft
No. of Tubes (Brass) including 32 Stay Tubes	1160
Length of tubes	5' 6"
Diameter of tubes	2¾" Ex
Heating Surface of Tubes	4558 sq ft
" " of Furnace & Flame Box	1092 sq ft
" " of Uptake	200 sq ft
Heating Surface	Total 5850 sq ft
Area of Tube opening	39.5 sq ft
Area of Funnel Dia 5' 6"	23.7 sq ft
	16 - 15 - 0
	4
Weight. Weighed at Crane with Door & Bearers	67 - 0 - 0

MASTS AND SPARS NO. 290
BASED ON LAIRD SAIL PLAN

		Fore mast			Main mast		
		Ft.	in.	Dia.	Ft.	in.	Dia.
Mast	Deck to Hounds	60	3	27	63	3	27
	Head	10	6		10	9	
	Housed (abt)	18	6		8	0	
	Over All (abt)	89	3		82	0	
Topmast	Heel to Stop	28	0	13	28	0	13
	Topgallant Mast	14	6	10	14	6	10
	Royal	8	0	7	8	0	7
	Pole	3	0		3	0	
	Overall	53	6		53	6	
Yard	over all	65	0	14	65	0	14
	Arms each	2	9		2	9	
Topsail Yard	overall	46	6	10	46	6	10
	Arms each	2	9		2	9	
Topgallant Yard	overall	31	0	7	31	0	7
	Arms each	2	0		2	0	
Royal Yard	overall	22	6	5	22	6	5
	Arms each	1	6		1	6	
Gaff	overall	36	0	8	37	0	8
	Pole	2	0		2	0	
Boom	overall	52		13	53		13

Mizen Mast

		Ft.	in.	Dia.
Mast	Deck to Hounds	52	6	23
	Head	8	6	
	Housed (abt)	10	0	
	Over All (abt)	71	0	
Topmast	Heel to Stop	35	0	9½
	Pole	3	0	
Gaff	overall	35	0	7½
	Pole	3	0	
Boom	overall	50	0	12

Bowsprit

		Ft.	in.	Dia.
Bowsprit	outboard	22	0	24
	Housed	17	0	
	Overall	39	0	
Jibboom	outside cap	24	0	13
	housed	19	0	
	Pole	2	0	
	Overall	45	0	

Alabama indicator diagram for 12 June 1862

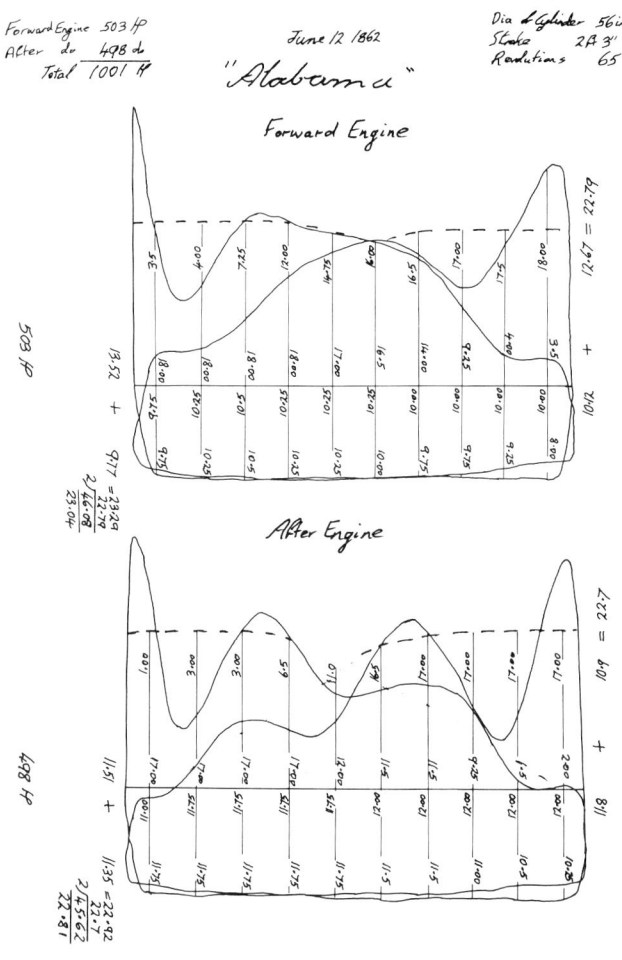

Boiler plan (scale = 1:96)

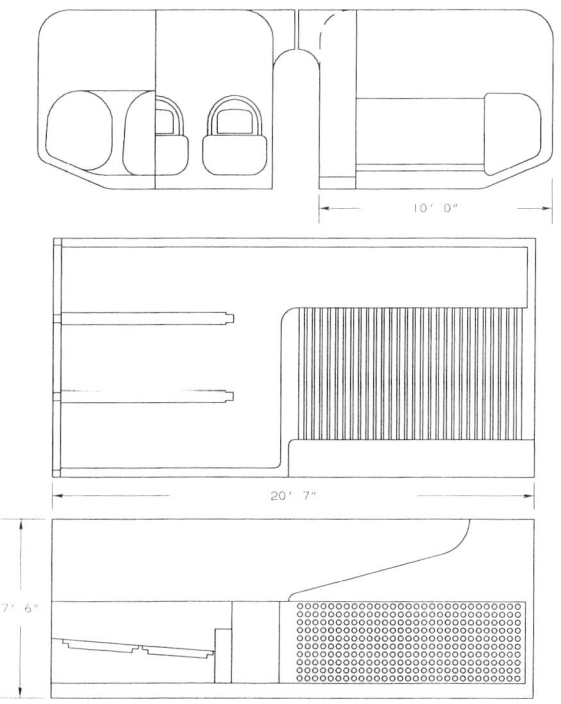

Alabama indicator diagram for 29 July 1862

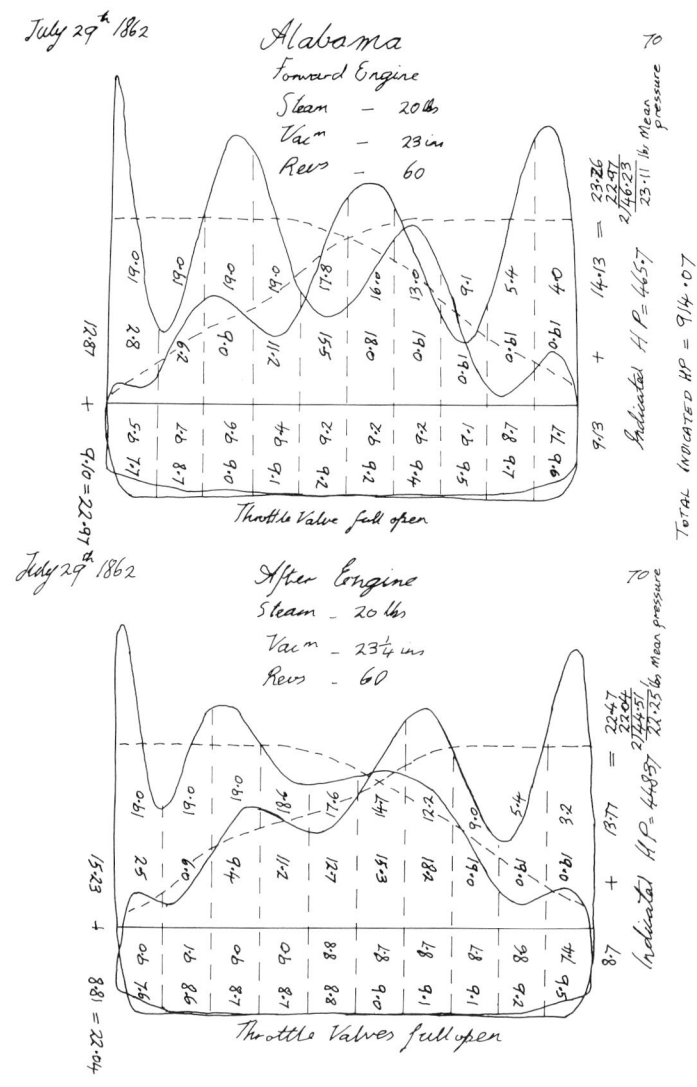

COPY OF MAGUIRE'S REPORT

'290' S.S. (Gunboat) now '*Alabama*' Confederate States Cruiser

The gunboat now building at Laird's yard, no person knows whom she is for, excepting Lairds themselves and the foreman carpenter. Mr. Laird declines to give any information. The information we shall endeavour to obtain from some person employed there.

(Reported Friday March 28th 1862)

The gunboat launched from Lairds' yard on Wednesday May 14th 1862, at which there was a very good attendance of gentlemen present, many Americans amongst them. There was no admittance to the yard, only those who were invited.

(Reported Tuesday May 6th 1862)

THE SHIP AS BUILT

Laird sail plan – original
(scale = 1:384)

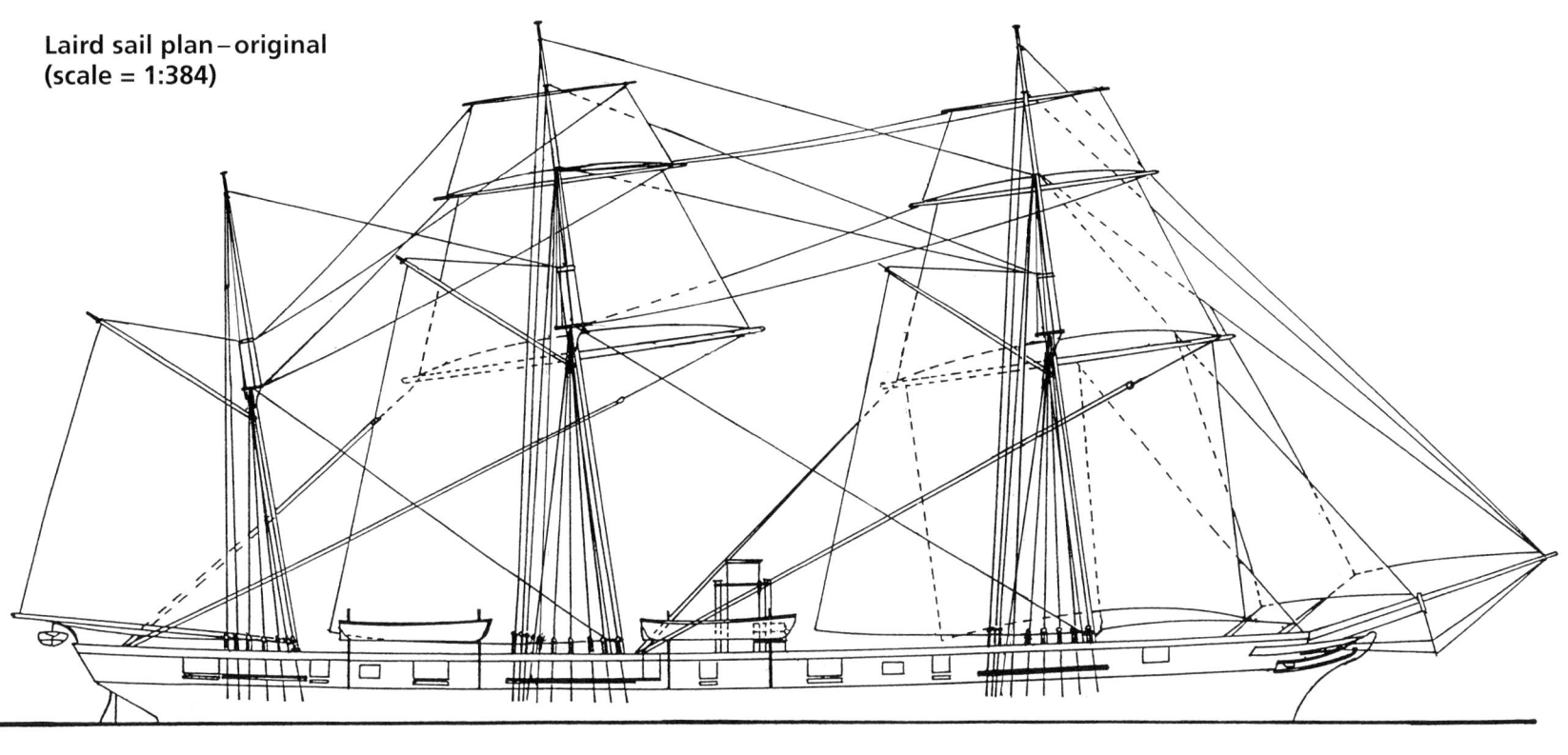

Laird sail plan as modified
(scale = 1:384)

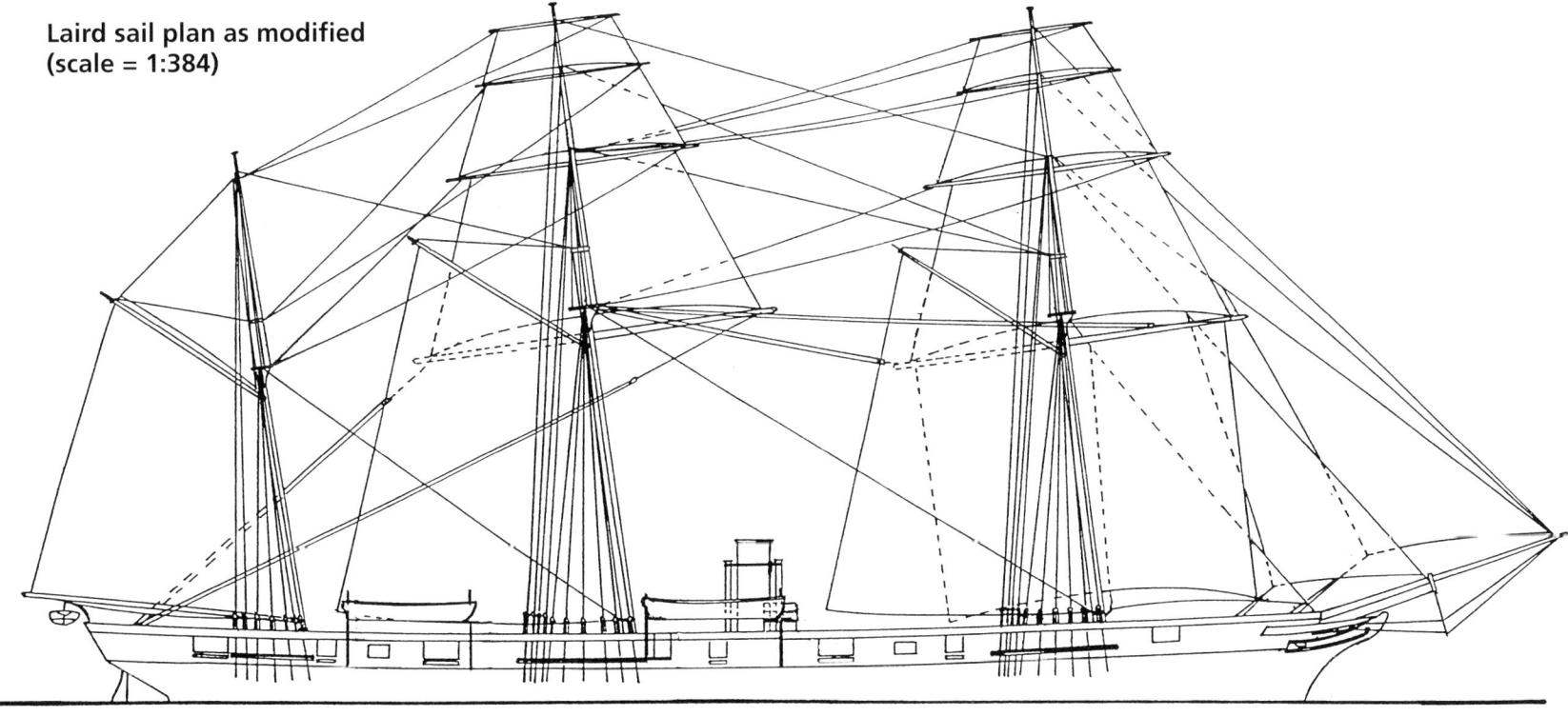

The gunboat built by Laird, is a sister boat to the 'Oreto' S.S. (gunboat) but is far superior. Her planks were caulked as they were put on; is built of the best English oak that could be obtained and that was picked. Every plank and timber of which she is built, was strictly examined after being worked up. A large quantity of this oak was condemned for what, the carpenter says, was no detriment whatever. Every timber in her is fastened with copper bolts 18 feet long and 2½ and 3½ inches in circumference. The stern gear is all copper and brass, in fact the gentleman who superintended her construction, says, 'they could not turn out anything better from Her Majesty's Dock Yard'.

The order, when given to build her, was, to build her of the

Comparison of Sail Areas (scale = 1:384)

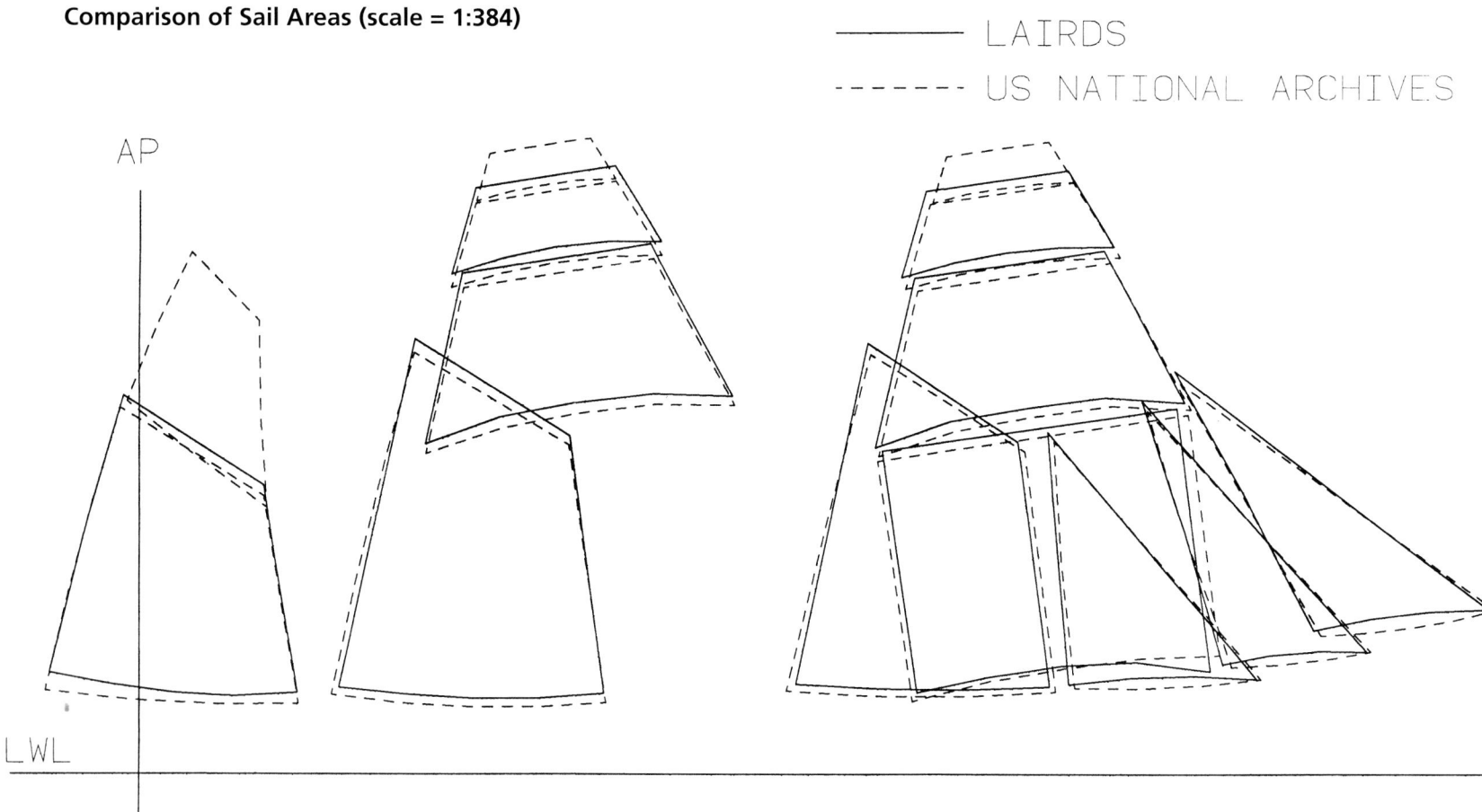

——— LAIRDS
------- US NATIONAL ARCHIVES

best materials that could be obtained; the order was strictly attended to throughout.

Messrs. Sidderley & Co. of William St. have got the order to make the copper powder cans which are of a new patent. It is a large order and is to be completed in a month.

She is allowed, by nautical gentlemen to be one of the best boats they ever saw, and the workmanship and materials are of the best that art and skill can put together. She has been nine months on the stocks.

(Reported Friday May 16th 1862)

The gunboat which was built at Laird's is in every respect similar to the 'Oreto' S.S. (gunboat), with the exception, that she has only one funnel; she is also similarly rigged. About 40 or 50 gentlemen went out with her on her trial trip which was to the Formby Light Ship. The Byrnes were there and also some from Messrs Fraser Trenholm & Co's firm. Everything connected with her, is kept a profound secret and her name is not known as yet, to any one in the yard. She went direct out of the dock and went direct in.

(Reported Friday June 13th 1862)

There are two hundred powder cases for her, sixty of which are delivered and the remainder to be delivered by the end of the week. The screws of them cost £2 each.

Her engines are on the oscillating principle and are 350 Horse Power. Her funnel is painted black and is forward of the main mast. Her hull is painted black. Billet head gilt, with shield painted red. Round stern, with blank gallery windows; carving on stern, gilt. Is 1050 tons burthen and when loaded will draw 14 feet forward. Barque rigged, what is termed 'Jackass' or 'Donkey' rig. Spars &c very light. Has a lifting fan, by steam power. Coppered and copper fastened, and is capable of going 15 knots an hour. Her masts yards &c bright; mastheads, topmastheads, topgallant-mastheads, yards &c tipped in black.

The frame work in which the fan works, is solid brass castings and weighs from one and a half to two tons.

(Reported Thursday June 17th 1862)

The gunboat at Laird's is being fitted out as a privateer and is to be commanded by Captain Bulloch. She is to carry eleven guns, ten and a pivot. The crew of the 'Sumpter' S.S. now on board the 'Julie Usher' S.S. late 'Annie Childs' S.S. alias 'North Carolina' S.S. will go on board the gunboat, if the 'Julie Usher' S.S. goes into dock and discharges, but up to the present, they have not decided what to do with the 'Julie Usher' S.S.. She has put on board the magazines 1616 barrels of gunpowder which she took on board at Cork.

The engineers cooks stewards and officers are appointed. She is now bending sail and has the ensign flying from her peak and will sail, if possible from here, before eight days, from the date of this report (now Friday June 20th/62). Her guns, if possible, will be Armstrong's patent & of the largest size they can get to work on board.

(Reported Friday June 20th 1862)

The gateman told me that the gunboat was going out to-day (Friday June 27th), but that he was not certain. He further said, if I go over to-night he will try & get to know more for me, from the watchman on board. Her stores are all on board and the men were working all night one or two nights this week, to finish something for her but what it was, he could not tell me. He said, it was rumoured some time ago, that she was for the Spanish Government; he (the gateman) said she was for the South.

(Reported Friday June 27th 1862)

Captain Butcher is to command her; Mr McNair is to be Chief and Mr Black second engineer. She may go out any tide and sail in two or three hours notice. The crew is engaged to go to a certain place, then they will be told <u>where they are to go to</u>; if they don't sign articles to go there, they will be told to go home. Everything as regards time of sailing, where she is bound for, name &c is kept a profound secret.

(Reported Tuesday July 1st 1862)

Captain Bulloch went over to Tranmere in the same boat as I (Matthew Maguire) this morning (Wednesday July 2nd 10 o'clock boat). Went to Laird's yard and on board the gunboat, where he seemed to be given orders to the men, who saluted him and who went and appeared as if they were carrying his orders into effect, whatever they were.

(Reported Friday July 4th 1862)

Internal Description

State room right aft. The entrance to the cabin from the deck, is abaft the mizen mast, raised about 2 feet 6 inches. The state room is seated all round, there are two small glass cases in it. At the bottom of the stairs, the communication to the right leads to a small saloon in the centre of which, is a small dining table and on each side are state cabins. Passing from this to a little more forward, is a large saloon, where the chief officers and chief engineers cabins are situated on each side, fitted up with book and chart cases. From this you pass through a doorway into the engine room. There is a platform over the engines (which are two in number) and which are most complete and handsome pieces of machinery, only occupying a small space and lying entirely at the bottom; they are on the oscillating principle.

From here also you can pass into the stoke holes. Forward of this, but no communication, are the men's berths, which are quite open and spacious and run entirely forward, in the centre is the cooking apparatus. The hooks are slung to the deck, for the men's hammock's. This also is seated all round. Under these seats are places for the men's bags with iron grating, which forms the front of the seats. The entrance to this department is directly forward of the foremast. At the bottom of the stairs, a little to the fore part of the ship is a small hatch, which leads to the magazines, two in number. The partition on each side of these magazines is of three thicknesses of oak, between each thickness is lined with lead. These magazines are under the main deck, of what I should call the men's berths in the fore part of the ship, about six or eight feet forward of the foremast. The cannisters are fixtures on their sides, the screws lying one over the other. The magazines and the entrance to them, are filled with water during action, by a pipe on each side and by a pipe in the middle of the floor, the water descends to the bottom of the ship and is pumped out by steam power. The entrance to the cabin is abaft the mizen mast; each side is a brass ventilator, about twelve inches high. Forward of the mizen mast is a skylight to the small saloon and forward of this skylight is a larger one, which gives light to the large saloon. These skylights do not stand more than a foot high on deck and which have iron bars across. Forward of this skylight and abaft the funnel, is a skylight 5 or 6 feet long, which gives light to the engine room. The base of the funnel forms a square, about 2 feet high; each corner is latticed with iron rails, to throw light and air into the stoke room. Each side abaft the funnel, are two ventilators with round bell mouths and which stand about 5 or 6 feet high; more forward of the main mast are two more ventilators, of the same description. The entrance to the stoke hole is abaft the foremast. The entrance to the men's sleeping apartment, is raised about 2 feet high. A small chimney or small brass or copper funnel, rises here from the cooking apparatus. Each side of the gangways is carved oak, with an anchor and rope carved on.

Richard Broderick a shipwright, states, that on the day of the launch of the gunboat 'No. 290' Captain Bulloch and his wife, with several American gentlemen, were in attendance. Captain Bulloch's wife was in one of the office windows, with other ladies. Her bonnet dropped from the window, he (Broderick) lifted it and passed it up to her. He also states, that one of the gentlemen who was present was tall, stout and wore red whiskers. He further states, that he is sure that Captain Bulloch is the owner of the gunboat and that she belongs to the same parties as the 'Oreto' S.S. (gunboat) (now the 'Florida') which was built by W. C. Miller Toxteth Dock and for the same purpose, viz:- for cruising about on the American Coast. He (Richard Broderick) says, in fact she is for the Confederate Government and that Captain Bulloch is a Southern Commissioner.

Captain Butcher, who is a young man, with light whiskers and beard, is, for the present in command of her and is appointing and shipping the crew. The chief officer whose name, at present he (Broderick) does not know, has been in the Peninsular and Oriental Company's Service. The chief steward has been on board the Royal Mail Steamer 'Africa', one of the Cunard Line. There are to be two carpenters, viz:- carpenter and carpenter's mate. Captain Butcher wanted him (Broderick) to go as carpenter's mate, but he (Broderick) would not go as the wages were too small, they offering only £6 and he (Broderick) wanted £7 per month and also a guarantee from Mr. John Laird that his (Broderick's) wages would be all right, as they refused to say who the owners were. Mr. Laird smiled when he was asked to be security as he (Mr. Laird) said, he had no doubt it would be all right. Broderick refused to go.

The stores are all on board. Some person of the name of Barnett is shipping the crew by direction of Captain Butcher.

Captain Bulloch is there every day.

The gentleman who inspected the timber was an American, but did not stop about the yard, but only came occasionally and examined the timber and selected that which was to be used. His name Broderick does not know, but will get it as soon as he possibly can as well as all particulars. As we (Maguire & Broderick) were sitting in the hotel, he (Broderick) said, as sure as you are sitting there, Captain Bulloch is the owner of the gunboat, he gave the order.

Dimensions

		Feet	inches
Extreme length		222	'
Keel		196	'
Distance⊗ from F'head		101	'
Breadth ditto		28	6
Depth		24	6
Section at 58 feet forward of⊗	Breadth	28	'
	Depth	26	'
Section at 77 feet aft of⊗	Breadth	26	'
	Depth	24	6
Distance of fore post from⊗		99	

Captain Butcher who is appointed to the gunboat was formerly a captain in the American trade, sailing from New York to Havannah and Nassau. For the last two years he has been sailing in the Royal Mail Steamer 'Arabia' as second officer.

Barnett, who is the Shipping Agent and servant to the Cunard Company, is shipping the crew of the gunboat, who are all picked men, from the Naval Volunteer Reserve Force.

The gunboat 'No. 290' will leave the Graving Dock (Laird's) to-morrow (Saturday July 12th) and go into the Great Float.

Captain Butcher is well known in New York and New Jersey having been in the Royal Mail Steamers 'Africa' and 'Arabia' as 2nd Officer. From the information I received, he is to be second in command when she gets outside.

(Reported Tuesday July 15th 1862)

William Passmore, signal man on board the '290' says, the men have no need to sign articles here as she is not a British vessel, she is for the Southerners. He believes her name to be the 'Florida'. He (Passmore) was in Her Majesty's Ship 'Terrible' during the Crimean War, was also a Garibaldian Volunteer and was in Palermo May 6th, the time they had a fight with the Neapolitans. There are men from all Navies, English, American, Brazilian &c. There are two men from the Sumpter S.S. There are one hundred men altogether.

(Reported Friday July 18th 1862)

William Passmore's Report

Met the seamen, say thirty in number, on Saturday (July 26th 1862) coming down Canning St. from the ship, playing 'Dixie's Land', on a fife, concertina and a cornopean and they all took the 4-30 Woodside boat for Liverpool. They still kept playing 'Dixie's Land' on board the ferry boat. Went up to one of the men and asked him when he thought the ship would be going out. He told me that their bed clothes and bedding were on board and that the boatswain told those who intended to go in her, to hold themselves in readiness for early next week.

Captain Butcher made enquiries for me this afternoon at pay time and wanted to know where I was. It is understood by all on board, that she will go to sea next week. It was also understood that she was to have hauled out into the river to-day.

There are about 50 men on board now and more are expected on Monday.

(Reported Saturday July 26th 1862)

I, William Passmore, heard last night, that the gunboat would haul into the river and sail to-day (Tuesday July 29th 1862) on a trial trip and would not return again. Her crew have been paid a half month's advance on Monday July 28th.

(Reported Tuesday July 29th 1862)

Description

'Donkey' rigged Barque 'No. 290' S.S. (gunboat) 1050 tons Captain Butcher. Hull painted black. Round Stern, with twenty-two blank gallery windows in same. Carvings on stern, gilt. Billet head gilt; a red shield for figurehead, with a gilt anchor, about 9 inches long on it. Bowsprit painted black. Jibboom scrape spar, heel painted black. Fore main mizen lower and topmasts bright. Spanker boom and gaff, yards crosstrees and booms, painted black. Black funnel or smoke stack with bright copper steam pipe fore part of same; funnel between fore and main masts. Mizen mast well aft and about 14 feet from stern rail, with a great rake aft. Rigging chains painted black, outside of bulwarks. A bridge forward of funnel on iron stanchions; railing round bridge painted red. Four iron swing davits, for two boats, each side between main and mizen masts; boats painted black outside and drab inside. Two iron swing davits at the stern for the captain's gig. Flush deck. Has a lifting fan, which can be hoisted by steam power. The fan is solid brass. Entrances to cabin and engine room abaft main mast. Wheel abaft mizen mast, which has the following inscription round the rim 'Aid Toi diever Dieu T-aidi-ra'.(translation) Ball racks forward of each of the masts. Skylights to cabin, engine room &c. covered with wooden gratings. Inside of bulwarks painted drab. According to the chalk marks on the deck, she will carry three swivel guns. She has three double ports each side viz:- forward, amidships and aft. She will carry sixteen guns in all, swivels included.

She is in a confused state and from her appearance will not be ready before the middle of next week.

She is built of oak and coppered. About 200 feet long and 18 feet deep. When loaded will draw from 10 to 14 feet and is about 1050 tons.

(Reported ? July 1862)

On Friday July 18th 1862, two dozen of swords were taken on board the '290' S.S.

Sailed Tuesday July 29th 1862 at 10 am

She has taken a crew (according to what the shipping master says) of between 90 and 100 men. The seamen signed articles to go to Nassau, Savannah or any other port or ports. They were told by the captain, that when they should arrive at Nassau, any one who was willing, might remain by the vessel; any other person who did not wish to remain, would get their passage paid back to England by the mail, as Captain Butcher was going to return by the mail. The captain who is to take charge of her when she gets to Nassau told the seamen that 'he wanted men not cowards'. One of the seamen asked him if they were going to run the blockade?, the captain said he would let them know. The captain is a low sized stoutish man, with black bushy whiskers, moustache and beard, appearantly a foreigner. The shipping master told Ulskelu (one of the seamen) that the wages would be £4/10/- per month, a half month's advance and from what he (the shipping master, Mr. Barnett) heard, it would be as good as £60 or £70 each man, if they were successful, besides their wages.

Mr. King, who was on board the gunboat says, that a barque, which he thinks was named the 'Burrington' of Bristol, came to Stiton and there put on board the '290' S.S. (gunboat) seven guns viz:- two 32 pounders, two 96 pounders and three swivels. He said he heard there was a 100 pounder on board, but he (King) did not see it. They also took on board shot and shell, small arms and some coals. He also states, that the gunboat is a failure, for when the engines are at work, it is impossible to stand it below. She cannot do more than 10 knots and that she rolls terribly, so much so, that they were obliged to cover up the guns to prevent them from getting wet. He also says, he believes it to be the captain's intention to cruise about the Channel for a while and then make west, to intercept the Californian Mails. He states that the 'Bahama' S.S. is a faster boat than the '290'. When Captain Semmes was asked by the men who they were to look to for their pay, he could not or would not name anyone. He also learned when on board, that there was a boat ('Japan' S.S. now 'Georgia' S.S. Capt. Maury) now building at Glasgow; that Capt Semmes told him, that if he (King) would stop by the ship he would be promoted. This, King did not believe, as, he says, there are too many young Southerners on board, whom the captain will push forward. He also states that her metal is too heavy for her and when they come to fire a broadside, it will try her. He says the Southerners have no acknowledged Government, that they, on board the '290' are no better than pirates and if taken, the British Government would not protect them, for their joining the service, was a violation of the Queen's Proclamation. This man resides at 59 Clarence St. Smithdown Lane.

(Reported Friday September 12th 1862)

From information I (Matthew Maguire) received the '290' S.S. (gunboat) is at Charleston. (This information is taken out of the Journal of Commerce of Friday or about Sept 26/62)

(Reported Friday September 26th 1862)

A fireman belonging to the privateer 'Alabama' was here some ten days ago, he having been sent home sick. He would not state where he had been landed; that he had recovered and was going out to join her again. He had his papers all right so as to enable him to get to her. He would go to Cardiff where he would ship in a vessel which is loading to go out to her. He states his share of prize money to be £1,000.

(Reported Tuesday February 24th 1863)

Michael Ganshela, one of the five men who came home in the 'Agrippina' from the 'Alabama', states that it is eight weeks to-day (Saturday February 28th 1863) since he left the 'Alabama' off the island of Cuba.

Copy of Discharge
November 28th 1862
This is to certify that Michael Ganshela is discharged from the Naval Service of the Confederate States, his discharge to take effect from the arrival of the barque ('Agrippina') in England. (signed) R. Semmes

Copy of Account

Please pay the bearer (Michael Ganshela) £26/19/2 Messrs M. G. Thingender & Co.

The above is the amount due to Michael Ganshela after deducting for shirts, clothes &c. Ganshela resides at Trafalgar Place Great Howard St.

Thomas Price another of the seamen who came home from the 'Alabama' per 'Agrippina' had his leg bruised with a cask of vinegar. He states, there were many who wanted to exchange places with the four who came home. They were offering money to the invalids to take their places, but the doctor would not allow the others to go, as they were in sound health.

Carries the following guns viz:-

One 120 pounder swivel gun forward, a Dahlgrin, which does execution at the distance of 3½ miles

Four 68 pounders, broadside guns

One 92 pounder swivel, aft

(Reported Tuesday March 3rd 1863)

In Service

The photographs taken on board the ship in South Africa in 1863 are a valuable source of information about the deck fittings and armament. There were at least seven photographs taken at the time, and these are discussed elsewhere (pages 48 to 54). The ship was undergoing repairs while the photographs were taken and some things have been moved, so care is required when interpreting them. The two photographs which have recently come to light showing the whole of the ship in Singapore are very useful.

The career of the *Alabama* has been very well covered and literally hundreds of books and articles written over the years. Those by her crew members, such as Semmes and Sinclair, should be the most accurate even if they were written many years after the event. Few of the works give much detail about the ship except for principle dimensions and the number and size of guns so that it takes a careful reading to extract information that could be useful to reconstruct the ship.

Similar comments apply to information supplied by people from the ships captured by the *Alabama*. Descriptions such as the one for the *New York Herald* have to be viewed with caution.

Following the battle between the *Alabama* and the *Hatteras* a profile of the ship was drawn showing the positions of the holes caused by the shot from the *Hatteras*. This is described as 'A correct sketch of the CSS *Alabama*'s Hull with the position of the shot holes after the fight with the *Hatteras*'. The layout of the ship is essentially the same as in the other plans with the most noticeable thing being in the position of the lower deck. There is also a Vice room marked as being above the Engine room and forward of the Steerage.

The ship's log gives very little help in reconstructing the ship.

DESCRIPTION OF THE CONFEDERATE STEAM PROPELLER '*ALABAMA*'
CAPTAIN SEMMES FORMERLY OF THE 'SUMTER'

The '*Alabama*' was built at Liverpool, or Birkenhead, and left the latter port in August last – is about 1200 tons burden, draft about 14 feet – engines by Laird & Sons of Birkenhead 1862 – She is a wooden vessel, propelled by a screw, coppered bottom, about 210 feet long, rather narrow, painted black outside, and drab inside – has a round stern, billet head, very little shear, flush deck fore and aft, has a bridge forward of smoke stack, carries two large black boats, on cranes, amidships, forward of the main rigging, two black quarter boats between the main and mizzen masts, one small black boat over the stern on cranes, the spare spars on a gallows between the bridge and foremast, show above the rail, carries three long 32 pounders on a side, and is pierced for two more amidships; has a 100 pound rifled pivot gun forward of bridge, and a 68 pound pivot gun on the main deck, has tracks laid forward for a pivot bow gun, and tracks aft for a pivot stern chaser, all of which she will take on board to complete her armament - Her guns are of the Blakeley pattern

She is barque-rigged, has very long bright lower masts, and black mast heads, yards black, long yard arms, short poles (say 1 to 2 feet) with small dog vanes on each and a pennant to the main, studdingsail booms on the fore and main, and has wire rigging – carries on her foremast, a square foresail, large trysail, with two reefs, and bonnet topsail with two reefs, topgallant sail and royal – on the main mast, a large trysail, with 2 reefs and a bonnet, no square mainsail bent, topsail, 2 reefs, topgallant sail and royal – on the mizzen mast, a very large spanker, and short three cornered gaff topsail – has a fore and fore-topmast staysail, and jib, has had no staysails to the main, or mizzen, bent, or royal yards aloft yet – Is represented to go 13 knots under canvas, and under steam 15 knots; can get up steam in 20 minutes; but seldom uses it, except in chase or emergency – has all National flags; but usually sets St. George's Cross on approaching a vessel, until she ascertains her nationality, when if American she substitutes the Confederate flag – Her present complement of men is 120 all told, but is anxious to ship more – has a man at the mainmast head from daylight to sunset to look out for vessels –

Description of sails - hemp canvas sails very roaching – topsails have 20 cloths on the head, 30 on the foot, top gallant sails 16 cloths on head and 22 on the foot. General appearance of the hull and sails decidedly English – She is generally under 2 topsails, fore and main trysails, fore and fore topmast stay-sails, some times topgallant and jib, but seldom any sails on the mizzen mast, except while in chase of a vessel. She is very slow in stays, generally wears ship.

She was built expressly for the business she is engaged in to <u>destroy</u>, <u>fight</u> or <u>run</u>, as the character of her opponent may be –

IN SERVICE

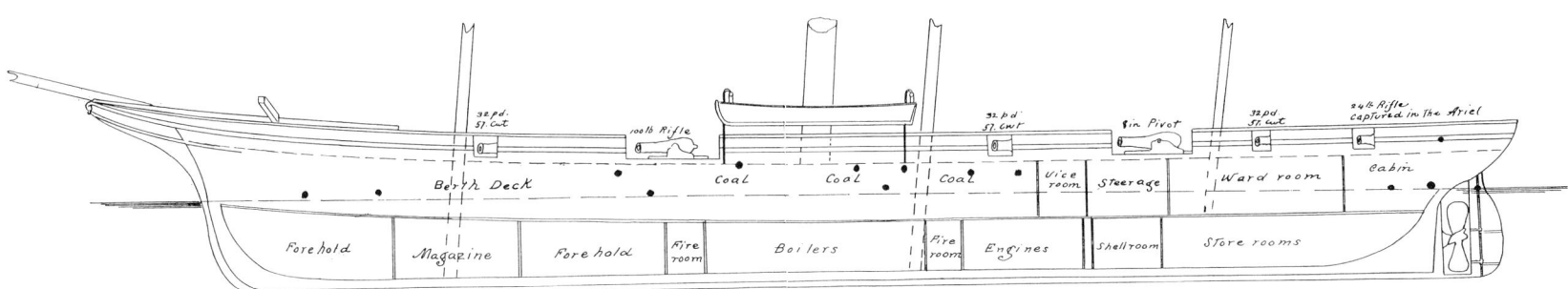

She took her armament and crew and most of her officers on board near Terciera (Western Islands) from an English vessel – Her crew are principally English, the officers Chivalry of the South.

P.S. All the water consumed is condensed – has 8 months provisions, besides what is being plundered, and about 400 tons of coal on board.

Names of the officers of 'Alabama'

Commander in Chief	Captain Semmes
1st Lieutenant	Kell
2nd "	Armstrong
3rd "	Wilson
4th "	Low
Sailing Master	Sinclair

'A correct sketch of the CSS *Alabama*'s hull with the position of the shot holes after the fight with the *Hatteras*. Also the position and weight of her armament.' (US National Archives)

Lieutenant of Marines	Howell	*Bro in law of Jeff. Davis*
Corpiral	Fullman	*FULHAM*
Gunner	Curdy	*Cuddy*
Captain's Clerk	Smith	
Midshipman	Maffitt	
do	Sinclair	
do	Bullock	*Bulloch*
Chief Engineer	Freeman	
Carpenter	Robinson	
Boatswain	McCaskie	*Macaskey*

Doctor, Surgeon and other Officers names unknown.

Lines plans of the *Alabama* redrawn from those in the Merseyside Maritime Museum.

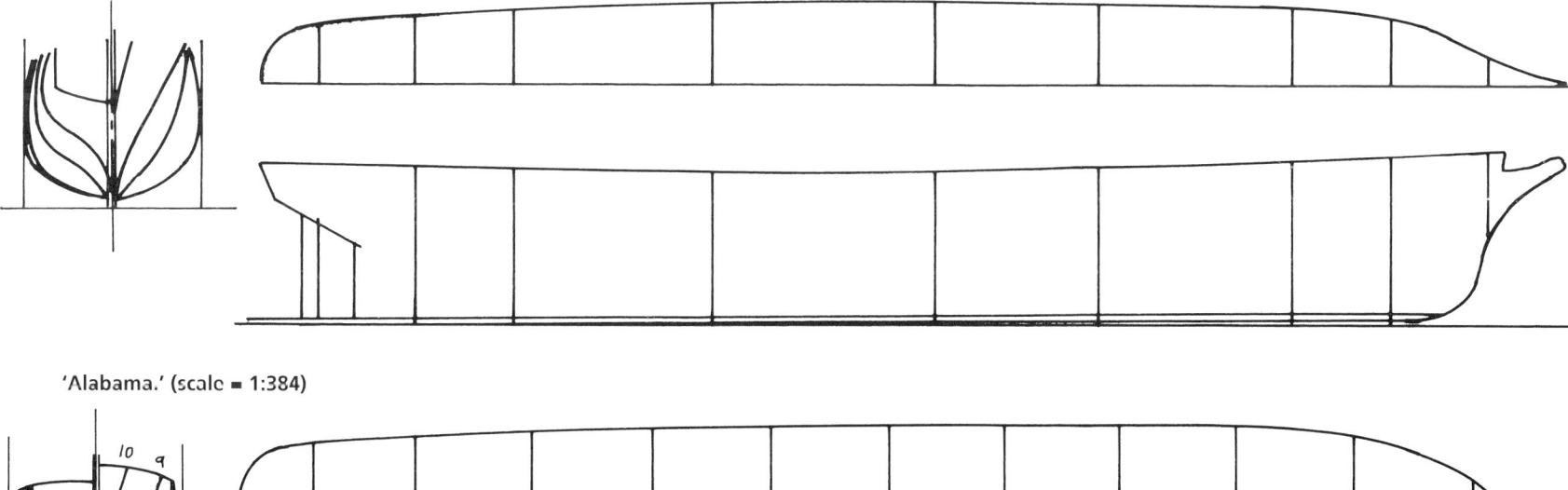

'Alabama.' (scale = 1:384)

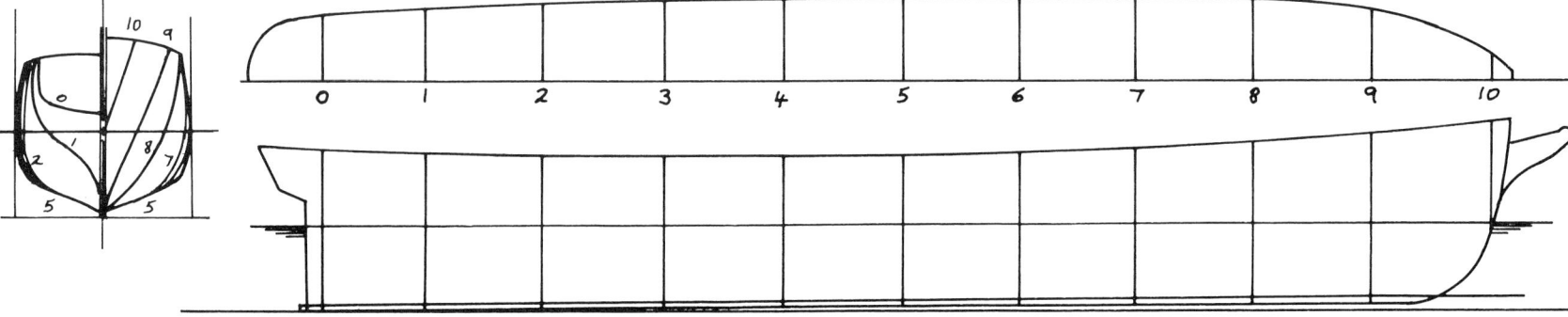

'Lines & sections of wooden corvette "Alabama", 1862.' (scale = 1:384)

Deck plan of the *Alabama* redrawn from that in the Merseyside Maritime Museum (scale = 1:384)

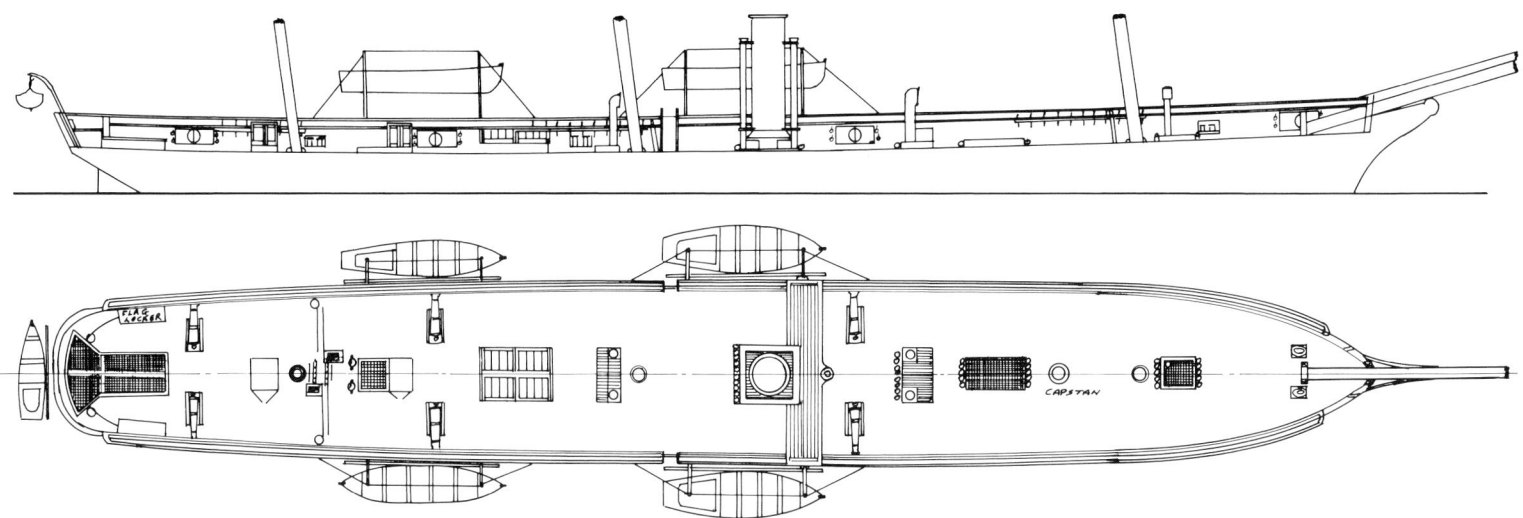

To the Editors:

Please publish the enclosed description of the steamer without one word being abridged as the information is <u>invaluable</u> to the <u>Government</u> and ship owners generally – Everything is faithfully described and she would be known by referring to it by any of our Navy Officers or Merchant Ship Masters that might fall in with her.

For the New York Herald

The Wreck off Cherbourg

The excavation work on the wreck of the ship will continue for a number of years. So far this work has been reported in only two articles, in the *National Geographic*, December 1994 and *The Archaeology of Ships of War*, 1995. No doubt further articles or papers will be published as the work progresses. Some of the published information is valuable in showing details that have not survived elsewhere, if they were ever recorded.

Miscellaneous

There are four plans of a ship called 'ALABAMA' in the Merseyside Maritime Museum (two lines plans, a deck plan/profile and a sail plan) which look similar to other plans. The museum knows little about them and the plans are undated. The four plans have been redrawn and are reproduced here for comparison.

The Sail Plan is compared with the two others in Appendix 5. The Upper Deck plan is very similar to the University of Alabama one and the two models. The two Lines Plans have so few sections it is not easy to compare them with the models but the most significant difference is that they both have a rake of keel, which the *Alabama* did not, according to the Book of Elements.

There are two excellent models of the ship which are worthy of close study. The first is in the Mariners' Museum (referred to as the Bulloch model) which is said to have belonged to James Bulloch and remained within his family until going to the museum in the 1980s. This model is unrigged and has stump masts, and even the funnel is incomplete. The second model was at Cammell Laird Shipbuilders and is now in the Williamson Art Gallery in Birkenhead. The age of this model is unknown but for many years it stood in the main entrance to the shipbuilding offices. The model is fully rigged but the rigging has been repaired over the years. Further details of these models are given in the following section.

Similarly the paintings of the ship are illustrated and discussed on pages 57 to 60.

Books

Either contemporary or by crew members (some have gone through many editions or been reprinted recently, however only one edition is listed). References are given in the text from these books, and are identified by the initial letter of the author followed by volume and page number.

Anderson	'Letters from a Georgia Midshipman on the CSS *Alabama*', *Georgia Historical Quarterly* (Winter 1975), pp416-32.
Bulloch	*The Secret Service of the Confederate States in Europe* (Thomas Yoseloff, 1959), 2 volumes – (B)
Fullam	*The Journal of George Townley Fullam* (The University of Alabama Press, 1973), edited and annotated by Charles G Summersell – (F)
Kell	*Recollections of a Naval Life* (The Neale Company, 1900) reprinted, with additions, as *Beneath the Stainless Banner* (Burd Street Press, 1999), edited by R Thomas Campbell – (K)

Kell	'Cruise and Combats of the '*ALABAMA*' by Her Executive Officer', *Century Magazine*, April 1886– (CMK)	Semmes	*Memoirs of Service Afloat* (The Blue & Grey Press, 1987) – (SM)
"	'Cruise and the Combats of the "Alabama"', *Battles and Leaders of the Civil War* (reprinted by Castle, no date), 4 volumes – (B + L)	"	*The Cruise of the Alabama and the Sumter* (London 1864), 2 volumes – (SC)
Low	*The Logs of the CSS ALABAMA and CSS TUSCALOOSA 1862-1863* (Confederate Publishing Company, 1972), edited by W Stanley Hoole.	"	*Ships Log.* Printed in ORN I, 1, 2 & 3 – (SJ)
		Sinclair	*Two Years on the Alabama* (Annapolis 1989) – (S)

The other main source of reference quoted is the *Official Records of the Union and Confederate Navies in the War of the Rebellion*. These are referred to as ORN Series, Volume and page

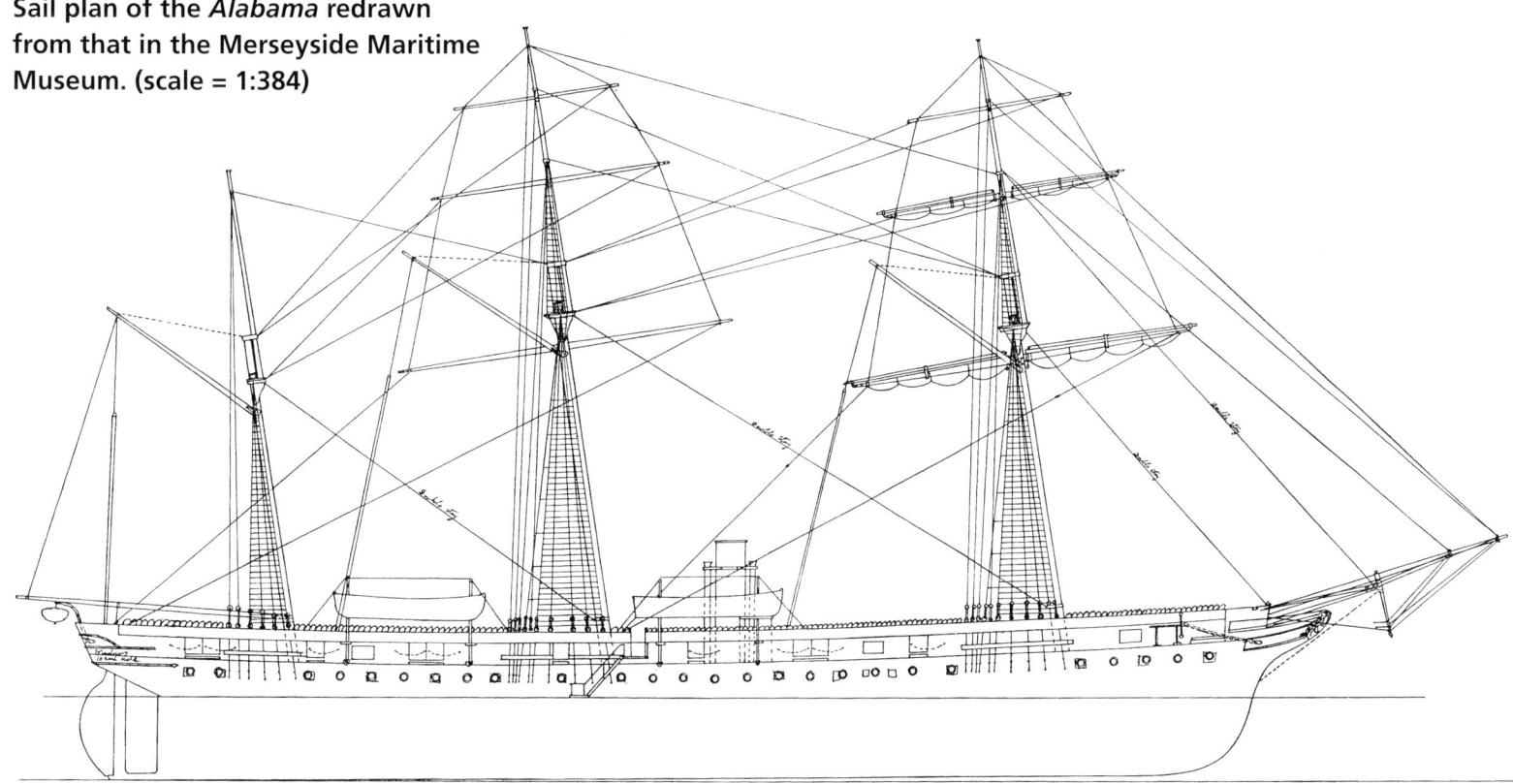

Sail plan of the *Alabama* redrawn from that in the Merseyside Maritime Museum. (scale = 1:384)

Visual Evidence

Photographs

Copies of what are hoped to be all the known photographs taken on, or of, the ship are included here, though I have no doubt that there are others which are unrecognised at present.

Semmes noted in his log on Wednesday 12 August 1863 'Photographers & visitors on board' when the ship was at Simon's Bay, South Africa. However, from the 9th to 14th there also appear to have been visitors on board, as well as repairs to, and recaulking, the deck. It is known that a photographer called Mr Green took pictures on board, and it would appear from looking at the photographs taken on board that they were taken at different times and by different people because of the work going on and the way men are posed.

1a

Photographs taken on board

1. This is probably the best-known photograph taken on board the ship and it shows both the Captain, Semmes, who is leaning on the carriage of the after pivot gun, and the First Lieutenant, Kell. On the left can be seen the breech of one of four identical 32pdr guns. Very little of the starboard rigging of the mizzen mast is shown, but the port side is shown more clearly (the blurred images in the top right hand corner are washing blowing in the wind, indicating a slow shutter speed for the camera). The two mizzen topmast backstays are not shown, presumably having been removed for maintenance.

There are three crewmen standing by the stern rail, the one on the left blurred because he moved as the shutter was released. The other two are just to the right of the mast and looking through telescopes (only the arm and telescope of one of the pair can be seen).

Semmes is leaning on the carriage of the 8in smoothbore gun on the centreline of the ship, secured against movement by the tackle just in front of the captain. Very little of the slide can be seen but the left cheek of the carriage is clearly shown along with the compressor frame. The fore and after sights are clearly shown, and can be compared with the drawings (pages 112 and 120). This photograph is available from several different sources and (apart from the comments below) the main difference is in how much of the right-hand side of the photograph is shown. Other prints give more detail of the breech of the pivot gun and its quoin. Part of the deck sweeps can be seen in the

foreground and can be compared with the original plans (page 130). Shot for the pivot gun is shown in the bottom right in a rack which is on the side of the engine-room hatch coaming.

Kell is standing by the gunroom skylight, leaning on the framework for a hoist. Just to the left of him is the ladderway to the ward room with someone just visible looking out at the camera. The twin steering wheels (with ten spokes on each wheel) are visible forward of the mizzen mast. Two binnacles can be seen, one forward of the wheels and the other between the horse block and the mizzen mast. The flag locker can be seen right at the stern, between the two davits for the dinghy.
((a) Courtesy George Eastman House)
((b) Courtesy US Naval Historical Center, Washington)

2. Kell is standing on the right-hand side of the 8in gun with his hand on the breech rope. This photograph shows the right cheek of the carriage and more of the quoin than the previous view. The gun is between the gunroom skylight and the engine-room skylight which is visible bottom left, clearly showing the bars over the glass.

On the right of the photograph next to the bulwark is the gunroom ladder with the companionway behind it, both of which have been removed, presumably for repairs. One of the davits for the aftermost boat on the port side can be seen, showing that the boat is in the water. Two mooring bollards can be seen set in the bulwark next to the companionway and just behind is a 32pdr gun run out through the gunport. The canvas cover for the hammock netting is in position.

This photograph appears to have been taken at about the same time as the first one, judging by the equipment lying about, the lack of backstays and the washing hanging in the rigging.
(Courtesy Cape Town Archives Repository: AG13080)

3. This photograph is looking forward to the bows of the ship from just aft of the fore mast shrouds. The main feature of this photograph is the 32pdr gun which is run out so that unfortunately its muzzle cannot be seen. The gun and carriage are well illustrated (it is one of two guns for which no plans have yet been found). The breeching rope is clearly shown, as is the side tackle. The after sight is just visible above the cascable.

The person standing to the left of the gun is identified on the back of the photograph (from George Eastman House) as Edward Anderson, a midshipman. However, the same photograph in Warren's paper (see photograph B on page 55) identifies him as the Gunner, Thomas C Cuddy. Comparing the pictures of the two men in the various books it would appear that it is Cuddy, not Anderson (who, according to Sinclair, was in charge of an after 32pdr at Cherbourg). The seaman standing behind the gun is unidentified.

The two crewmen leaning on the bulwark show the flare of the bows, and judging by the shadow on the bulwark below them, they are standing on a grating. To the right of the men is the gunport for the pivot gun in its forward position. On the deck below this gunport can be seen marks that are probably the sweeps laid for use with the pivot gun (these are shown on the plan, page 129). Part of the anchor cable is visible on the left of the photograph, going round a riding bitt. In the bottom right foreground is one of the wooden shot racks that has been moved and the shot on the deck will be for the 32pdr.

The arrangement of the shrouds and backstays for the fore mast is clearly illustrated and shows that none of the four backstays cross the shrouds, as is shown in the sail plans of the ship. A yard with sail bent is shown lashed to the foremost shroud. The extreme tip of the jibboom with a lowered sail can be seen on the left of the photograph.
(Courtesy George Eastman House)

4. There is a tremendous amount of detail shown on this photograph which is not very well known. The fore side of the bridge structure is clearly shown except for the centre section which is hidden behind one of the ventilators to the fore stokehold. On the right of the bridge (the port side of the ship) can be seen the screen for the port navigation light, the starboard one being hidden in the shadow cast by the hammock netting. The boat on the port side is swung in and resting upon the bridge, whereas the davits for the starboard boat are swung out. The funnel is held by four guys which are of chain judging by the shadows cast.

The 32pdr shown on the left is the same one as in the previous view but seen from the other side. Very little additional detail is visible except to show the curve to the bottom of the cheek of the carriage. Just above the breech of this gun can be seen the breeches of two other 32pdrs, the different shape of the breech being obvious.

PHOTOGRAPHS

The hatch above the crew accommodation is clearly shown and has the ladder at the after part of the hatch and not at the fore part as is usually shown in the plans. The fore part of this hatch is covered by a grating which lifts off to provide access to the stores beneath the lower deck. There are four sections of grating visible, one in place and three sitting on top of the first. The forward corner of the coaming appears to have a piece of metal around it, probably to protect it from rubbing by the anchor cable as it comes off the capstan and goes down the chain pipe in to the locker. The fore side of this coaming has a shot rack fitted which contains five shot for the Blakely rifled gun. Similar shot can be seen in a rack on the fore side of the coaming to the fore stokehold. The Blakely, the forward pivot gun, should be positioned between the bridge and the hatch to the fore stokehold. Unfortunately because of the men and the ventilator it is not possible to see it.

The starboard ventilator to the fore stokehold is clearly shown in the hatchway, the port ventilator is mostly obscured by the gantry which carries the spare spars. To the left of the hatchway there appears to be a mat on the deck which is presumably at the top of the ladder down to the stokehole (so that the stokers do not get coal dust all over the decks).

Two yards can be seen lashed to the shrouds of the mainmast, the one on the left with a sail bent, the one on the opposite side without a sail (possibly the royal yard).

On the extreme right of the picture can be seen a wheel, but unfortunately it is not possible to see what sort of pump or machine it is part of.

I do not know the identity of the man standing by the top of the ladderway. Comparing him with photographs in other books he looks similar to the boatswain, Benjamin Mecaskey, but this could just that they both have beards. According to the number of buttons on his cuffs he should be either a Midshipman or a Passed Midshipman, depending on the size of the buttons. *(Courtesy Cape Town Archives Repository: AG13079)*

5. This photograph shows two of the lieutenants, Sinclair (on the left) and Armstrong, leaning against one of the 32pdr guns which is positioned almost level with the twin wheels. The axle tree band and the linch pin on the front axle show clearly, and can be compared with the drawings of the gun. The lower bolts in the bulwark either side of the open gunport are for the breeching rope, the upper eyebolts are for the side tackle.

This photograph and the following one were taken at a different time to the first two because the 8in gun has been pivoted to the port side of the deck so that the deck on the centreline can be recaulked. The shot in the racks on the coaming of the engine-room hatch has also been moved.

The aft side of the starboard ventilator to the aft stokehold can be seen on the left of the picture and shows what appears to be a door. This could be a means of raising the ash from the boilers from the boiler room (by means of a bucket and winch within the ventilator) for disposal over the side. If so, there should be a similar one for the fore stokehold.

The inside of the bulwarks is shown clearly in way of the gunport and in the bottom right of the picture is one of the lead scuppers. Resting on the pin rail are two handspikes, used for training the gun.
(Courtesy Cape Town Archives Repository: AG13081)

6. This photograph is taken at about the same time as the previous one and from a few feet further forward. The bottom right hand corner shows the breech of the 32pdr seen in the previous photograph. The 8in gun has been pivoted to the port side of the deck which is being recaulked between the

5

6

gunroom and engine-room skylights. Part of the barrel of the 8in gun is visible on the left just below the deadeyes, the cascable is just visible to the right of the open hatchway. The muzzle of one of the 32pdrs is shown side-on just above the engine-room skylight. Shot has been removed from the racks alongside the engine-room skylight but is still in position in the racks on the bulwark forward of the gunport. The rail and hammock netting in way of this gunport are moveable to allow the 8in gun to be run out when moved across (the barrel of the gun is approximately the same height as the rail).

Both the two forward boats have been swung in and are supported by their davits and are partly resting on the bridge. The starboard one appears to have a support under the keel towards the stern.

The shrouds and backstays of the rigging for the mainmast are clearly shown and provide a lot of detail. On the port side there is a gap in the six shrouds (with three on each side). This is around a gunport and so the spacing has been increased. The stay from the top of the mizzen mast to the mainmast can be seen to be attached to the mainmast by a band about 7ft above the deck. The main trysail can be seen brailed up to the main mast and the mast hoops show clearly. There are two yards lashed to the shrouds of the main mast. However, unlike in photograph 4, there is a sail bent to the one on the port side. The two ladders up to the bridge (one on either side of the funnel) can be seen. In the foreground, just to the right of the companionway to the gunroom can be seen part of one of the handspikes for the pivot gun.
(Courtesy Cape Town Archives Repository: AG13082)

7. There are three engraving in the *Illustrated London News* of 10 October 1863 which are all taken from photographs. Two of these engravings are photographs Numbers 2 and 5. An original photograph for the third has only recently come to light. This shows Semmes sitting on a chair which has been placed next to the binnacle which is between the horse block and the mizzen mast. This photograph has been cropped compared with the engraving in the *ILN*, the most obvious difference being that all the binnacle can be seen.

The photograph has clearly been posed, and it appears that the background has been modified. Starting on the left, there is part of a gunport which should be a larger one, for the pivot gun aft of the mizzen mast. The hammock netting comes to a break at this point enabling the rail to be removed to allow the pivot gun to be run out. There do not appear to be any sweeps visible on the deck for the pivot to run on (they are just visible under the cascable of the 32pdr in Photograph No. 2). Immediately forward of this gunport is the pinrail for the mizzen mast, with the shrouds and deadeyes running through the hammock netting, which would not therefore have a canvas cover. These shrouds can be seen in Photograph No. 2 (which is looking aft along the bulwarks). It would appear that the whole of this pinrail has been removed from the picture (though something still remains by the right-hand side of Semmes head).

To the left of the binnacle, and partly obscured by Semmes, can be seen the top of one of the vents (the top lifts off, leaving a small rim protruding above the deck). Comparing this photograph with Nos. 1 and 2 shows the binnacle and the vents in different relative positions. It is not clear if the top of the vent or the binnacle has been moved for this picture. However, it is clear that if a pivot gun was placed on the sweeps at this point both the vents and the binnacle would have to be moved to allow the gun to pivot.

Overall, while this is a good photograph of Semmes, it is of very little help in reconstructing the ship. Even though the binnacle is clearly seen, it can be moved, and is not necessarily in the same position at sea.
(From a private collection)

7

8. As mentioned earlier most of the photographs of the *Alabama* are available from several different sources, the differences between them being in the quality of the reproduction and the cropping.

For Photo 1 I got a high quality copy from George Eastman House, but subsequently noticed the same photograph in a book from a second source which was of poorer quality but included more of the details of the gun. When I obtained a copy of this second photograph (from the Naval Historical Center) I placed it next to the first one and realised that even though they were basically the same there were significant differences. Part of the two photographs are shown to explain the differences.

The position of both Semmes and Kell is the same, as is the blurred figure of the crewman on the left by the stern rail indicating they were both taken at the same time. Looking to the right of Semmes's head there is a light patch on the lower photograph between his head and the rope of the davit. On the right hand side of the photographs the lock (firing mechanism) of the 8in gun is clearly shown. In the lower photograph there is a line which just touches the

left side of the lock but in the top photograph there is a good clearance between these two. As both photographs were taken at the same time (as shown by the blurred figure at the stern) the explanation for these differences is that they are the left (top) and right of a pair of stereo photographs.

Stereo photography consisted of taking two photographs at the same time with a camera that had two lenses spaced about 2¾in apart (the same spacing as between the eyes). When comparing two objects, one close to the camera and one far away, there is a difference in their relative position depending which lens (eye) is used. This can be seen when comparing other parts of the photographs.

One of each of these two photographs have been copied and reprinted at a suitable size for a stereoscope (a viewer which produces a three-dimensional image) which confirms the idea. An advertisement for the photographer in *The South African Advertiser and Mail* lists stereoscopic views.

Despite a number of copies of the other photographs I have been unable to locate a second stereo pair. The most likely will be of Kell standing by the gun (No. 2) as it appears to have been taken at the same time.
(Courtesy George Eastman House (top), US Naval Historical Center (bottom))

9. This shows a stereoscope with a part of the 'left' and 'right' photograph mounted on a card suitable for the viewer. When held up to the eyes only a single image will be seen.

External Photographs

A. This photograph shows the *Alabama* moored alongside the P&O coal wharf in Singapore, where the ship was from 22 to 24 December 1863. The photograph was taken on either of the first two days as the ship sailed early in the morning of the last day. Because of the distance involved it is not possible to see some details very clearly. A lot of the rigging can be seen where it is in front of the buildings and trees. The braces for the fore yard are shown on the original plans as going to the bulwarks around the entry port. However, because of the position of the boats this would not be possible as they would interfere with the operation of the braces. The paintings show the braces

PHOTOGRAPHS

The approximate position and direction of each photograph taken on deck.

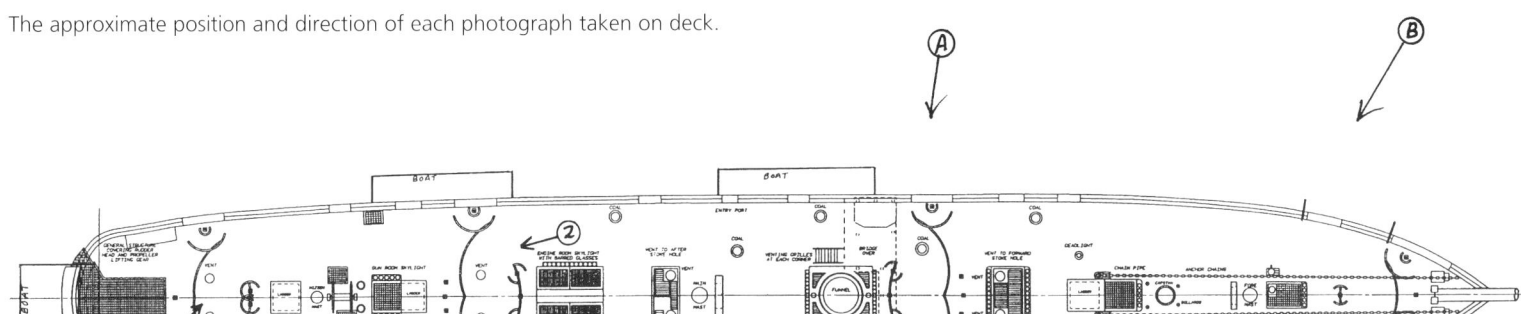

A

B

going to the head of the mainmast. As the fore braces cannot be seen going to the bulwarks it would be reasonable to assume they went to the mast head (the main braces can be seen going to the stern).

The big trysails are shown as brailing up to the mast, not to the mast and gaff as had been assumed before seeing this photograph. Sails can be seen on the yards, but there is not one on the main yard, confirming a previous description of the ship (page 44). A flag is flying (or rather hanging because of the lack of wind) from the mizzen gaff. The Laird model has quite large tops on the fore and main masts but it is hardly possible to see anything on this photograph.

Two windsails can be seen above the bulwarks, one above the hatch to the crew accommodation and the other above the hatch to the engine-room. A windsail, or ventilator, is a tube made of canvas and used to take fresh air down into the lower part of the ship. An awning is covering the quarter deck from the mizzen mast to the stern. Only four boats can be seen, the dinghy at the stern, the two quarter boats and one on the port side at the bridge level.
(Courtesy Tennessee State Library and Archives)

B. This photograph was also taken in Singapore, on the morning that the *Alabama* left. It is an enlargement from a microphotograph, that is to say a very small photograph mounted on a slide and meant to be viewed through a microscope. The microscope slide, which is 3in by 1in, is shown with the microphotograph in the centre. In this microphotograph the length of the ship

is 1.3mm. (0.05in) long. The full story of this microphotograph is in a paper in the magazine *Microscope* Vol. 46:2 (1998), pp41-60, by Stanley E Warren and Budd J LaRue.

This photograph is obviously very similar to the previous one, except that the ship is ready to sail with steam up. The different angle the ship is viewed from makes it easier to see the rigging where it is outlined against the hill behind. The fore braces can clearly be seen going to the head of the mainmast, as shown in the paintings, and as had been assumed from the previous photograph. It is possible to see the studdingsail booms on the fore and main topsail yards on both sides of the ship.

A second boat appears to be suspended from the same davits as the port quarter boat.
(Courtesy Stanley E Warren)

COMPARISON OF THE TWO SINGAPORE PHOTOGRAPHS

The *Alabama* anchored off Singapore on the evening of Monday 21 December 1863. The following morning they took a pilot on board and ran up to the New Harbour and moored alongside the P&O coaling depot. The coaling finished that night, after taking no more than ten hours, and (according to Fullam) 250 tons of coal were loaded. The next day (the 23rd) the *Alabama* was open to inspection by the public. That night a ship, the *Kwang Tung* (various spellings are used) moored in front of the ship. By coincidence she was also built by Lairds (Yard No. 297) and the stern of the ship visible in Photograph B is very similar to the painting of this ship by Samuel Walters in the Williamson Art Gallery. The *Kwang Tung* sailed on the morning of Thursday 24 December, followed by the *Alabama*. Photograph B was taken on the morning of sailing, but it is not immediately clear on which of the two preceding days the other photograph was taken.

Looking at (A) the muzzles of two 32pdrs that have been run out are just visible (aft of the fore mast and forward of the mizzen mast), and they each cast a shadow on the hull. According to an Admiralty chart of 1858 the P&O coaling wharf lay in almost an exact east-west line. As the ship is moored with her bows pointing to the west the shadows imply that the sun was high, but it was before noon. Therefore the photograph was taken either just after the ship moored, or on the following day, after loading her coal.

The 250 tons of coal loaded on the 22nd would increase the draught of the ship by approximately 21in. From the Book of Elements, at the load draught, it took 12.35 tons to increase the draught by 1in (the TPI). This figure (12.35) will vary slightly as it is dependant upon the waterplane area and therefore changes with draught. Therefore, the increase in draught is found by dividing the increase in load by the TPI, assuming level trim before and after loading. From the drawing of the 32pdr gun by Fawcett Preston (page 122) the gunport is 32in deep. Therefore the change of draught (for 250 tons) is roughly equal to two-thirds of the depth of a gunport.

Comparing both photographs, the distance from the waterline to the bottom of the gunport next to the bridge is less in B than in A. However, the difference is not equivalent to 21in, more like a quarter of that. The boat hanging at the port quarter davits will cause the ship to heel over on that side, thereby giving the impression that the draught is greater. (On the starboard side it gives the impression that the draught has reduced.) Checking the draughts at the bow and stern, as they are not affected by the heel, shows that there is a very small change between the two photographs, not as much as 21in. Therefore it would appear that the photograph A was taken after the ship had been loaded with coal on the 23rd, and on the day the ship was open to visitors.

OTHER PHOTOGRAPHS

(a) Liverpool

There is no record of a photograph being taken of the ship in Liverpool or Birkenhead before she sailed. However, a letter from Acting Rear-Admiral Lee, dated November 4, 1862 (*Alabama* sailed July 29, 1862) stating 'I send herewith a rough draft taken from a photograph of the 290, or *Alabama*' (ORN I, 8 p192) seems to imply that there was one taken. If there was a photograph taken it would almost certainly have passed through the hands of Thomas

PHOTOGRAPHS

This photograph of a line engraving has the title 'The Confederate Privateer Steamer "*Alabama*" ("290") Captain Raphael Semmes - from a photograph taken in Liverpool, where she was built'. This is virtually identical to the painting by Samuel Walters (page 58) and is probably the photograph referred to in the letter dated 4 November 1862. (Courtesy US Naval Historical Center: NH58740)

Dudley. Enquiries with the Dudley collection at the Huntington Library revealed that there is no photograph of the ship in the collection but there is a photograph of a painting or lithograph. This would appear to be the lithograph which appears elsewhere with the caption 'from a photograph taken in Liverpool, where she was built'. It can be seen that this is almost identical to the painting by Samuel Walters (page 58). The most obvious difference is in the boats which are bigger and look out of proportion. The background varies, especially the sea, and the seagull under the jibboom is in a slightly different position.

(b) Cherbourg

There are no known photographs of the *Alabama* taken in Cherbourg which is surprising considering her fame. Photographs were taken during the battle (from the shore) so it is difficult to believe no one attempted to photograph the ship while in harbour. It might be that photographs were taken but the ship not recognised for the following reason.

The *Alabama* was normally rigged as a barque, that is with square sails on only the fore and main masts and not the mizzen. However, when she entered Cherbourg the rig was varied and 'a crossjack yard was got up across the mizen-mast, with mizen topsail and topgallant yards to match; and the *Alabama* assumed for the time the appearance of a full-rigged ship' (*Semmes, Cruise of the Alabama and the Sumter*, 1864). All the topgallant and mizzen yards were sent down a few days later during the preparations for battle. For part of her stay in Cherbourg the *Alabama* was rigged as a ship and the rest of the time had yards sent down prior to the battle, neither case being the normal rig. Therefore is it possible that photographs have not been identified because of this change in rig.

(c) Elsewhere

The *Alabama* stayed in different ports long enough for photographs to be taken. It is possible there are still photographs lying unrecognised in archives.

Paintings

There have been many paintings done of the *Alabama* over the years, some more picturesque than accurate. However, some of the contemporary ones are worthy of study, and they are listed below.

1. This painting was by the well-known Liverpool artist Samuel Walters and the original is now in the Williamson Art Gallery, Birkenhead. This portrays the ship passing the Tuskar Rock Lighthouse off the south-east corner of Ireland and is dated 1862.
(Courtesy Williamson Art Gallery and Museum, Birkenhead, Wirral)

2. This painting is also by Samuel Walters and is now in the collection of the Merseyside Maritime Museum in Liverpool. Dated 1863 this shows the ship off Cork Harbour off southern Ireland. This and the previous painting probably assumed that the *Alabama* would leave the Irish Sea by the southern route, but instead she went around the northern coast. The ship is flying the first Confederate flag, known as the 'Stars and Bars'. The Merseyside Maritime Museum also have two photographic prints of this painting which are identical to the painting except that the ship is not flying a flag. There are also slight differences in the cloud formations, and the smoke from the funnel.

This painting has also been issued as a *carte de visite*, in the same style as the photographs, *ie* the ship has no flag and there is plenty of smoke from the funnel.
(Courtesy of the Board of Trustees of the National Museums & Galleries on Merseyside (Merseyside Maritime Museum)).

3. This is a photographic print of another painting by Walters. The fate and whereabouts of the original are unknown at present. This print came from the Laird photographic collection at the Williamson Art Gallery, and the Peabody & Essex Museum also have an identical copy. In this view the ship is shown off Cape Town. The second Confederate flag is being flown, which was adopted after 26 May 1863. See the frontispiece for a larger version of this painting.
(Courtesy Williamson Art Gallery and Museum, Birkenhead, Wirral)

4. This view is a *carte de visite* in the photograph album of Midshipman Edward Maffitt Anderson, now at the University of Alabama. Underneath the picture is written '*Alabama* or 290 in Chase'. The style of the ship and the sea is very similar to that of Samuel Walters. On 12 March 1863 Samuel Walters registered for copyright at Stationer's Hall, London a photograph of his painting 'The *Alabama* in Chase'. Unfortunately this photograph is no longer among the records of Stationer's Hall, which are now at the Public Record Office at Kew. The flag being flown by the ship is the 'Stars and Bars', which was not superseded until May 1863. It would appear that it is possible that the *carte de visite* in Anderson's album is a copy of Walter's painting. The whereabouts of the original painting is unknown. This is one of the few illustrations showing the ship with topgallants set.
(Courtesy W S Hoole Special Collections Library, The University of Alabama)

PAINTINGS

5. This view is from Sinclair's book *Two Years on the Alabama*. The general setting is identical to the previous picture, except for the royals being set. It would appear that this picture is a copy of the previous one, but of not quite the same standard. The wave pattern along the hull and even the flag are the same. *(Courtesy US Naval Historical Center)*

6. This view is from *The Cruise of the Alabama and the Sumter*, 1864 and is the frontispiece to Volume II. The lithographs of the *Sumter* and the *Alabama* are described (Volume I, page viii) as follows 'the latter vessel being represented in chase of a prize, the former running the blockade of New Orleans in face of the powerful United States steamer *Brooklyn* – are taken from two curious and extremely accurate etchings, executed on walrus teeth, with a penknife and coal dust, by Fireman Mason, of the *Alabama*.' Underneath the lithograph is the caption 'The *Alabama* (in chase of the '*Morning Star*')'. The *Morning Star* was captured on 23 March 1863. Just to be pedantic the *Alabama* is flying the second Confederate flag, which was not in use for another two months.

7. This is an engraving from *Harper's Weekly*, 1862 and 'certified to be correct by Captain Hagar of the *Brilliant*'. Despite the claim that it is correct there are a number of obvious discrepancies. The braces from the fore yard are taken right to the stern by the main braces, a very unusual position. All the four boats appear to be suspended from davits on the port side, but there is a dinghy at the stern.
(Courtesy US Naval Historical Center)

There is also a sketch (not reproduced here) which appears in the book *Battles and Leaders of the Civil War* (Volume IV, page 601), where the caption reads – 'This sketch was made from a photograph (of a drawing) which Captain Semmes gave to a friend, with the remark that it was a correct picture of his ship.' This picture would appear to be based on one of Samuel Walters (No. 2 above),

the wave pattern along the hull is similar to this painting and it even has the same flag. The main difference is that there is no land in the background.

The first three paintings are of a high quality and contain a lot of information. At first glance, ignoring the background, the ship appears to be identical in each, however there are slight differences. For example, in 1 the backstays on the fore and main masts are aft of the shrouds, whereas in 2 and 3 the foremost backstay crosses the aftermost shroud as it does on the sail plans. The photographs taken in South Africa and Singapore show that the first painting is the correct one. If either of the two sail plans is laid over one of these paintings there is a very good match with the position and height of the masts. The lower masts in 2 do appear to be slightly longer than on the other two, and similar to the longer lower mast on the Laird sail plan.

Models

There are two models of the ship which are worthy of close examination. The one I am most familiar with is the one which was at Cammell Laird Shipbuilders and is now in the Williamson Art Gallery in Birkenhead. The second model is in the Mariners' Museum, Newport News, and is said to be Bulloch's model. Each of the models is discussed below, and for convenience are referred to as the Laird Model or the Bulloch Model respectively.

Laird Model

According to an article in a magazine in 1874 Lairds kept models of all the vessels they built in a model room. Included amongst these should have been one of the *Alabama*. Unfortunately we do not know for certain if the model that exists today was built at the same time as the ship, but it has undoubtedly been in the company for a long time. I have been told that there was an estimate done to build a model of the ship in the 1930s, but I have not been able to see this estimate, so cannot comment.

The model is at a scale of 1:48 which gives a hull approximately 56in long overall. As can be seen from the photographs the model is fully rigged and goes in to considerable detail in terms of deck fittings. The most noticeable, and most commented on, feature is that the guns are wrong. This, along with other differences when compared with the University of Alabama deck plan, such as the position of the coal scuttles, has led people into believing that the model is not genuine and therefore has no real value.

The hull lines of the model have been taken off on two separate occasions in 1936 and 1990 and their accuracy in relation to the ship as built is discussed in Appendix 6. The deck plan of the model was drawn over a period of time. A comparison of this deck plan with the copy of the original plan at the University of Alabama and based about the common point of the AP was drawn (not included here). Basically the two plans are very similar, the only significant difference being in the position of the capstan and the companionway to the crew quarters, which have been moved aft by about five feet. From the original plans the forward part of the hatchway has a ladder and the after part is above the hatch, in the lower deck, to the provision store. One of the photographs (No. 4, page 51) clearly shows the ladder was at the after part of the hatchway at the time the photograph was taken. It is not possible to see on the model where the ladder would be, unlike with the gunroom skylight where it is clearly shown.

The sweeps for the guns are significantly different to those fitted to the ship, yet there are marks on the deck which correspond to those on the ship. This can be seen by looking at the sweeps between the gunroom and engine room skylights. The correct sweeps are drawn with the details of the model superimposed and shown by dotted lines. The position of six pivot points near the centreline on the plan can be seen as small squares (partly obscured) on the deck of the model in the photograph. The guns are fixed to

CSS *Alabama*: lines lifted off the model at Cammell Laird Shipbuilders. Modified to 213ft 8in LBP and 32ft beam by A O Bowcock October 1990. (Scale = 1:384)

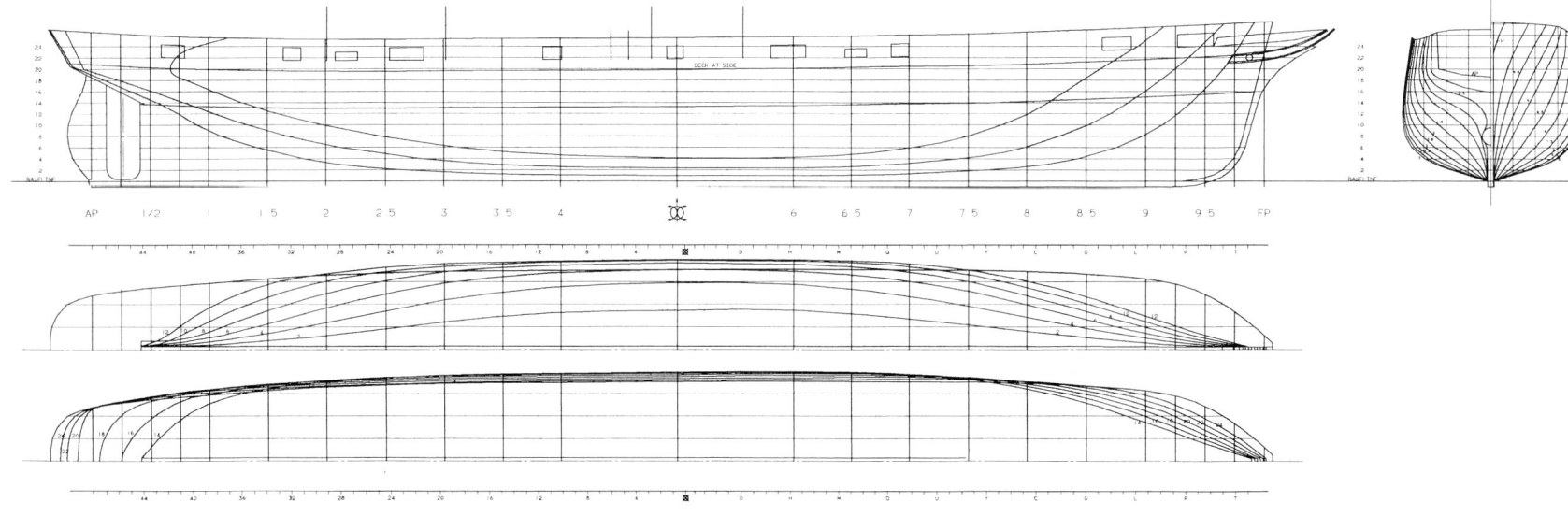

MODELS

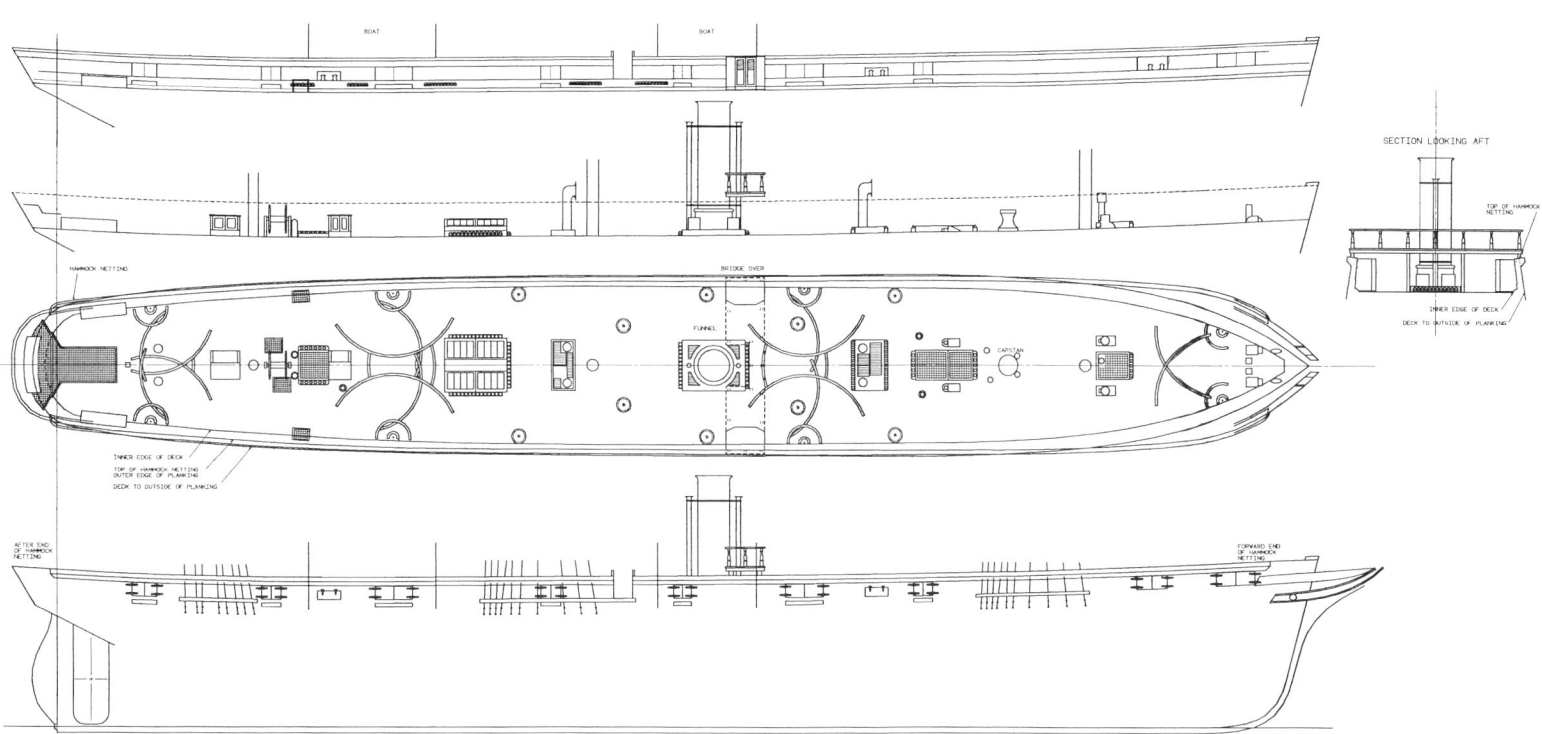

Drawing based on the model at Cammell Laird Shipbuilders. Information taken from model November 1992 and March 1993 by A O Bowcock. (Scale = 1:384)

the deck of the model and so it is not possible to see if there are also similar square marks corresponding to those on the original plans. There are similar marks on the deck of the model for the other three pivot positions which all agree with the original plans.

This model is rigged and has masts and most spars (unlike the Bulloch model), although there are no royal yards on the fore and main masts. The length of the masts agree with the table on the original sail plan but the rake of the masts is different. The rake of the fore mast is greater than the other two masts, which are nearly the same, and all the angles are less than measured from the sail plan.

The biggest differences, however, come in the length of the yards. The fore yard is the equivalent of about 2ft shorter than the figure listed in the table on the sail plan. The fore topsail yard is 10ft shorter and the fore topgallant yard is about 14ft shorter (there is no fore royal yard). The yards on the main mast are the same as on the fore mast (as they are on the ship). The gaffs on the fore and main masts are slightly short (1 or 2ft) but both the boom and gaff on the mizzen mast are about 5ft shorter. Depending on the angle the model is viewed from it is only the upper yards on the masts that look wrong. Over the years various parts of the rigging have been repaired or replaced.

Even if this model is not contemporary with the ship I think it is probable that it was built using the original plans. The marks for the pivot points for the guns on the deck support this. At the time of building the ship it was reported – 'is pierced for guns, the sockets for the bolts of which are laid down' (ORN II, 2 p382). It would appear that this refers to the marks on the deck of the model, which implies that it is based on the original plans. The comparison between the lines of the model and the figures for the original ship (given in Appendix 6) tend to agree.

A propeller is fitted but unfortunately the wrong way round. What should be the leading edge has been placed to the rear. The propeller is of the Griffiths type which was widely used in the nineteenth century.

Bulloch model

This model, which is in the Mariners' Museum, Newport News, Virginia, is said to have belonged to Bulloch and was given to the museum in 1985. As can be seen from the photographs it is unrigged and has stump masts and funnel. The two models, which are to the same scale, are very similar in terms of hull shape and deck layout, so it is probably easier to list the differences between them.

The most obvious (apart from the lack of masts, rigging and guns) is that the gunports are open, except those for the bow pivot gun. There are also gangways at the entry ports and ladders to the bridge. The forward pair of boats are slightly further aft, with the aftermost davit aft of the entry port, which agrees with the photographs in Singapore, but disagrees with the Laird model and the paintings by Walters. There is what appears to be a compass binnacle just aft of the vent to the after stokehold. Two anchor-handling davits are fitted on each bow. Some are missing from the Laird model, but it is possible to see where they were fitted. The sweeps for the guns appear to be identical on both models. There even appear to be the marks on the deck for the pivots in the correct place for the original sweeps. The propeller on this model is placed correctly, unlike the Laird model.

VISUAL EVIDENCE

The Laird model: View on starboard bow.

View on stern, showing decoration, hammock netting and gunport. Dinghy in davits over the stern.

View on starboard quarter.

View of bridge and funnel.

View on bow showing figurehead.

MODELS 63

View on deck showing fore mast, capstan and entrance to crew quarters.

View on deck showing mizzen mast, steering wheels and up to the engine room skylight.

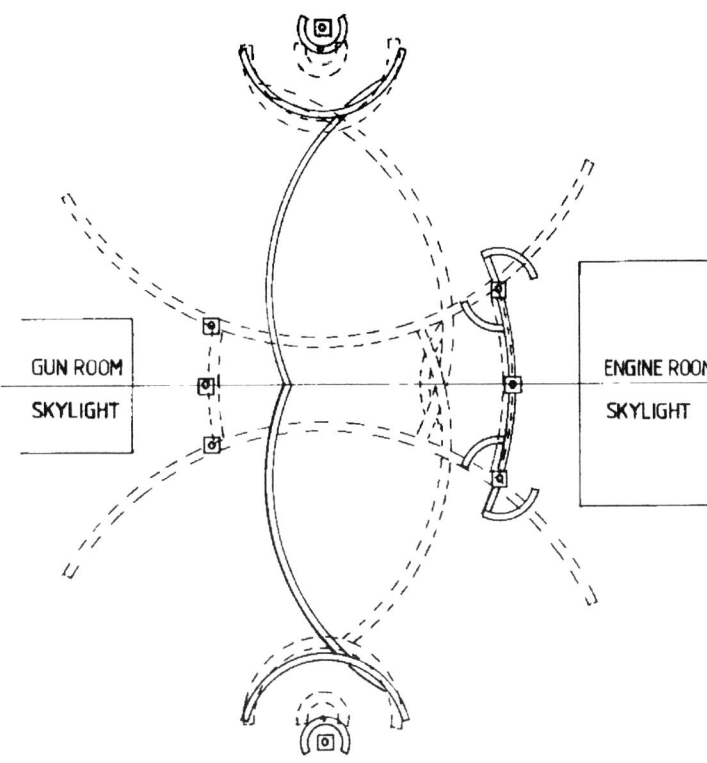

Sweeps for the pivot gun with those for the Laird Model shown by the broken lines. The photograph shows the same area on the deck of the model. Marks on the deck show the pivot points.

Photographs below and on the next page: The Bulloch Model. (From the Collections of The Mariners' Museum, Newport News, Va.)

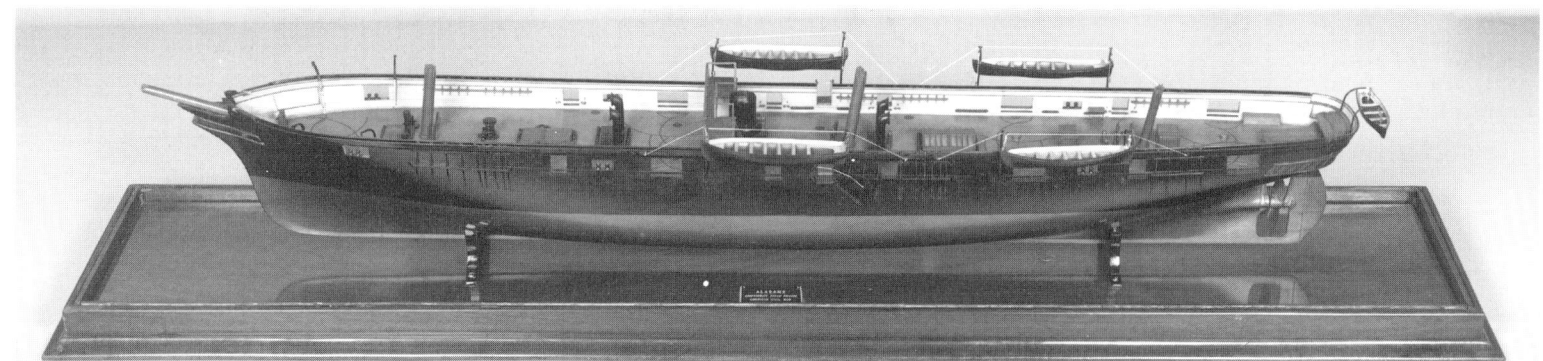
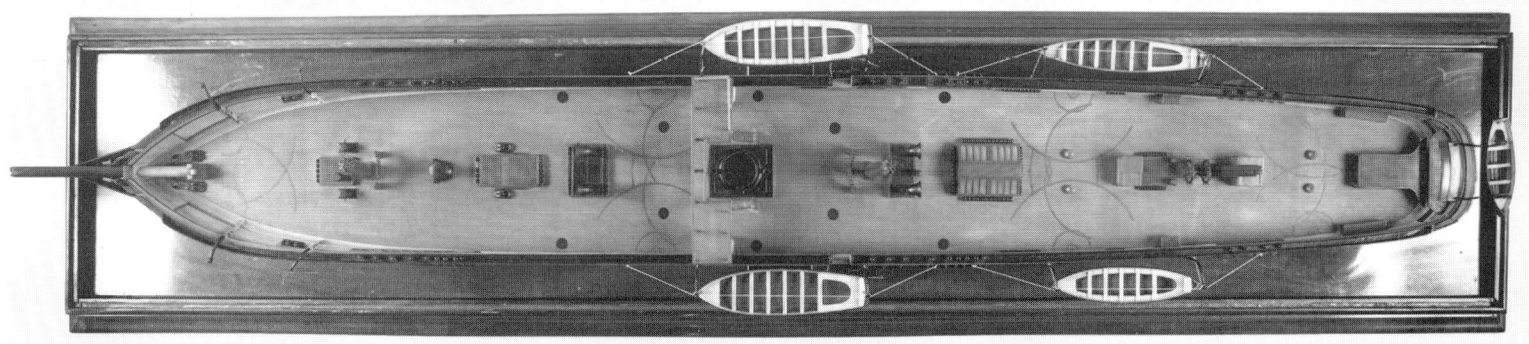

MODELS

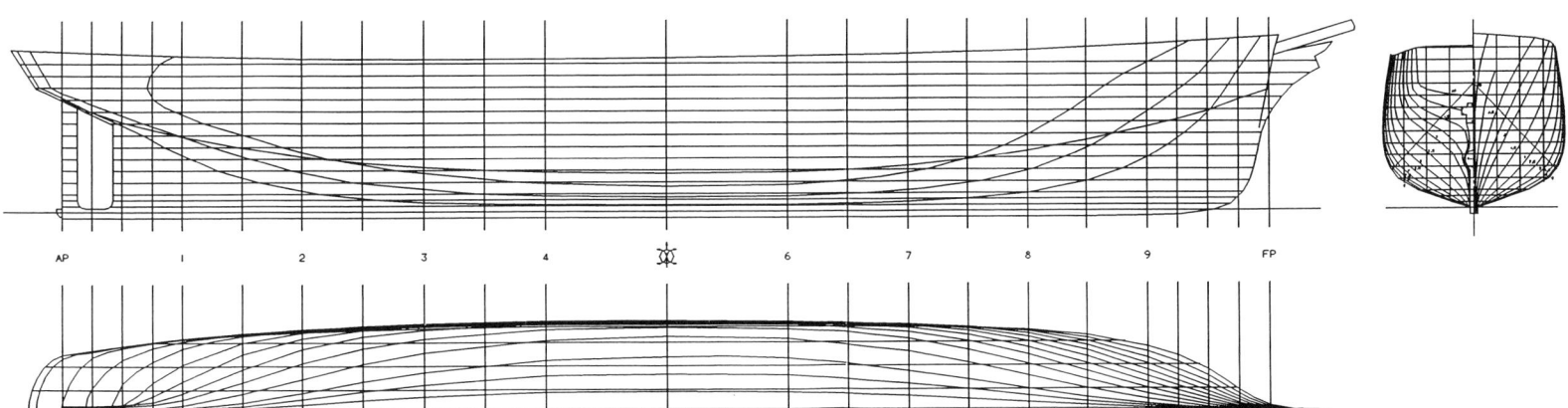

CSS *Alabama*: lines lifted from the model in the Mariners' Museum (the Bulloch Model). Redrawn by A O Bowcock October 1990/August 1992. (Scale = 1:384)

The Drawings

Hull and Decks

Hull

Dimensions

The dimensions of the ship as proposed are given in the specification and are listed below:

Length: 210ft
Beam Extreme: 32ft
Depth: 17ft 3in.

The ship as built was slightly different, and had the following dimensions:

Length: 213ft 8in
Beam Extreme: 32ft
Depth: 18ft 0in

The following definitions have been used for the dimensions:

Length between perpendiculars – from the intersection of fore side of the stem with the upper deck to aft side of the rudder post.
Length on load water line – from fore side of rabbet of stem to after side of rabbet of fore stern post.
Depth in Hold – from top of the limber strake to top of upper deck beam.
Depth at Side – from lower side of rabbet to top of upper deck beam.

The original plan Profile of Inboard Works only has one dimension marked which is the height between the top of the lower deck and the top of the upper deck beams (or underside of the upper deck). This dimension is 6ft 9½in but the height scaled off the drawing at that point is 5ft

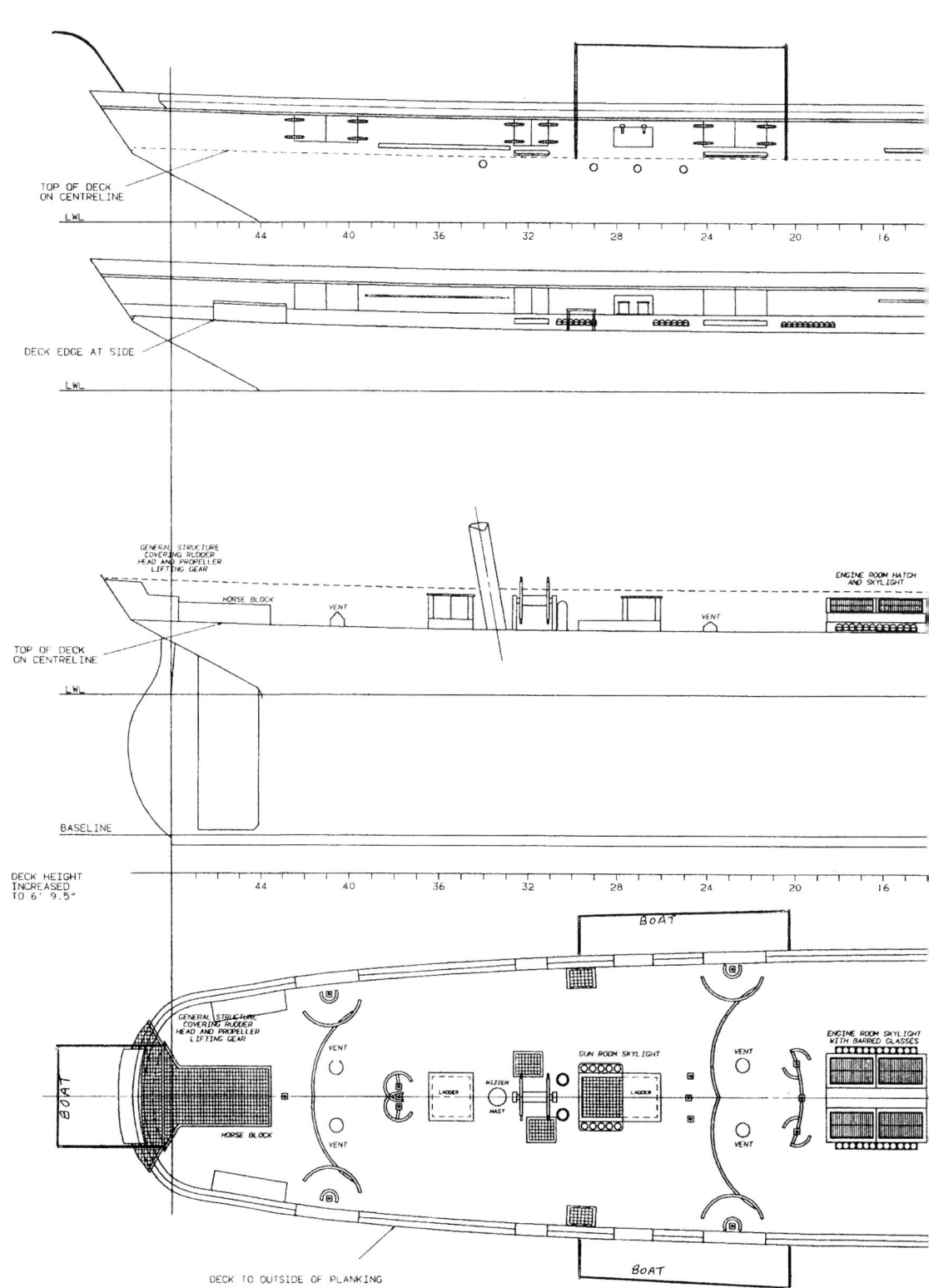

HULL AND DECKS

Profile and Upper Deck (scale = 1:192)

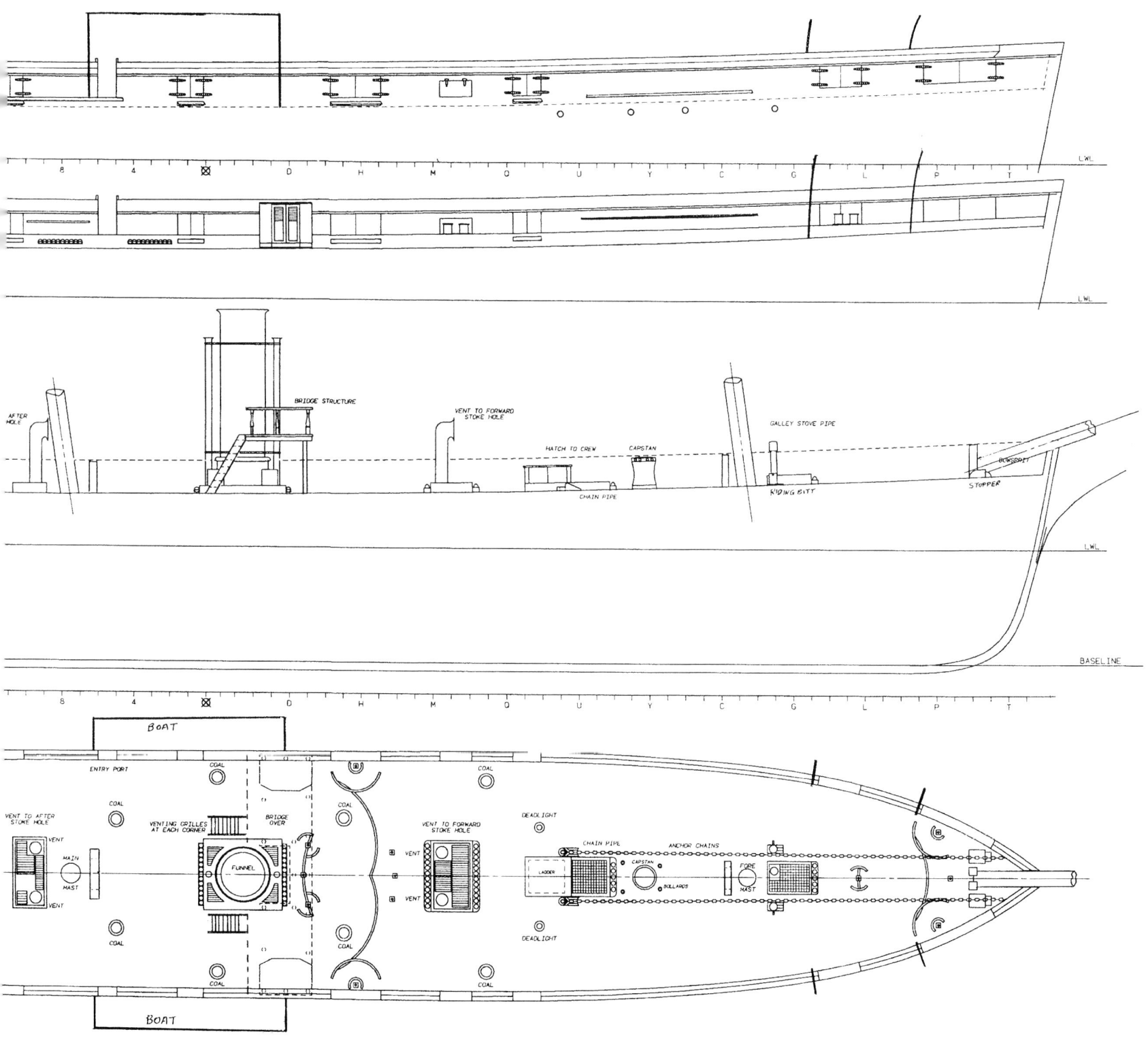

68 THE DRAWINGS

11in. It would appear that the 'tween deck height was increased at some stage (to increase the headroom) so the original drawings just had the new height marked but were not redrawn. As discussed earlier the hull lines of the Laird model are considered to be those of the finished ship, and the drawings in this section are based on these lines and the Profile of Inboard Works which has been modified in the following way.

The depth at side for both models is the same (bearing in mind the fact that the dimensions have been lifted from models) and is equal to the 19ft 9in quoted in the Book of Elements (page 34). Using the structure described in the Specification gives the correct distance for the Depth in Hold, and therefore the line of the upper deck. The position of the top of the lower deck beams has therefore been drawn at 7ft 0in below the top of the upper deck

Profile of Inboard Works, Lower Deck and below Lower Deck (scale = 1:192)

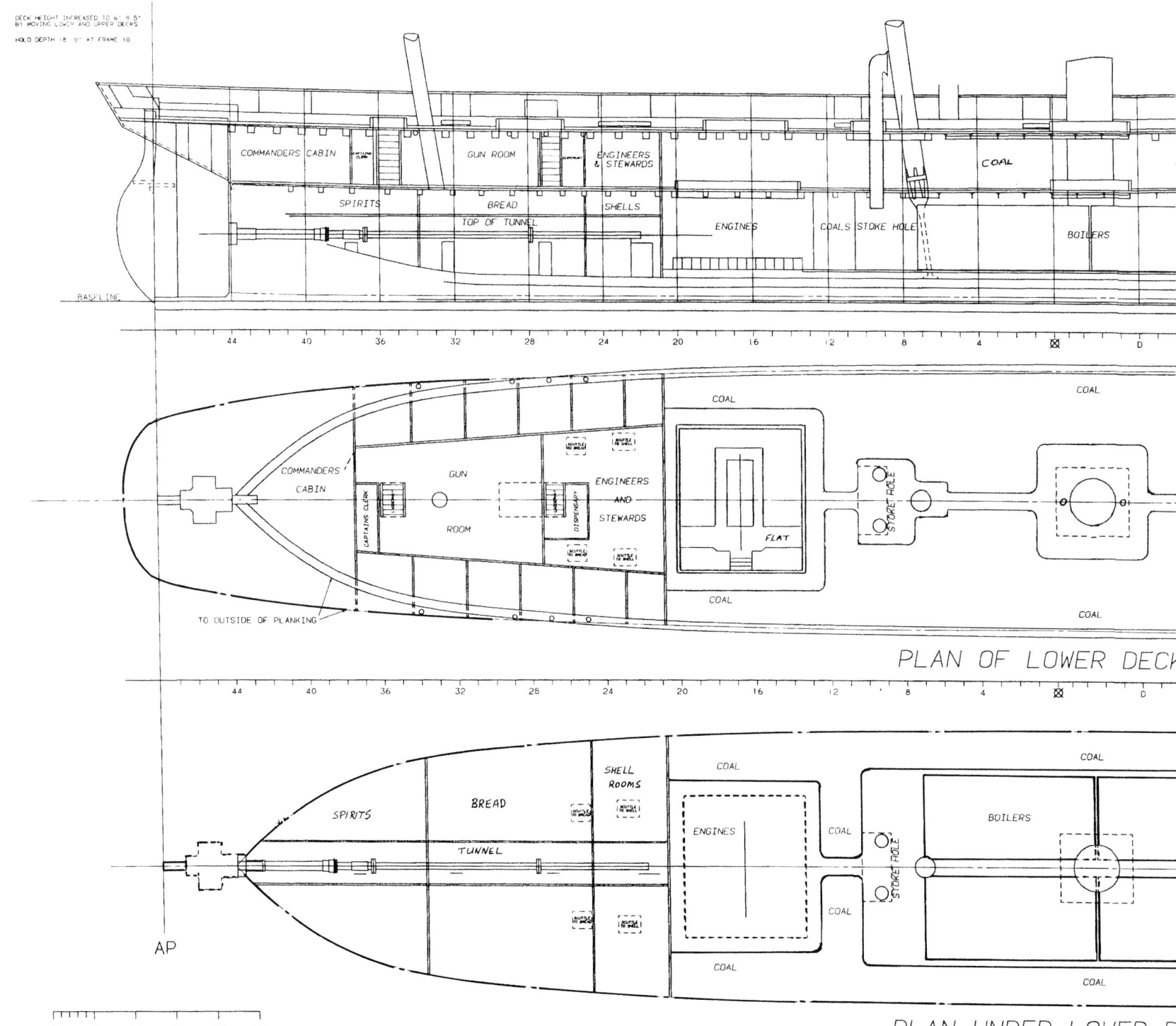

beams. The distance is taken from the 6ft 9½in marked on the original plan plus the thickness of the lower deck planking of 2½in. The plan of the engines is the only other plan to give the position of a deck, that is to say the lower deck at the aft end of the engine-room. The position of the lower deck above the centreline of the propeller shaft agrees with the profile with the decks drawn as described above.

Hull Structure

The Specification gives all the sizes and types of the timbers in the hull. The two main drawings show the decks which are based on the originals, but are modified where necessary to fit the hull lines, and the increase in deck height. Other changes are described as appropriate in the following sections.

The keel and frames form the backbone of the ship and are joined together by copper bolts. A hole is drilled through the pieces of timber to be joined and the copper bolt driven through and clenched over washers. The drilled hole is slightly smaller than the diameter of the copper bolt. Towards the bow and stern these copper bolts could be over 6ft long in order to pass through the deadwood.

Inside the frames the diagonal iron riders and the wooden diagonal truss pieces provide additional strength by joining the frames together. A partial elevation shows how these items are fitted.

The deck beams, going across the ship, complete the strength of the hull and provide the platforms from which the ship is worked. The beams have camber (are curved) to allow water to run off the deck, but it also increases the strength as the ends are fixed. The ends of the beams rest upon the shelf, and their position fixes the ends of the hatch coamings.

Transverse sections at eleven points along the hull have been drawn, and show the different parts of the structure described in the Specification. Iron deck beams are shown on the lower deck over the boilers and on the upper deck around the funnel. These were two angle irons with a piece of plate with a bulb on the lower part riveted together. They appear to be the same depth as the wooden beam they replace. There would be an iron stringer plate riveted on the top of the beams (under the waterway). These iron deck beams would probably also be held in place by a wooden lodging knee (lying fore and aft and between the waterway and the shelf to stop them twisting).

The size of the iron beam knees are determined by their weight, those for the

Frames (scale = 1:192)

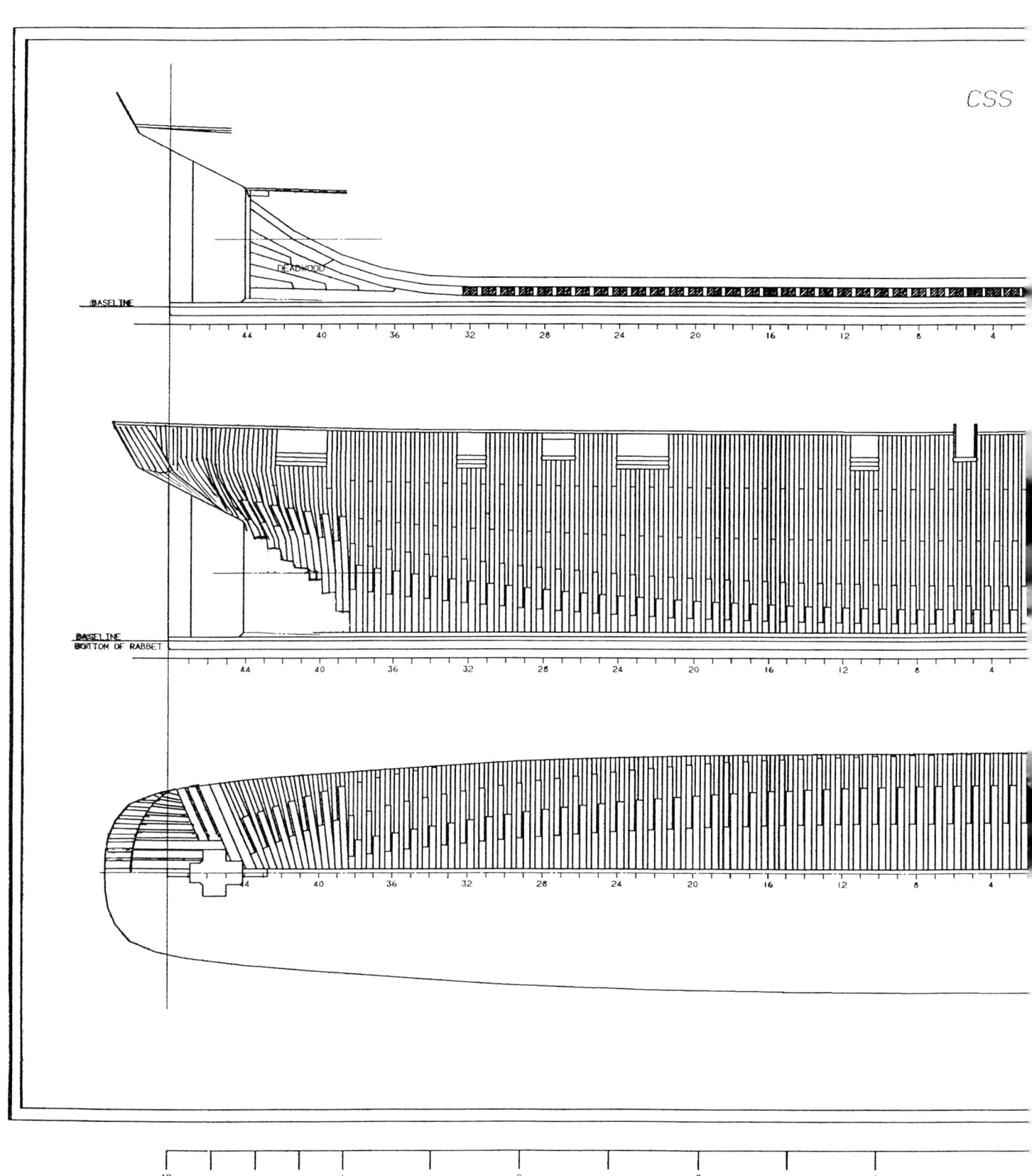

HULL AND DECKS

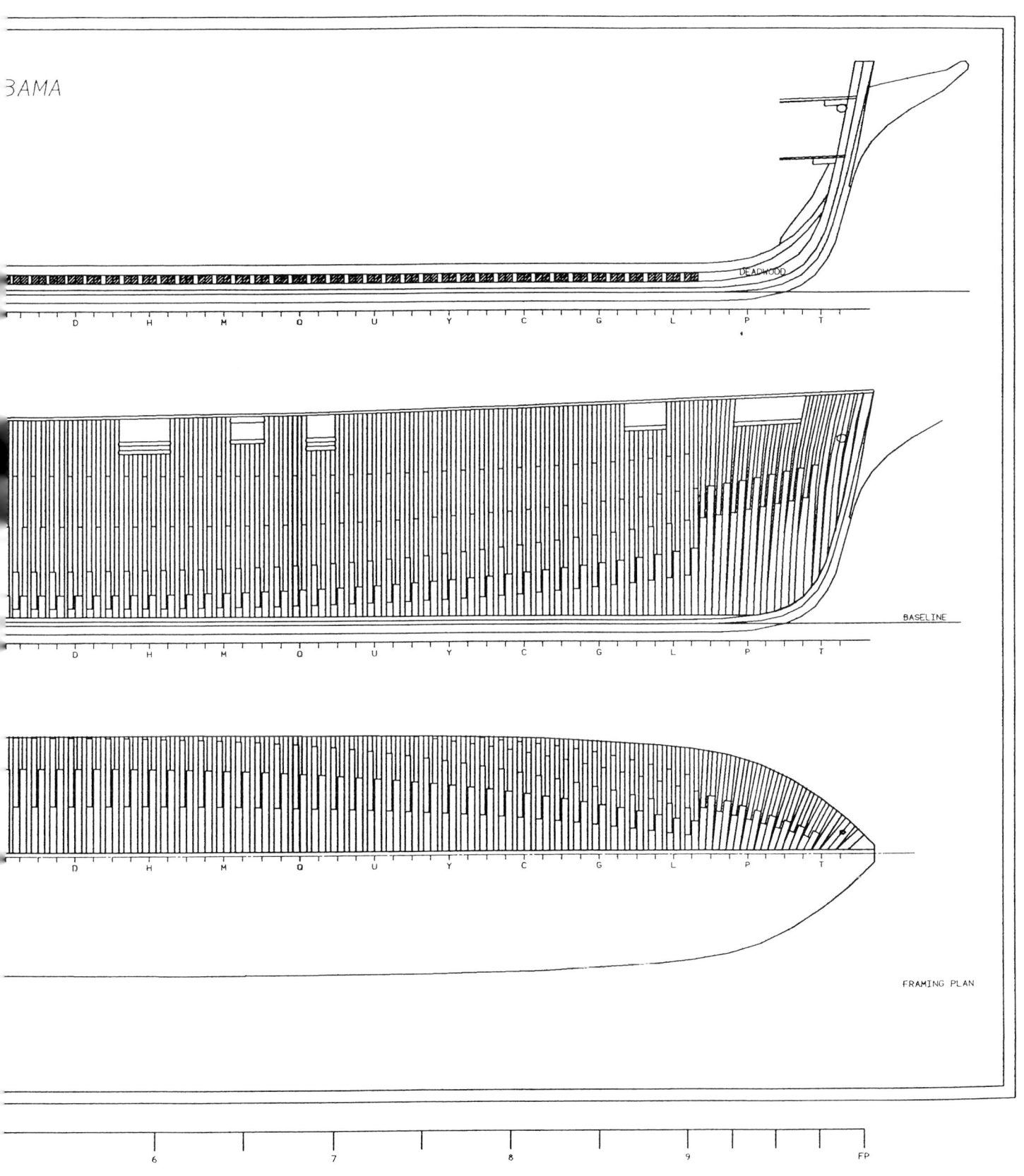

FRAMING PLAN

Deck Beams (scale = 1:192)

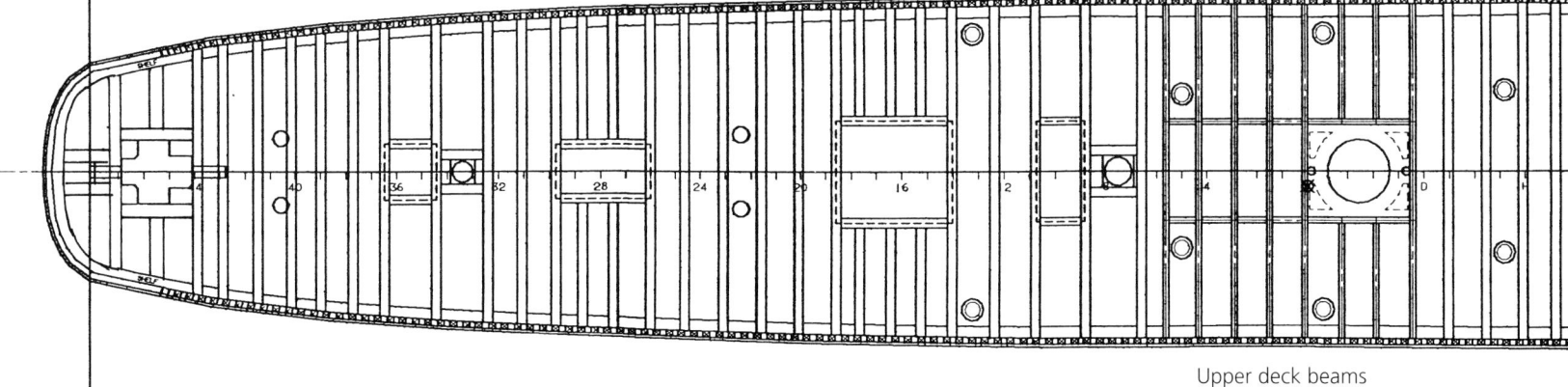

Upper deck beams

Coal scuttles from model moved slightly to fit within beams.

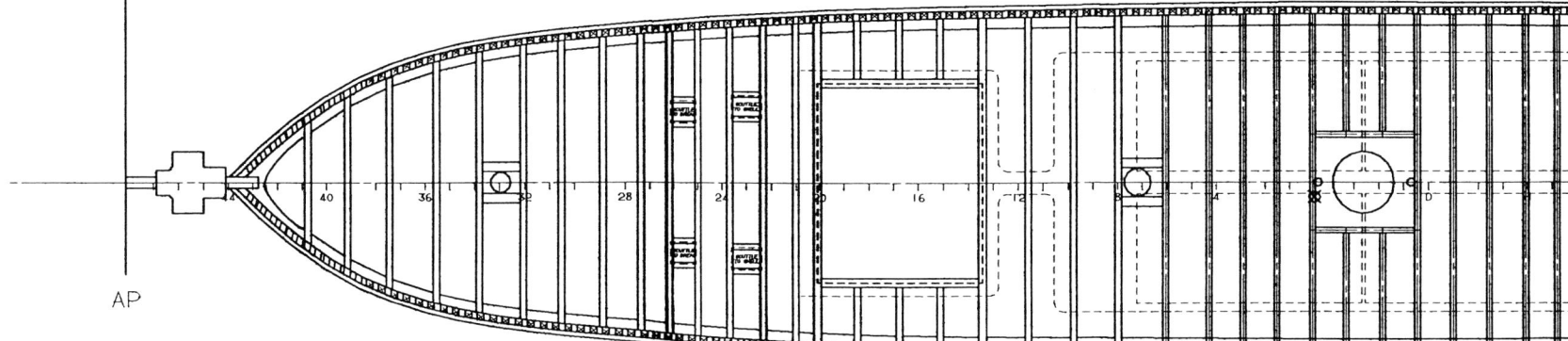

Lower deck beams

AP

Part elevation on centreline looking to port. Diagonal iron riders and truss pieces

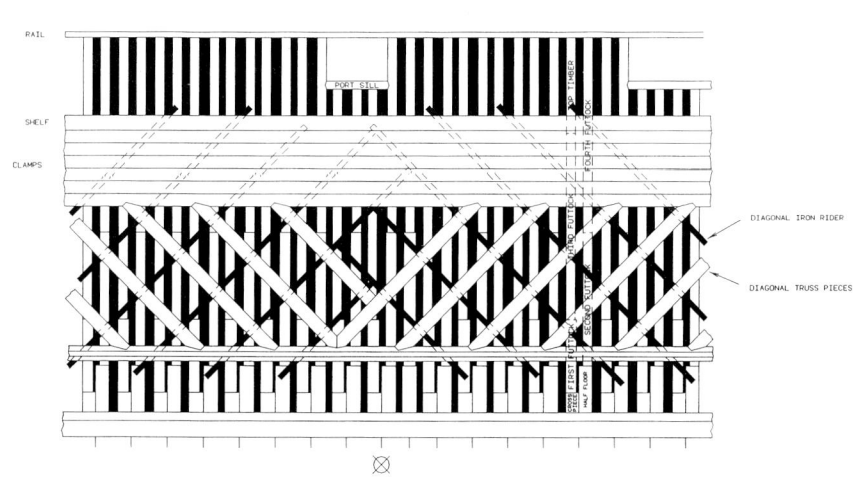

Frame 40 – Looking Forward (scale = 1:192)

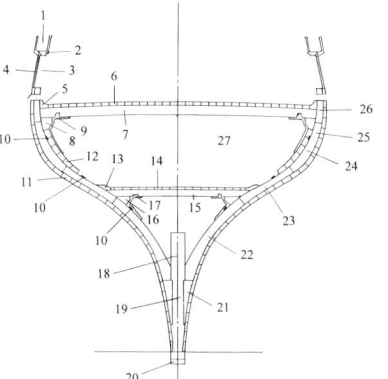

1. Hammock netting
2. Rough tree rail
3. Gunport
4. Gunport lid
5. Upper deck waterway
6. Upper deck planking
7. Upper deck beam
8. Upper deck shelf
9. Upper deck beam knee
10. Diagonal iron riders
11. Wales
12. Upper deck clamps
13. Lower deck waterway
14. Lower deck planking
15. Lower deck beam
16. Lower deck shelf
17. Lower deck beam knee
18. Propeller shaft
19. Deadwood
20. False keel
21. Deadwood
22. First futtock
23. Second futtock (behind)
24. Third futtock
25. Fourth futtock (behind)
26. Top timber
27. Cabin (Captain)

HULL AND DECKS

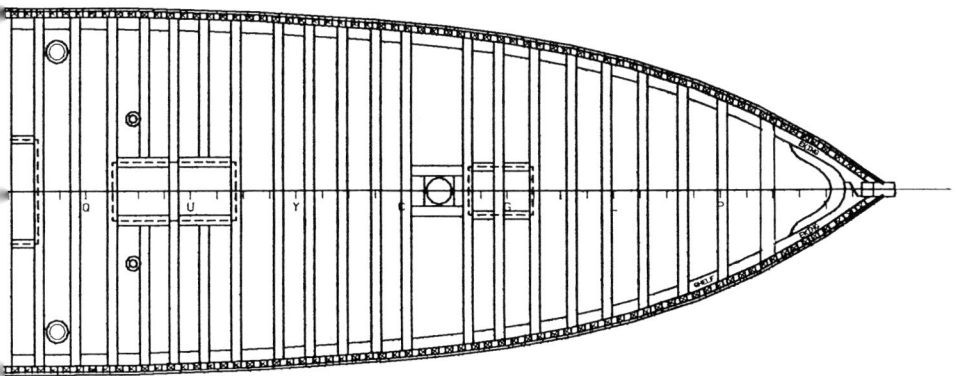

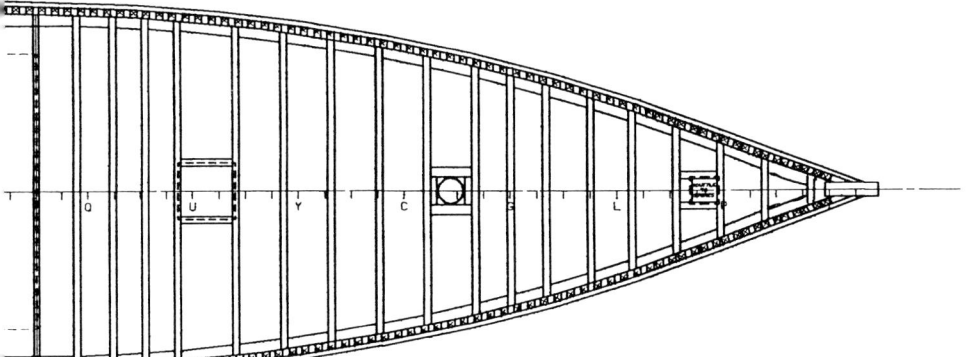

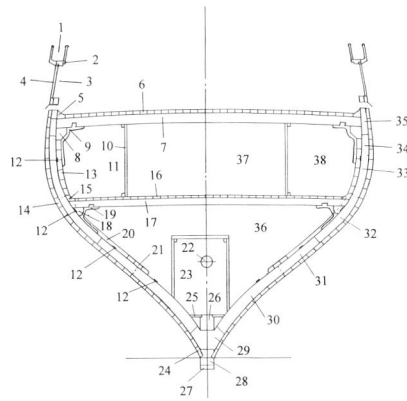

Frame 32 – Looking Forward (scale = 1:192)

1 Hammock netting
2 Rough tree rail
3 Gunport
4 Gunport lid
5 Upper deck waterway
6 Upper deck planking
7 Upper deck beam
8 Upper deck shelf
9 Upper deck beam knee
10 Wooden bulkhead
11 Cabin (Lieutenant)
12 Diagonal iron rider
13 Upper deck clamps
14 Wales
15 Lower deck waterway
16 Lower deck planking
17 Lower deck beam
18 Lower deck shelf
19 Lower deck beam knee
20 Diagonal truss piece
21 Bands at floor heads
22 Propeller shaft
23 Shaft tunnel
24 Garboard strake
25 Limber strake
26 Keelson
27 False keel
28 Keel
29 Cross piece
30 Half floor (behind)
31 First futtock
32 Second futtock (behind)
33 Third futtock
34 Fourth futtock (behind)
35 Top timber
36 Bread room
37 Wardroom
38 Cabin (Lieutenant)

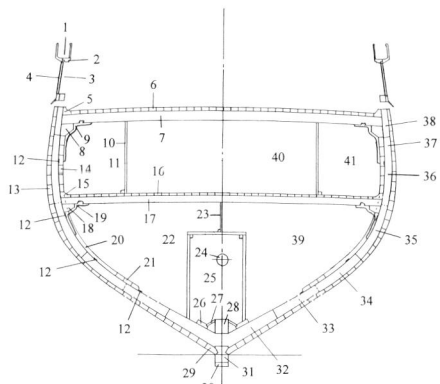

Frame 24 – Looking Forward (scale = 1:192)

1 Hammock netting
2 Rough tree rail
3 Gunport
4 Gunport lid
5 Upper deck waterway
6 Upper deck planking
7 Upper deck beam
8 Upper deck shelf
9 Upper deck beam knee
10 Wooden bulkhead
11 Cabin (Engineer)
12 Diagonal iron rider
13 Wales
14 Upper deck clamps
15 Lower deck waterway
16 Lower deck planking
17 Lower deck beam
18 Lower deck shelf
19 Lower deck beam knee
20 Diagonal truss piece
21 Bands at floorheads
22 Shell room (elongated shells)
23 Bulkhead
24 Propeller shaft
25 Shaft tunnel
26 Limber strake
27 Limber board
28 Keelson
29 Garboard strake
30 False keel
31 Keel
32 Cross piece
33 Half floor (behind)
34 First futtock
35 Second futtock (behind)
36 Third futtock
37 Fourth futtock (behind)
38 Top timber
39 Shell room (spherical shells)
40 Gunroom
41 Cabin (Midshipman)

Frame 16 – Looking Forward (scale = 1:192)

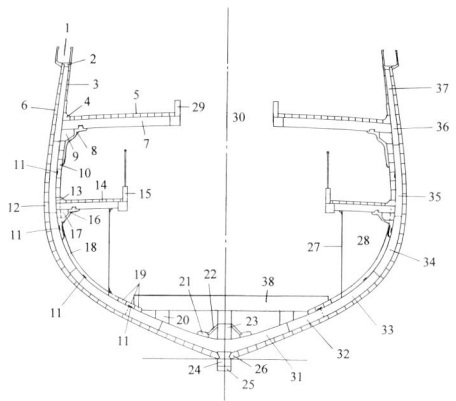

1 Hammock netting
2 Rough tree rail
3 Quickwork (or spirketting)
4 Upper deck waterway
5 Upper deck planking
6 Outer planking
7 Upper deck beam
8 Upper deck beam knee
9 Upper deck shelf
10 Upper deck clamps
11 Diagonal iron riders
12 Wales
13 Lower deck waterway
14 Lower deck planking
15 Lower deck coaming
16 Lower deck beam knee
17 Lower deck shelf
18 Diagonal truss piece
19 Bands at floor heads
20 Side keelson
21 Limber strake
22 Limber board
23 Keelson
24 Keel
25 False Keel
26 Garboard strake
27 Iron bulkhead
28 Coal bunker
29 Upper deck coaming
30 Engine room skylight
31 Cross piece
32 Half floor (behind)
33 First futtock
34 Second futtock (behind)
35 Third futtock
36 Fourth futtock (behind)
37 Top timber
38 Engine bed

Frame 8 – Looking Forward (scale = 1:192)

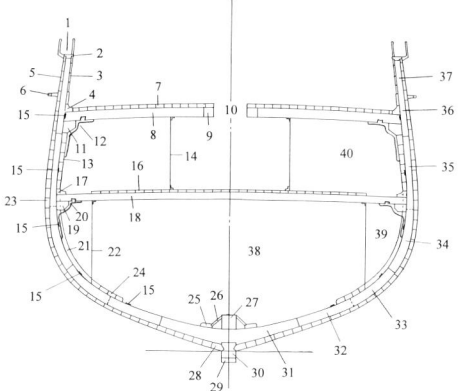

1 Hammock netting
2 Rough tree rail
3 Quickwork (or spirketting)
4 Upper deck waterway
5 Planking of topsides
6 Channel
7 Upper deck planking
8 Upper deck beam
9 Carling
10 Main mast partners
11 Upper deck shelf
12 Upper deck beam knee
13 Upper deck clamps
14 Iron bulkhead
15 Diagonal iron riders
16 Lower deck planking
17 Lower deck waterway
18 Lower deck beam
19 Lower deck shelf
20 Lower deck beam knee
21 Diagonal truss piece
22 Iron bulkhead
23 Wales
24 Bands at floorheads
25 Limber strake
26 Limber board
27 Keelson
28 Garboard strake
29 False keel
30 Keel
31 Cross piece
32 Half floor (behind)
33 First futtock
34 Second futtock (behind)
35 Third futtock
36 Fourth futtock (behind)
37 Top timber
38 Boiler room
39 Coal bunker
40 Coal bunker

Deadflat – Looking Forward (scale 1:192)

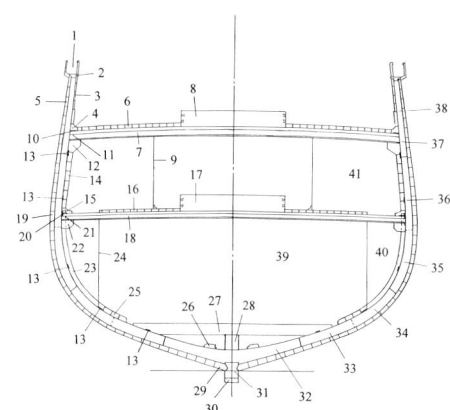

1 Hammock netting
2 Rough tree rail
3 Spirketting (or quickwork)
4 Upper deck waterway
5 Planking of topsides
6 Upper deck planking
7 Upper deck beam – iron
8 Headledge
9 Iron bulkhead
10 Iron stringer
11 Lodging knee
12 Upper deck shelf
13 Diagonal iron riders
14 Upper deck clamps
15 Lower deck waterway
16 Lower deck planking
17 Headledge
18 Lower deck beam – iron
19 Wales
20 Iron stringer
21 Lodging knee
22 Lower deck shelf
23 Diagonal truss piece
24 Iron bulkhead
25 Bands at floor heads
26 Limber strake
27 Bed for boilers
28 Keelson
29 Garboard strake
30 False keel
31 Keel
32 Cross piece
33 Half floor (behind)
34 First futtock
35 Second futtock (behind)
36 Third futtock
37 Fourth futtock (behind)
38 Top timber
39 Boiler room
40 Coal bunker
41 Coal bunker

Frame H – Looking Forward (scale = 1:192)

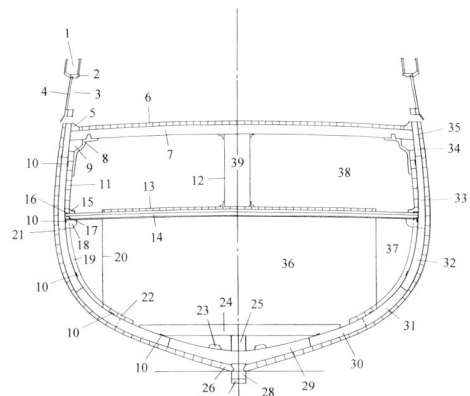

1 Hammock netting
2 Rough tree rail
3 Gunport
4 Gunport lid
5 Upper deck waterway
6 Upper deck planking
7 Upper deck beam
8 Upper deck knee
9 Upper deck shelf
10 Diagonal iron riders
11 Upper deck clamps
12 Iron bulkhead
13 Lower deck planking
14 Lower deck beam – iron
15 Lower deck waterway
16 Iron stringer
17 Lodging knee
18 Lower deck shelf
19 Diagonal truss piece
20 Iron bulkhead
21 Wales
22 Bands at floor heads
23 Limber strake
24 Bed for boiler
25 Keelson
26 Garboard strake
27 False keel
28 Keel
29 Cross piece
30 Half floor (behind)
31 First futtock
32 Second futtock (behind)
33 Third futtock
34 Fourth futtock (behind)
35 Top timber
36 Boiler room
37 Coal bunker
38 Coal bunker
39 Passageway

HULL AND DECKS

Frame Q – Looking Forward (scale = 1:192)

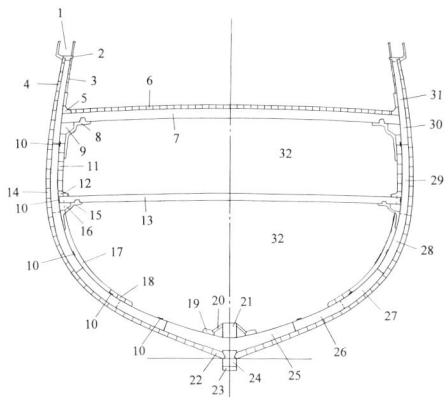

1. Hammock netting
2. Rough tree rail
3. Spirketting (or quickwork)
4. Planking of topsides
5. Upper deck waterway
6. Upper deck planking
7. Upper deck beam
8. Upper deck beam knee
9. Upper deck shelf
10. Diagonal iron riders
11. Upper deck clamps
12. Lower deck waterway
13. Lower deck beam
14. Wales
15. Lower deck beam knee
16. Lower deck shelf
17. Diagonal truss piece
18. Bands at floor heads
19. Limber strake
20. Limber board
21. Keelson
22. Garboard strake
23. False keel
24. Keel
25. Cross piece
26. Half floor (behind)
27. First futtock
28. Second futtock (behind)
29. Third futtock
30. Fourth futtock (behind)
31. Top timber
32. Coal bunker

Frame Y – Looking Forward (scale = 1:192)

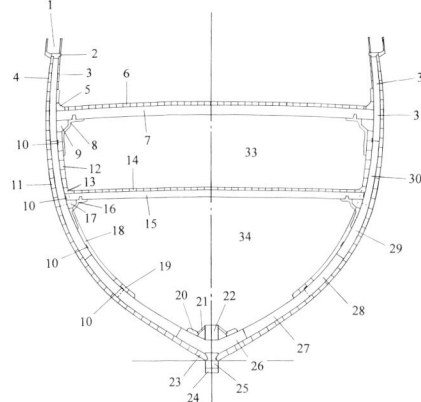

1. Hammock netting
2. Rough tree rail
3. Spirketting (or quickwork)
4. Planking of topsides
5. Upper deck waterway
6. Upper deck planking
7. Upper deck beam
8. Upper deck beam knee
9. Upper deck shelf
10. Diagonal iron riders
11. Wales
12. Upper deck clamps
13. Lower deck waterway
14. Lower deck planking
15. Lower deck beam
16. Lower deck beam knee
17. Lower deck shelf
18. Diagonal truss piece
19. Bands at floor heads
20. Limber strake
21. Limber board
22. Keelson
23. Garboard strake
24. False keel
25. Keel
26. Cross piece
27. Half floor (behind)
28. First futtock
29. Second futtock (behind)
30. Third futtock
31. Fourth futtock (behind)
32. Top timber
33. Crew accommodation
34. Stores, water, magazine etc

Frame G – Looking Forward (scale = 1:192)

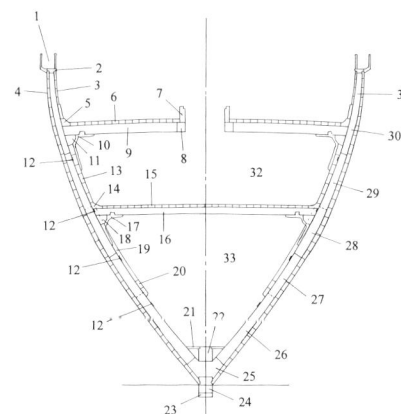

1. Hammock netting
2. Rough tree rail
3. Spirketting (or quickwork)
4. Planking of topsides
5. Upper deck waterway
6. Upper deck planking
7. Coaming
8. Carling
9. Upper deck beam
10. Upper deck beam knee
11. Upper deck shelf
12. Diagonal iron riders
13. Upper deck clamps
14. Lower deck waterway
15. Lower deck planking
16. Lower deck beam
17. Lower deck beam knee
18. Lower deck shelf
19. Diagonal truss piece
20. Bands at floor heads
21. Limber board
22. Keelson
23. False keel
24. Keel
25. Cross piece
26. Half floor (behind)
27. First futtock
28. Second futtock (behind)
29. Third futtock
30. Fourth futtock (behind)
31. Top timber
32. Crew accommodation
33. Stores

Frame P – Looking Forward (scale = 1:192)

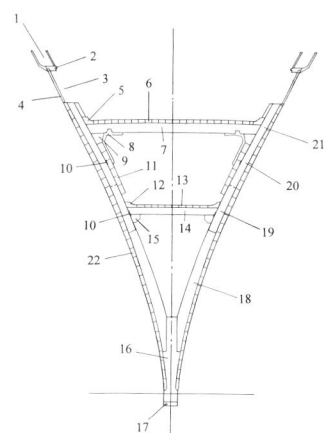

1. Hammock netting
2. Rough tree rail
3. Gunport
4. Gunport lid
5. Upper deck waterway
6. Upper deck planking
7. Upper deck beam
8. Upper deck beam knee
9. Upper deck shelf
10. Diagonal iron riders
11. Upper deck clamps
12. Lower deck waterway
13. Lower deck planking
14. Lower deck beam
15. Lower deck shelf
16. Keel and deadwood
17. False keel
18. First futtock
19. Second futtock (behind)
20. Third futtock
21. Top timber (behind)
22. Hull planking

Rudder (scale = 1:48)

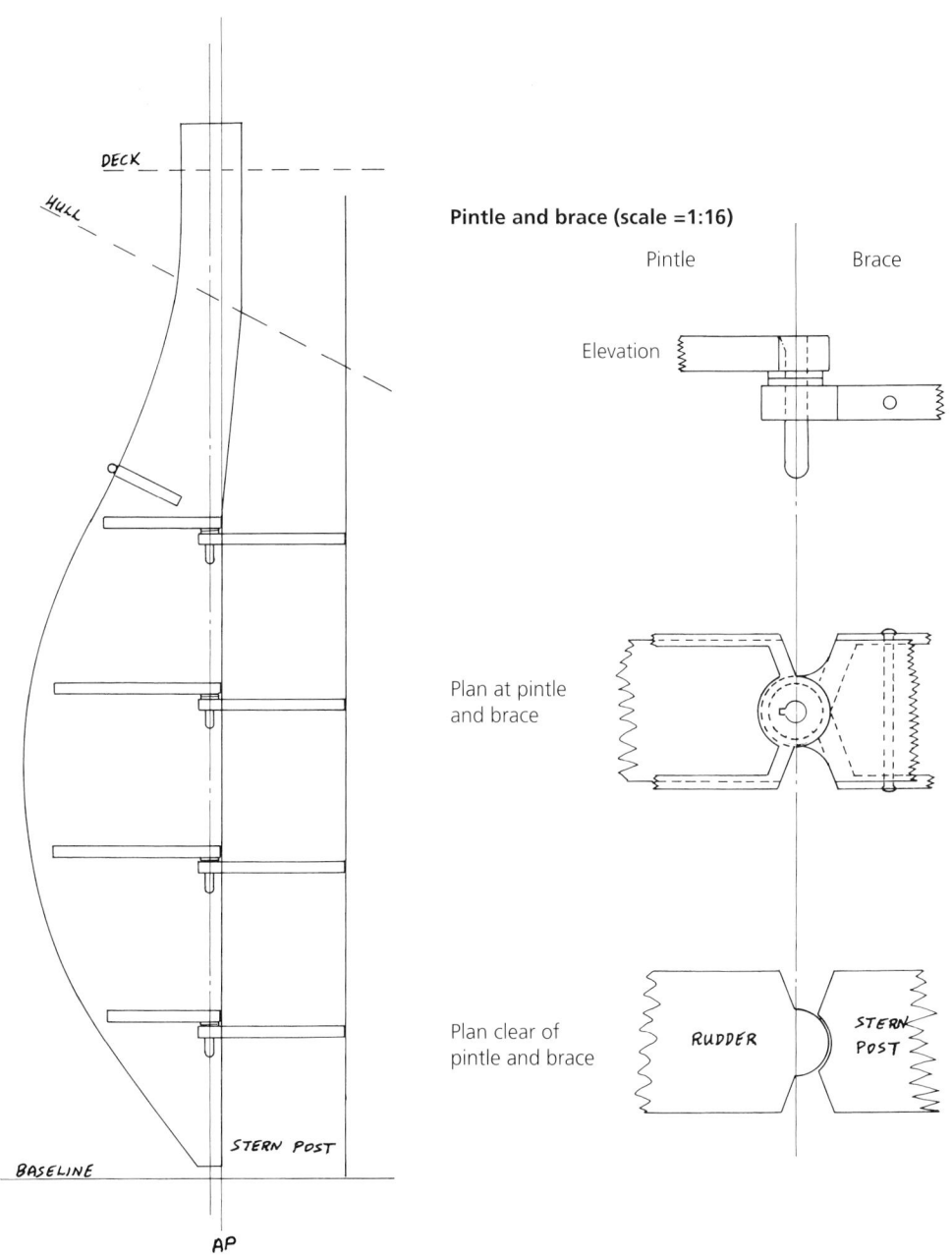

Stern decoration (not to scale)
19 dummy windows

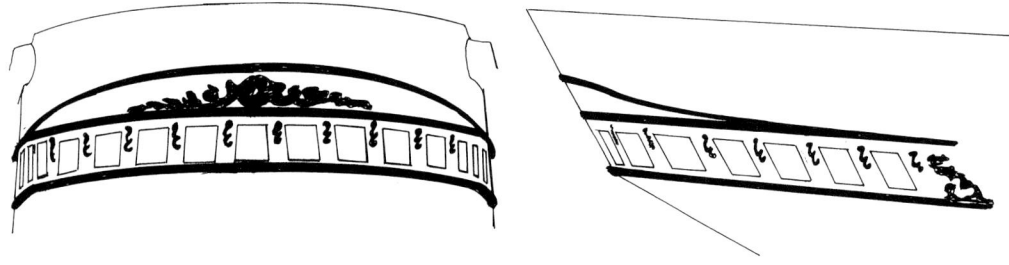

upper deck are to weigh not less than 1 cwt (112lbs). Those for the lower deck were smaller and were to weigh 'about 3 qrs', that is to say about three quarters of a hundredweight (about 84lbs).

Rudder
According to the Specification the rudder was to have four pintles and braces 'fitted on the late Captain Lihon's plan'. Captain Lihon, RN, took out a patent on the means of hanging the rudder, and this is illustrated in the drawing.

Stern decoration
The round stern had a number of dummy windows, twenty-two according to Maguire but only nineteen on the Laird model. These windows are above the level of the upper deck and therefore serve no useful purpose other than decoration. The carving around these windows was gilt, according to Maguire. The drawing of the decoration is based on the Laird model.

Bow and figurehead
The cheeks and berthing boards of the bow are shown in the drawing, but the actual figurehead used is not clear. The original sail plan shows what appears to be a figure. The Laird sail plan has a dotted line around the area where the figurehead would be. According to Maguire she had a 'Billet head gilt; with red shield for figurehead, with gilt anchor, about nine inches long on it'. The paintings by Walters seem to agree with this, as far as it is possible to see because of the scale. The photograph of the Laird model shows a head painted gold with what appears to be a shield with a fouled anchor on it. Overall it would appear that the figurehead was similar to that on the Laird model, but with a red shield.

Copper sheathing
The outside of the lower hull was covered with copper sheets to prevent attack by sea-worm which tended to live in tropical

Hull and Decks

waters. The hull was first covered with tar or pitch and then brown paper was laid on top. The copper sheets (sized about 4ft by 1¼ft) were nailed on top of the paper, each sheet overlapping the one below and astern of it. The copper extended to about 18in above the waterline, and the sheets along the waterline and at the bow were slightly thicker than the rest (because they were likely to suffer greater wear).

Upper Deck

At the extreme after end of the upper deck is the flag locker. This sits on the structure covering the rudder head and tiller. There are twin steering wheels immediately forward of the mizzen mast. Each of the steering wheels has ten spokes. The motto 'Aide toi, et Dieu t'aidere' is engraved on the rim of the wheel. According to the Laird model the ropes run from the drum between the two wheels down to the deck then across to the bulwarks, then along the waterway to the tiller, pulleys being fitted as appropriate to keep the rope close to the side. However, there are gunports directly opposite the steering wheels which would mean that the trucks of the guns would run over the steering ropes. Unless the steering ropes are under the deck (and shown in position above deck) they must run in some other way. Looking at the pho-

Head (scale =1:96)

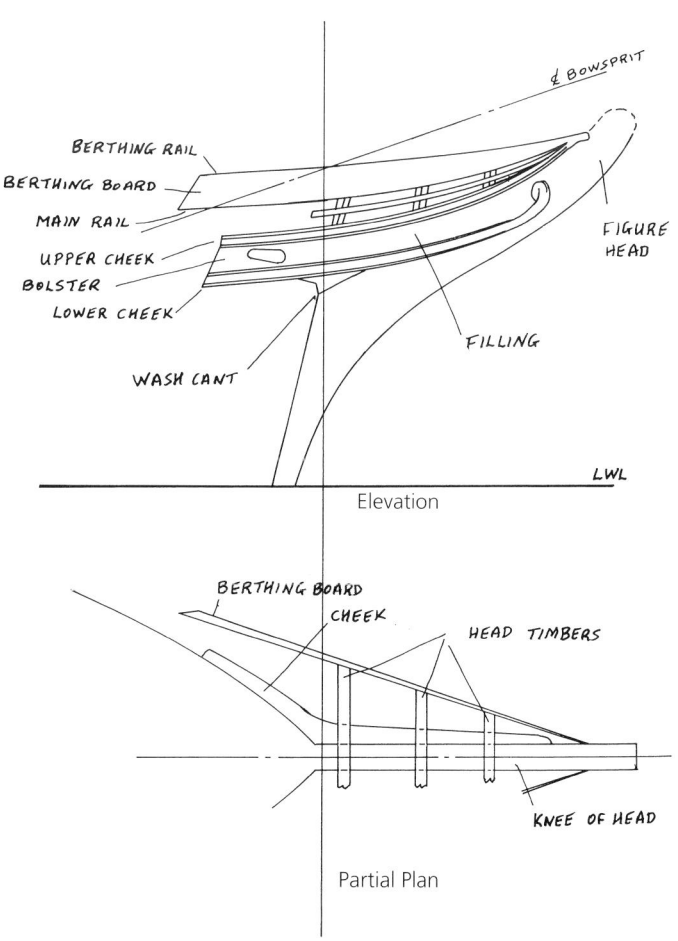

Chain Plates and Bulwarks (scale = 1:24)

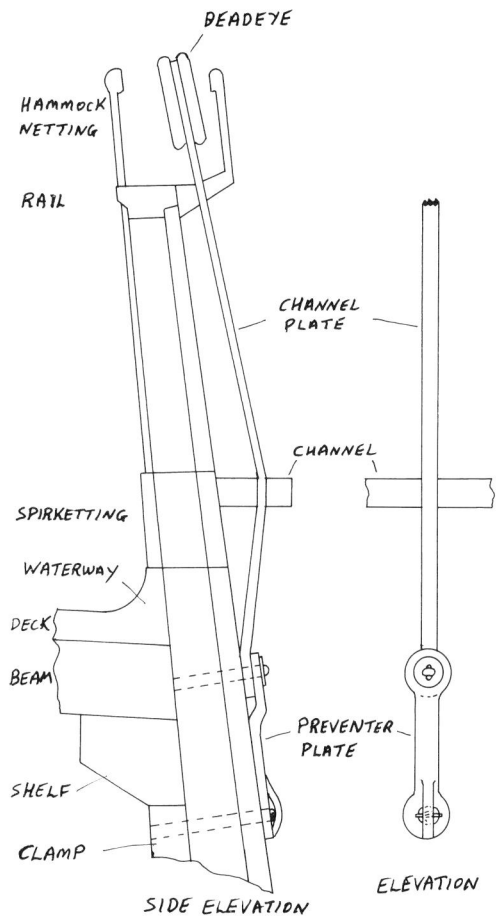

tographs of this part of the deck it is not clear where they run.

The photographs show two binnacles, one by the wheels and the other further aft between the horse block and the ladderway. The sweeps for the aftermost position for the pivot guns are in the same area as this second binnacle, and therefore it would have to be moved if a pivot gun was on those sweeps.

Arms chests are fitted next to the bulwarks, one on each side, each of which contains two small cases of pistols. All around the bulwarks and hatch coamings are shot racks. Generally those for spherical shot being of iron, and those for solid shot for the Blakely are of wood because of the shape of the projectiles (as can be seen in Photograph No. 4, page 51).

Almost all the way around the top of the bulwarks is the hammock netting, the exceptions being at the extreme ends of the deck. Despite its name, it is a wooden structure, and is shown in the drawings and is clearly seen in the photographs with the canvas cover. Because of the height of the barrels of the two pivot guns the rail and hammock netting is removable in way of the gunports to allow the guns to be run out.

There are four ventilators providing air to the two stokeholds, situated either side of the funnel. The top part of each ventilator will be able to turn to ensure the best draught for the boilers. The

Profile on centreline (scale = 1:384)

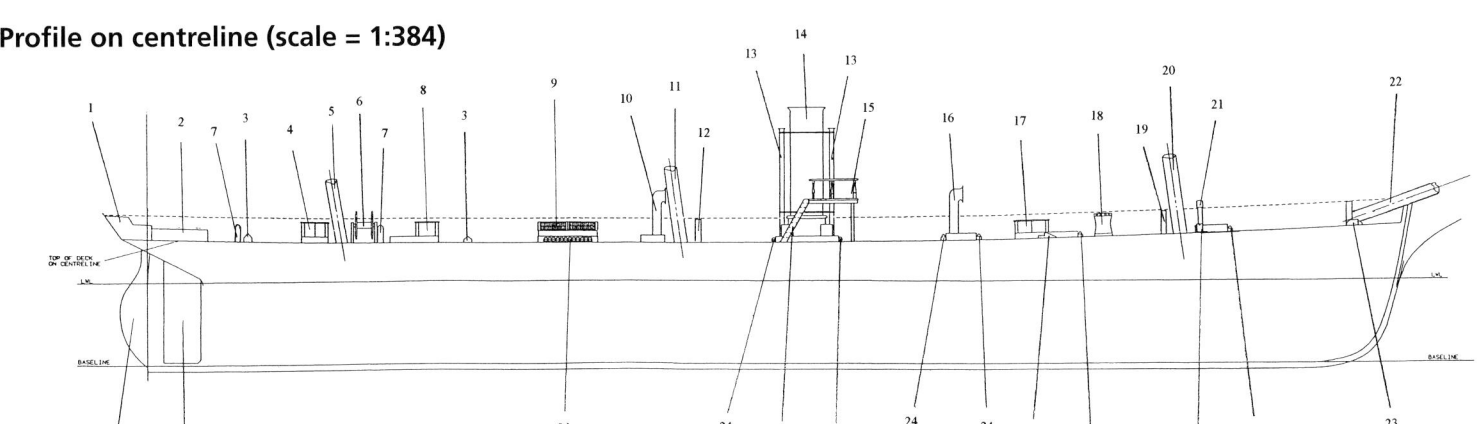

1	Flag locker	8	Ladderway to Gunroom	14	Funnel
2	Horse block	9	Engine room skylight	15	Bridge structure
3	Vent	10	Ventilator to after stoke hole	16	Ventilator to fore stoke hole
4	Ladderway	11	Main mast	17	Ladderway to crew accommodation
5	Mizzen mast	12	Fife rail	18	Capstan
6	Steering wheels	13	Steam pipe		
7	Compass binnacle				

19	Fife rail	26	Deck pipe stopper (chain pipe)
20	Fore mast	27	Ladder to bridge
21	Galley stove pipe	28	Propeller aperture
22	Bowsprit	29	Rudder
23	Bow cable stopper		
24	Shot rack		
25	Riding bitts		

Bulwarks – inner and outer (scale = 1:384)

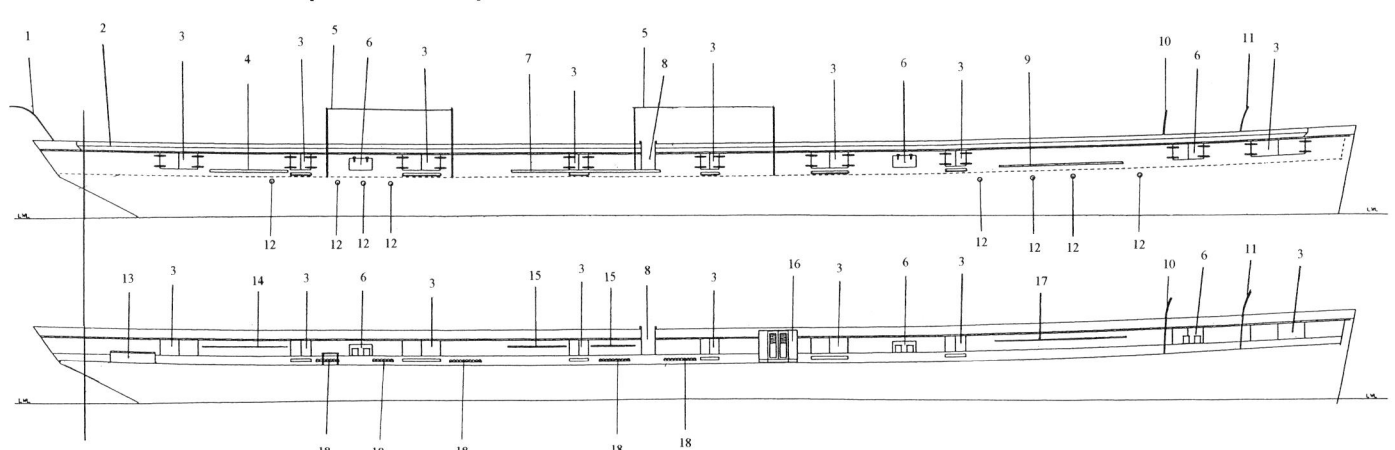

1 Stern boat davits
2 Hammock netting
3 Gun port
4 Mizzen mast channel
5 Boat davits
6 Port for bollards
7 Main mast channel
8 Entry port
9 Fore mast channel
10 Anchor davit
11 Anchor davit
12 Side scuttle (porthole)
13 Arms chest
14 Mizzen rail
15 Main rail
16 WC
17 Fore rail
18 Shot rack

Capstan and Riding Bitts (scale = 1:48)

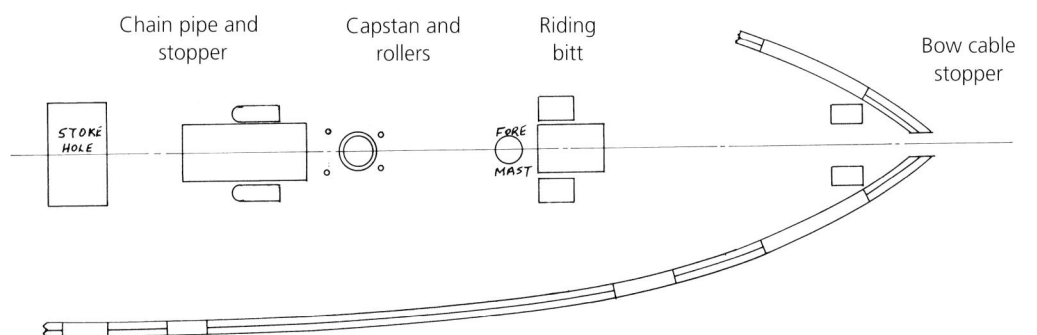

Chain plate and stopper

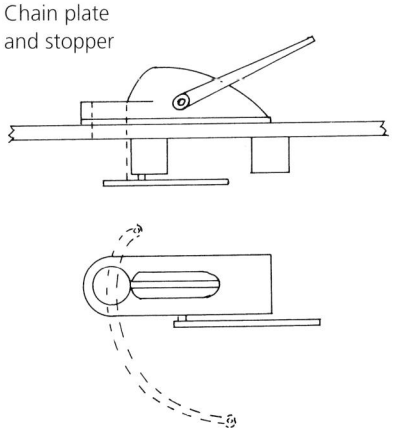

HULL AND DECKS

Upper Deck (scale = 1:384)

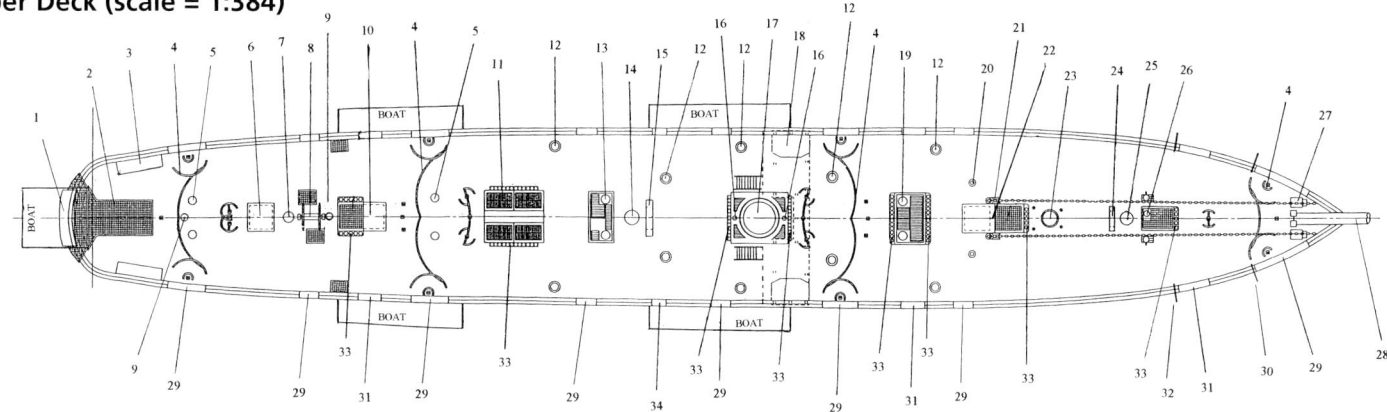

1. Flag locker
2. Horse block
3. Arms chest
4. Sweeps for pivot gun
5. Vent
6. Ladderway
7. Mizzen mast
8. Steering wheels
9. Compass binnacles
10. Ladderway to Gunroom
11. Engine room skylight
12. Coal scuttle
13. Ventilator to after stoke hole
14. Main mast
15. Fife rail
16. Steam pipe
17. Funnel
18. WC
19. Vent to fore stoke hole
20. Deadlight
21. Deck pipe stopper (chain pipe)
22. Ladderway to crew accommodation
23. Capstan
24. Fife rail
25. Fore mast
26. Galley stove pipe
27. Bow cable stopper
28. Bowsprit
29. Gun port
30. Anchor davit
31. Port for bollards
32. Anchor davit
33. Shot rack
34. Entry port

Ventilator (4 off) (scale = 1:96)

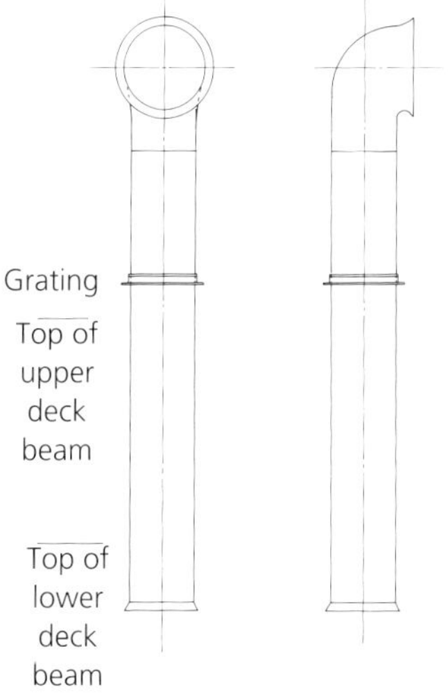

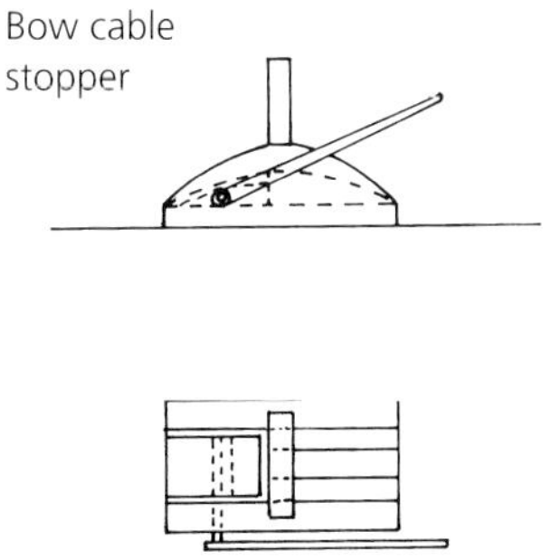

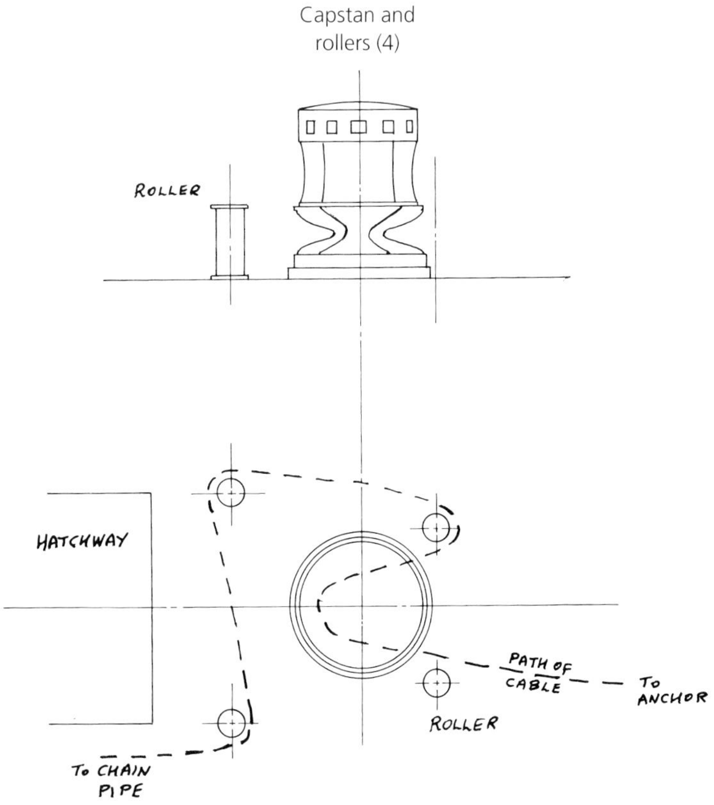

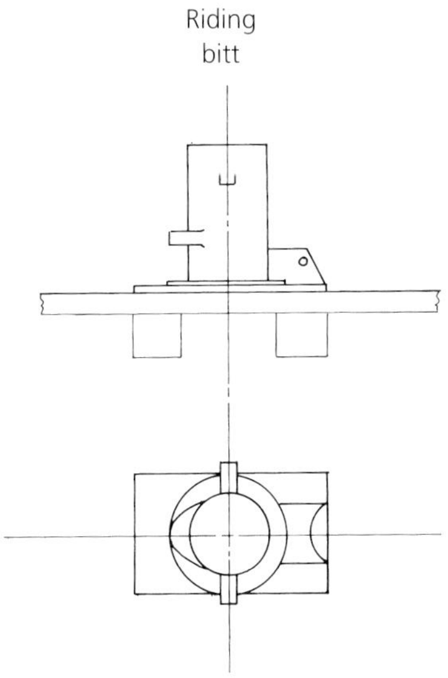

Anchor (not to scale)

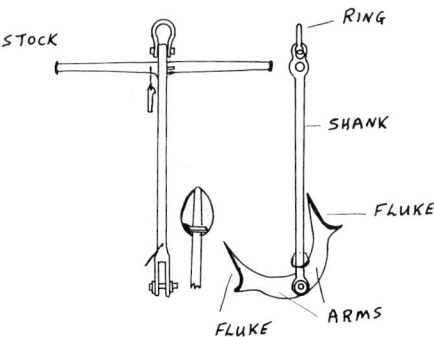

funnel, as shown by the previous drawing, is capable of being raised or lowered. The mechanism for this is on the lower deck. On the forward side of the funnel, supported on iron stanchions, is the bridge with a ladder up to it on each side. The rail round the bridge is, according to Maguire, painted red. Parts of this rail are removable as it is possible to swing the boats in and rest the forward part on the bridge. Based on the photographs showing the position of the ladder on the starboard side, it appears that the bridge is longer than on the models. The forward extent of the bridge is limited because of the position of the pivot gun, so it appears that it extends further aft along the side of the funnel. This is shown in the drawing of this deck.

The main difference between the original plans and the Laird model is in the position of the hatch to the crew quarters. The model shows it to be further aft than the plans. Also the plan shows the ladder on the forward half of the hatchway, and Photograph No. 4 shows it at the after end. From the model and the photograph it seems that the hatchway has been moved aft, and has the ladder at the after half. This seems logical looking at the capstan and the space required for turning it using the capstan bars. Based on the original plan there would not be enough room for the capstan bars.

From the Specification the capstan and riding bitts were to be on Brown & Harfield's Patent. These two gentlemen took out a number of patents over the years for improvements to capstans, winches and mooring equipment. Based on their patents the individual items in the layout have been drawn. After coming through the hawse pipe the cable passes over the Bow Cable Stopper (also known as a Controller). The chain cable runs freely over this when the tongue is raised by the lever. When the tongue is lowered the chain is caught. When riding to an anchor the cable was passed round the Riding Bitts. Keys would stick out from the iron bitt to support the cable, there being a shelf at the rear to support the first coil. The Capstan was of wrought iron and had a chain flange, into which the links of the chain fitted. The rollers guided the chain into the bottom of the capstan and it then followed the path shown in the drawing, being guided around the hatchway towards the Chain Pipe. It is not clear from the photograph (No. 4) but the chain pipe would probably be fitted with a stopper and a compressor. The stopper would work in the same way as the bow cable stopper. The compressor would be fitted below the deck beams and is simply a curved lever which applies pressure to check the cable when running out. The pressure being applied by means of a block and tackle under the deckhead.

There are two small iron anchor davits at the bow. When the anchor was hoved up the stock was just above the water. A hook was then attached to the ring of the anchor from the blocks on the cathead – the foremost davit. The anchor was then fished by attaching the bottom of the shank to the second davit, and hauling

Inboard Profile (scale = 1:384)

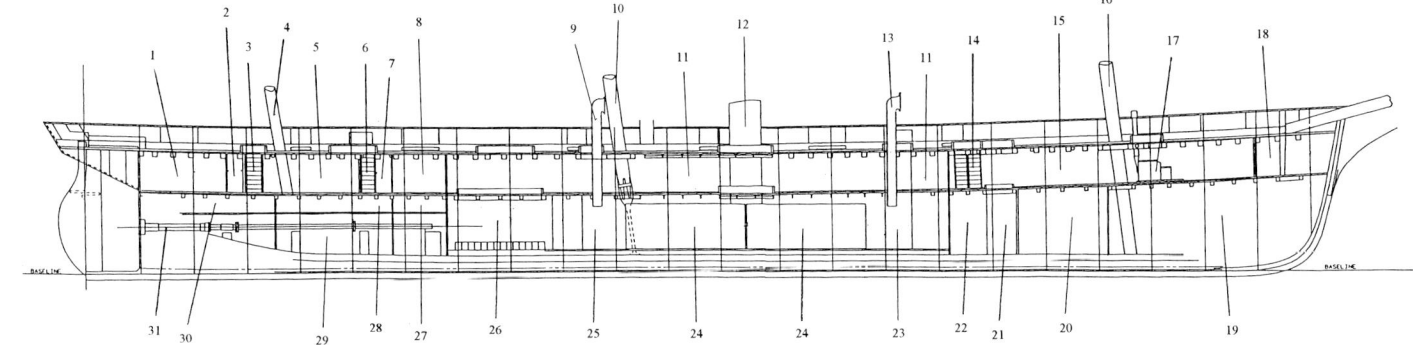

1	Captain's cabin	7	Dispensary	13	Vent to fore stoke hole	18	Sail room	25	After stokehold
2	Captain's clerk	8	Steerage			19	Stores	26	Engine room
3	Ladderway	9	Vent to after stoke hole	14	Ladderway to crew accommodation	20	Magazine and water tanks	27	Shell rooms
4	Mizzen mast							28	Bread
5	Gun room (wardroom)	10	Main mast	15	Crew accommodation	21	Stores	29	Shaft tunnel
		11	Coal bunker			22	Chain lockers	30	Spirits
6	Ladderway to gun room	12	Funnel	16	Fore mast	23	Fore stokehold	31	Propeller shaft
				17	Galley stove	24	Boilers		

HULL AND DECKS

Boats (scale = 1:192)

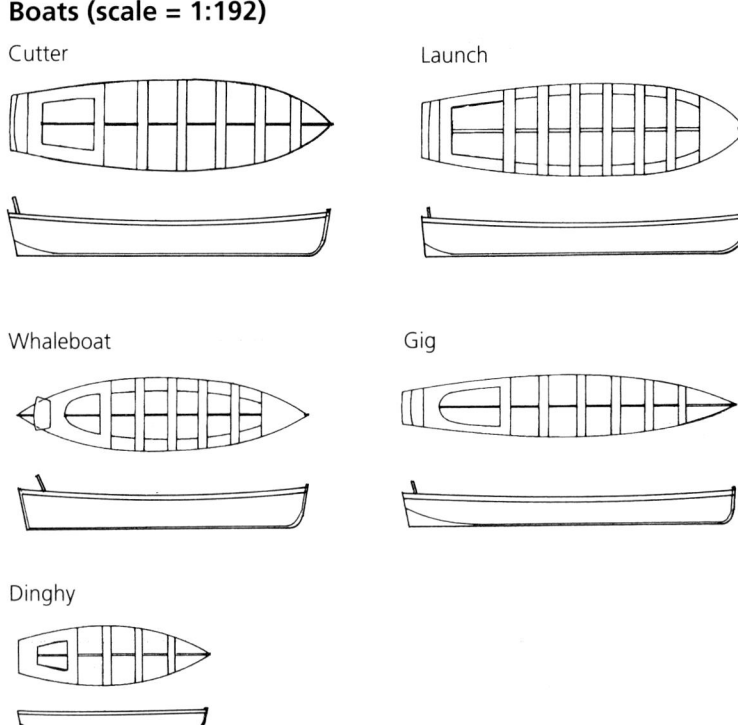

it up until the shank was horizontal. It appears from diving on the wreck that the anchors were of the Trotman patent type. This type has a hinge at the bottom of the shank which enables the arms and flukes to rotate.

Boats

Five boats were carried, all on iron davits, a dinghy over the stern, and a gig and whale-boat between the main and mizzen masts. Amidships were a cutter and launch which could be swung in and partially rested on the bridge (this is shown in some of the photographs).

Semmes's own boat was a beautiful gig, furnished with scarlet cushions and fancy yoke and steering ropes, fitted with a lug sail (SM pp518 & 533)

The boats as fitted to the Laird model are as follows:

Position	Length	Breadth	Type
Port side fwd	28ft 0in	7ft 6in	Cutter
Stbd side fwd	28ft 0in	7ft 6in	Launch
Port side aft	25ft 0in	6ft 0in	Whaleboat
Stbd side aft	28ft 6in	5ft 3in	Gig
Stern	16ft 6in	5ft 3in	Dinghy

The boats on the Bulloch model are similar.

Over the course of her career I think all the boats were replaced because of damage or other problems. For example, the Captain's gig had the planks started when firing the 8in gun, and a quarter boat was swept from its davits during a gale. The drawings show typical boats of the types on board.

There is slight variation in the position of the davits, which is not important, except at one point. This is the after davit for the boats alongside the bridge. The Laird model and sail plan both have this davit forward of the entry port but the Bulloch model and the photographs taken in Singapore have it aft of the port. Therefore, it has been moved to agree with the photographs, which would also make it easier to swing the boats in and out.

Lower Deck

At the after end of the lower deck is the captain's cabin which was semi-circular with a small stateroom opening out from it on the starboard side. The cabin was seated all round, a large mirror adorned the after part of the cabin and there was a painting of the ship (which was subsequently destroyed during the battle off Cherbourg). During heavy weather in October 1863 water leaked in to Semmes's cabin and 'down a little into my bookcases, etc'.

Lower Deck (scale = 1:384)

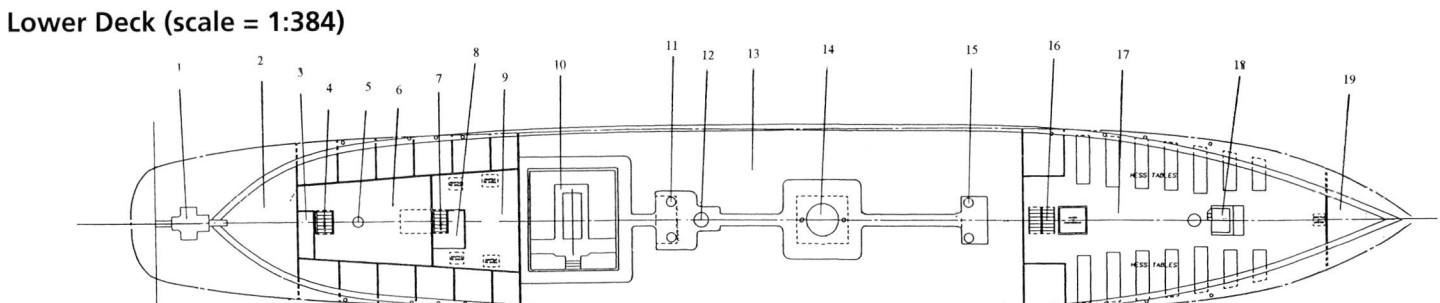

1 Propeller well
2 Captain's cabin
3 Captain's clerk
4 Ladderway
5 Mizzen mast
6 Gun room (wardroom)
7 Ladderway
8 Dispensary
9 Steerage
10 Engine room flat
11 Ventilator to after stokehold
12 Main mast
13 Coal bunker
14 Funnel and lifting gear
15 Ventilator to fore stokehold
16 Ladderway to crew accommodation
17 Crew accommodation
18 Galley stove
19 Sail room

Section through Side Scuttle (scale = 1:8)

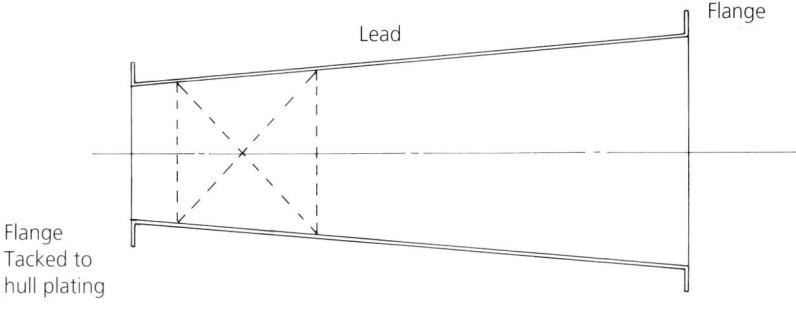
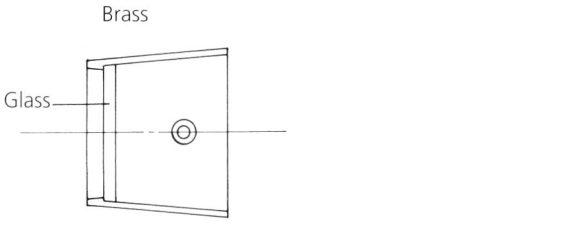

Chronometers taken from the captured ships were screwed to the transom. Semmes slept in a swinging cot, commenting at one point, 'the ship occasionally rolled and pitched with violence, frequently thumping my cot against the beams overhead and awaking me' (SC II p187).

Further forward was the wardroom—or gunroom—with the cabins for the officers. Kell, in his article in *Century Magazine* (April 1886, pp911-22) said those in this mess were the five Lieutenants, the Acting Master, the Surgeon and Assistant Surgeon, the First Lieutenant of Marines and the Chief Engineer. If there were any women aboard one of the ships that were captured they were given one of these cabins and the lieutenant had to move out. Sinclair (p106) says that 'they are to empty, for the use of the ladies, or lock up, their bureau drawers', and 'Get your tin basin and camp-stool'. There were also bunks for sleeping in. There was a table in the middle of the mess and the steward had his pantry near by. Next to the wardroom was the steerage mess, in which were the junior officers—midshipmen, young master's mates and engineers. The star-

Two views of a porthole recovered from the *Alabama*, 29 June 2000. The two parts have been separated.

Below Lower Deck (scale = 1:384)

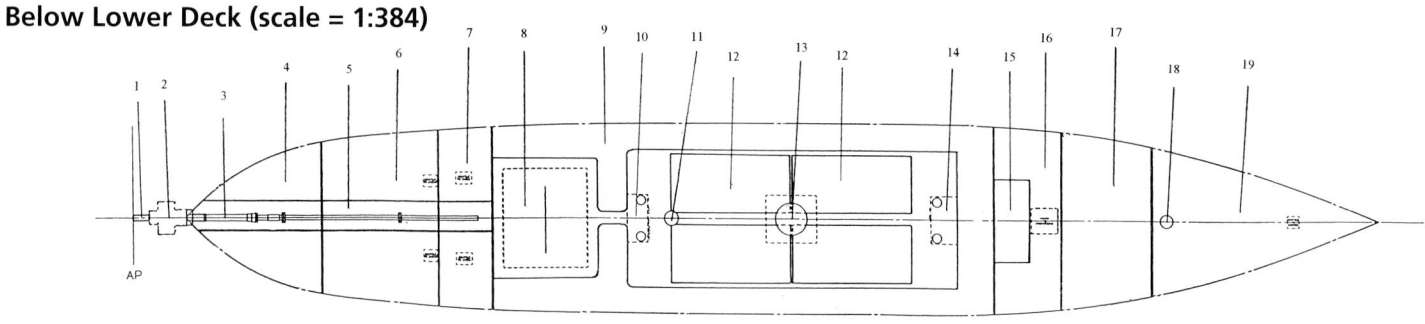

1 Stern post	5 Shaft tunnel	9 Coal bunker	13 Funnel	17 Magazines and water tanks
2 Propeller	6 Bread	10 After stokehold	14 Fore stokehold	
3 Propeller shaft	7 Shell rooms	11 Main mast	15 Chain lockers	18 Fore mast
4 Spirits	8 Engine room	12 Boilers	16 Stores	19 Stores

board side was for the midshipmen and the engineers were on the port side (B&L IV, p601). In the forward bulkhead to this mess was a door through to the engine-room and stokeholes.

The engine controls are on top of the engine on the flat which is only a few steps below the level of the lower deck. Almost all this deck, between the steerage and crew accommodation, is a large coal bunker. There are iron bulkheads either side of the centre-line, which provide a walkway to the two stokeholes and to the base of the funnel, where the gear for raising it is located.

The forward part of the lower deck is taken up with the crew accommodation. Access is to the rear of the compartment by ladder from the upper deck. There is also a hatch over the galley stove, which is just forward of the fore mast. Maguire reported about this space as follows: 'the men's berths, which are quite open and spacious and run entirely forward, in the centre is the cooking apparatus. The hooks are slung to the deck, for the men's hammocks. This also is seated all round. Under these seats are places for the men's bags with iron grating, which forms the front of the seats.' There are side scuttles (portholes) to allow light to enter along both sides. One of these side scuttles recovered from the wreck is shown in the photograph and drawing. The anchor chains pass through this space, one on each side of the hatchway, before descending into the chain locker below.

Below Lower Deck

The propeller shaft, bearings and tunnel take up a significant part of the space between the stern and the after engine-room bulkhead. Based on other ships the shaft tunnel would not be symmetrical, but wider on the port side, to allow access to the bearings. On either side and above the shaft tunnel were various stores. Right at the stern was the spirit store, the access probably from the wardroom, then there was the bread room.

Next were the shell rooms, one for the spherical shells on the starboard side with the elongated (Blakely) shells on the port side. All the shells were stored in boxes of the correct size for the shell. There would probably be engineers' stores immediately next to the after engine-room bulkhead.

The engine was bolted on a solid wooden bed, with coal bunkers along the sides. In fact the coal bunkers extended along the sides right up to the bulkhead at the forward end of the boiler room. The coal was loaded through the coal scuttles on the upper deck into the space below which would be continuous down to the bilges along the ship's side. There would be access into the coal bunkers to trim the coal and move it as required to the stokeholes for the boilers.

The chain lockers should be immediately in front of the bulkhead which forms the forward end of the coal bunkers. Stores surround the chain lockers with access to them through a hatch in the lower deck, and one directly above in the upper deck. Somewhere in this area will be the fresh water condenser. Steam will come from the boilers and the fresh water will pass straight into the holding tank to cool down. Forward of these stores was the magazine and water tanks. Bulloch describes it: 'The magazine was placed so that the top would be 2½ feet below the waterline, and the water tanks, which were of iron, were fitted on each side and in front of it, and were carried up to the berth deck beams' (B I p287). These tanks only held a few weeks supply of fresh water as it was condensed once a week. The allowance of water was 1 gallon per man per day, and it took 1lb of coal to produce the steam to make 1 gallon of fresh water.

There were two magazines side by side, and, according to Maguire, 'The partition on each side of these magazines is of three thicknesses of oak, between each thickness is lined with lead.' The magazines contained the powder canisters, and also must have had a handling room. The light for the magazines will have come from lamp rooms outside, the light shining in through glass windows. The hold forward of the magazine and water tanks contained stores, with access from the crew accommodation.

Sails and Rigging

General

The *Alabama* was rigged as a three-masted barque. Semmes described her as follows:

> The *Alabama*, or as she should as yet be called, 'No. 290,' was barque-rigged, her standing gear being formed throughout of wire rope; thus combining strength with lightness to the utmost possible extent. Her ordinary suit of sails consisted of the usual square sails in the foremast, fore topmast staysail and jib, large fore and main topsails, maintop sail, topgallant sail and royal, and on the mizzen-mast spanker and gaff topsail. Occasionally, this rig would be varied, as was the case in entering Cherbourg, just before the close of her eventful career, when a crossjack yard was got up across the mizzen-mast, with mizzen topsail and topgallant yards to match; and the *Alabama* assumed for a time the appearance of a full rigged ship. (SC I p267)

However, later in his memoirs (p402), she was described as a 'barkentine'. This is a strange way to describe the ship because a barkentine (or barquentine) has no square sails on the mainmast, and the *Alabama* most definitely did.

The *Alabama* seems to have been a good ship under sail and easily handled. A sailing ship cannot sail directly into the wind and so makes progress into the wind by tacking (a zigzag motion with the wind first on one side then the other). To change direction either the bow is turned through the wind (tacking) or the ship turns the opposite way so that the wind blows over the stern (wearing). There are more references to wearing than tacking in the litera-

Jibboom (scale = 1:96)

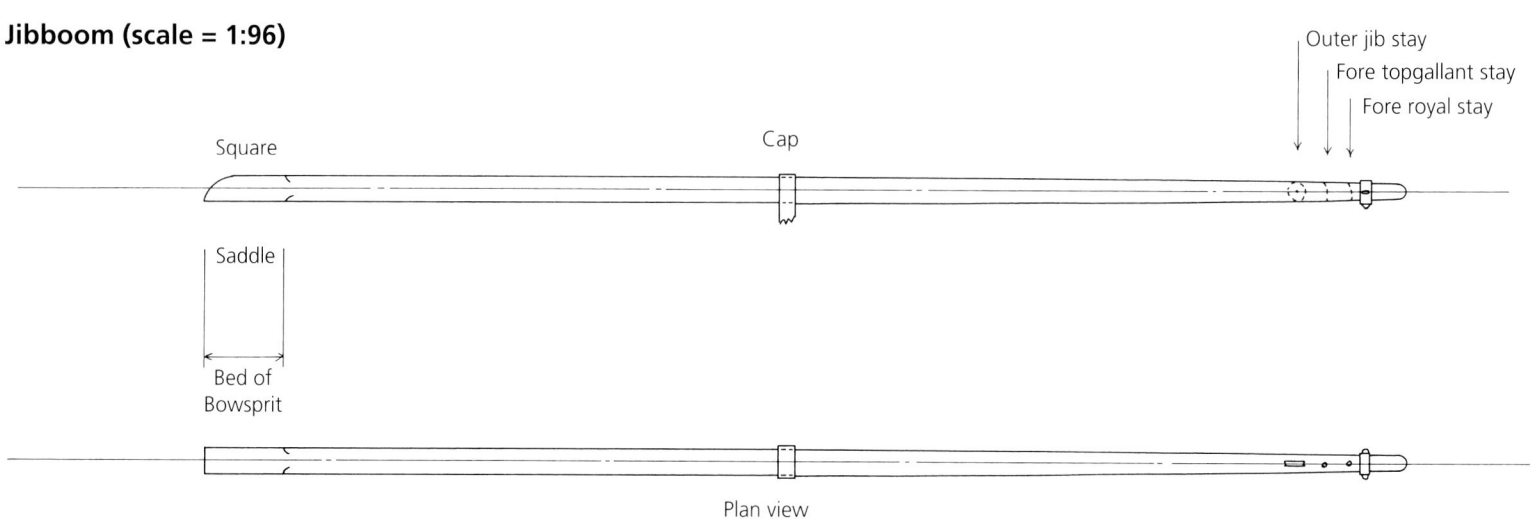

Lower Fore Mast (scale = 1:96)

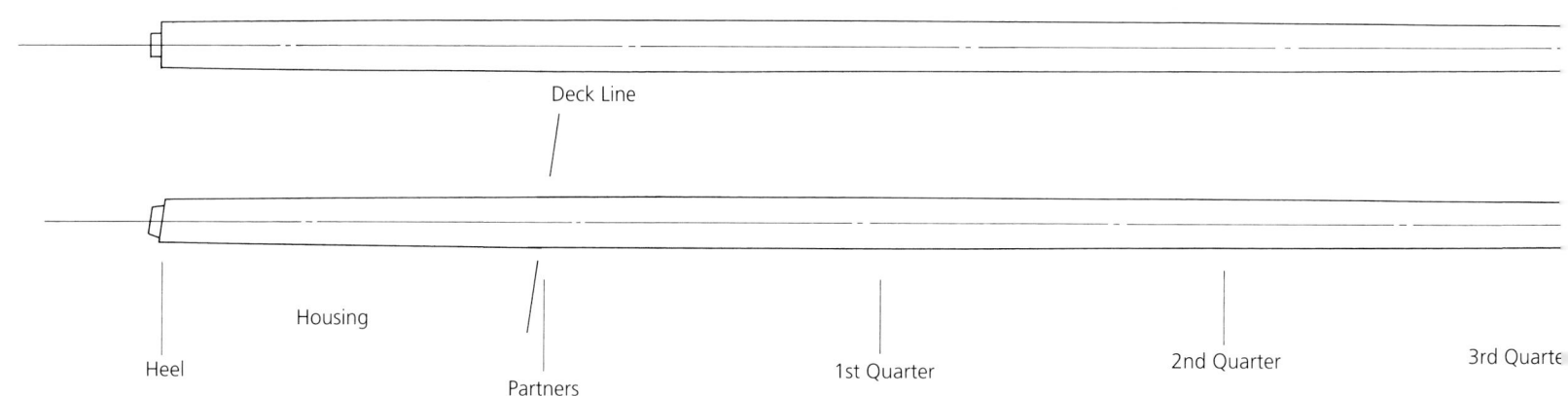

Lower Main Mast (scale = 1:96)

SAILS AND RIGGING

Bowsprit (scale = 1:96)

Heel–square Housing–octagonal Bed–square Fore Topmast Stay–double

Bobstay–chain

Dolphin Striker

Guys–chain

Top (fore and main masts) (scale = 1:96)

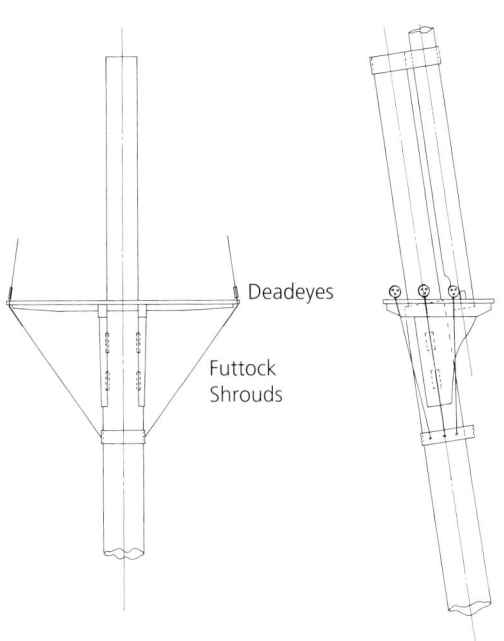

Deadeyes

Futtock Shrouds

Main mast foot (scale = 1:192)

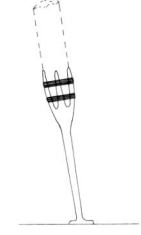

Top fore and main masts (scale = 1:96)

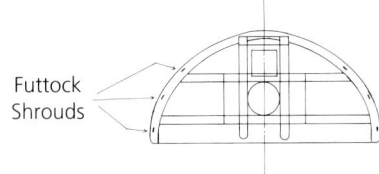

Futtock Shrouds

Head

Hounds

ture, and this might be the reason for some comments about her being a poor sailer. However, it was considered by some that it was safer and less likely to cause damage to wear than tack when convenient. Semmes would be mindful of the fact that to lose a mast, or have problems with the rig, would probably end the cruise because of the difficulties of making repairs.

In redrawing the original masts, yards and sails the following books have been found to be helpful. However, rigging was an individual thing and could vary between ships.

Lieut. G S Nares, *Seamanship* (1862)
R Kipping, *Elementary Treatise on Sails and Sailmaking* (1862)
R Kipping, *Rudimentary Treatise on Masting, Mast-making, and Rigging of Ships* (1928 [identical to 1856 edition])

Masts and Yards

The length of both the upper and lower masts have been increased (by variable amounts), compared to those listed in the original drawing. It would appear that these lower masts were a single piece of pine (Semmes says 'yellow' and Sinclair says

Topmast, Topgallant and Royal Masts (fore and main) (scale = 1:96)

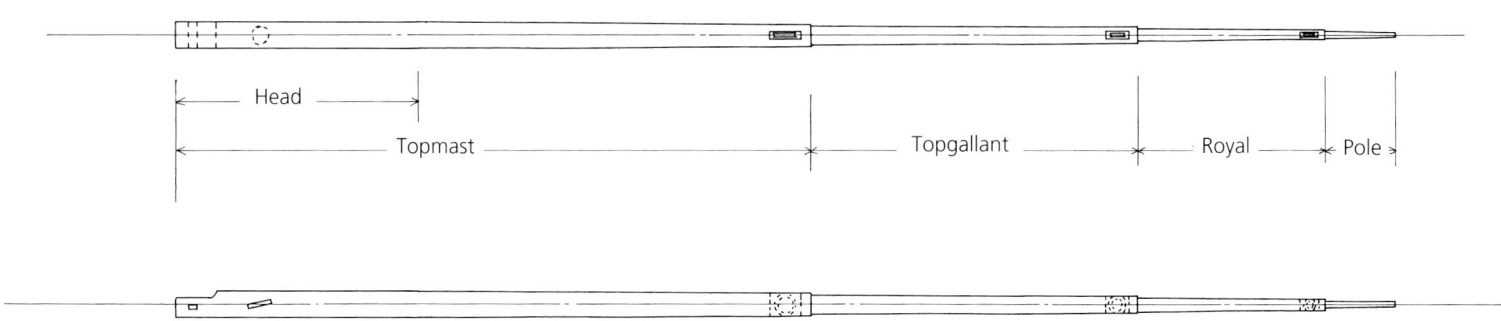

Head (scale = 1:48)

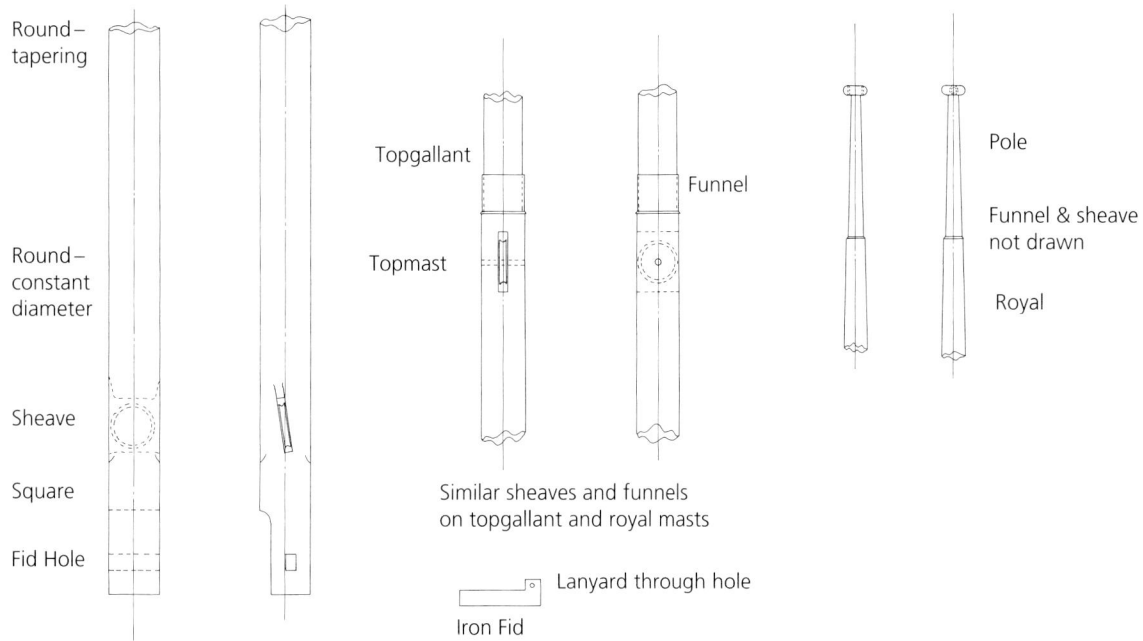

Lower Mizzen Mast (scale 1:96)

SAILS AND RIGGING

Mizzen Topmast (scale = 1:96)

Head (scale = 1:48) **Copper funnel (scale = 1:24)** **Pole (scale = 1:48)**

Iron Fid (scale = 1:48)

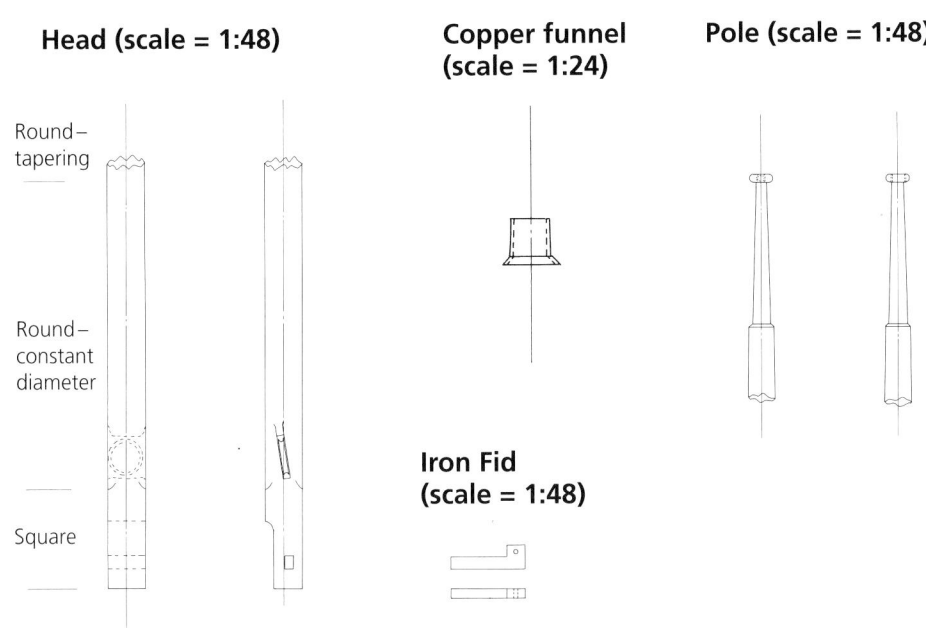

Top (scale = 1:96)

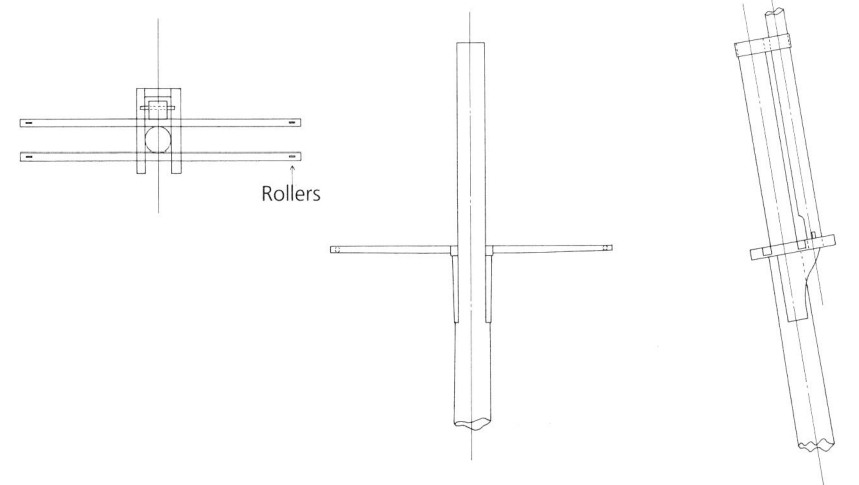

'Georgia'). According to the Laird model the masts and yards were 'bright' except for the mastheads and the yardarms which were black. Most of the main lower mast was also black, down to the level of the funnel, presumably to avoid discoloration by smoke.

The sizes of the masts and yards are given in the original drawing, and each individual mast and yard has been redrawn separately, using the longer masts from the later drawing. The diameter of each spar is given in the table, and this is what is called the 'given diameter', and is the maximum size. The diameter at various points along the spar is a set (smaller) proportion of this given diameter. Looking at the plan of the lower fore mast the given diameter is at the partners, or deck line. The diameters at points such as the 1st, 2nd or 3rd Quarters are a proportion of the given diameter. The position of the given diameter varies according to the spar, but the proportions are given in most books on mastmaking.

The tops on the fore and main masts on the Laird model appear to be quite large and similar to those on a warship, such as *Warrior*. However, looking at the photographs taken in Singapore (Photographs A & B, page 55) virtually nothing can be seen of them. The conclusion has to be that those on the ship were smaller and lighter than those on the model. The top drawn for the fore and main masts is based on this assumption.

Rake of masts
Fore mast   20in in 12ft (8°)
Main mast   21¼in in 12ft (8½°)
Mizzen mast   24in in 12ft (9½°)
Bowsprit   48in in 12ft (18½°)

The top, topgallant and royal masts on the fore and main are in one piece. There is a step, or change in diameter, at the top of each individual section. A copper funnel sits at this point to protect the wood from the wire standing rigging which is round the mast. The sheaves on the end of the lower yards are for the sheets for the topsails which were iron chains of about 2in in diameter (S, p38).

The studding sails, or stunsails, were additional sails that were used temporarily to increase the area of canvas. They were light sails that were laced between a yard at the head and a boom at the foot. When not in use the booms were run in by means

Lower Yard, Fore and Main (scale = 1:96)

Boom irons (scale = 1:24)

Jackstay stanchions (scale = 1:4)

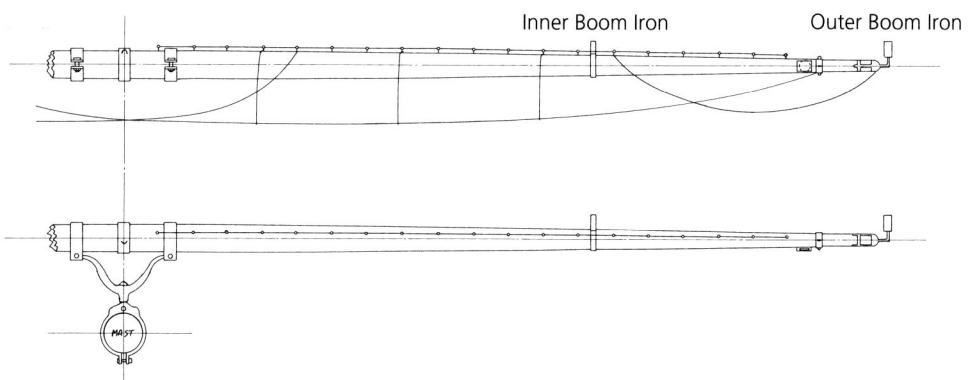
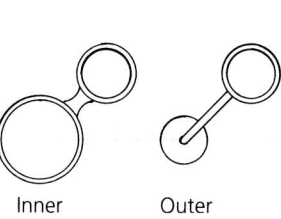
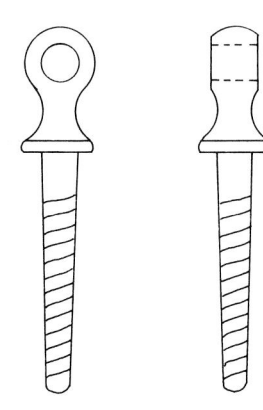

Topsail yard, Fore and Main (scale = 1:96)

Boom irons (scale = 1:24)

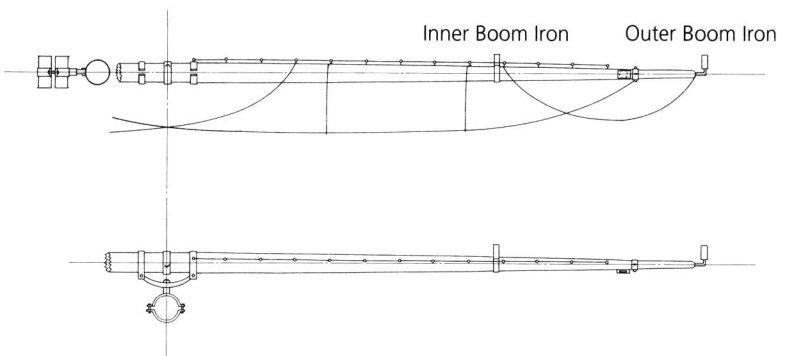
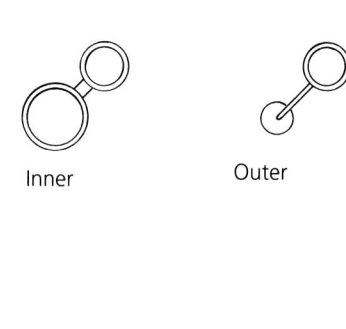

Topgallant Yard, Fore and Main (scale = 1:96)

Royal Yard, Fore and Main (scale = 1:96)

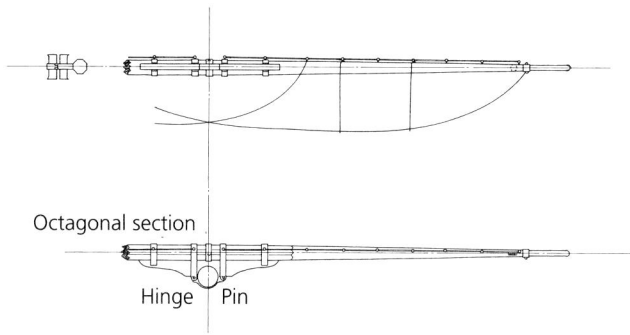
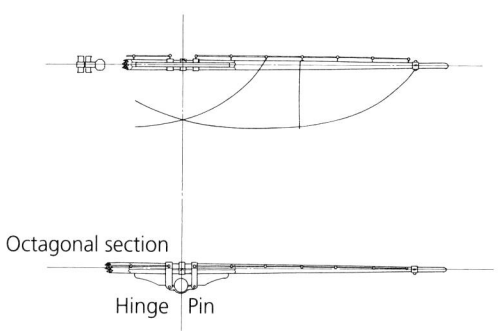

of the booms irons on each yard. The Laird model has stunsail booms on the lower and topsail yards which is confirmation of Semmes's journal (9 October 1863) that says there are topgallant stunsails as well. A boom is used to spread the foot of the sail above it, therefore there would be a topgallant stunsail. There would be at least two sets of yards and booms because Semmes refers to studding sails 'alow and aloft' and 'set on both sides' (SC I, pp352 & 376).

A lightning conductor was fitted from the top of each mast down to the deck. From there it probably went via the ship's beams to the copper sheeting on the hull, and then into the sea. An alternative route for the copper conductor was down to the keel and connected to a copper bolt. The lightning conductor should be on the aft side of the mast and be continuous at the mast head, or any break in the mast. There are several references to the conductors in the literature: 'Almost a continual stream of lightning ran down our conductors, and hissed as it leaped into the sea' (SM, p736) and 'The lightning ran down the three conductors to the masts in constant streams, entering the water with a hissing sound, and jumping from gun to gun, and even to the engine below' (S, p210).

Gaff, Fore and Main (scale = 1:96)

Gaff, Mizzen (scale = 1:96)

Mizzen Boom (scale = 1:96)

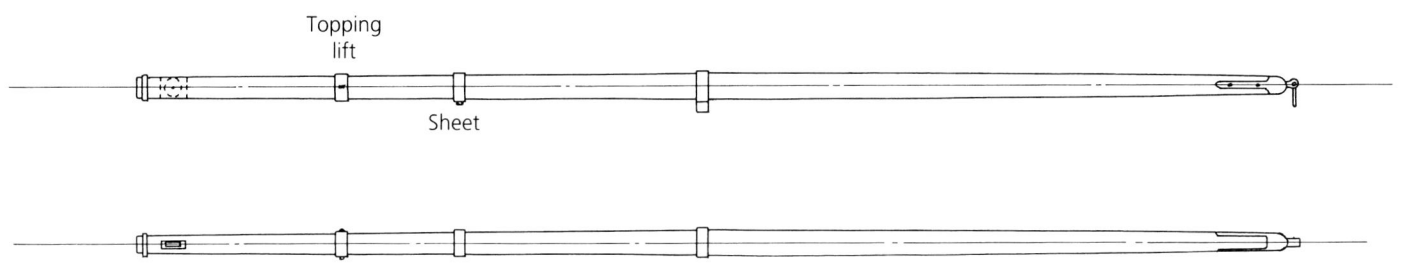

Studding Sail Booms (scale = 1:96)

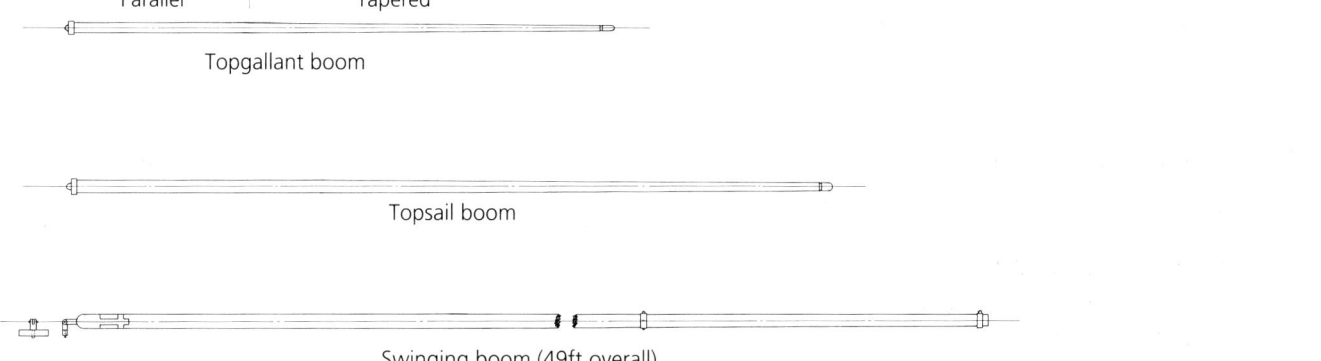

Studding Sail Yards (scale = 1:96)

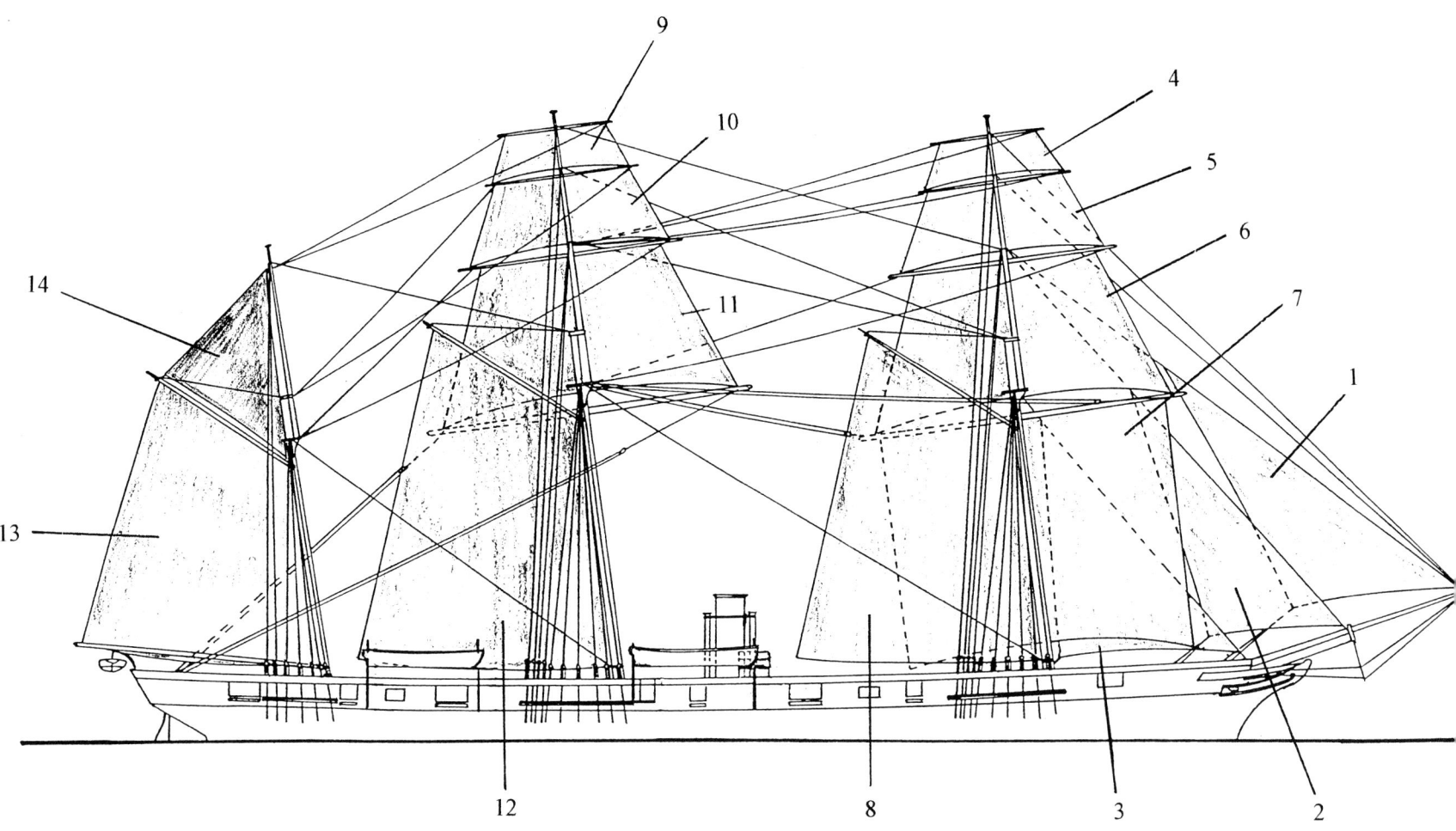

Sails

1. Jib
2. Fore-topmast staysail
3. Fore staysail
4. Fore royal sail
5. Fore topgallant sail
6. Fore topsail
7. Fore sail
8. Fore trysail
9. Main royal sail
10. Main topgallant sail
11. Main topsail
12. Main trysail
13. Spanker
14. Gaff topsail

Sails and Rigging

The sails described at the start of this section are illustrated in the accompanying drawings. The ship also carried studding sails on the fore and main mast. Also given are sketches showing the names of the different parts of the various types of sail.

Based on the photographs of the ship, and the books listed above, each sail with its associated running rigging has been drawn. The approximate position of each block has been shown, though in some cases it has been moved to show things clearly. Each line is labelled and has the number of the pin to which it is belayed. The estimated position of these pins is shown on the Belaying Pin drawing, and the drawing of the individual sail needs to be used in conjunction with this. The vast majority of the lines are symmetrical about the centreline of the sail, and in some cases, to avoid confusion, they have not been drawn on both sides. The photographs clearly show the fairleads attached to the shrouds, and that more than one line can pass through a fairlead.

The size of the sails in terms of number of cloths has been given in the description of the ship earlier (pages 44-45), however for convenience they are repeated here – 'carries on her foremast, a square foresail, large trysail, with two reefs, and bonnet topsail with two reefs, topgallant sail and royal – on the main mast, a large trysail, with 2 reefs and a bonnet, no square mainsail bent, topsail, 2 reefs, topgallant sail and royal – on the mizzen mast, a very large spanker, and short three cornered gaff topsail – has a fore and fore-topmast staysail, and jib, has had no staysails to the main, or mizzen, bent, or royal yards aloft yet' and 'Description of sails – hemp canvas sails very roaching – topsails have 20 cloths on the head, 30 on the foot, top gallant sails 16 cloths on head and 22 on the foot.'

Some sails had reef points, the two topsails, the fore stay sail and the three trysails. The fore staysail and the trysails on the fore and main masts also had a bonnet which was laced to the foot of the sail. The royals are rarely mentioned but it seems from the book by Nares that they were worked from the top, except for the braces which went to the deck.

Rigging

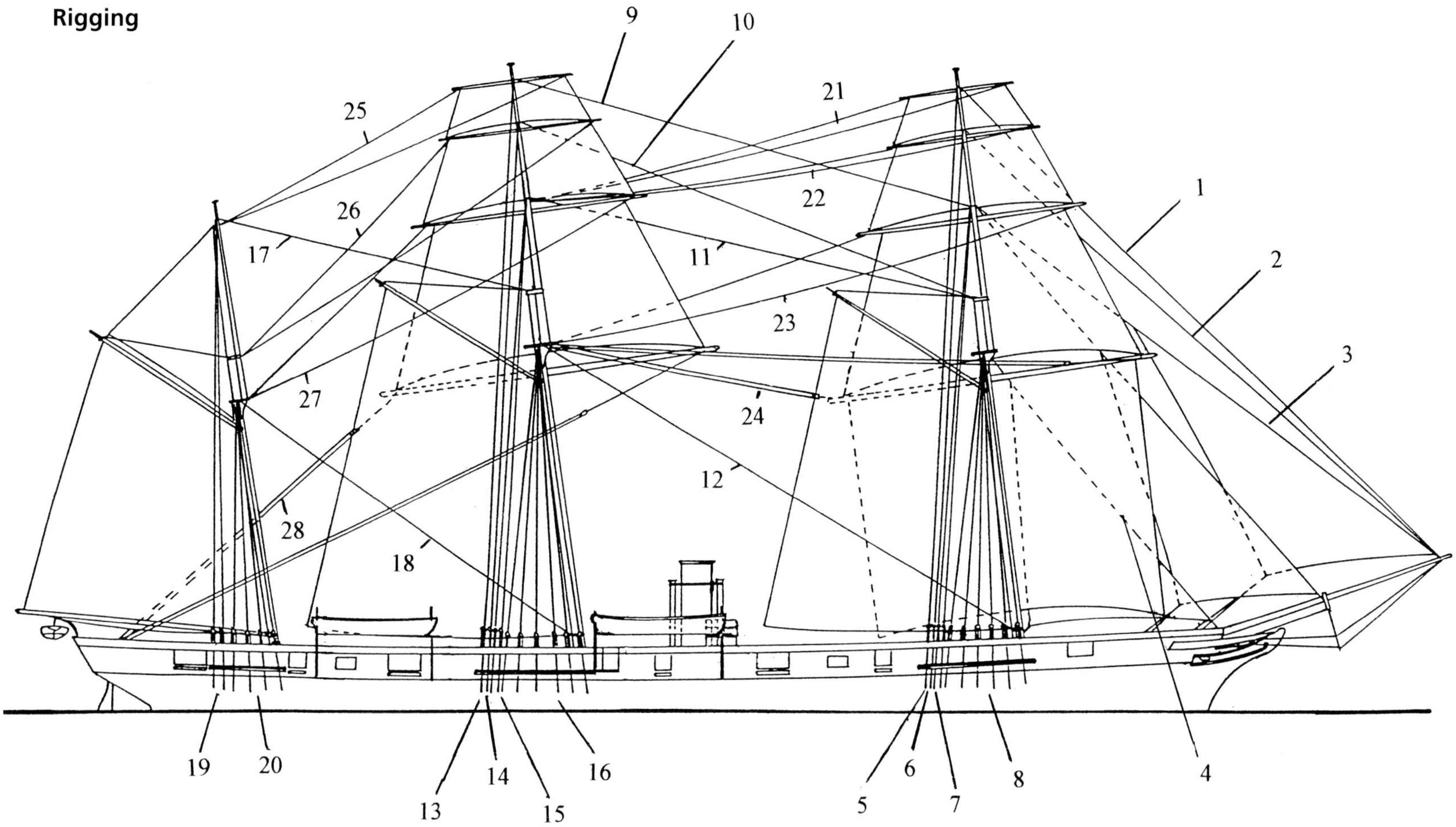

Standing Rigging
1. Fore royal stay
2. Fore topgallant stay
3. Fore topmast stay
4. Fore stay
5. Fore royal backstay
6. Fore topgallant backstay
7. Fore topmast backstays (2)
8. Fore shrouds (6)
9. Main royal stay
10. Main topgallant stay
11. Main topmast stay
12. Main stay
13. Main royal backstay
14. Main topgallant backstay
15. Main topmast backstays (2)
16. Main shrouds (6)
17. Mizzen topmast stay
18. Mizzen stay
19. Mizzen topmast backstays (2)
20. Mizzen shrouds (4)

Running Rigging
(one side only marked)

21. Fore royal brace
22. Fore topgallant brace
23. Fore topsail brace
24. Fore brace
25. Main royal brace
26. Main topgallant brace
27. Main topsail brace
28. Main brace

Parts of a Square Sail (no scale)

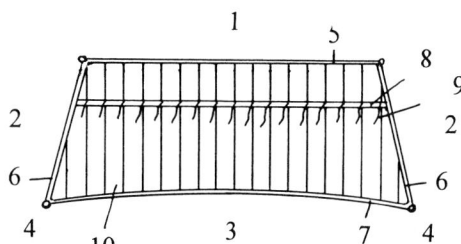

1. Head
2. Leech
3. Foot
4. Clew
5. Head rope
6. Leech rope
7. Foot rope
8. Reef band
9. Reef point
10. Cloth

The collective name for 5, 6 & 7 is boltropes.

Parts of a Staysail (triangular sail) (no scale)

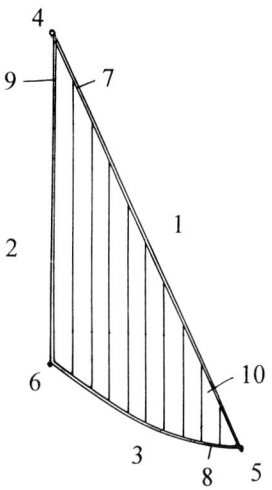

1. Luff
2. Leech
3. Foot
4. Head
5. Tack
6. Clew
7. Luff rope
8. Foot rope
9. Leech rope
10. Cloth

The collective name for 7, 8 & 9 is boltropes

Parts of a Gaff Sail (no scale)

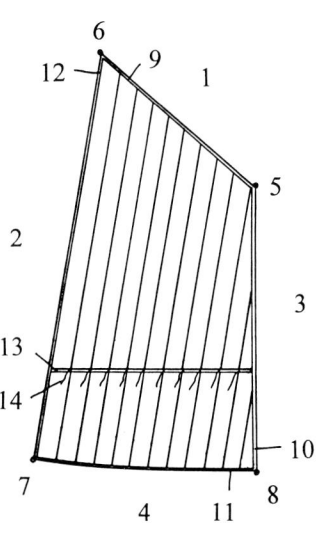

1. Head
2. Leech
3. Luff
4. Foot
5. Throat
6. Peak
7. Clew
8. Tack
9. Head rope
10. Luff rope
11. Foot rope
12. Leech rope
13. Reef band
14. Reef point

The collective name for 9, 10, 11 & 12 is boltropes

RUNNING RIGGING

Line	Pin Number	Number Off
Bowsprit Jibboom		
Jib		
Halliard	41P	1
Downhaul	3	1
Sheets	7	2
Fore Topmast Staysail		
Halliard	41S	1
Downhaul	4	1
Sheets	8	2
Fore Staysail		
Halliard	13	1
Downhaul	5	1
Sheets	30	2
Fore Mast		
Fore Yard		
Lifts	21 & 23	2
Bunt lines	32	4

Line	Pin Number	Number Off
Leech lines	32	2
Clew lines	31	2
Reef tackle	33	4
Tack	1 & 6	2
Sheets	43	2
Braces	52 & 53	2
Fore Topsail Yard		
Halliard	37P	1
Bunt lines	35	2
Clew lines	34	2
Reef tackles	36	4
Sheets	20 & 24	2
Braces	70	2
Fore Topgallant Yard		
Halliard	37S	1
Bunt lines	39	2
Clew lines	38	2
Sheets	12 & 14	2
Braces	78	2

Belaying Pins (not to scale)

- B   Bollard
- EP   Entry Port
- G   Gunport
- RB   Royal Backstay
- TGB   Topgallant Backstay
- TB   Topmast Backstay
- S   Shrouds

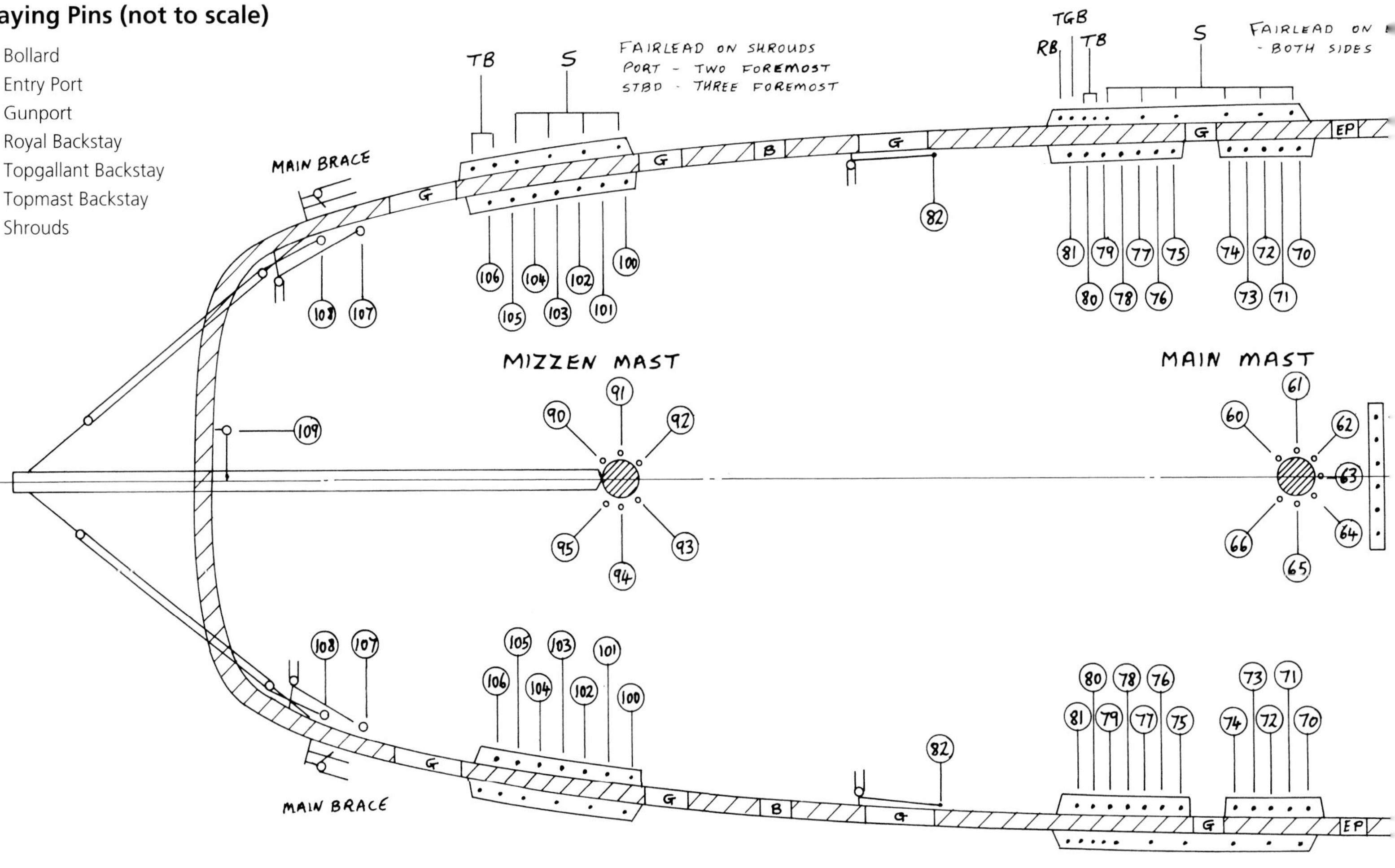

SAILS AND RIGGING

Line	Pin Number	Number Off	Line	Pin Number	Number Off	Line	Pin Number	Number Off
Fore Royal Yard			Bunt lines	72	2	Brails	61 & 65	6
Halliard	42P	1	Clew lines	71	2	Vangs	83	2
Clew line	Top	2	Reef tackles	73	4	Sheets	104	2
Sheets	Top	2	Sheets	50 & 55	2	Peak Halliard	79S	1
Braces	82	2	Braces	100	2	Throat Halliard	79P	1
Fore Trysail			*Main Topgallant Yard*			**Mizzen Mast**		
Outhaul	10	1	Halliard	77P	1	*Mizzen Spanker*		
Downhaul/inhaul	16	1	Bunt lines	76	2	Gaff Outhaul	91	1
Brails	11 & 15	6	Clew lines	75	2	Downhaul/inhaul	94	1
Vangs	44	2	Sheets	62 & 64	2	Brails	92 & 93	6
Sheets	45	2	Braces	101	2	Vangs	107	2
Peak Halliard	40S	1	*Main Royal Yard*			Peak Halliard	105S	1
Throat Halliard	40P	1	Halliard	80S	1	Throat Halliard	105P	1
Main Mast			Clewline	Top	2			
Main Yard			Sheets	Top	2	Boom Outhaul	90	1
Lifts	51 & 54	2	Braces	102	2	Inhaul	95	1
Braces	106	2	*Main Trysail*			Guys	108	2
Main Topsail Yard			Outhaul	60	1	Sheet	109	1
Halliard	74S	1	Downhaul/inhaul	66	1	Topping Lift	103	2

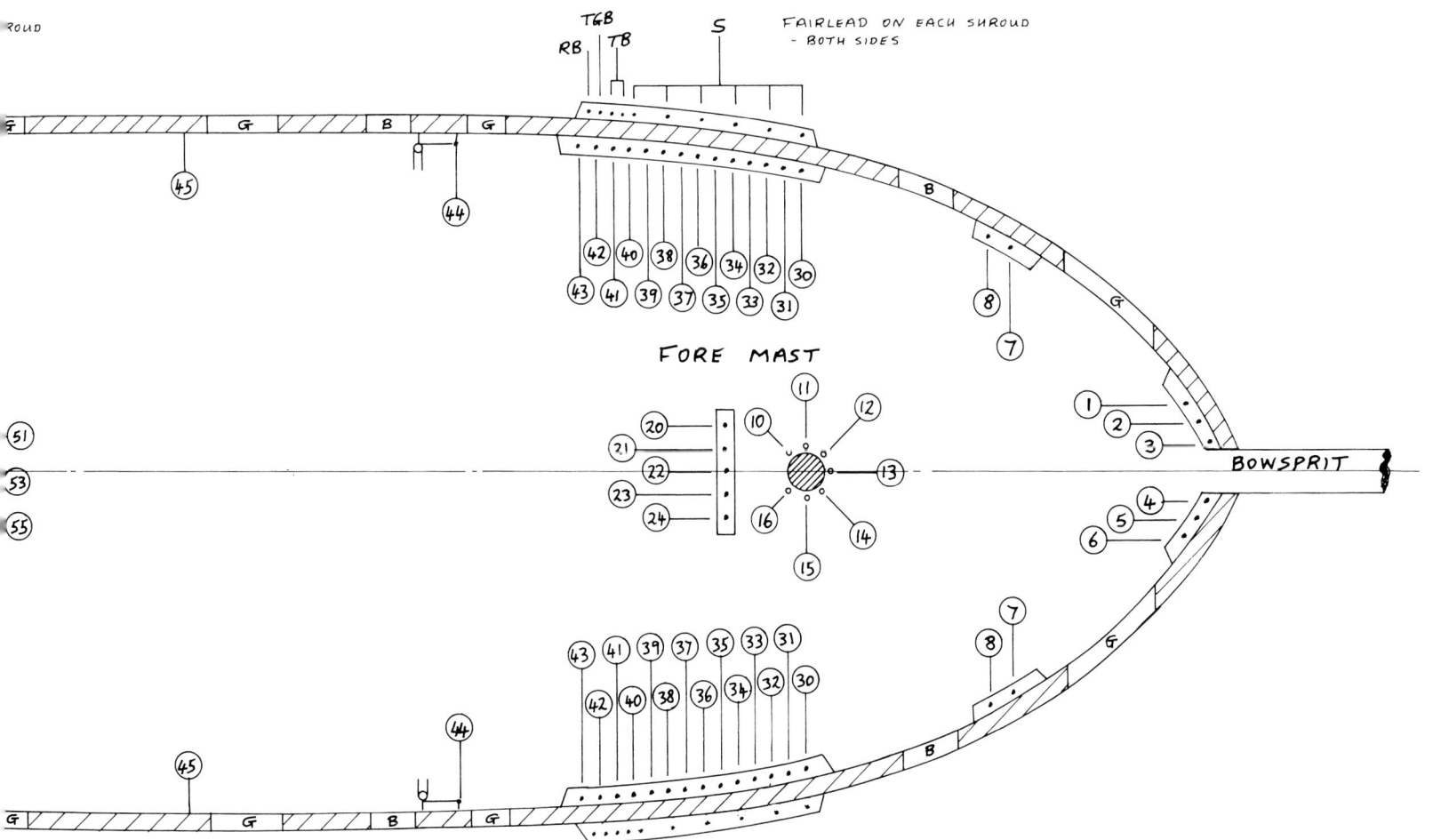

Pin Numbers

1	Fore course	Tack	37S	Fore topgallant yard	Halliard	75	Main topgallant yard	Clew lines
2	Spare		38	Fore topgallant yard	Clew lines	76	Main topgallant yard	Bunt lines
3	Jib	Downhaul	39	Fore topgallant yard	Bunt lines	77P	Main topgallant yard	Halliard
4	Fore topmast staysail	Downhaul	40P	Fore trysail	Throat Halliard	77S	Spare	
5	Fore staysail	Downhaul	40S	Fore trysail	Peak Halliard	78	Fore topgallant yard	Braces
6	Fore course	Tack	41P	Jib	Halliard	79P	Main trysail	Throat Halliard
7	Jib	Sheets	41S	Fore topmast staysail	Halliard	79S	Main trysail	Peak Halliard
8	Fore topmast staysail	Sheets	42P	Fore royal yard	Halliard	80P	Spare	
10	Fore trysail	Outhaul	42S	Spare		80S	Main royal yard	Halliard
11	Fore trysail	Brails	43	Fore yard	Sheets	81	Main royal yard	Sheets
12	Fore topgallant yard	Sheets	44	Fore trysail	Vangs	82	Fore royal yard	Braces
13	Fore staysail	Halliard	45	Fore trysail	Sheets	83	Main trysail	Vangs
14	Fore topgallant yard	Sheets	50	Main topsail yard	Sheets	90	Mizzen boom	Outhaul
15	Fore trysail	Brails	51	Main yard	Lifts	91	Mizzen gaff	Outhaul
16	Fore trysail	Inhaul	52	Fore yard	Brace	92	Mizzen gaff	Brails
20	Fore topsail yard	Sheets	53	Fore yard	Brace	93	Mizzen gaff	Brails
21	Fore yard	Lifts	54	Main yard	Lifts	94	Mizzen gaff	Inhaul
22	Spare		55	Main topsail yard	Sheets	95	Mizzen boom	Inhaul
23	Fore yard	Lifts	60	Main trysail	Outhaul	100	Main topsail yard	Braces
24	Fore topsail yard	Sheets	61	Main trysail	Brails	101	Main topgallant yard	Braces
30	Fore staysail	Sheets	62	Main topgallant yard	Sheets	102	Main royal yard	Braces
31	Fore yard	Clew lines	63	Spare		103	Mizzen boom	Topping lift
32	Fore yard	Bunt lines and Leech lines	64	Main topgallant yard	Sheets	104	Main trysail	Sheets
			65	Main trysail	Brails	105P	Mizzen gaff	Throat halliard
33	Fore yard	Reef tackle	66	Main trysail	Inhaul	105S	Mizzen gaff	Peak halliard
34	Fore topsail yard	Clew lines	70	Fore topsail yard	Braces	106	Main yard	Braces
35	Fore topsail yard	Bunt lines	71	Main topsail yard	Clew lines	107	Mizzen gaff	Vangs
36	Fore topsail yard	Reef tackles	72	Main topsail yard	Bunt lines	108	Mizzen boom	Guys
37P	Fore topsail yard	Halliard	73	Main topsail yard	Reef tackles	109	Mizzen boom	Sheet
			74P	Spare				
			74S	Main topsail yard	Halliard			

Flags

The Confederate flags flown by the *Alabama* changed during the period of her cruise. The first Confederate flag was adopted on 5 March 1861 and was known as the 'Stars and Bars'. It was also the ensign of the Confederate Navy and it is clearly shown in the painting by Walters (page 58). The parts of a flag are the top (or head), bottom (or foot), the hoist which is next to the pole and the fly which is the rest. A special emblem or symbol in the top corner next to the hoist is called the canton. The size of flags is usually described in terms of the ratio of length to breadth (the hoist). The 'Stars and Bars' consisted of three equal stripes of red, white and red with a large square blue canton containing seven white stars.

In May 1863 this flag was replaced by the Second Confederate Flag which had an all-white field (instead of the three stripes). The canton was replaced by the Battle Flag, of a red background with a blue cross with white stars on it. On 11 November 1863 Semmes writes in his log 'hoisted our own colors (new flag)'. This flag can be seen in the painting by Walters showing the ship at Cape Town (page 59). The photograph (A) (page 55) showing the *Alabama* at Singapore has a flag hanging loosely from the mizzen gaff which appears to be this one. All the flags were kept in the flag locker which was right at the stern, on the horse block.

SAILS AND RIGGING

Jibboom and Bowsprit Rigging (scale = 1:96)

1. Martingale stay – chain
2. Martingale backstay (2) – chain (P&S)
3. Bobstay – chain
4. Outer jib stay. Port side of martingale attached by deadeye and heart
5. Fore topgallant stay. Starboard side of martingale attached by deadeye and heart
6. Fore royal stay. Starboard side of martingale attached by deadeye and heart
7. Jibboom guy. P&S to whisker beam
8. Fore topmast stay (double). P&S to sheave on bowsprit to hearts
9. Fore stay (double)

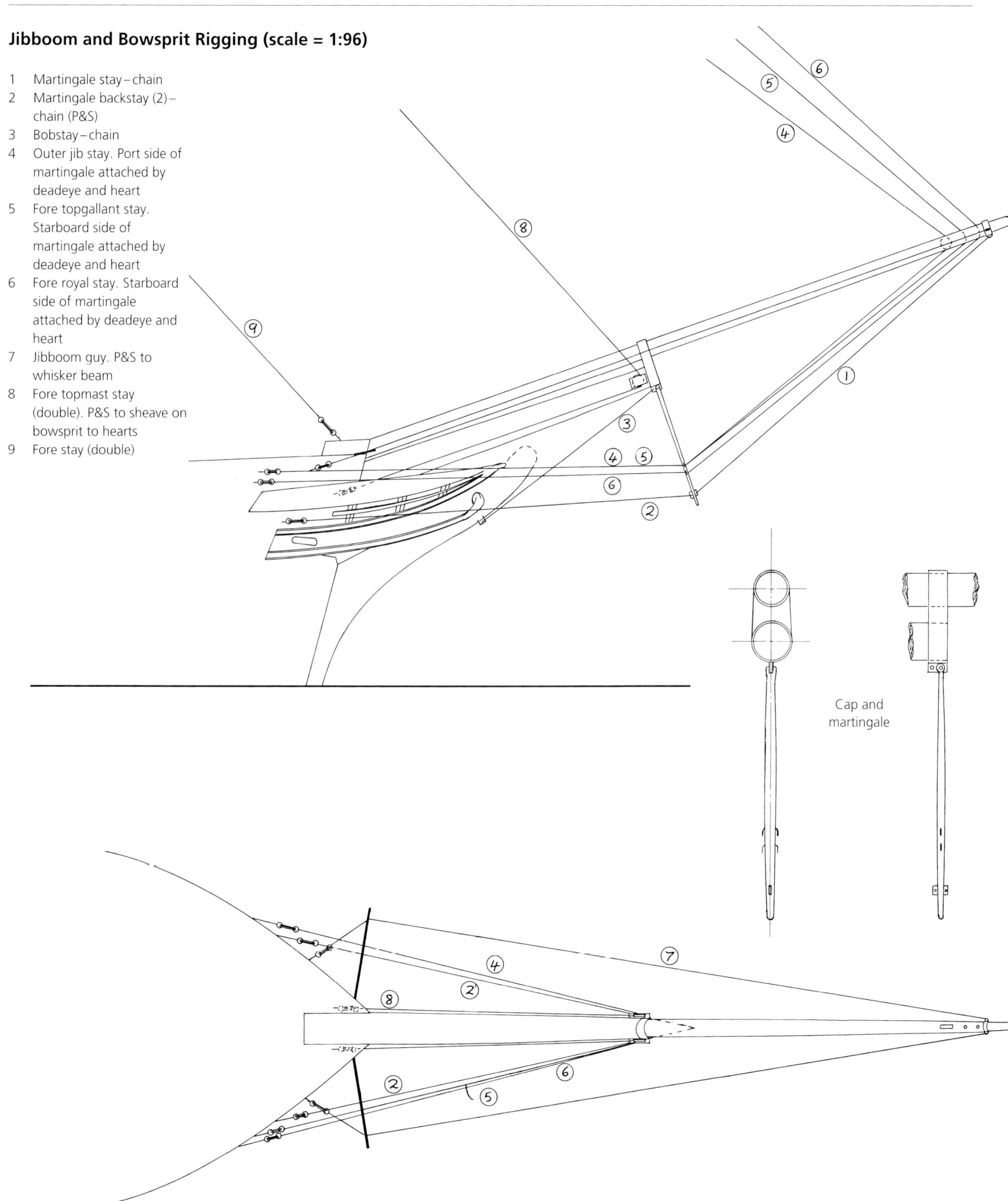

Cap and martingale

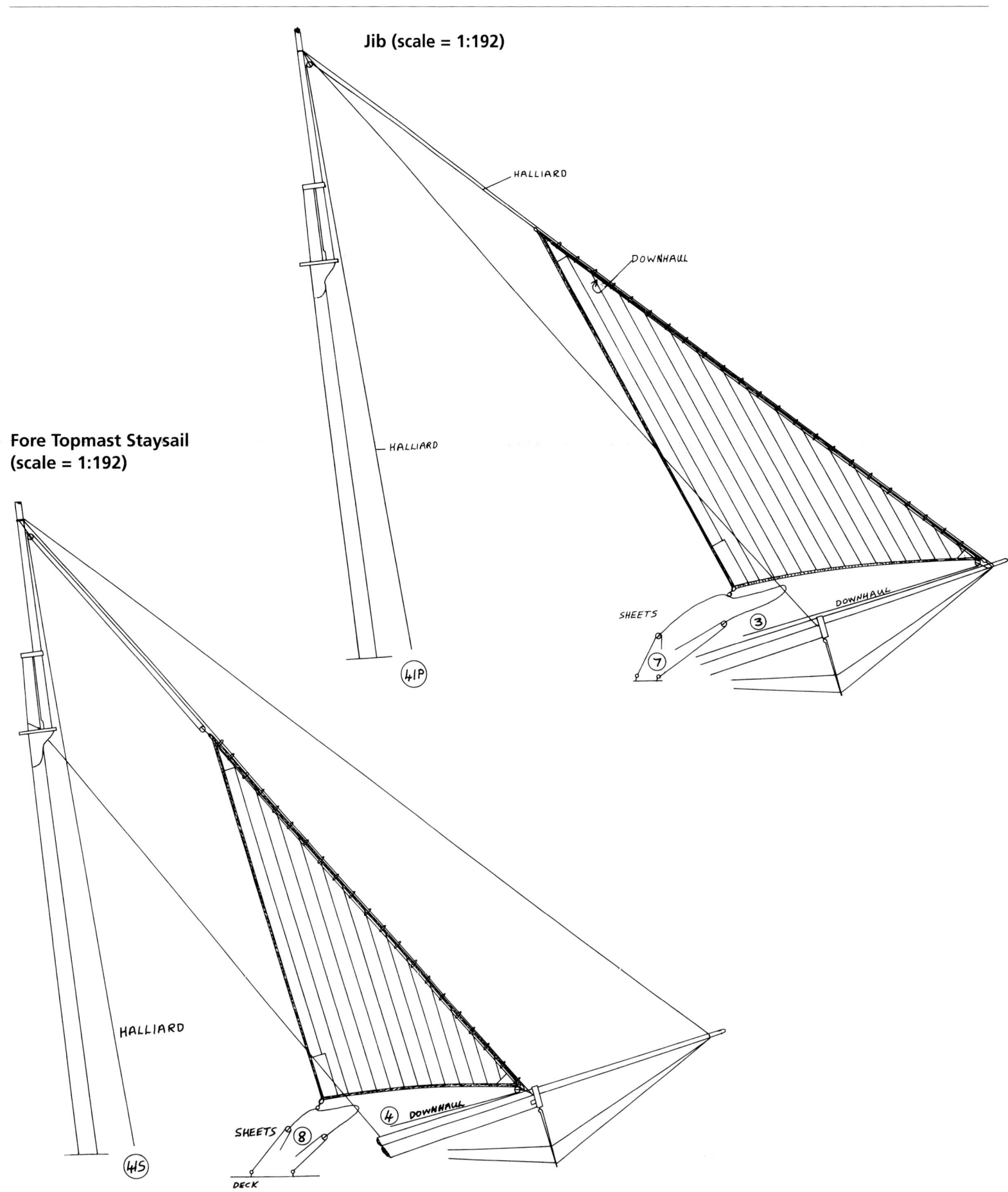

SAILS AND RIGGING

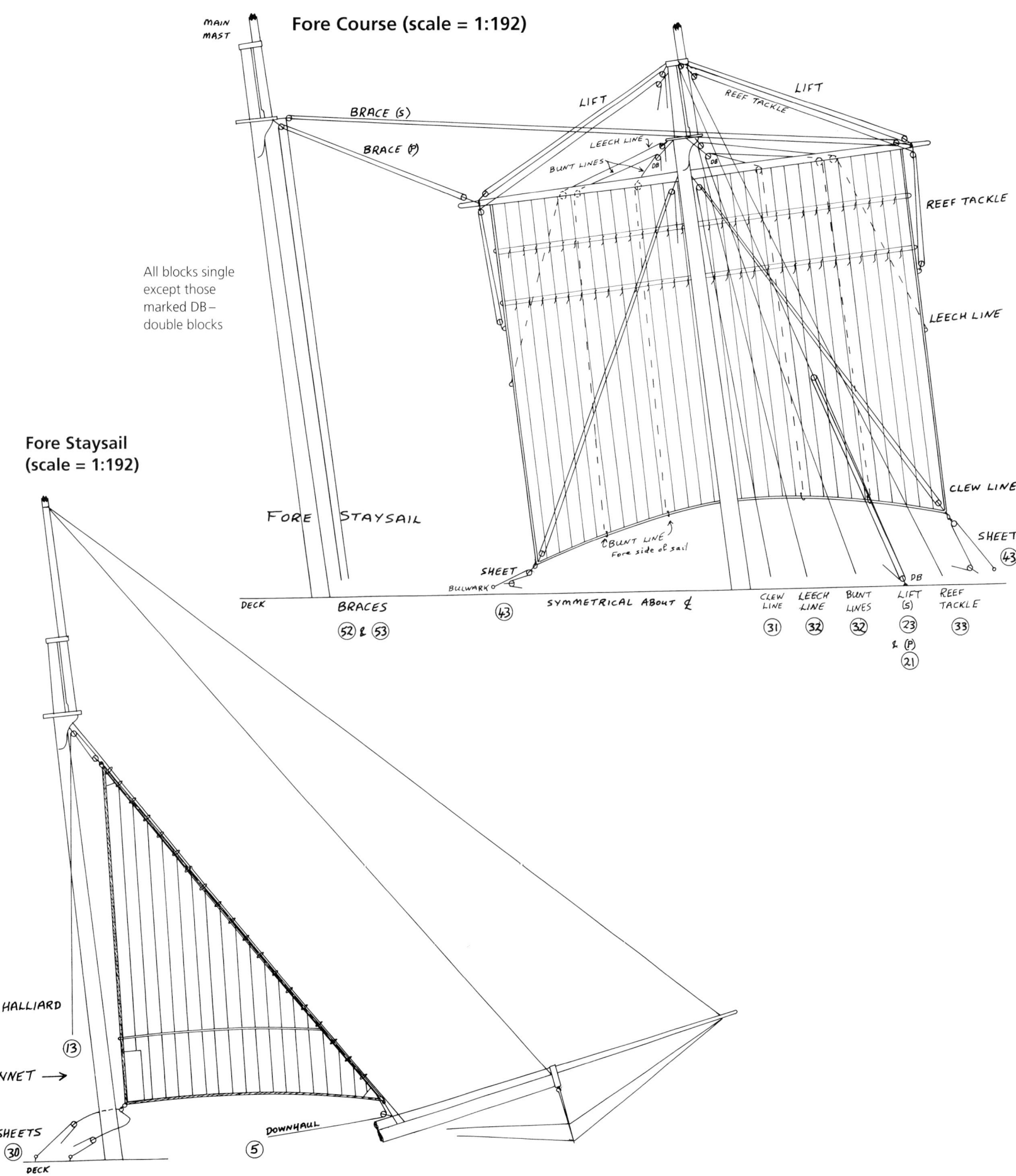

Fore Topsail (scale = 1:192)

All blocks single except those marked DB – double blocks, and SB – sister blocks

Fore Topgallant (scale = 1:192)

All blocks single except those marked DB – double blocks

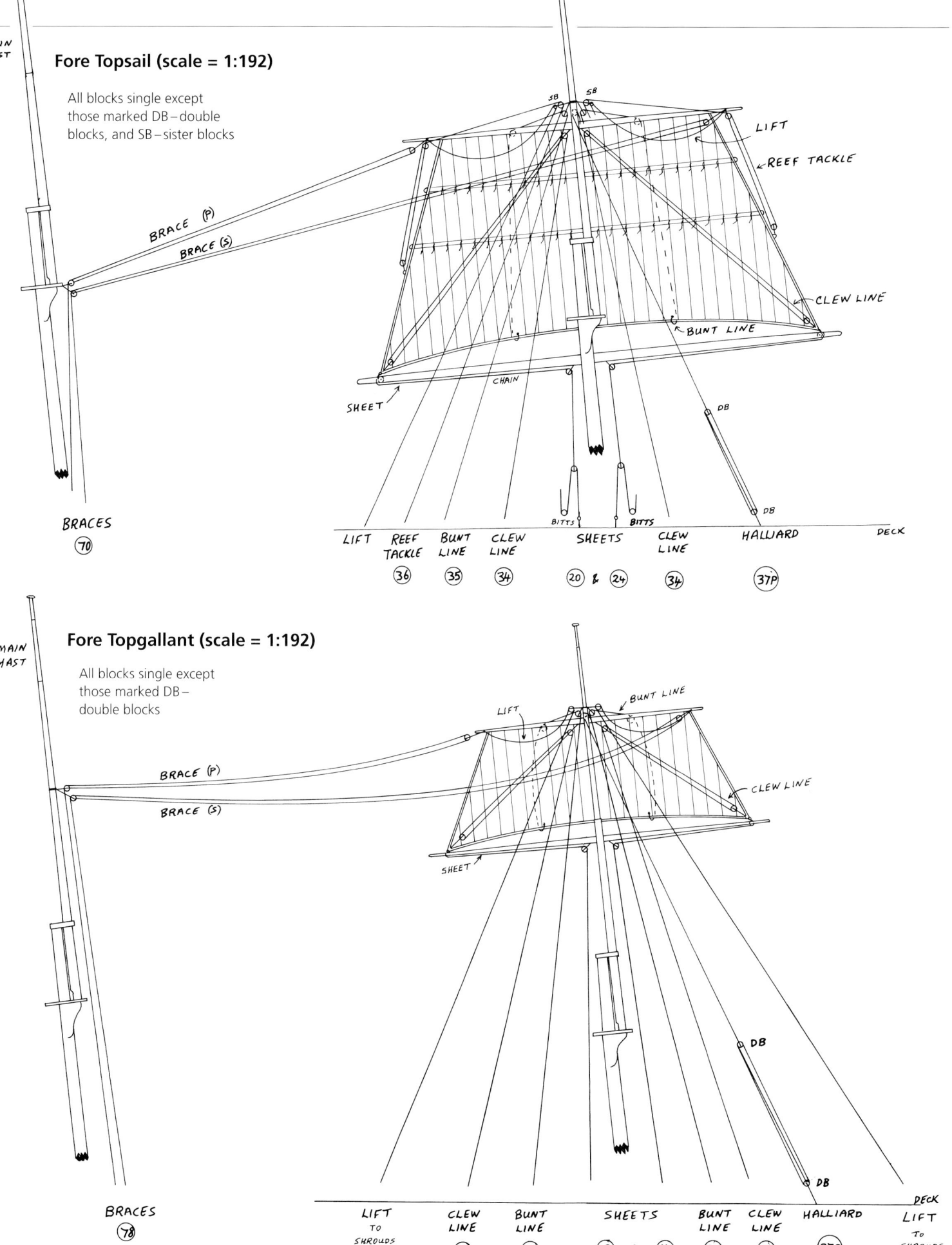

SAILS AND RIGGING

Fore Royal (scale = 1:192)
Sheet and clew lines worked from top

Fore Trysail (scale = 1:192)
All blocks single except those marked DB – double blocks

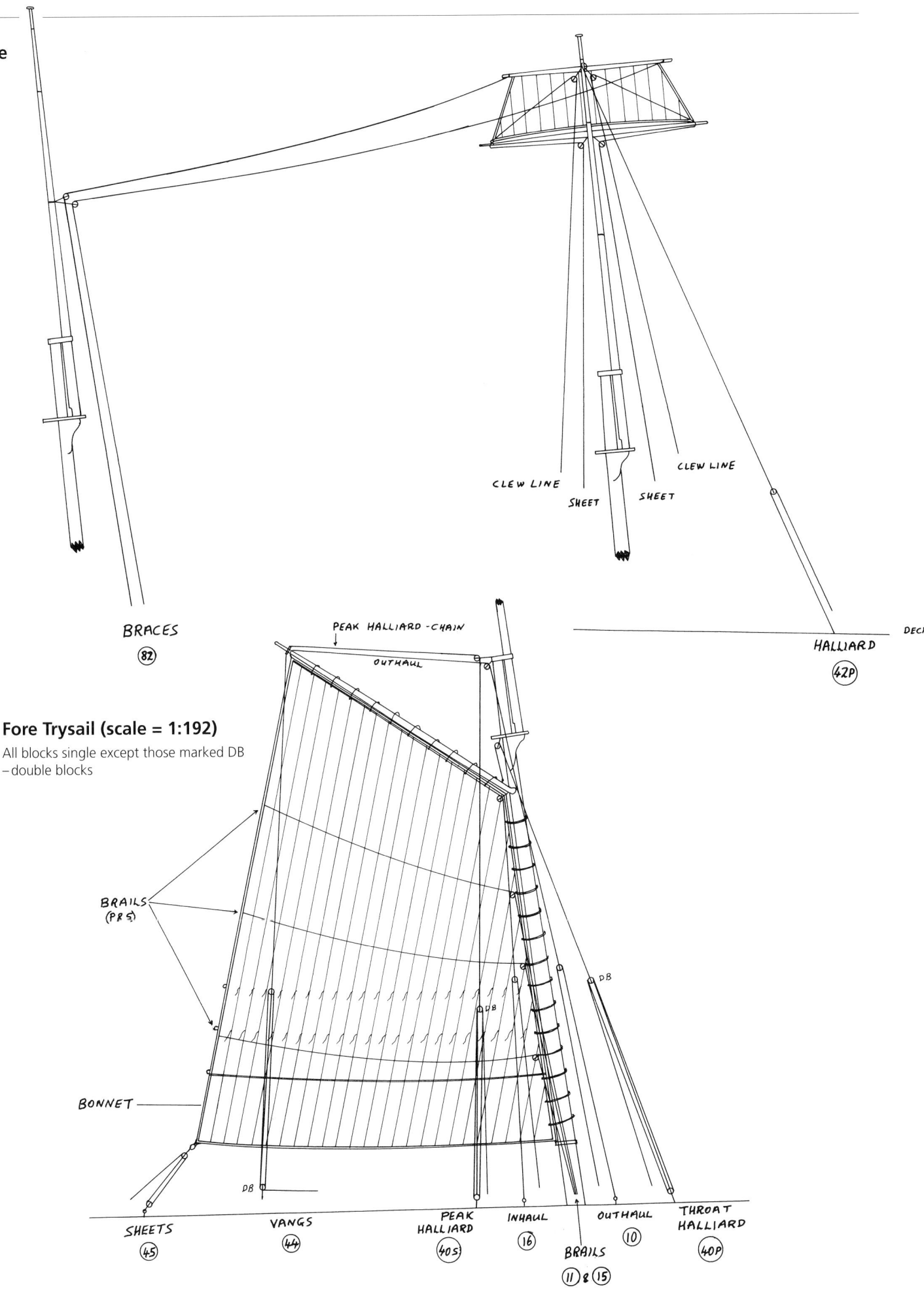

Main Yard – no sail (scale = 1:192)

All blocks single except those marked DB – double blocks

Main Topsail (scale = 1:192)

All blocks single except those marked DB – double blocks, and SB – sister blocks

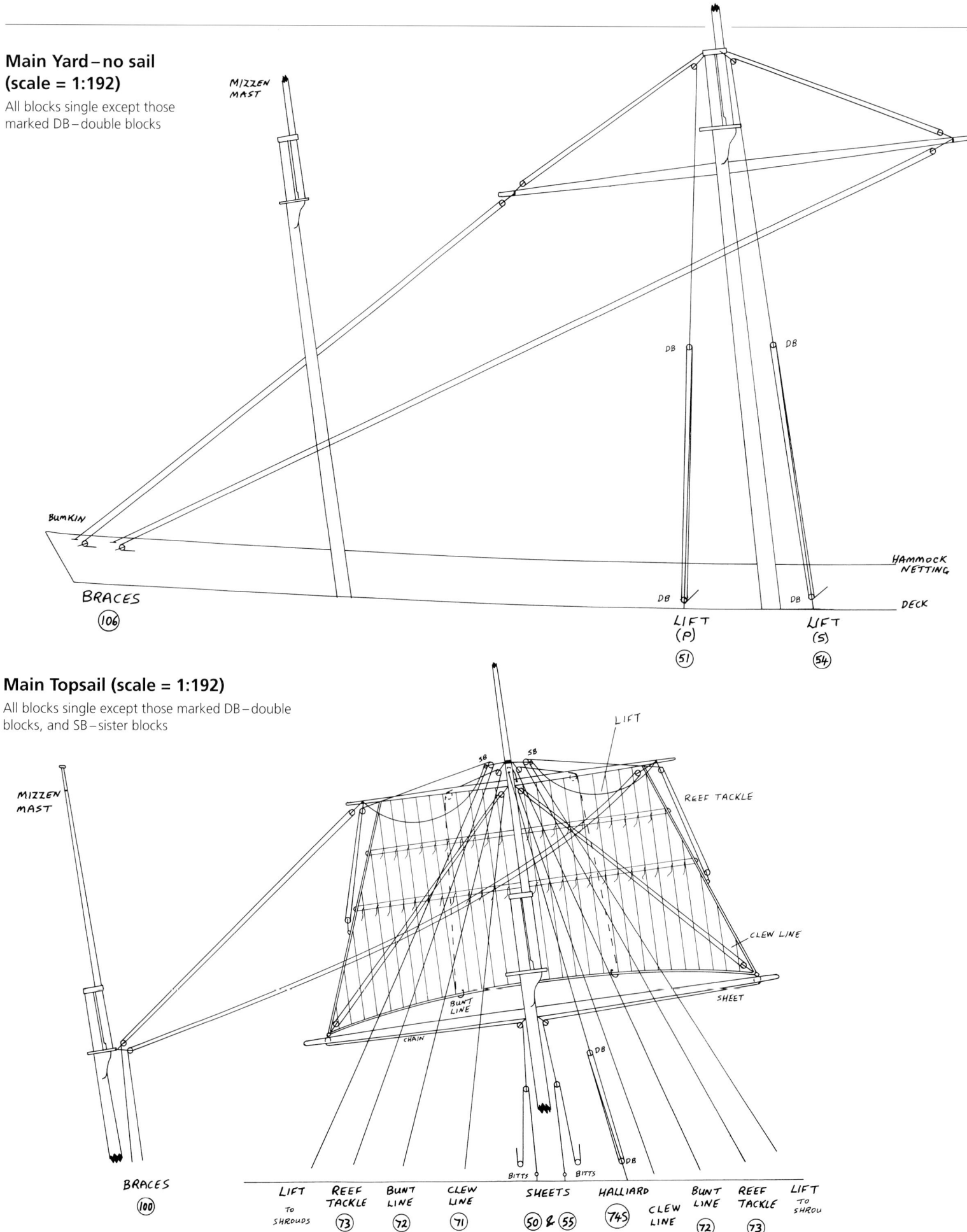

SAILS AND RIGGING

Main Topgallant (scale = 1:192)

All blocks single except those marked DB – double blocks

Main Royal (scale = 1:192)

All blocks single
Clew lines and sheets worked in top

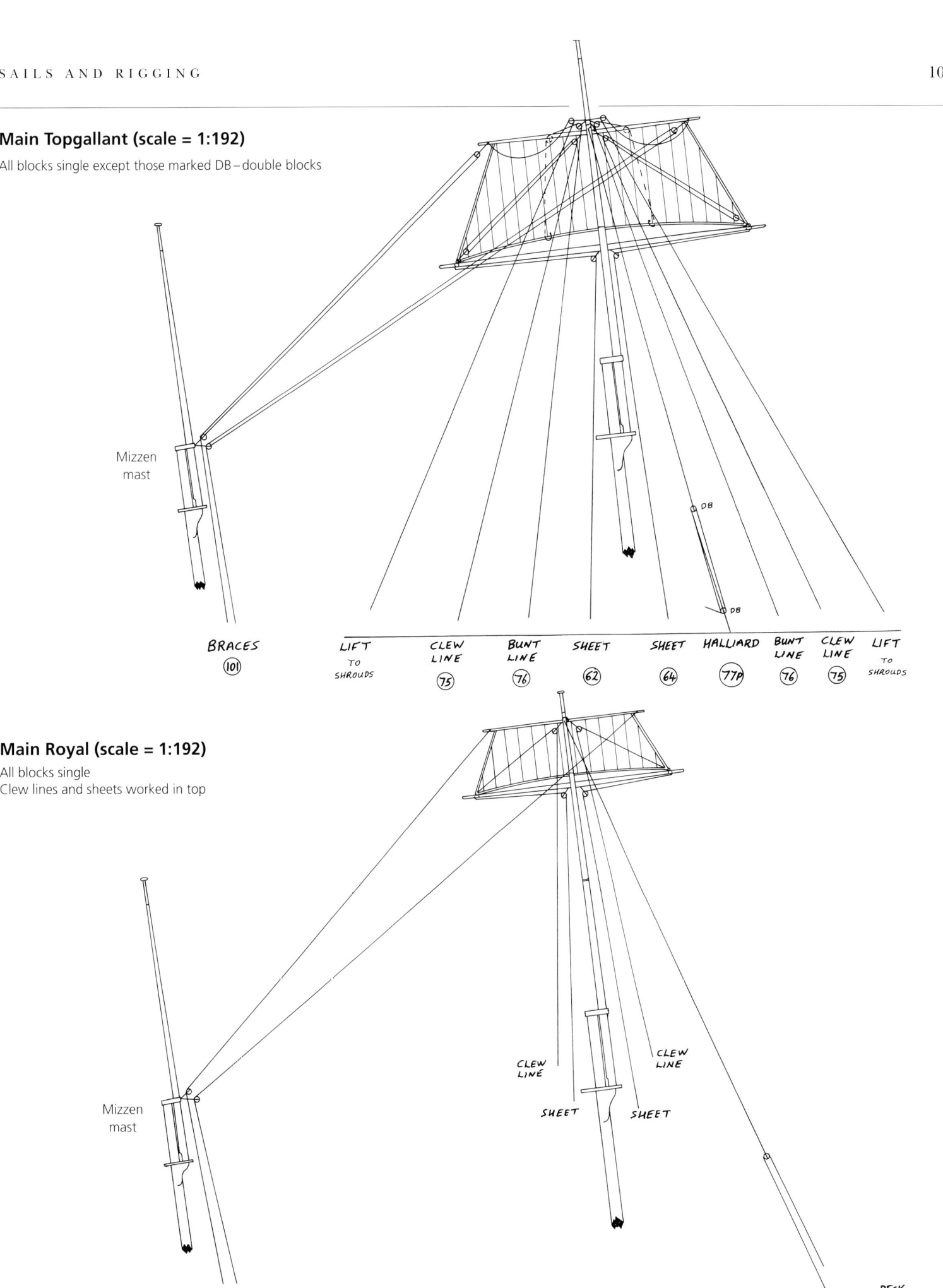

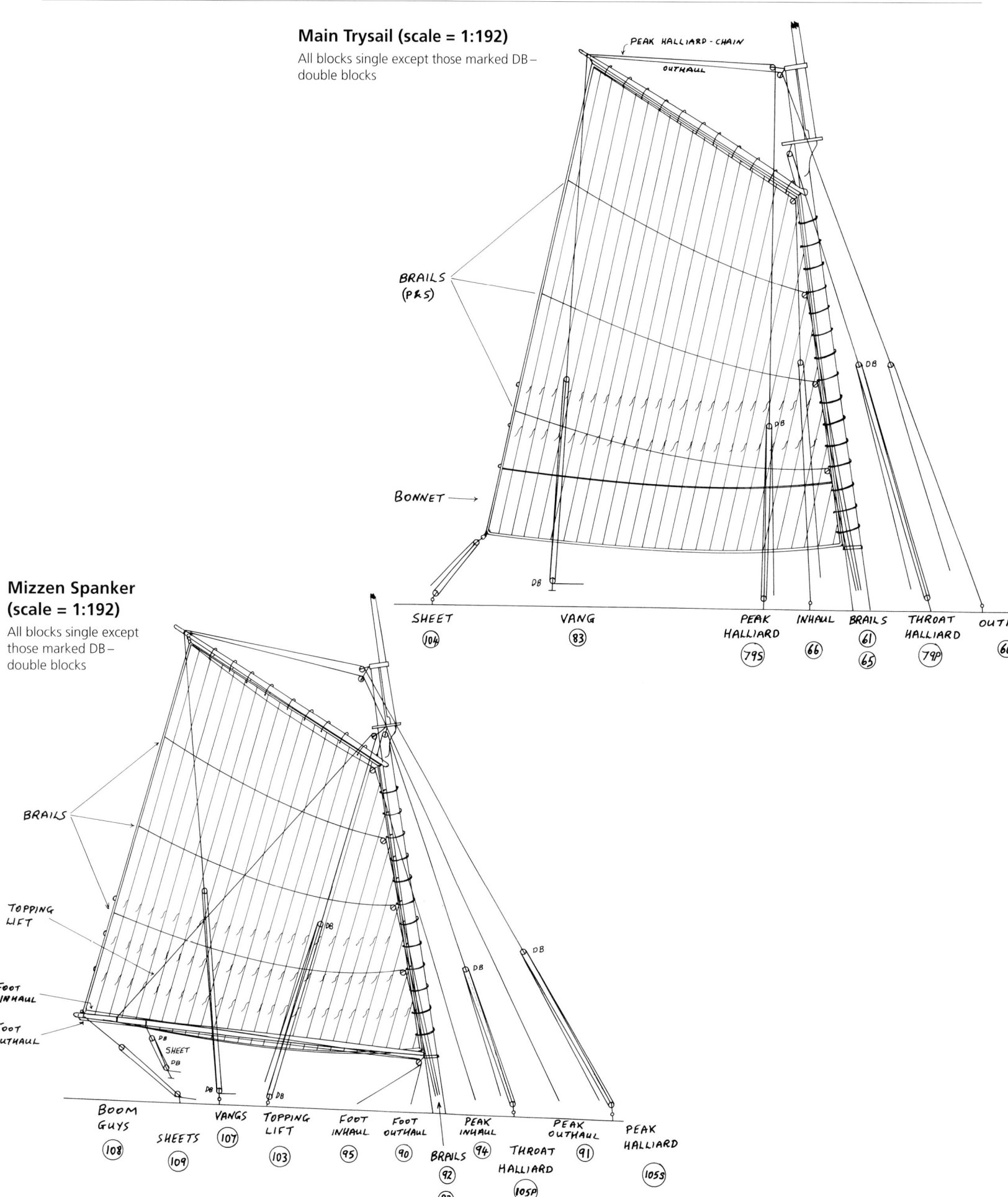

Main Trysail (scale = 1:192)
All blocks single except those marked DB – double blocks

Mizzen Spanker (scale = 1:192)
All blocks single except those marked DB – double blocks

SAILS AND RIGGING

Mizzen Gaff Topsail (scale = 1:192)

Fore Mast Studding Sails (scale = 1:192)
View looking forward

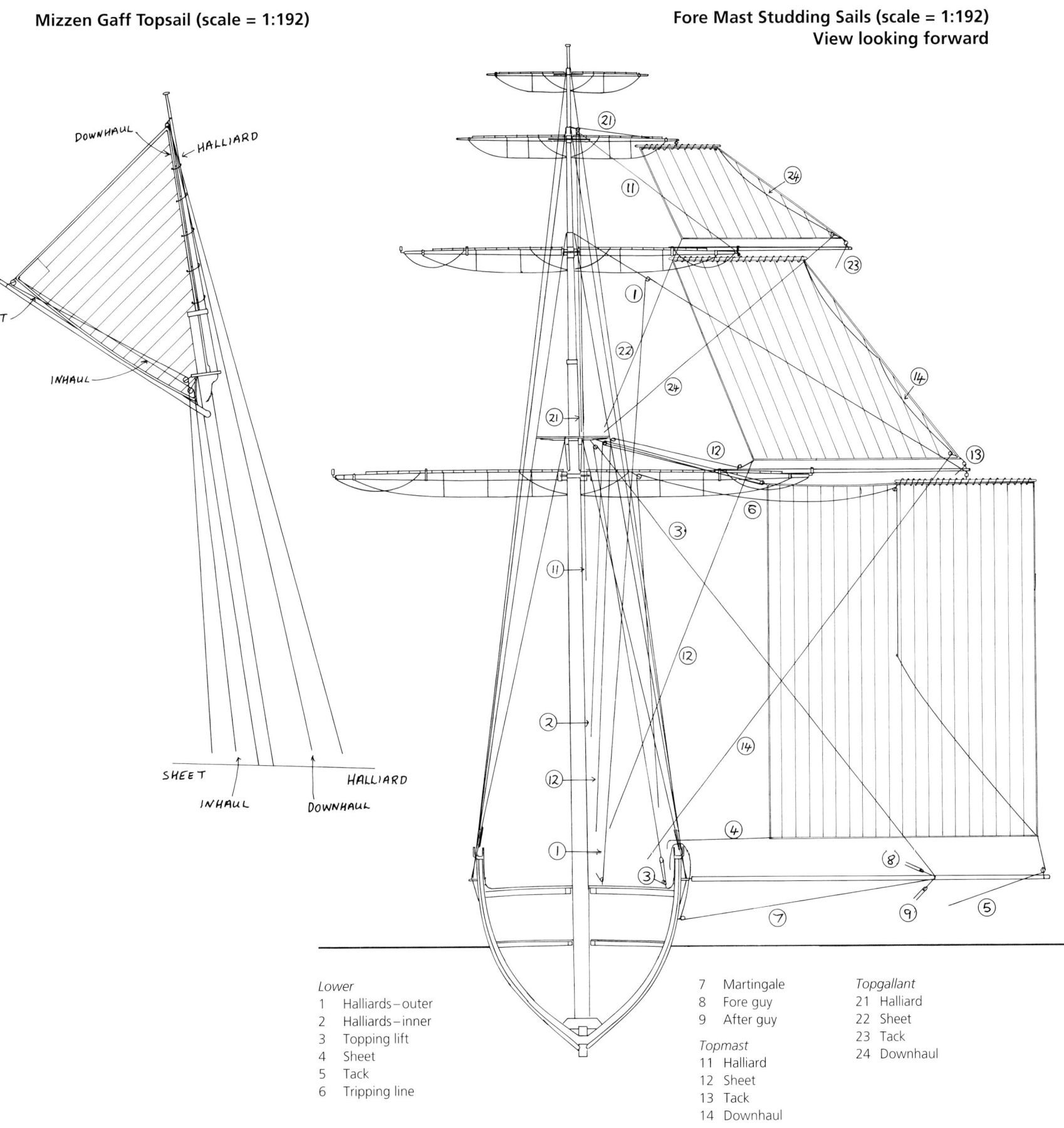

Lower
1. Halliards – outer
2. Halliards – inner
3. Topping lift
4. Sheet
5. Tack
6. Tripping line

7. Martingale
8. Fore guy
9. After guy

Topmast
11. Halliard
12. Sheet
13. Tack
14. Downhaul

Topgallant
21. Halliard
22. Sheet
23. Tack
24. Downhaul

Armament

GUNS

According to Semmes 'The armament of the *Alabama* consisted of one 7-inch Blakely rifled gun, one 8-inch smooth-bore pivot-gun, six 32-pounders, smooth-bore, in broadside' (SC II, p288).

Bulloch gave a little more detail when writing to the Secretary of the Navy. 'When finally armed the *Alabama* will have a battery consisting of a 7-inch 100 pounder rifled gun, Blakely pattern, 84cwt; one 8-inch solid shot 68-pounder, smooth bore, 108cwt; and six 6-inch 32-pounder guns, 55cwt each. The 8-inch gun is of course provided with shell as well as shot, and I have provided seventy 42-pound spherical shot for the rifled gun in addition to the elongated shell and shot peculiarly adapted to its character' (ORN II, 2 p236).

A copy of the authorisation granted to Raphael Semmes to attack ships of the United States of America signed by Jefferson Davis is reproduced. This states that the *Alabama* was to carry ten guns. As noted before, when the ship was commissioned off the Azores she carried eight guns. It appears that she was to receive an extra two guns during the cruise. This is mentioned by Bulloch and Semmes and the extra guns were apparently to be delivered by the *Agrippina* while the *Alabama* was at the island of Fernando de Noronha in April 1863 (B I, p267 & ORN I, 2 p740). However, as the two ships did not in the event meet there, or subsequently, the additional guns were not delivered. I have seen no reference to the size or type of these guns.

The eight original guns will be described below, separated into the two types – pivot and broadside. All the original drawings used

A copy of the authorisation granted to Raphael Semmes to attack US ships, signed by Jefferson Davis, President of the Confederate States of America, dated 22 June 1862. This gives the armament of the Alabama as ten guns. (US Naval Historical Center: NH47169)

ARMAMENT

Gun (not to scale)

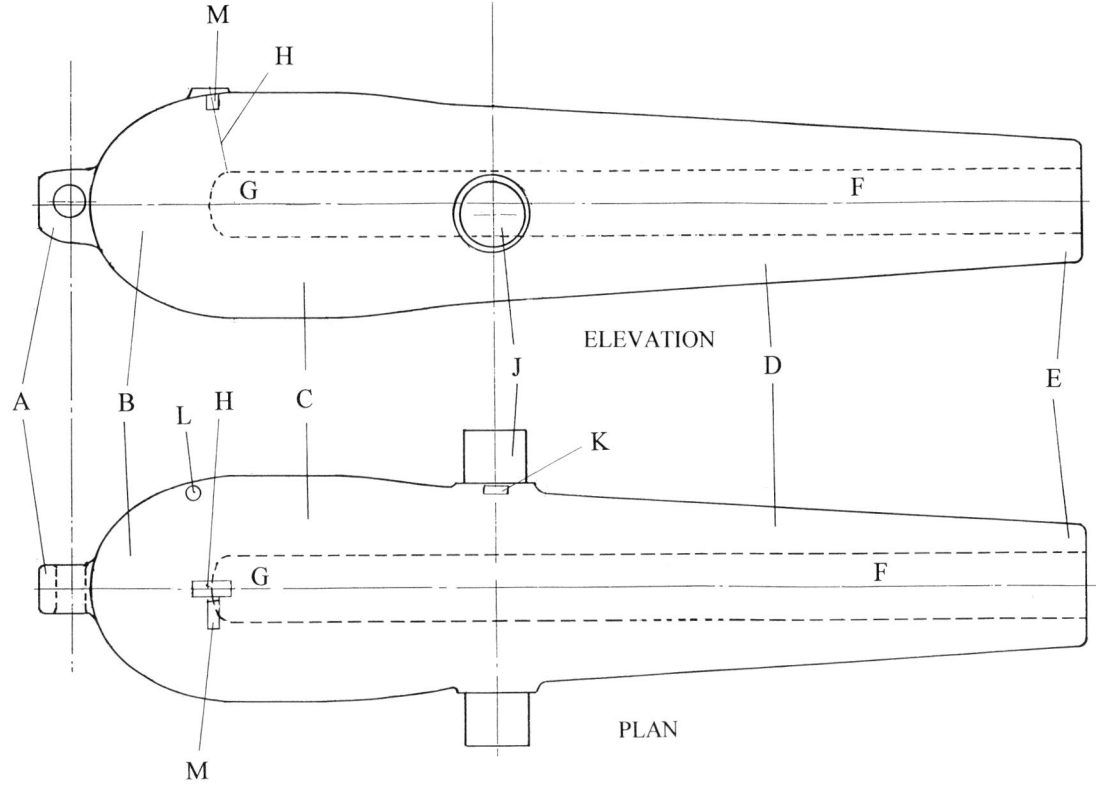

Parts of a barrel
A   Cascable
B   Breech
C   Reinforce
D   Chase
E   Muzzle
F   Bore
G   Chamber
H   Vent
J   Trunnion
K   Fore sight
L   After sight
M   Lock

7in Gun No 145 (reconstruction) (scale = 1:24)

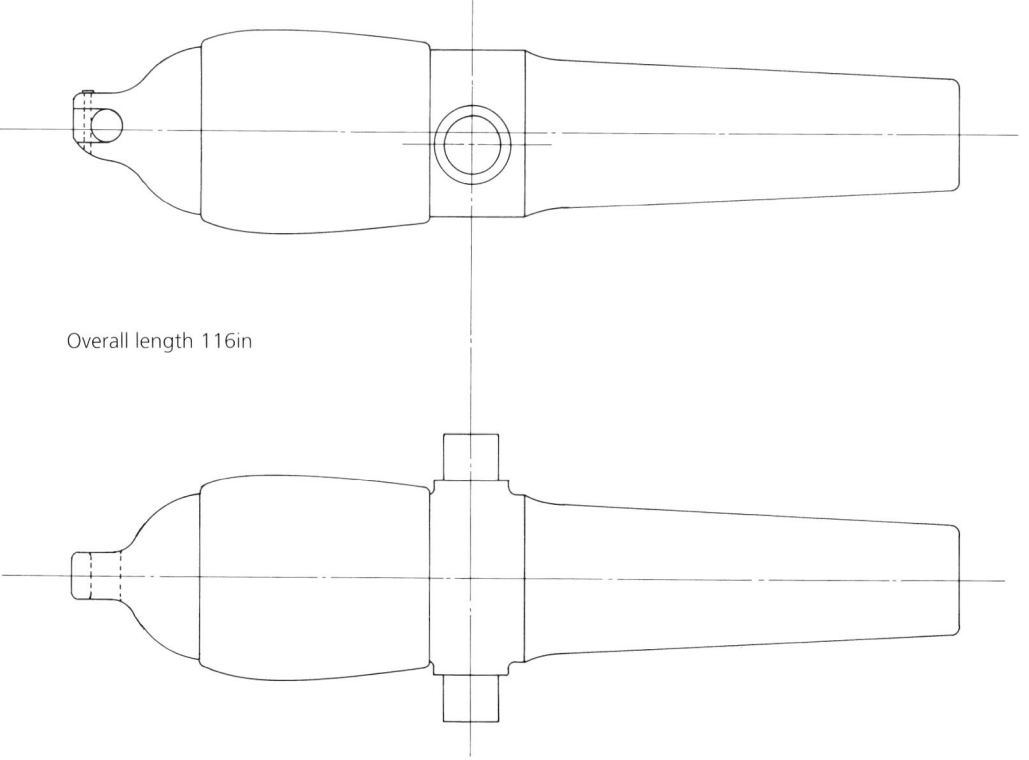

Overall length 116in

are now in the Fawcett Preston Archive in Liverpool, and have been redrawn. A lot of these original drawings are damaged or torn. In some cases they have also been cut so that they will fit on the page before being glued down. Therefore there can sometimes be difficulty in interpreting the drawings. Any drawing which is marked with the word 'Reconstruction' is redrawn using the best information, or may possibly be based on details from another similar gun from the collection.

The following drawings illustrate the different parts of the each type of carriage and also the slide and a gun. The position of the items on the various detailed drawings, for example the wrought iron work, is shown and has the same number. The brackets (or cheeks) of a carriage are made of two pieces of timber bolted together. Points specific to each gun will be described as appropriate under that heading, but I think most things are fairly obvious.

Carriage and Slide for 7in Rifled Gun (1 July 1862) (scale = 1:24)

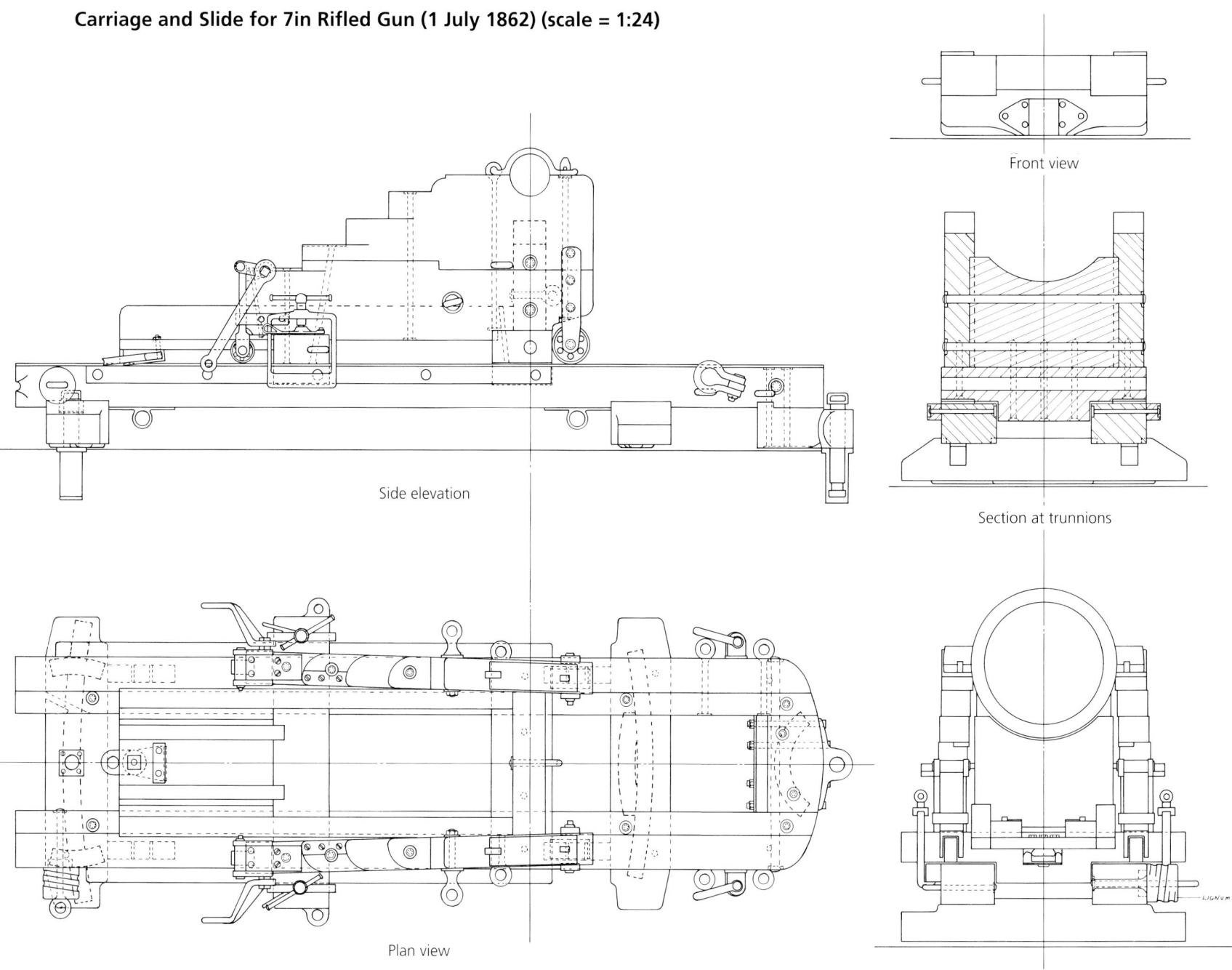

Pivot guns

<u>7in Blakely - Fawcett Preston Number 145</u>

'Her armament consisted of eight guns; six 32-pounders, in broadside, and two pivot guns amidships; one on the forecastle, and the other abaft the main mast – the former a 100-pounder rifled Blakely, and the latter, a smooth-bore eight inch. The Blakely gun was so deficient in metal, compared with the weight of shot it threw, that, after the first few discharges, when it became a little heated, it was of comparatively small use to us, to such an extent were we obliged to reduce the charge of powder, on account of the recoil' (SM, p403).

The term Blakely refers to the principle invented by Captain Blakely, which gives strength to the gun, and lightness. The gun starts off as a solid casting, which includes the trunnions. The gun is then bored out to the required diameter. A series of reinforcing rings are then bored to the appropriate diameter, and after being heated, are placed on the breech extending from the trunnions. These rings increase the strength of the gun, and hence also the range.

The only drawing of the gun is one that shows it in outline on the carriage. The *Florida* also had two 7in Blakely rifled guns by Fawcett Preston, one of which survives and is on display at the

ARMAMENT

Carriage Gun No 145. Preliminary. No Date (scale = 1:24)

Note: This drawing is superseded by a new one dated 1 July 1862 (see above)

Carriage modified by increasing the depth of the three lower steps by 2in each, *ie* 6in in total

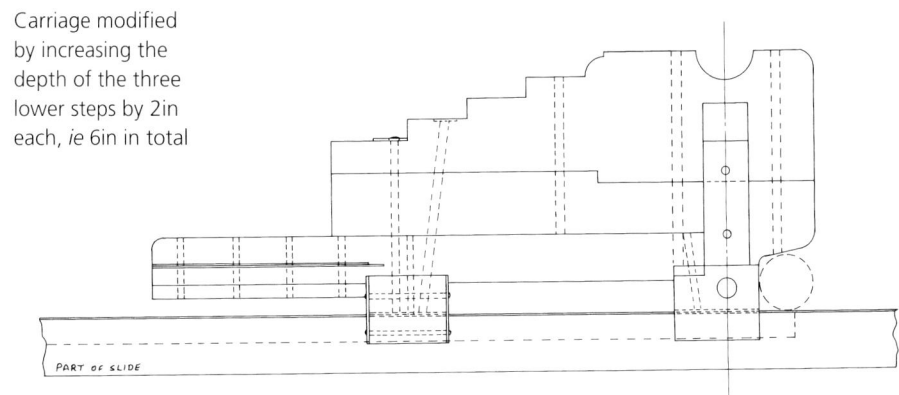

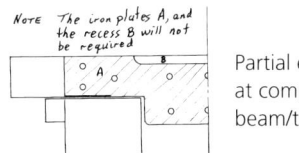

Partial elevation at compressor beam/transom

Washington Navy Yard. Looking at photographs of this gun, it appears to be identical to the one on the *Alabama*, except for the shape of the cascable. When Fawcett Preston cast a gun to an existing plan they just wrote a note on the plan giving the new gun number and order details. Therefore the plan of the *Alabama*'s gun would probably be among those for the *Florida*, but unfortunately they appear to be lost. However, the carriage was apparently sufficiently different for it to be drawn again, and these plans survive.

There are two drawings of the carriage and slide still available. The first is undated and shows a carriage that is incomplete, that is to say with no fittings. There is a note on this plan to say that it has been superseded by a later one, dated 1 July 1862. This second plan is complete and (presumably) shows the carriage and slide as finished and as it was on board the ship. There are only two significant differences between the plans of the two carriages and they are firstly that three of the steps of the brackets (or cheeks) are 2ins lower, meaning that the rear part of the carriage is therefore

Wrought Iron Work for 7in Gun No. 145 (reconstruction) (scale = 1:12)

Note: Numbers refer to key to Carriage and Slide drawings on pages 108-9

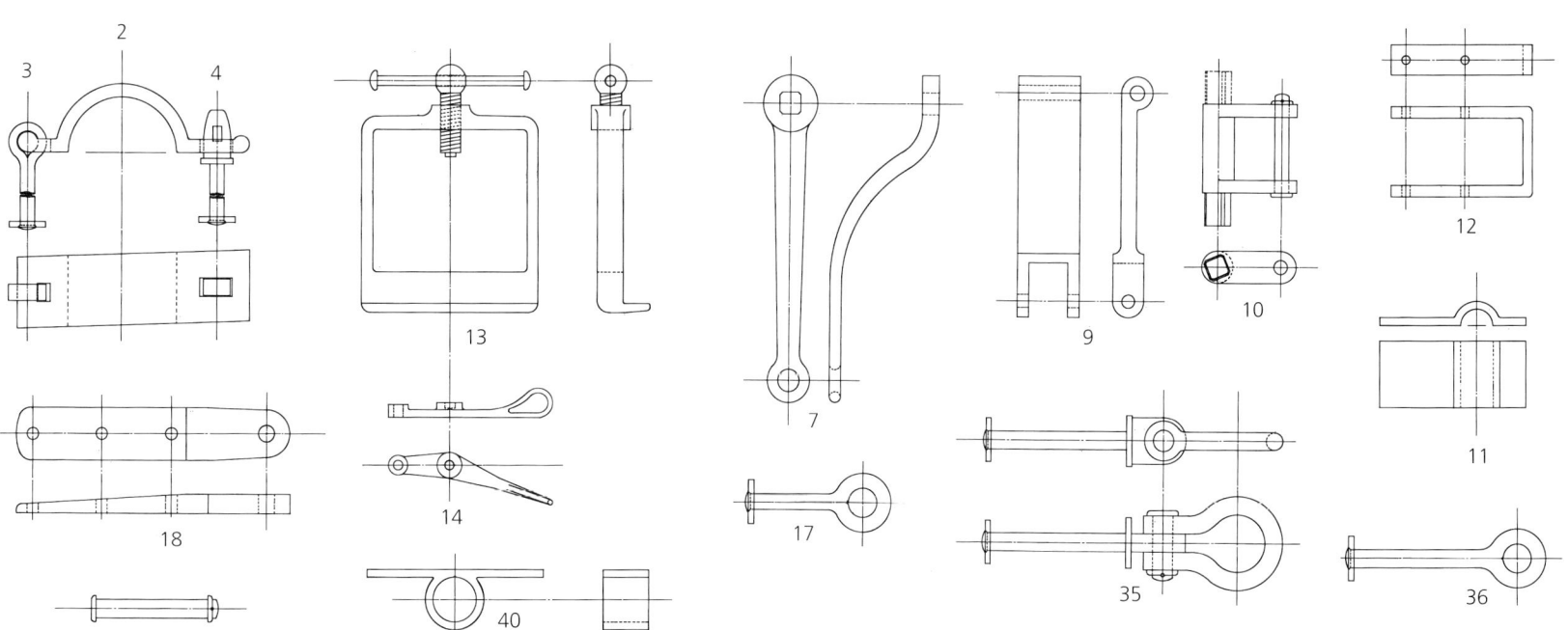

2, 3, 4	Capsquare with bolts (1 and 1 to opposite hand)	14	Compressor thimble lever (1 and 1 to opposite hand)	10	Rear lever (1 as drawn, 1 to dotted lines)	36 Slide front loops (4 off)
13	Compressor frame (2 off)	40	Axle eye (4 off)	12	Rear guides (2 off)	11 Lever cap (2 off)
18	Front wheel bracket (2 off)	7	Rope lever (2 off)	17	Transom loop (1 off)	
	Front wheel pins (2 off)	9	Rear lever slide (2 off)	35	Breeching tackle (2 off)	

Carriage and Slide – Pivot Guns (scale = 1:24)

Plan view

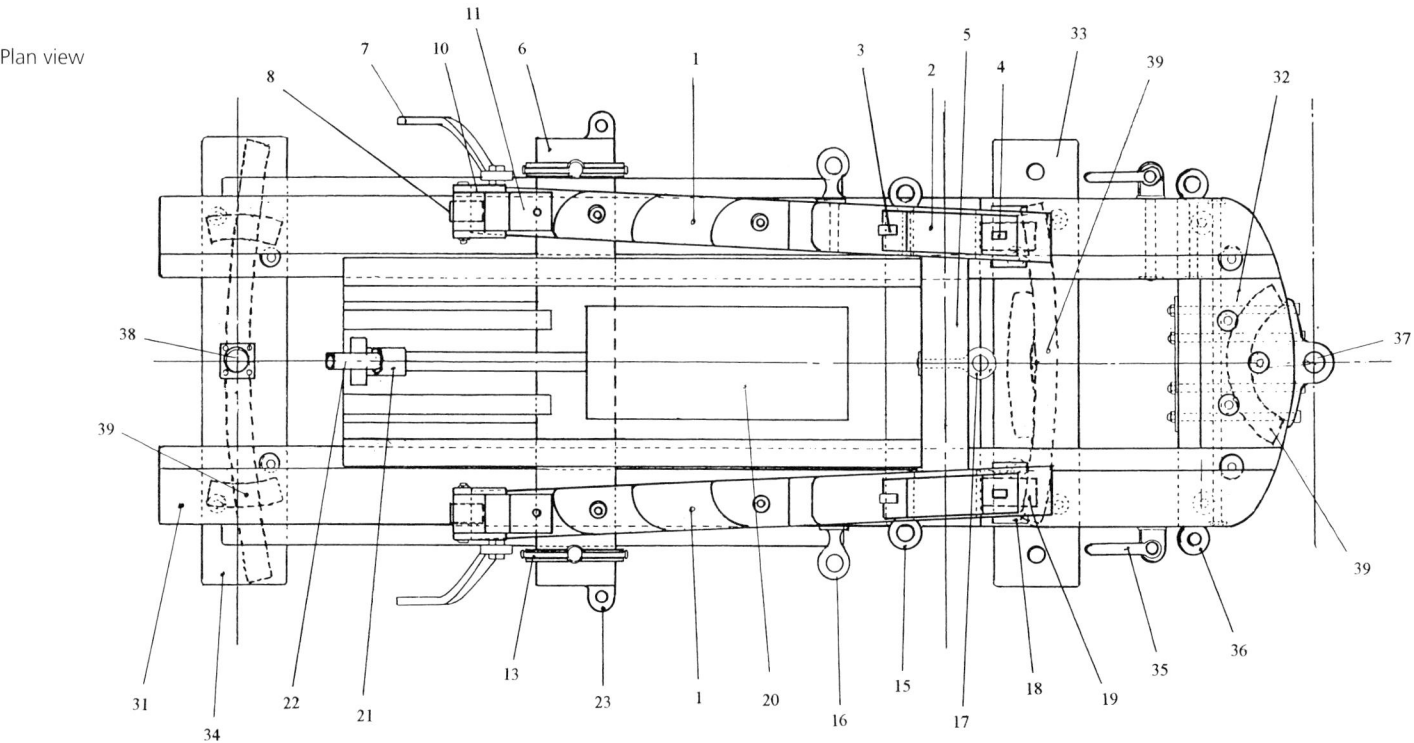

Carriage
1. Bracket
2. Capsquare
3. Capsquare bolt
4. Capsquare bolt with key
5. Transom
6. Transom - compressor beam
7. Rope lever
8. Rear roller
9. Rear lever slide
10. Rear lever
11. Lever cap
12. Rear guides
13. Compressor
14. Compressor thimble lever
15. Loop
16. Loop
17. Transom Loop
18. Front wheel bracket
19. Front roller
20. Quoin
21. Ratchet motion
22. Handle for ratchet motion
23. Loop (outhaul)

Slide
31. Rail
32. Transom – front
33. Transom – middle
34. Transom – rear
35. Breeching shackle
36. Loop (outhaul)
37. Pivot
38. Pivot
39. Sweeps on underside of transom
40. Axle eye

Elevation

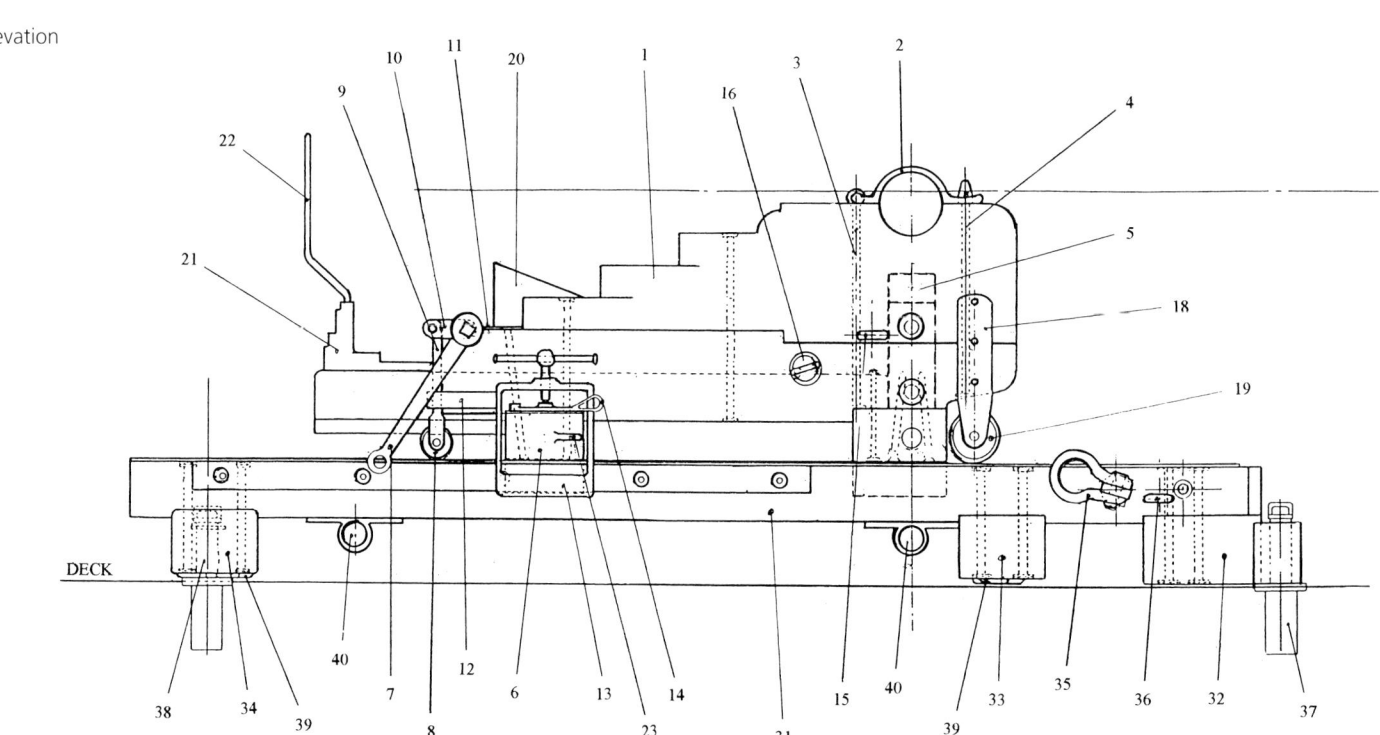

ARMAMENT

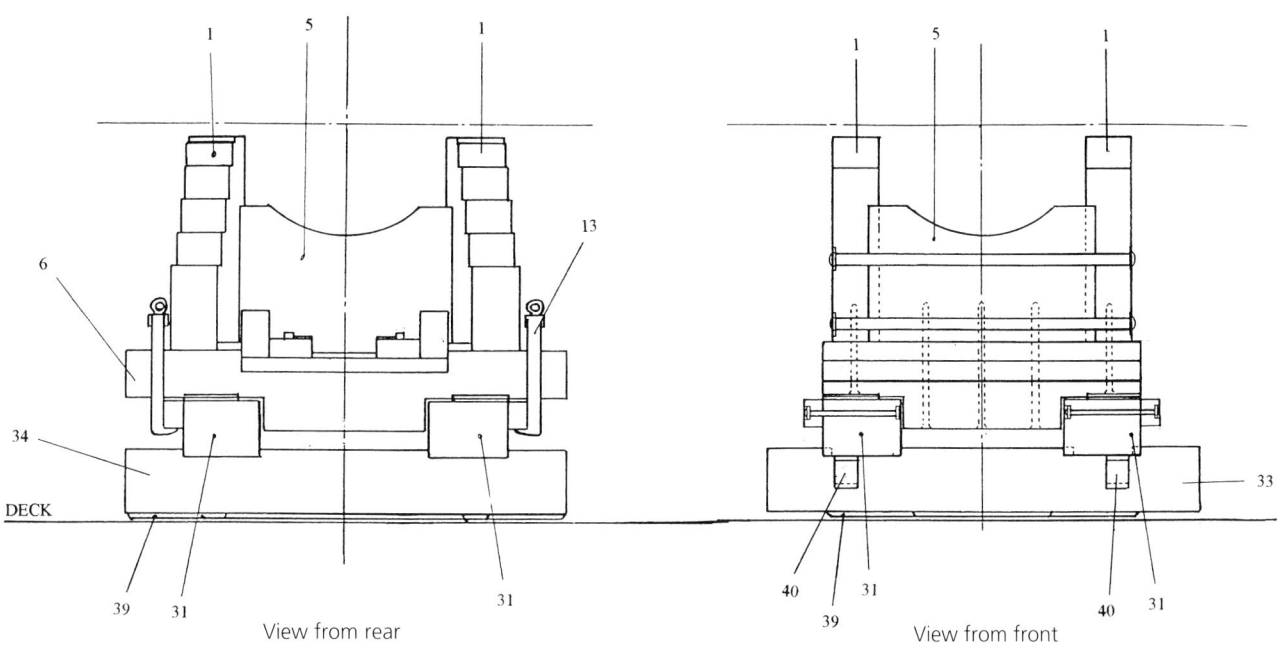

View from rear

View from front

Wrought Iron Work for 7in and 8in Guns (reconstruction) (scale = 1:8)

Note: Numbers refer to key to Carriage and Slide drawings opposite

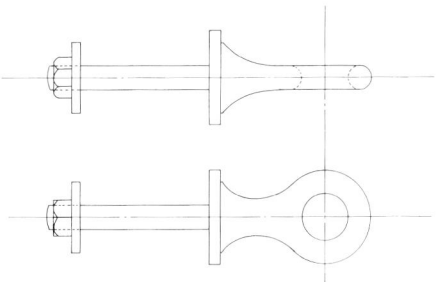

16 Carriage loop (2 off for 7in gun; 2 off for 8in gun ½in longer)

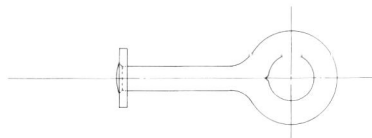

15 Carriage loop (2 off for 7in gun; 2 off for 8in gun ½in longer)

8. Rear Rollers for Pivot Gun Carriages (3 June 1862) (scale = 1:4)

Note: Numbers refer to key to Carriage and Slide drawings opposite

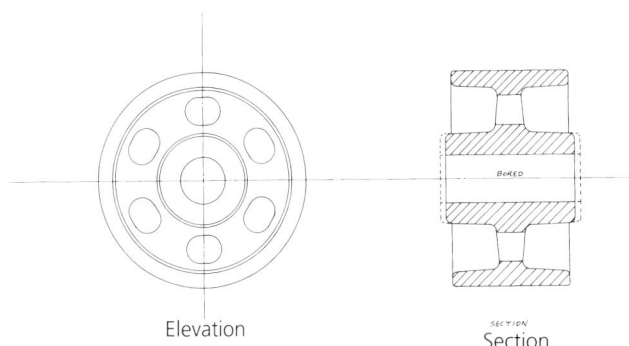

Elevation

Section

2 off to dotted lines for 8in gun No 144
2 off to solid lines for 7in gun No 145

Axle (scale = 1:16)

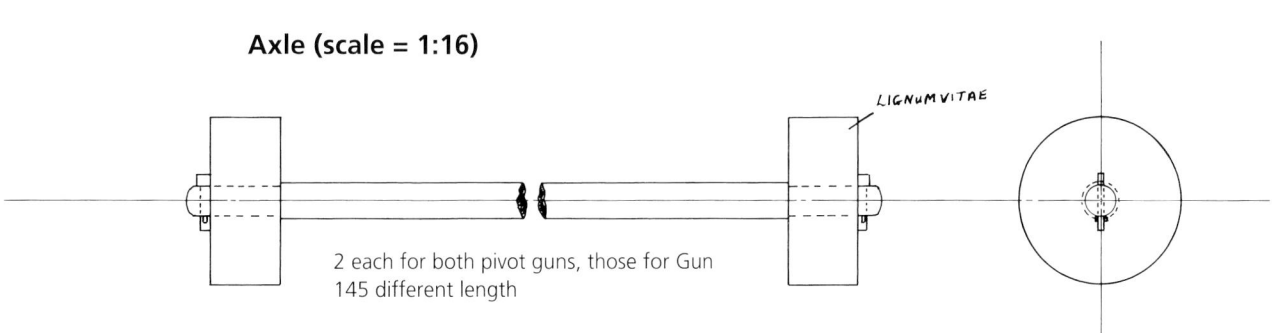

2 each for both pivot guns, those for Gun 145 different length

19. Front Rollers for Pivot Gun Carriages
(3 June 1862) (scale = 1:4)

Note: Numbers refer to key to Carriage and Slide drawings on pages 108-9

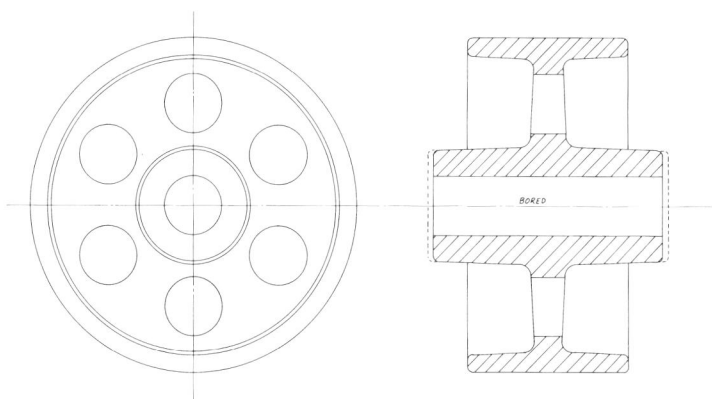

2 off to dotted lines for 8in gun No 144
2 off to solid lines for 7in gun No 145

21. Ratchet Motion for Gun Quoins
(26 May 1862) (scale = 1:4)

Note: Numbers refer to key to Carriage and Slide drawings on page 108

1 for 8in gun No 144 Order 81 Stock
1 for 7in gun No 145 Order 81 Stock

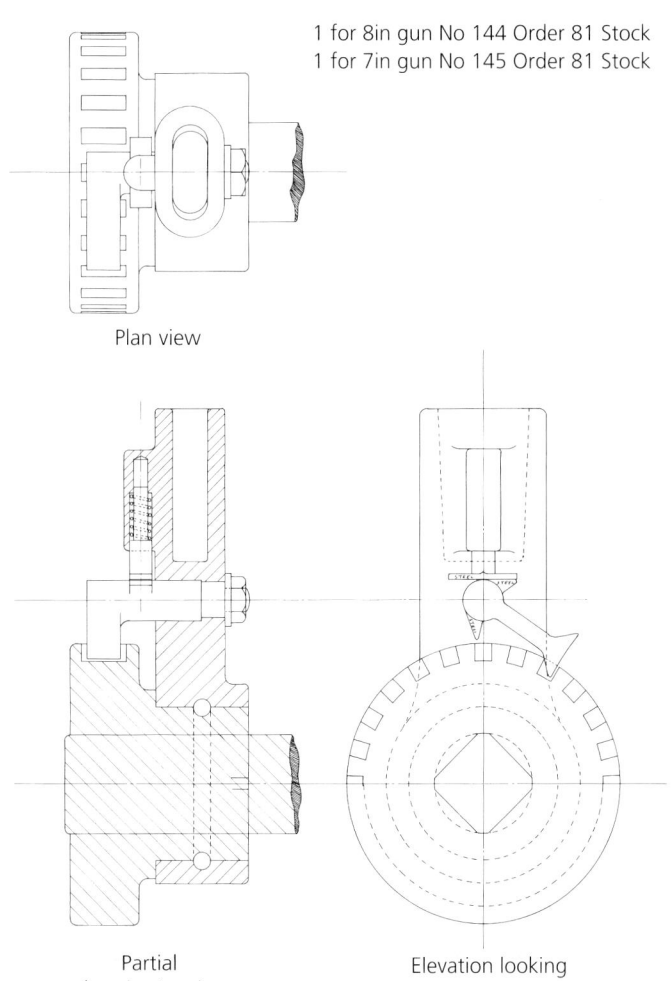

Plan view

Partial elevation/section

Elevation looking from quoin

Elevating Mechanism for 7in Rifled Gun No 145
(scale = 1:16)

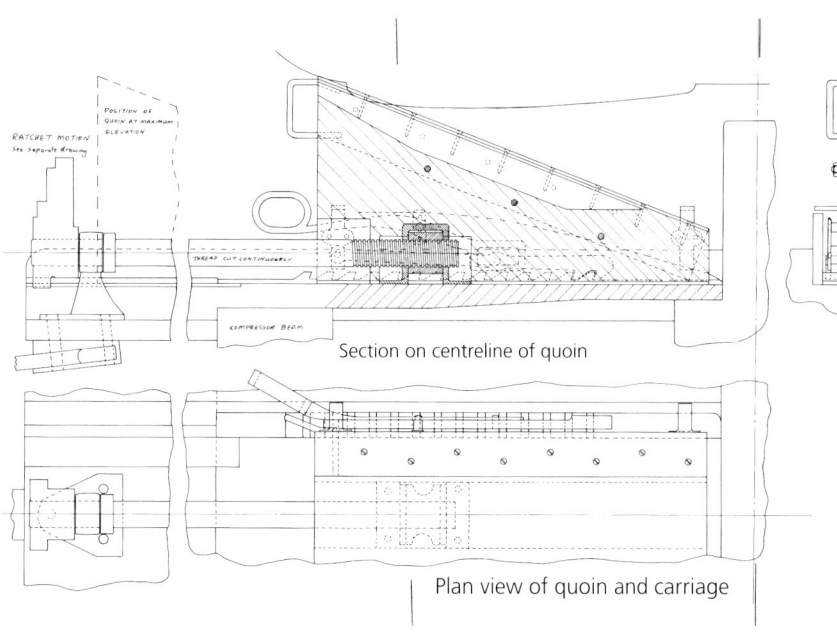

Section on centreline of quoin

End elevation of quoin

Plan view of quoin and carriage

The original drawing is torn and only part remains. The two thick black vertical lines, top and bottom of this drawing, show the approximate position of the edges of the original. Everything outside these lines has been reconstructed using the plans of the ratchet motion and carriage, and photographs of the 8in smoothbore gun.

ARMAMENT

22. Handle for Gun Quoin Ratchets (27 May 1862) (scale = 1:8)

Note: Numbers refer to key to Carriage and Slide drawings on pages 108-9
1 for 8in gun No 144
1 for 7in gun No 145

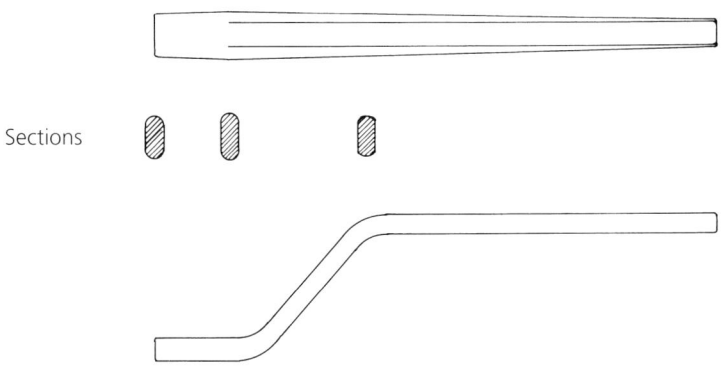

Sections

Pivot Guard Plates for Traversing Gun Carriages (scale = 1:4)

Note: Numbers refer to key to Carriage and Slide drawings on pages 108-9
Order 81   1 for 7in gun No 145 'Stock' May 1862
           1 for 8in gun No 144 'Stock' May 1862

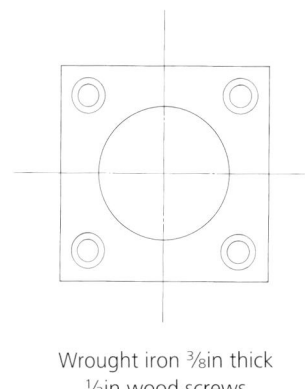

Wrought iron ⅜in thick
½in wood screws

37. Brass Pivots for Traversing Gun Carriages (scale = 1:8)

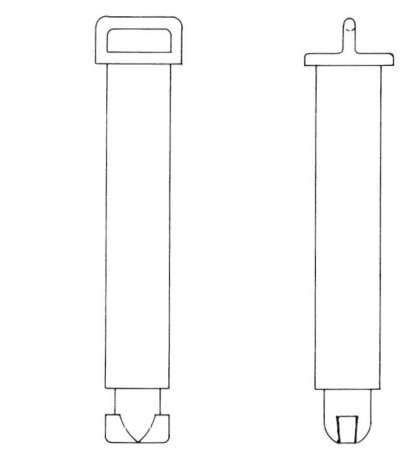

4 for Gun 145

Faces for Tangent Sight 7in Gun No 145 (reconstruction) (scale = 1:3)

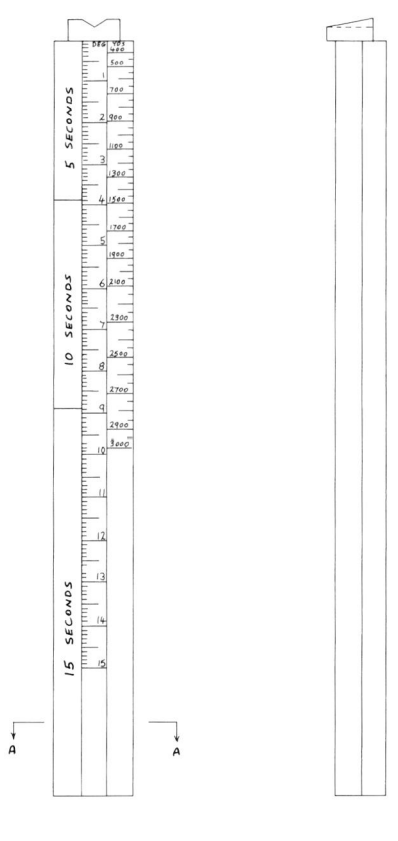

Section A-A

Fore Sight Guns 144 and 145 (re-drawn from the one recovered with No 145) (scale = 1:2)

After Sight 7in Gun (reconstruction) (scale = 1:3)

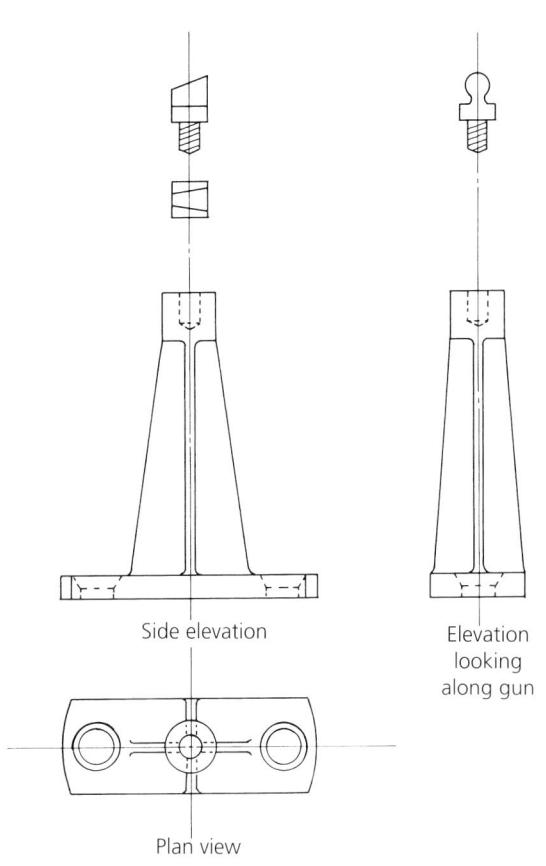

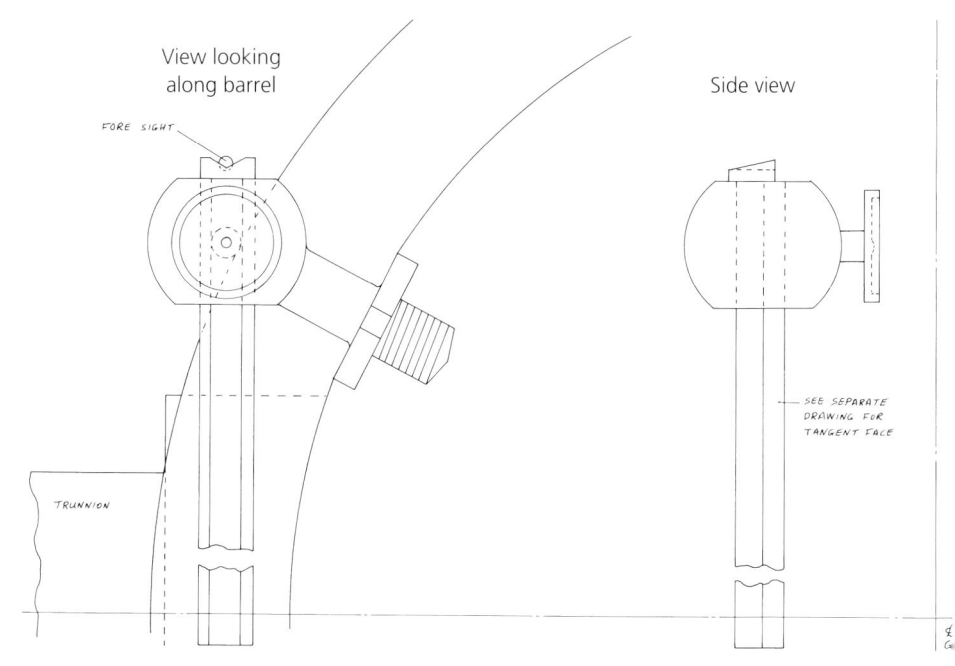

Lock for 7in Gun No 145 (reconstruction) (scale = 1:3)

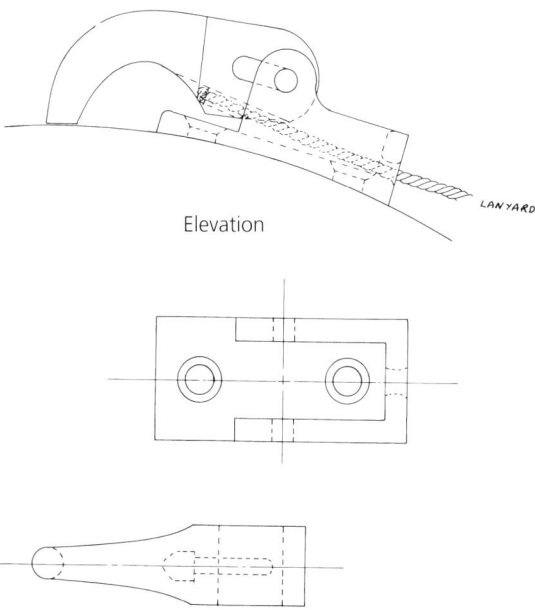

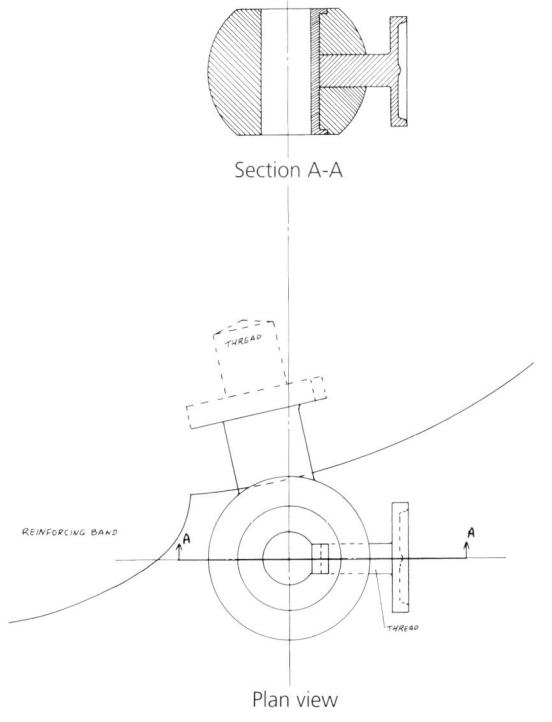

ARMAMENT

6ins lower, and secondly that there is a metal plate on both the front and rear sides of the compressor beam which are through-bolted.

There is very little difference between the two drawings of the slides for this gun as the position of the sweeps on the deck define the layout of those on the underside of the slide, and therefore the position of the transoms.

The brackets of the carriage are made of two pieces of wood, which are bolted together, several of the bolts having other uses such as the capsquare bolts. There appears to be no existing drawing showing the wrought iron work for this carriage so it has been reconstructed using the drawing of the carriage and that for the 8in gun.

The arrangement of the rear wheels appears to be straightforward in operation. A pulley block is attached to the lower end of the rope lever, with another pulley block attached to a loop at the front of the slide. As the rope lever (7) rotates, the rear lever (10) is turned, which in turn pushes the rear lever slide (9) down forcing the rear roller (8) into contact with the slide. The rear of the carriage is thus raised slightly which ensures that the front rollers (19) are in contact with the slide, enabling the carriage to move forward easily and be run out. The rollers run on a metal strip screwed on top of the slide, and there is a corresponding metal piece on the underside of the transoms (5 & 6). The purpose of the compressor (13) is to prevent the recoil during firing the gun. The compressor is tightened down before firing, and slackened off to allow the gun to be run out after loading. The extent of travel during recoil is limited by the breeching rope which is attached to the front of the slide (35) – see sketch of ropes.

The quoin (20) and elevating mechanism for this gun is unlike anything I have seen before and its reconstruction presented many problems, not least because only a small part of the original drawing remained. The actual quoin is made of wood with a channel in the top, sloping, surface. This is to take the cascable at high elevations so that the weight and recoil of the gun are taken on the breech, not the cascable. The ratchet mechanism (21) must be attached to the extreme end of the carriage. This mechanism rotates a bar which is cut with a continuous thread along it, which runs through what is effectively a captive nut in the base of the quoin. As the ratchet mechanism rotates the bar the quoin is moved either towards or away from the mechanism, thereby changing the angle of elevation of the barrel. The quoin is held in position by a pawl which engages in a rack which is alongside. There is one pawl on each side of the quoin, and each pawl is pivoted about the rear end. There is a small lug about half way along the length of the pawl. This engages with a cutout on the end of a lever which has a handle at the other end and a pivot point towards the middle. Pressing down on the handle will raise the pawl which will enable the quoin to be moved.

Shell for 7in Gun (reconstruction) (scale = 1:8)
Weight of shell 55.75lbs
Powder charge 2.44lbs

Shot for 7in Gun No 145 (reconstruction) (scale = 1:8)

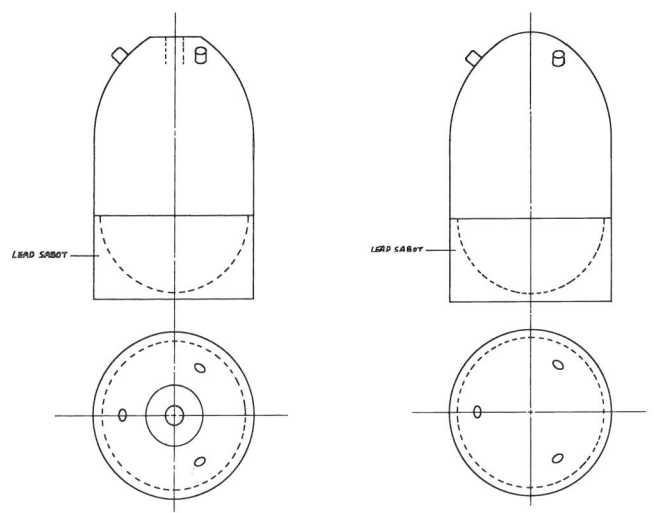

The shell that lodged in the stern frame of the *Kearsarge* during the battle off Cherbourg is preserved in the museum at the Washington Navy Yard. The photograph below shows the shell on display, and the details on the attached plaque are:

Weight of shell	55.75lbs
Powder charge for shell	2.44lbs
Diameter of shell	6.96ins

The shell that lodged in the stern frame of the *Kearsarge* in the Washington Navy Yard. The wooden stern frame is protected by a metal mesh covering, and the photograph is taken through the top.

7in Rifled Gun – Ropes (not to scale)

For general guidance see photograph of Semmes standing by the 8in gun.

Breeching Rope
8in circumference of hemp, three-stranded rope, shroud laid.
Length sufficient to allow travel to end of slide, plus through thimble and seized on itself.

Side Tackles
(from rope levers on carriage to eyebolt on slide)
3in circumference, of a similar quality to the breeching rope.
Two double blocks, each fitted with a hook.
Length of block = 9in.

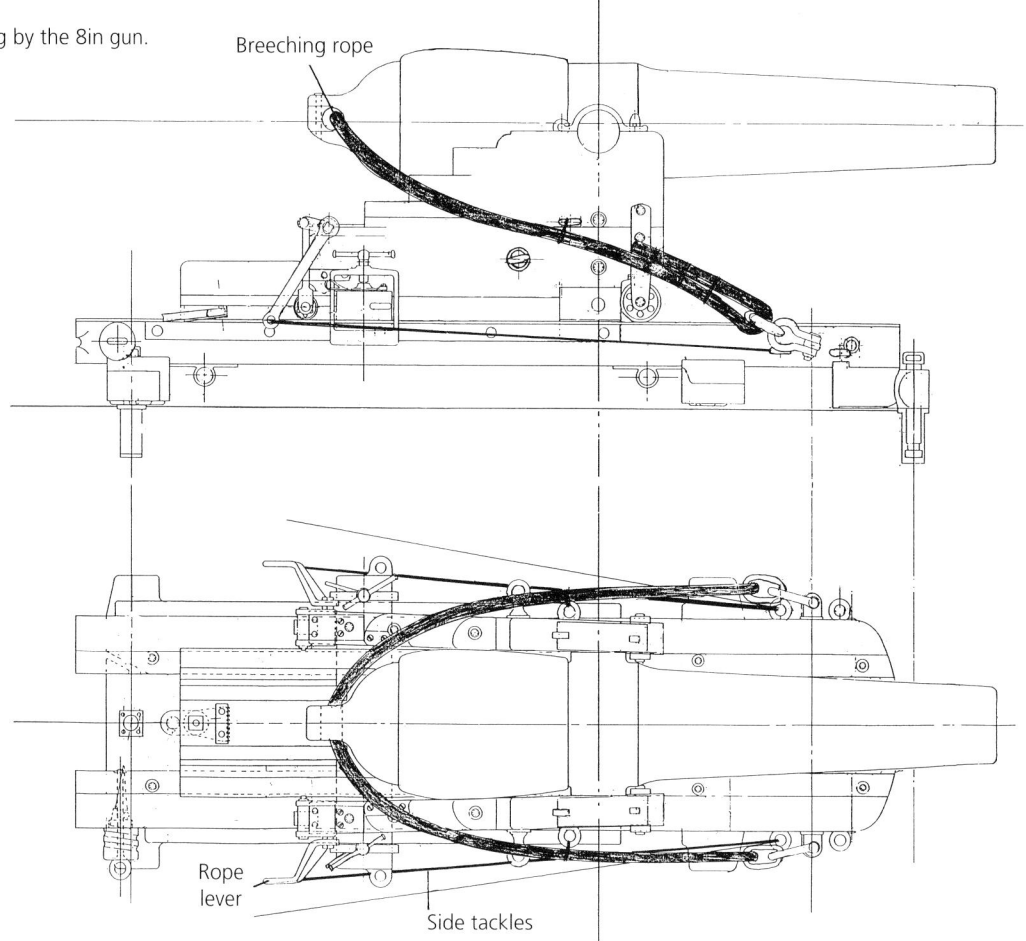

Full-size replica of the *Alabama*'s 7in Blakely gun and carriage built by the CSS *Alabama* Association (USA), and displayed at the City Museum, Mobile, Alabama. The gun is based on the one recovered from the wreck, and the carriage and slide from the drawings that appear in this book.
(Courtesy Phillip Nassar, CSS *Alabama* Association (USA))

ARMAMENT

Shell Lifter for Gun No 145 (reconstruction) (scale = 1:8)

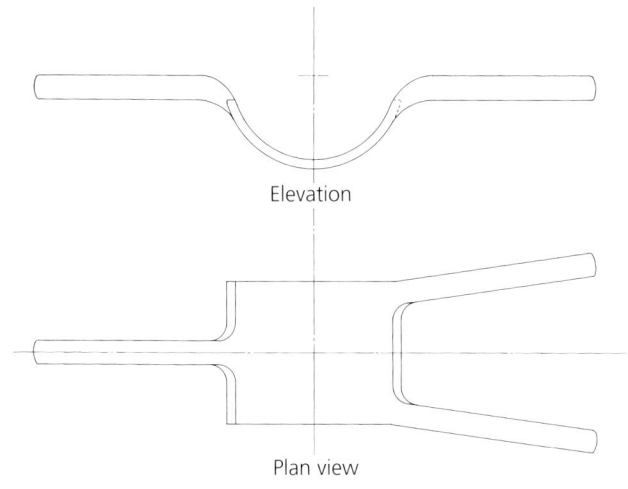

Shell Extractor for Gun No 145 (reconstruction) (scale = 1:8)

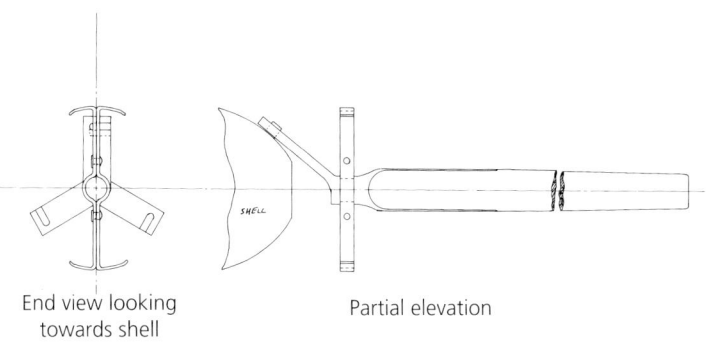

Rammer for Gun No 145 (reconstruction) (scale = 1:8)

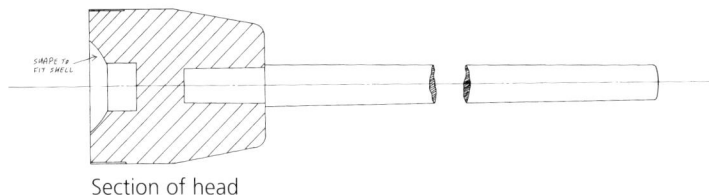

Gimlet/Priming Wire for Gun No 145 (reconstruction) (scale = 1:8)

1 pointed to puncture cartridge bags
1 flat ended to clear vent of burnt particles

Sponge and Worm for Gun No 145 (reconstruction) (scale = 1:8)

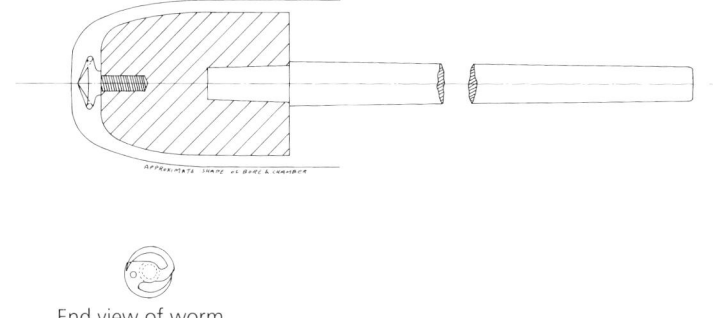

Handspike (6 off) for Gun No 145 (reconstruction) (scale = 1:8)

The end of the shell on display must have been filled in because it is not possible to fit the fuse. The drawing is based on this shell and the picture of the one recovered when the barrel was raised from the wreck.

Shot for this gun can be seen in Photograph 4 (page 51). The equipment and implements necessary for the gun are drawn, mainly reconstructions based on similar guns. The use of these is illustrated elsewhere by the firing of the gun (pages 134-7).

The weight of the gun is not known but Blakely made the following response to a letter in the *Times* newspaper on 29 June 1864: 'J G G, in his very interesting letter, published in The Times of to-day, makes a slight mistake, which I shall feel greatly obliged if you will correct. He imagines the Blakely rifle on board the *Alabama* weighed 16,000lb, the same as the 11-inch Dahlgren guns on board the *Kearsarge*. In reality the one Blakely rifle weighed less than half the two Dahlgren smoothbores pitted against it, making the odds four to one at close quarters. At long range the advantage would have been with the one rifled gun, for it could make tolerable practice at a distance a full mile further than the smooth bores. The *Alabama* had not one steel shot or shell on board. Any gun she had, even the little 32-pounders, could have fired a steel shot through the *Kearsarge*'s armour; no gun on earth could throw thin iron shell through it.'

8in GUN

8in Smoothbore Gun (4 April 1862) (scale = 1:24)

As finished – revised cascable and turned down at the muzzle

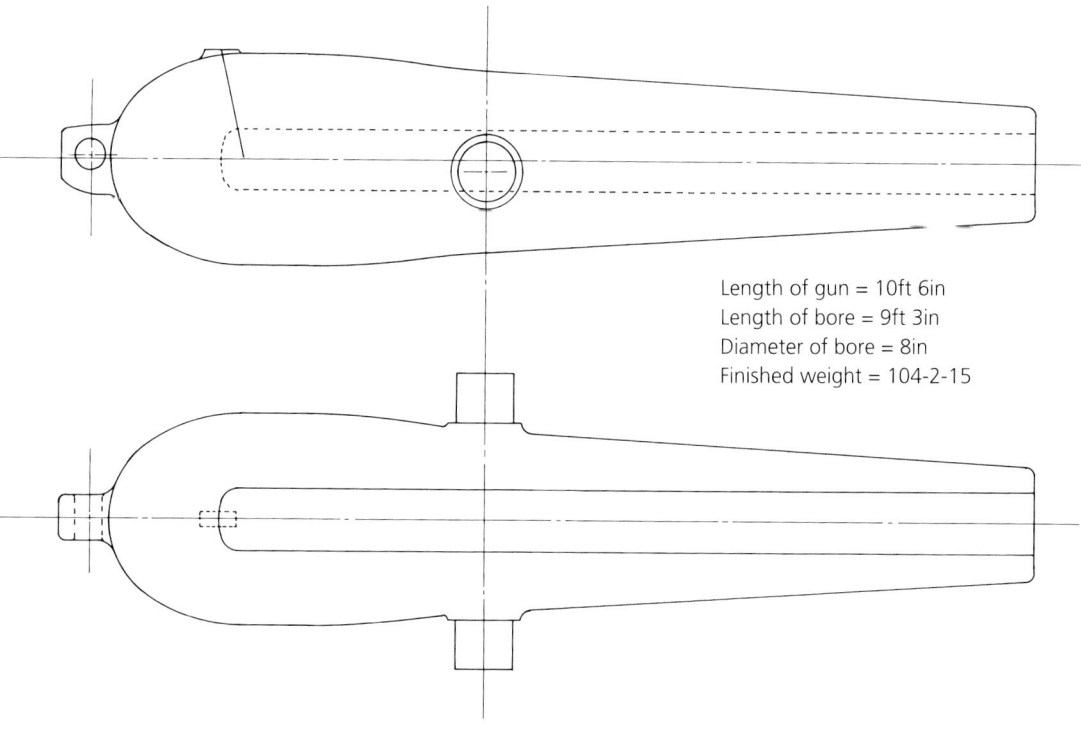

Length of gun = 10ft 6in
Length of bore = 9ft 3in
Diameter of bore = 8in
Finished weight = 104-2-15

8in Smoothbore Gun, No 144 'Stock' (4 April 1862) (scale = 1:24)

Note: July 1862. This gun as drawn was 2¼cwt more at muzzle than at breech. The gun was finally turned down to 15in at the muzzle, shown in dotted lines. Finished weight 104-2-15.

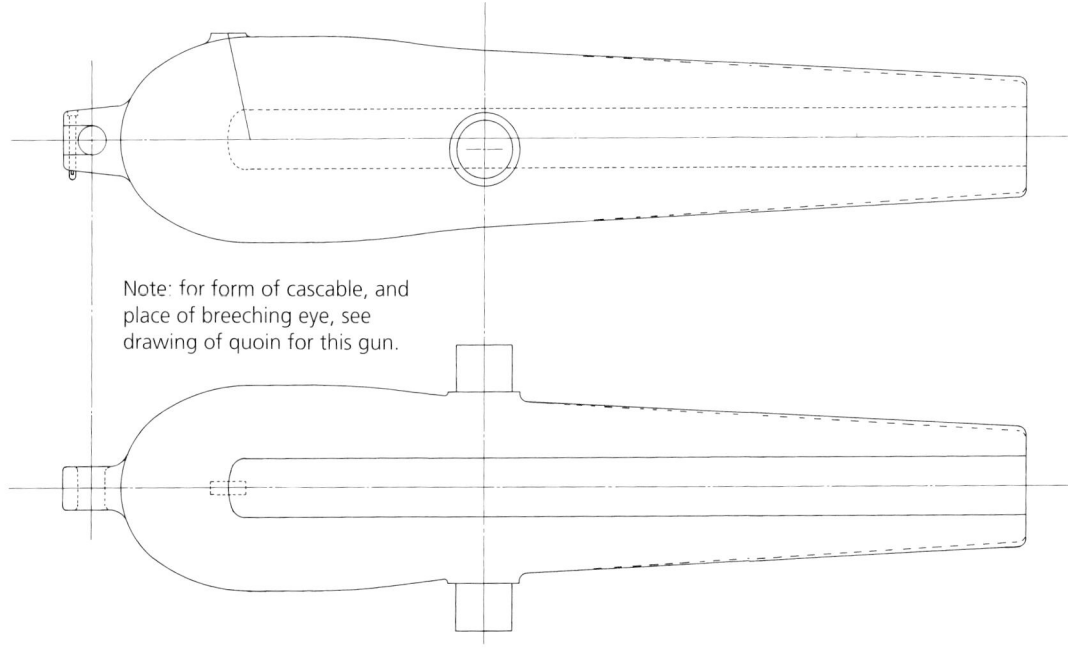

Note: for form of cascable, and place of breeching eye, see drawing of quoin for this gun.

This implies that the weight of the gun was less than 8000lbs (about 71 cwt), however Bulloch describes it as 84 cwt (quote at the start of this chapter).

The maximum range of this rifled gun was about 4 miles. This is greater than the range marked on the tangent sight but would be achieved by firing at the correct point during rolling.

<u>8in smoothbore – Fawcett Preston Number 144</u>

According to the drawing there were problems with this gun as initially cast because it was too heavy at the muzzle. All guns are heavier at the breech than at the muzzle, the difference being called the 'preponderance'. With this gun the muzzle had to be turned down to achieve a satisfactory preponderance. The shape of the cascable was also changed from that originally drawn. Two drawings show the gun in its initial and final forms. The final weight of the gun was 104 cwt 2 quarters 15 pounds (11,719lbs). Bulloch describes the gun as 108 or 112 cwt, which raises questions about his descriptions of the other guns (even if he takes a hundredweight as 100lbs not 112lbs).

This carriage also had two forms, the second of which will have influenced the shape of the cascable. The first carriage (dated 9 May 1862) is fairly low in comparison with the later but the principle difference is that it has a fairly standard type of quoin. The second carriage is higher than the first and has been extended to the rear so that a quoin similar to the Blakely can be fitted. The shape of the new quoin meant that the cascable had to be raised and its lower face shaped to fit in the channel of the quoin at large angles of elevation. I have seen no information at all on the second quoin for this gun, although it must have been similar to that for the Blakely. This gun used an identical ratchet mechanism (21) to the Blakely, as well as the extension to the rear of the carriage.

ARMAMENT

Carriage and Slide for 8in Gun No 144
(9 May 1862) (scale =1:24)

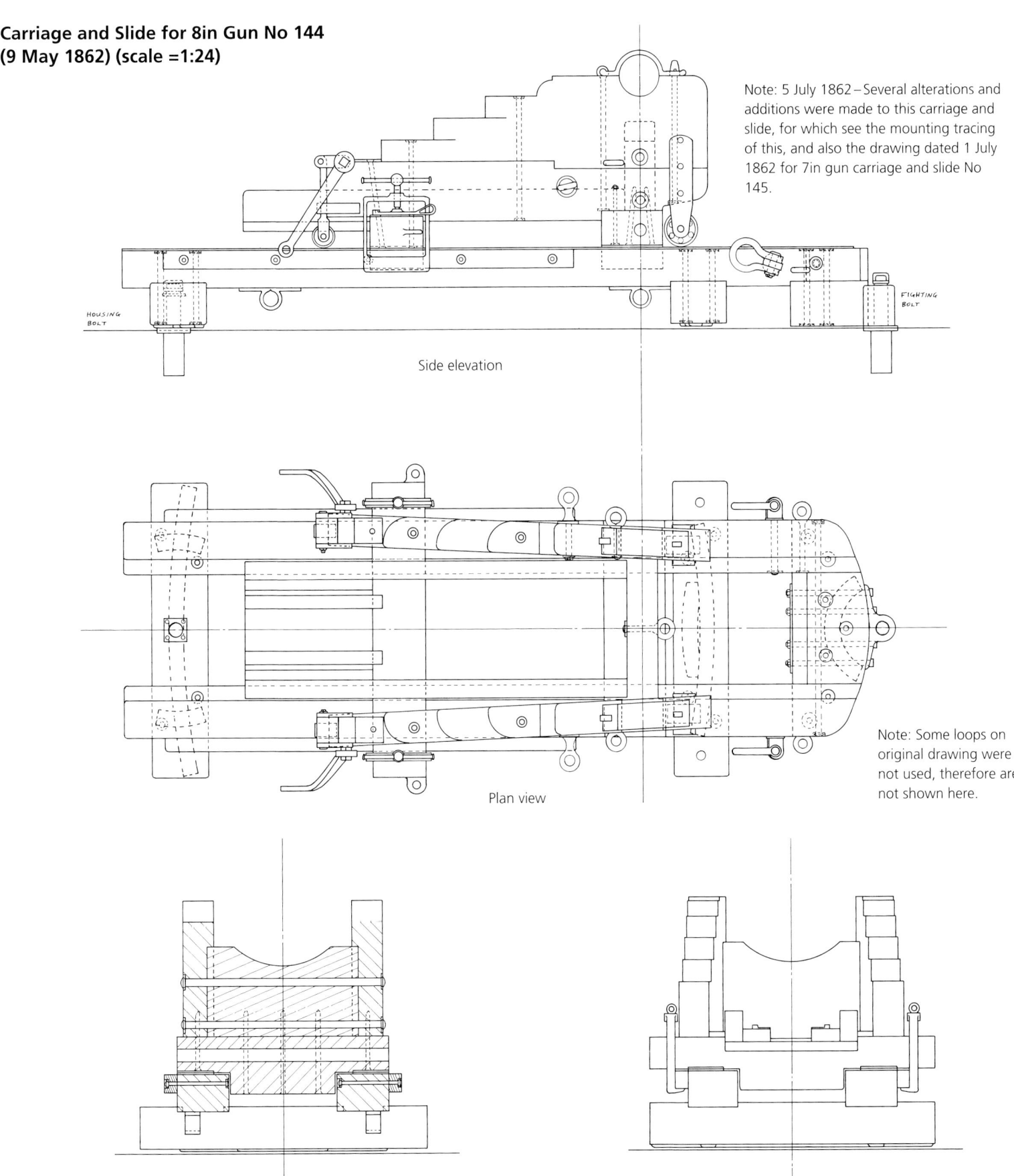

Note: 5 July 1862 – Several alterations and additions were made to this carriage and slide, for which see the mounting tracing of this, and also the drawing dated 1 July 1862 for 7in gun carriage and slide No 145.

Side elevation

Note: Some loops on original drawing were not used, therefore are not shown here.

Plan view

Section at trunnions

View looking forward

Original Carriage of 8in Gun No 144, date 9 May 1862 (scale =1:24)

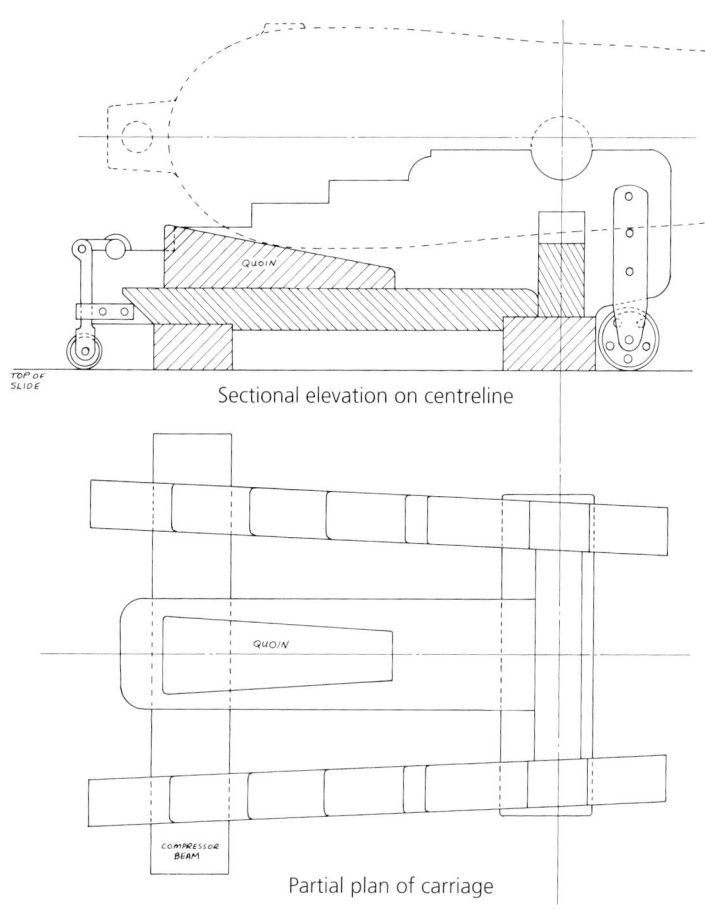

Wrought Iron Work of 8in Gun No 144, original dated 29 April 1862 (scale = 1:12)

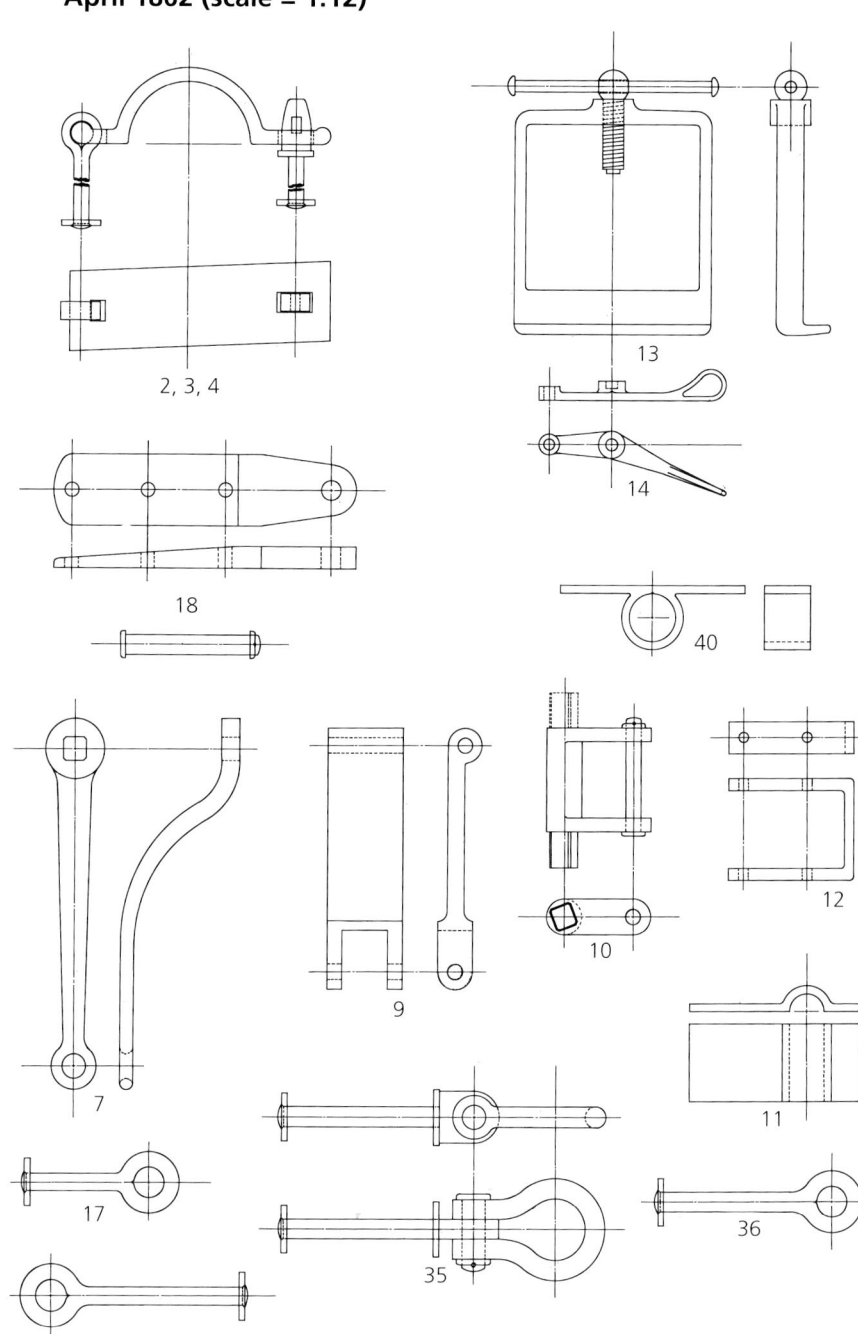

Note: Numbers refer to key to Carriage and Slide drawings on page 108.

2, 3, 4	Capsquare with bolts (1 and 1 to opposite hand)	10	Rear lever (1 as drawn, 1 to dotted line)
13	Compressor frame (2 off)	12	Rear guide (2 off)
14	Compressor thimble lever (1 and 1 to opposite hand)	17	Transom loop (1 off) Rear loop (1 off, position unknown so not shown)
18	Front wheel brackets (2 off) Front wheel pins (2 off)	35	Breeching shackle (2 off)
40	Axle eyes (4 off)	11	Lever cap (2 off)
7	Rope lever (2 off)	36	Slide front loop (2 off)
9	Rear lever slide (2 off – pins as for rear lever but 1¾in shorter)		

Wrought Iron Work for 8in Gun No 144. Items not used (29 April 1862) (scale = 1:12)

No 4 Slide loops

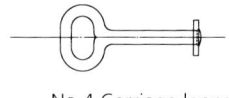

No 4 Carriage loops

ARMAMENT

Therefore I think it reasonable to assume that they worked in exactly the same way, and the drawing of the quoin is based on this.

The slide was the same as that for the Blakely except that it was wider because the gun and hence the carriage was wider. The transoms and the sweeps on the underside were the same as the Blakely and so either gun could be used on any one of the four sets of sweeps.

The drawing for the wrought iron work survive for this gun and have been redrawn. The original drawing is dated 29 April 1862 and therefore shows the items that were to go on the original carriage. Some items are marked 'not used' because they were not required for the second, later, carriage. These items are also redrawn but just consist of loops for the carriage and slide, with four of each being required. There was also one loop drawn which does not appear on the finished carriage and slide, so the position of it is not known.

The drawings for the after sight and the faces for the tangent sight survive and are reproduced. There is no drawing for the fore sight, but from the photograph (No. 1) it appears to be the same as the one on the Blakely.

According to the drawing the following are the weights of the shot and shell for this gun:

Estimated weight of shell empty, without mountings	41lbs
Actual weight of shell empty, without mountings	40lbs
Actual weight of this shot	63¾lbs

Quoin for 8in Gun No 144 (reconstruction) (scale = 1:12)

Note: Quoin fittings same as for 7in No 145. Positions different as marked. Top surface of quoin different because of radius of gun and trough for cascable. Means of working identical to 7in and only differences from 7in drawn.

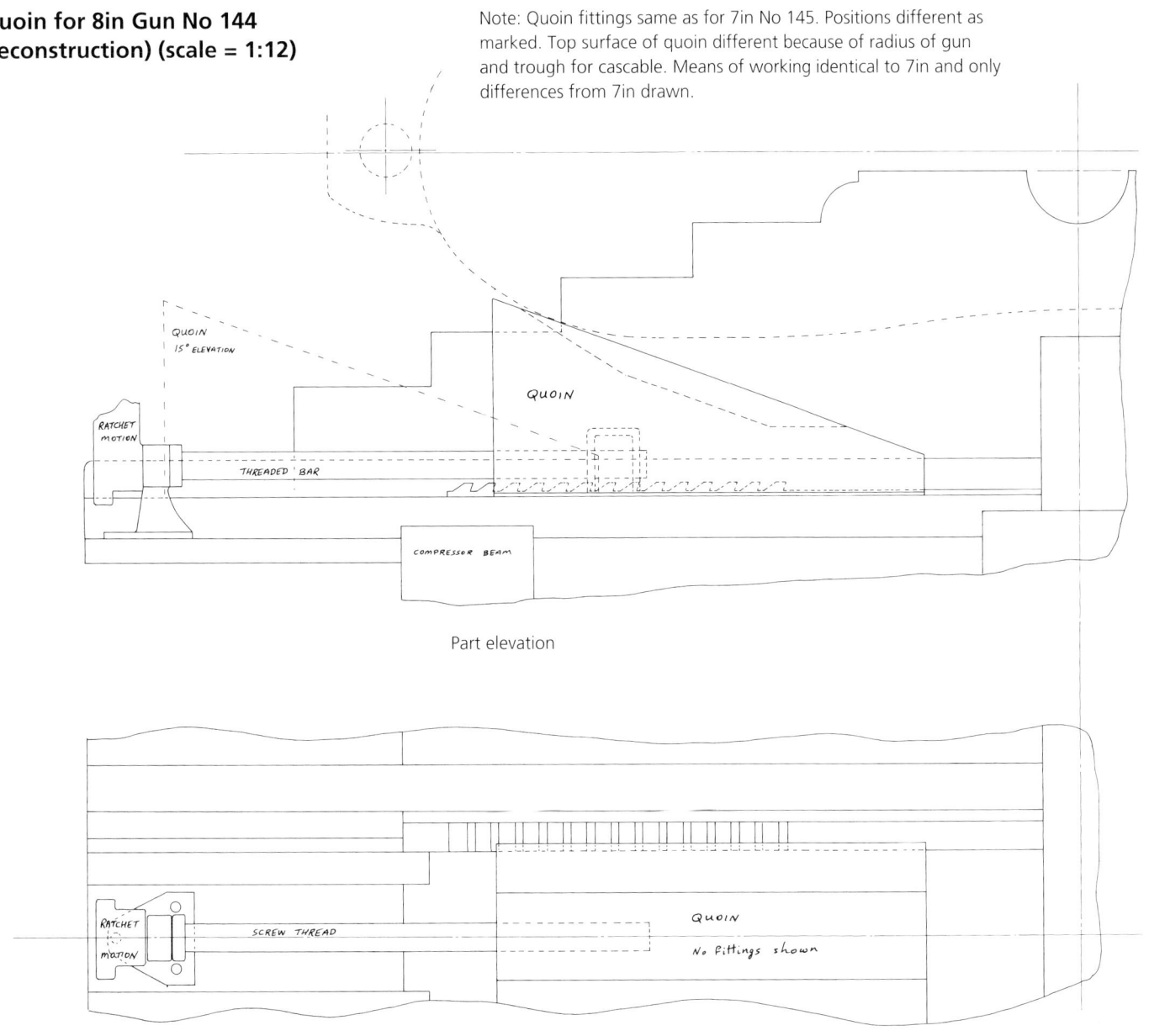

Part elevation

Part plan

Tangent Sight Face for 8in Gun No 144 'Stock' (scale = 1:4)

Note: Length of point blank base line as per drawing of arrangement of the sights 42.75in

After Sight for 8in Gun No 144 (reconstruction) (scale = 1:3)

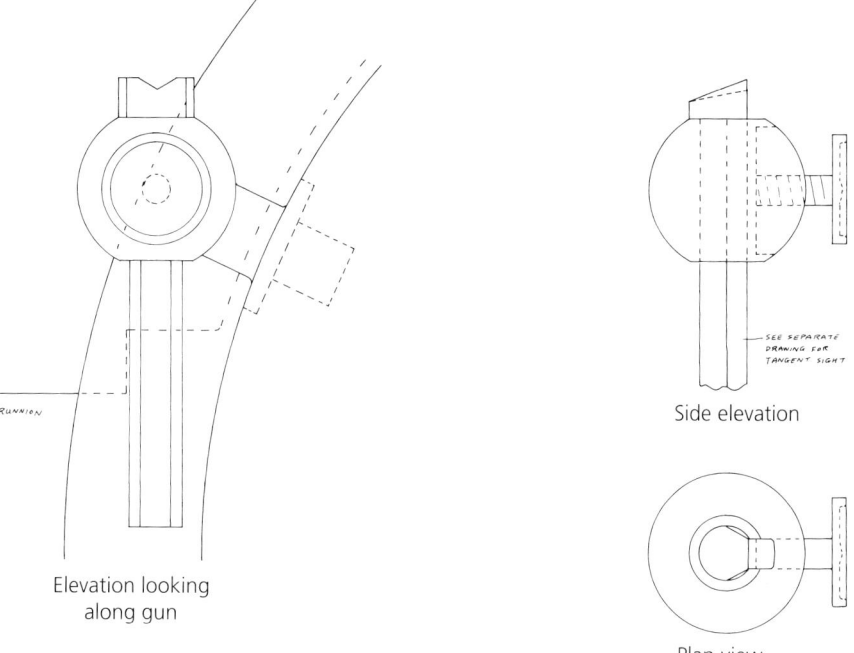

Shell for 8in Gun No 144 (April 1862) (scale = 1:4)

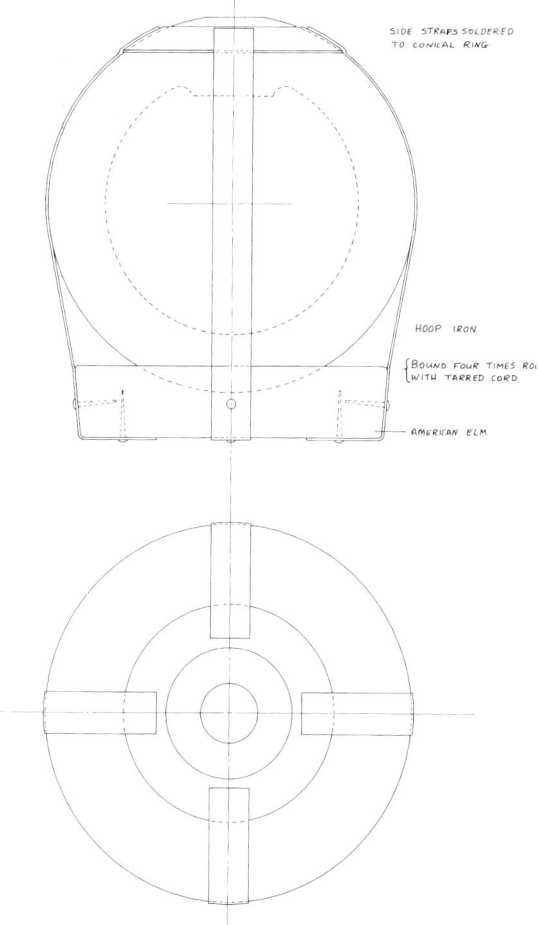

The number of shells ordered 'for 68 pr gun No. 144' varied. The first figure has been so well crossed out that it cannot be read, but it has three numbers, that is to say it would appear to be 100 or greater. This unknown number was then replaced by 80, which number was in turn replaced by 70. It would appear therefore that the ship carried 70 shells of this type.

32pdrs

Fawcett Preston guns – four, Numbers 153 to 156

The original order was for two of these guns, but it was subsequently increased to four. The drawing is dated 7 May 1862 but there is no date for the increase in numbers ordered. There looks to be a close resemblance between these guns and the 8in smoothbore, and they are unlike the Blakely in both shape and construction.

A section of the original carriage is shown to illustrate the condition of some of the plans now in the Fawcett Preston Archive. Usually enough remains for the drawing to be reconstructed with some confidence. However, the plans for the wrought iron work for these guns do illustrate the difficulties. On the original drawings next to the title of the piece is the number required for each carriage (not the total number required), for example there are four axle tree bands for each carriage at one per truck. There is one item which appears to be from this gun but has no name to say what it is. The dimensions written on it are illegible but scaling off the drawing gives the following dimension – 6in diameter – and the

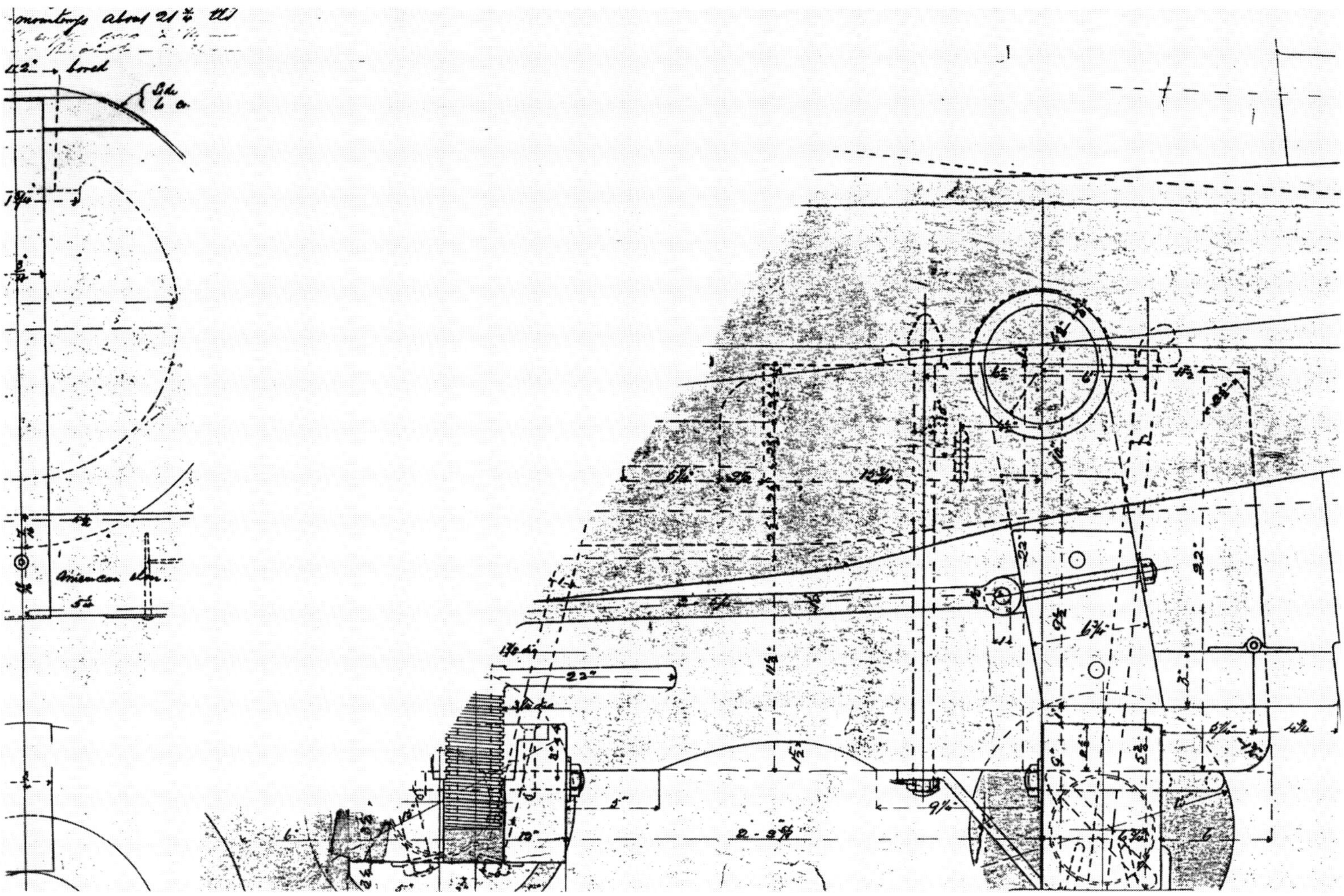

ARMAMENT

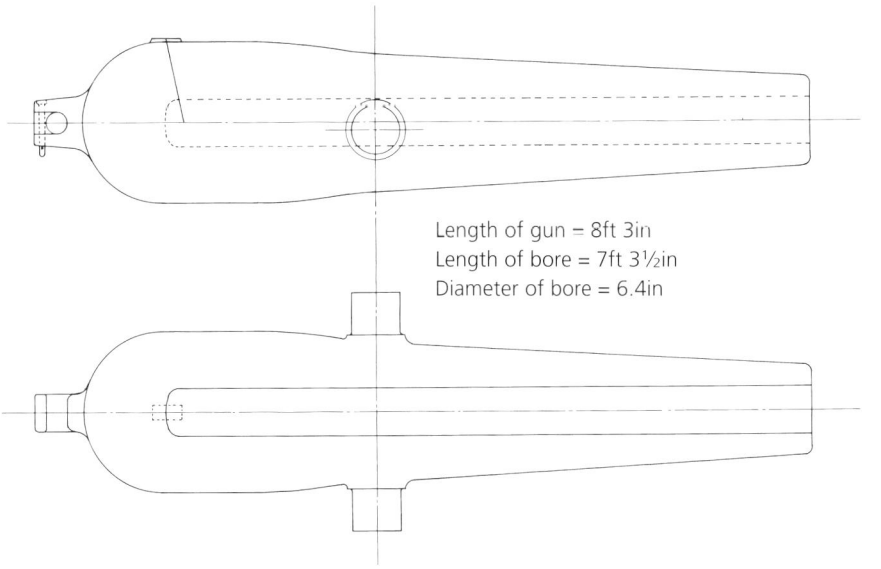

32pdr Guns Nos 153-156 Order 107 'Stock' (7 May 1862) (scale = 1:24)

Length of gun = 8ft 3in
Length of bore = 7ft 3½in
Diameter of bore = 6.4in

32PDR GUNS

Above: Part of the Fawcett Preston drawing of the 32pdrs Numbers 153-156. Also shown is part of the drawing for a 32pdr shell for the guns. This illustrates how badly torn some of these drawings are, and a lot of reconstruction is sometimes required.

fact that there are four per carriage implies they are for the axles or trucks, but nothing is shown on the main drawing of the carriage that looks like them.

The drawings showing the fore and aft sights and the faces for the tangent sights survive for these guns, the only complete set for any of the *Alabama*'s guns.

The shell for these guns is shown and the weights given are:

Weight of empty shell without mountings	21¾lbs
Actual weight of this shell, empty, was	21¼lbs
Weight of this shot	32¾lbs

The total number ordered was 160, or 40 per gun, the drawing does not state whether this is shot or shell. However it is reasonable to assume that it is 160 each of shot and shell – see page 132.

A badly-torn drawing (which has also been cut into three parts) survives for some of the implements for these guns, they are reproduced but in a few cases it is not clear what they are. The drawing title is 'Rammers, sponges etc for (missing) No. 153 to 156'. The implements shown are as follows, with the total number for the four guns:

Sponge (torn)	5
Priming wire	6
Gimlet	6
Handspike (torn)	16
Scoop	1
Scraper	1
Worm	4
?Rammer (torn)	5

There is so little of the head of the implement at the bottom of the list that it is not clear what it is. As there is so little remaining it has not been reconstructed, but has been reproduced as it is. It may be a rammer because they are listed in the drawing title, and none are shown on the drawing. However, it is possible that part of the drawing may be lost, including the rammer. One of the implements is assumed to be a scraper, which when closed would have a diameter slightly less than the bore of the guns.

Other guns – two

There are no plans available for these two guns and the best information appears to be what is shown in the two photographs (3 and

32pdr Gun Carriage. 4 for Guns 153-156 Order No 107 'Stock' (scale = 1:24)

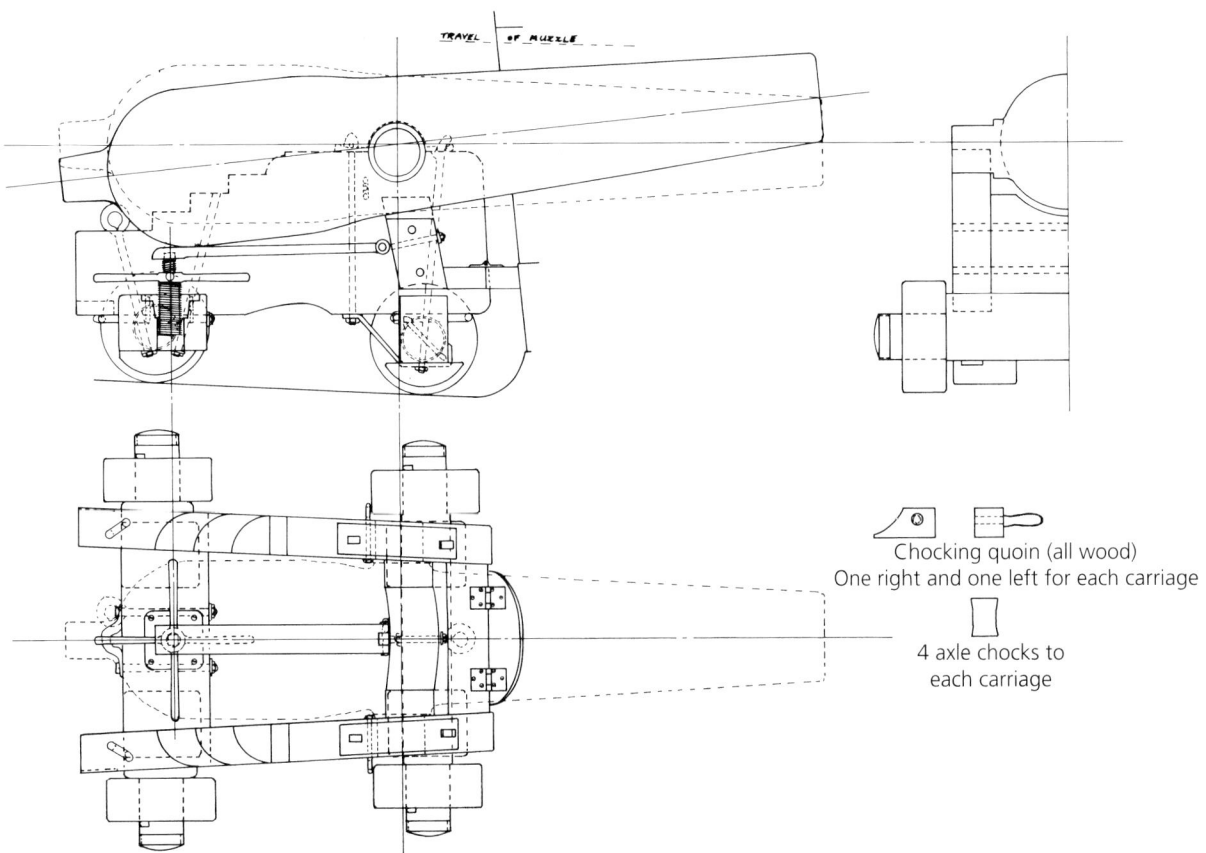

Chocking quoin (all wood)
One right and one left for each carriage

4 axle chocks to each carriage

ARMAMENT

32pdr Gun Carriage (scale = 1:24)

Elevation and part plan

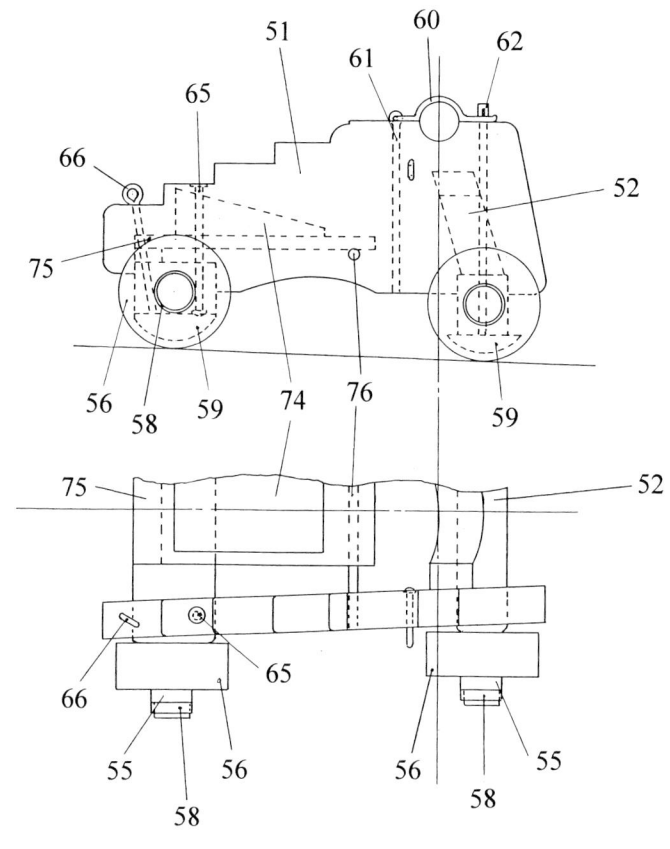
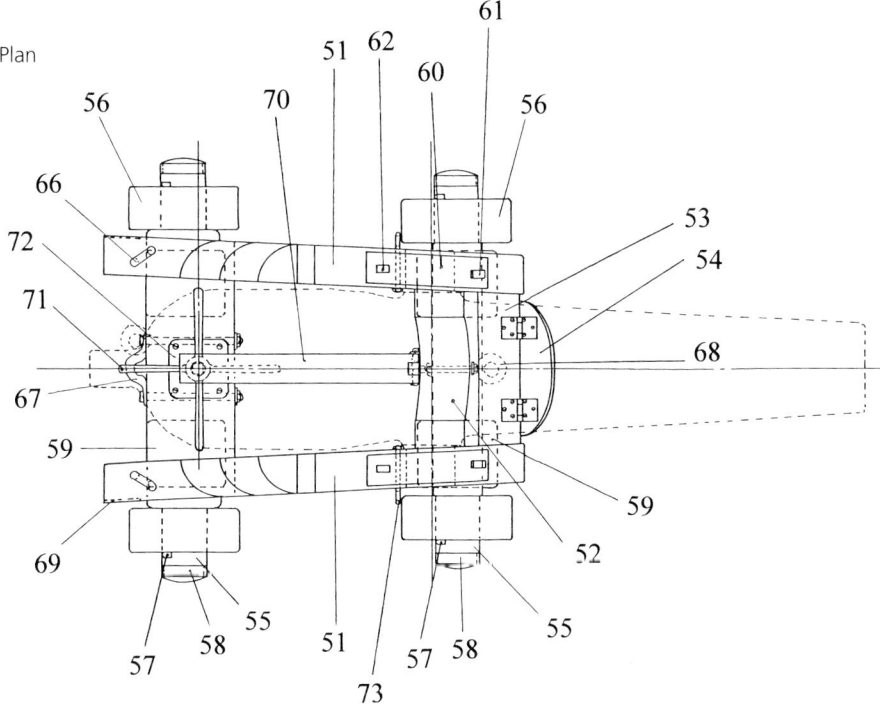
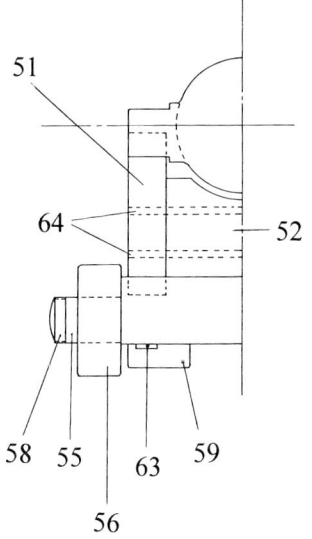

Key

- 51 Bracket
- 52 Transom
- 53 Breast piece – inner
- 54 Breast piece – outer
- 55 Axle tree
- 56 Truck
- 57 Linch pin
- 58 Axle tree band
- 59 Dumb truck
- 60 Capsquare
- 61 Capsquare bolt
- 62 Capsquare bolt with key
- 63 Axle stay
- 64 Transom bolt
- 65 Rear axle tree bolt
- 66 Side tackle eye bolt
- 67 Train tackle loop
- 68 Transporting eye bolt
- 69 Chafing piece
- 70 Elevating bar
- 71 Elevating screw
- 72 Nut for elevating screw
- 73 Eye bolt
- 74 Quoin
- 75 Bed and stool
- 76 Bed bolt

Wrought Iron Work for 32pdr Guns Nos 153-156 (19 May 1862) (scale = 1:12)
NB Numbers refer to carriage drawings on page 123

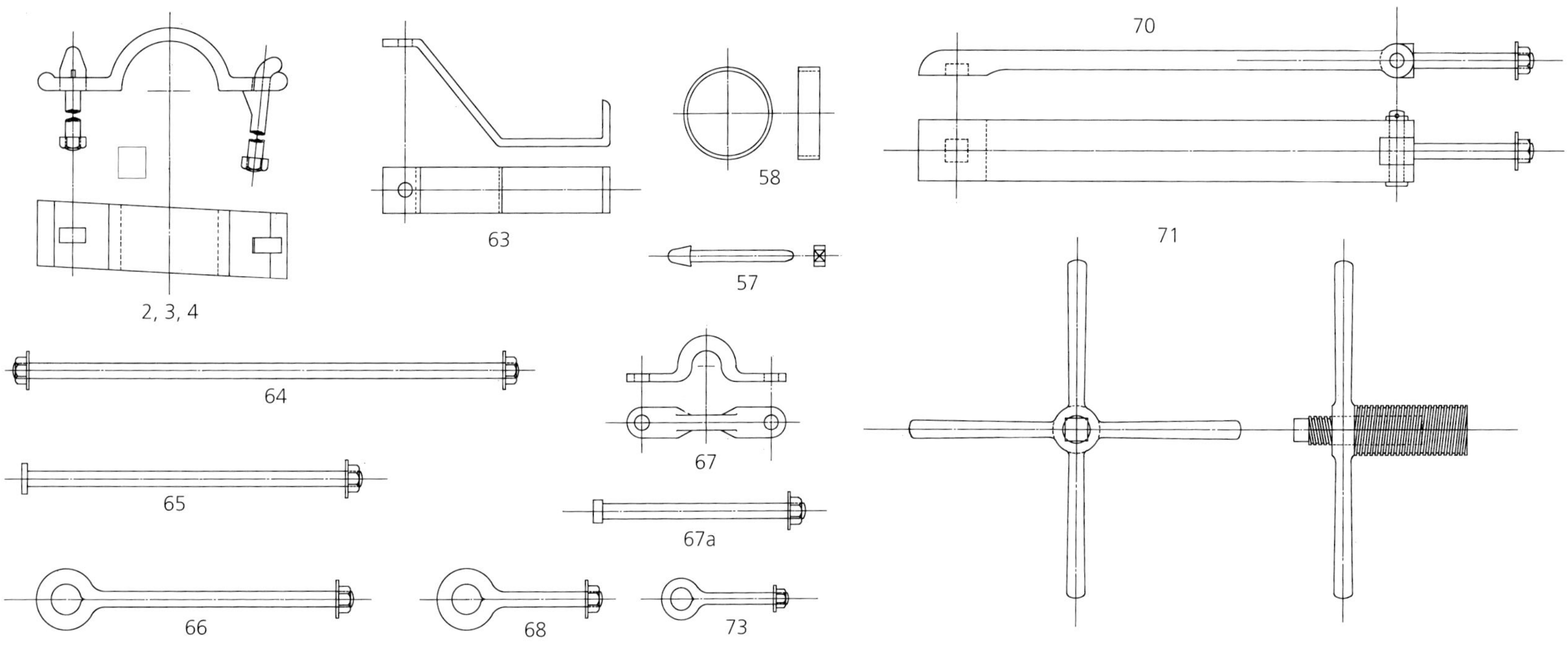

60, 61, 62	Capsquare (1 and 1 to opposite hand – left one drawn)		66	Side tackle eye bolt (2 off)
			68	Eye bolt – transom (1 off)
63	Front axle stay (2 off)		73	Eye bolt – bracket (2 off)
58	Axle tree band (4 off)		70	Elevating bar (1 off)
57	Lynch pin (4 off)		71	Elevating screw (1 off)
64	Transom bolt (2 off)		A	No 4 Part of wheel/truck?
67	Rear loop/train tackle loop (1 off)		69	No 2 Chafing piece – ³⁄₈in thickness
67a	Rear loop bolt (2 off)		72	Nut for elevating screw
65	Rear axle tree bolt (2 off)		72a	View from underneath

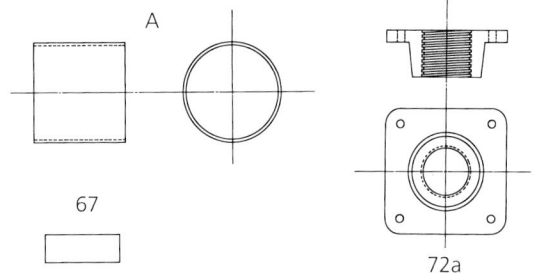

Note: in this elevation the three faces are supposed to be spread out to their full breadth.

Tangent Sight Faces for 32pdr Guns Nos 153-156 Order 107 'Stock' (June 1862) (scale = 1:4)

Note: Length of point blank base line as per drawing of arrangement of sight 37.25in

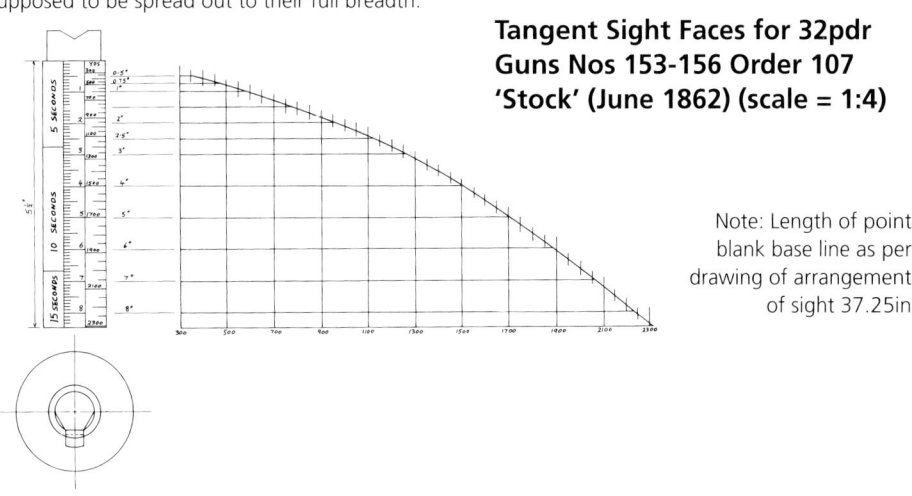

ARMAMENT

After Sight of 32pdr Guns Nos 153-156 (scale = 1:3)

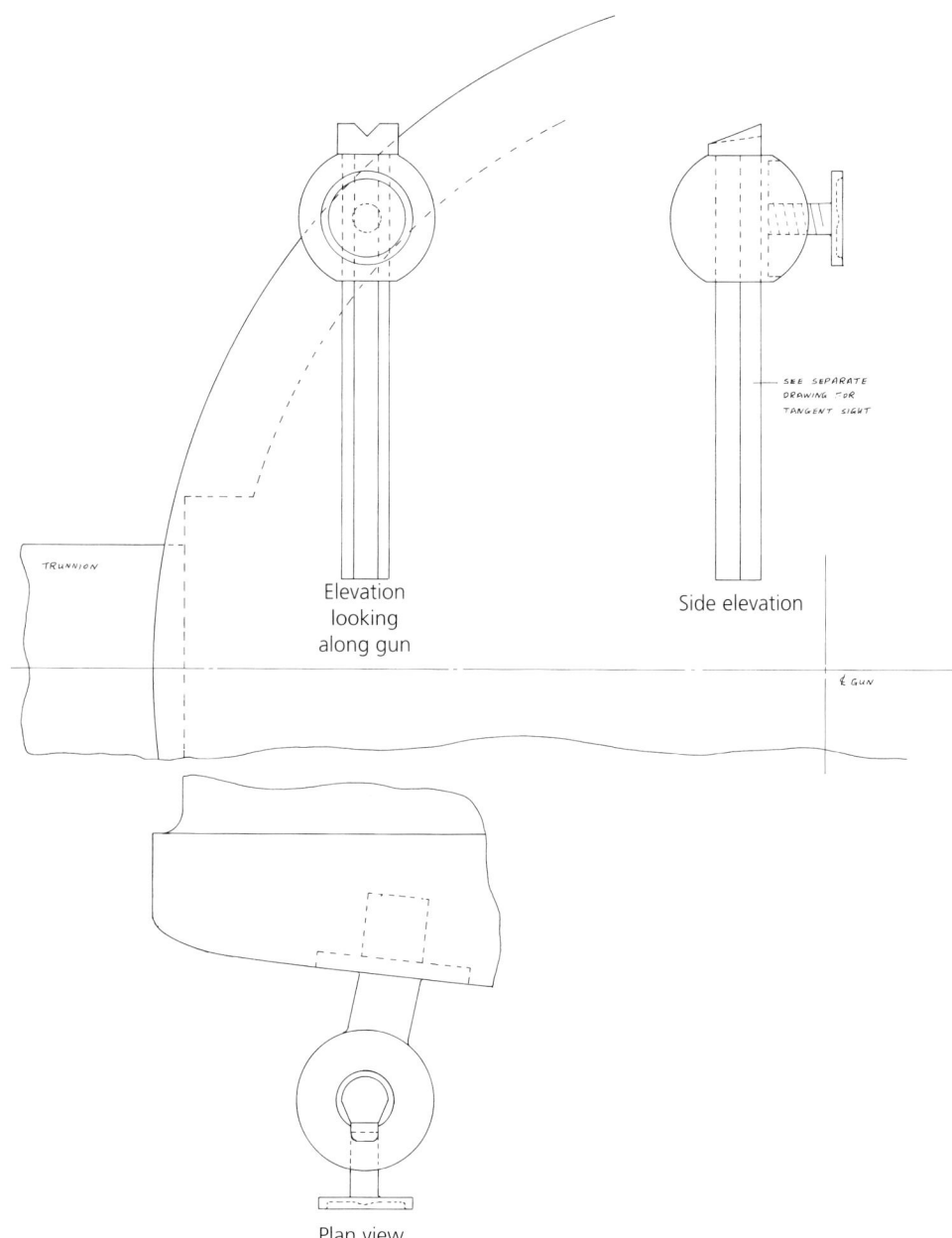

Fore Sight of 32pdr Guns Nos 153-156 (scale = 1:3)

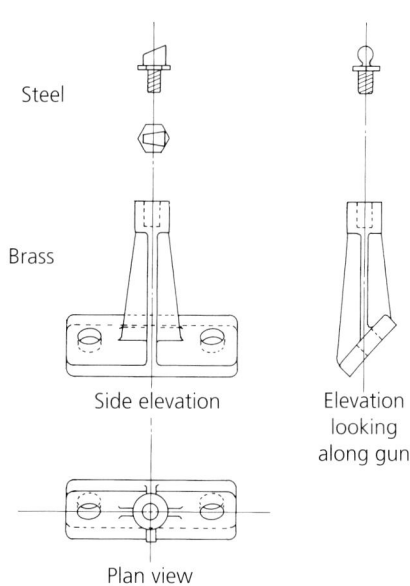

Shell for 32pdr Gun (scale = 1:4)

Weight of empty shell without mountings = c21¾lbs
Actual weight of empty shell = 21¼lbs, and of this shot 32¾lbs

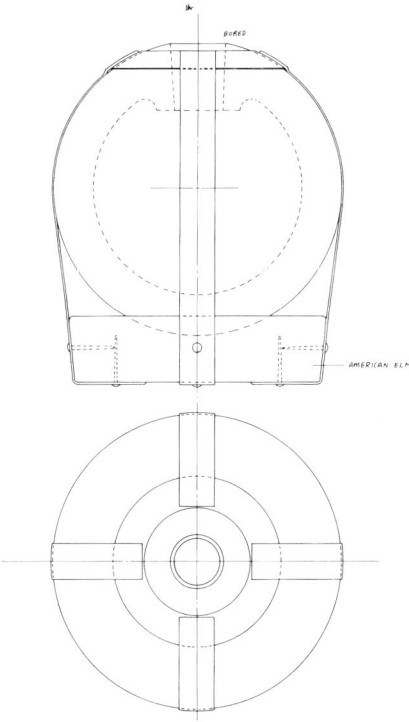

Scraper for Guns Nos 153-156 (scale = 1:8)

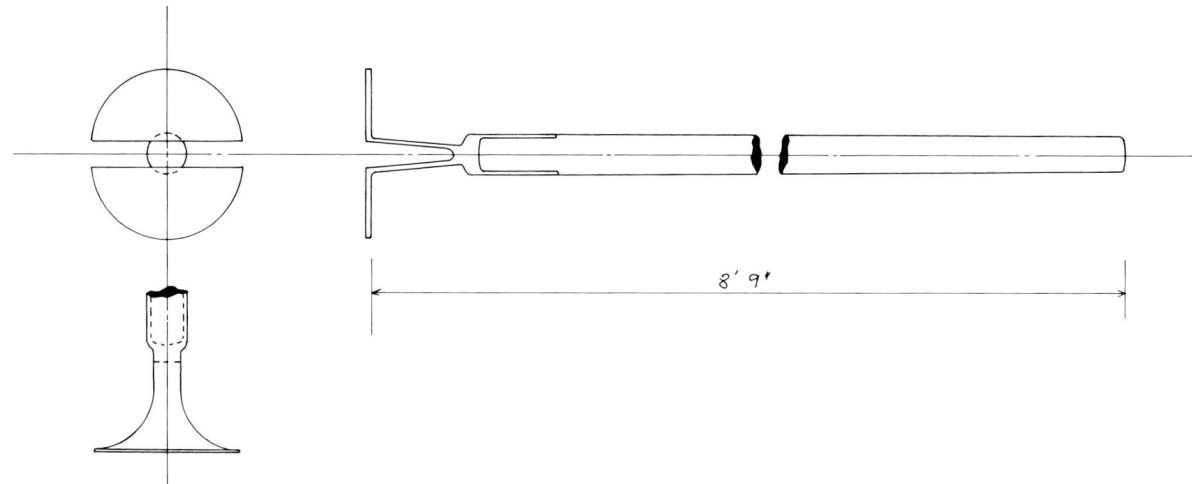

Worm for Guns Nos 153-156 (scale = 1:8)

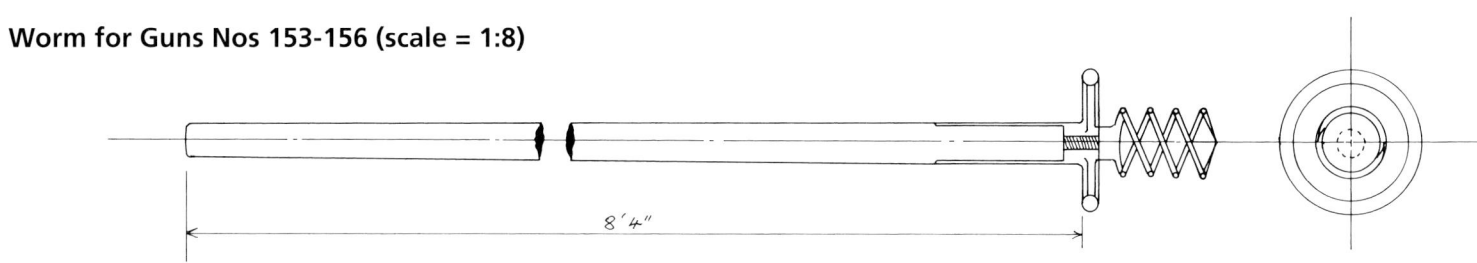

Scoop for Guns Nos 153-156 (scale = 1:8)

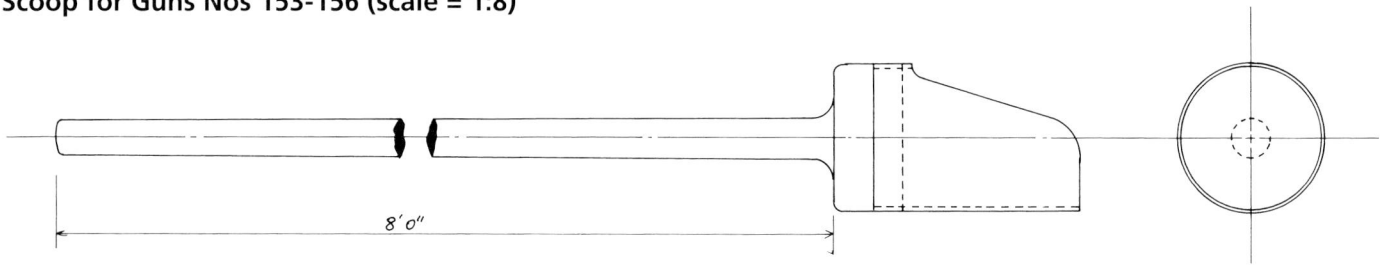

Gimlet and Priming Wire for Guns Nos 153-156 (scale = 1:8)

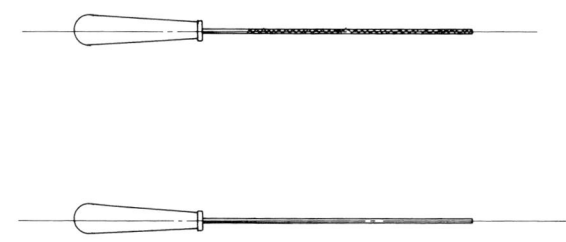

Sponge for Guns Nos 153-156 (scale = 1:8)

8′ 2½″

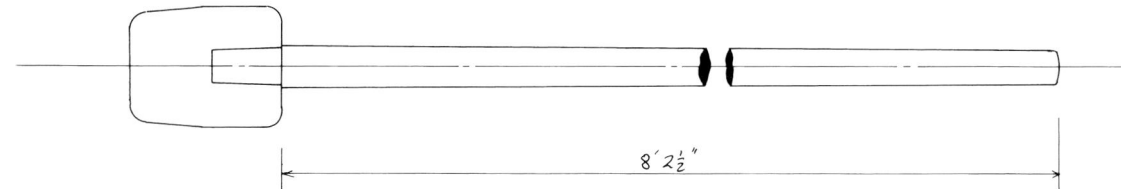

? for Guns Nos 153-156 (scale = 1:8)

Drawing
torn
8′ 1″

Handspike for Guns Nos 153-156 (scale = 1:8)

Square
Round
4′6″

32PDRS (NOT FAWCETT PRESTON)

32pdr Gun (2 off) (reconstruction) (scale 1:24)

Length = 8ft

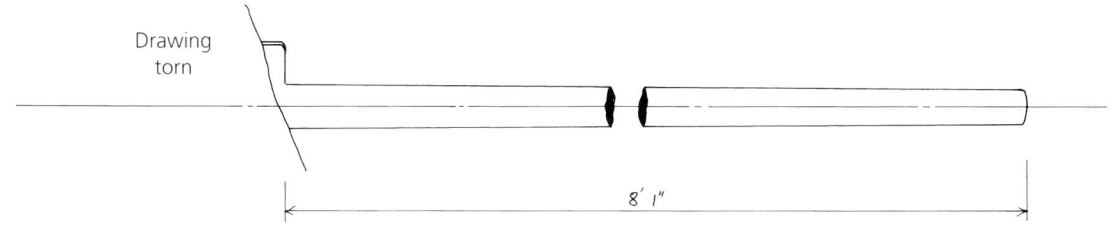

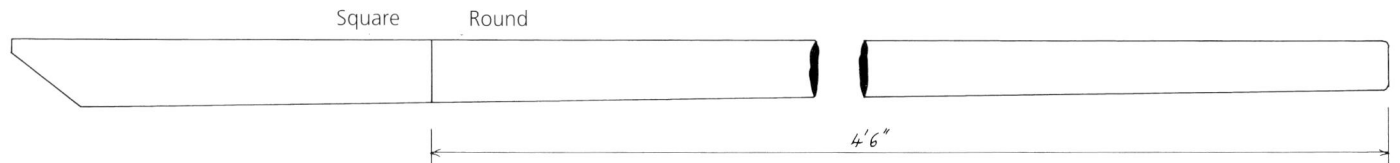

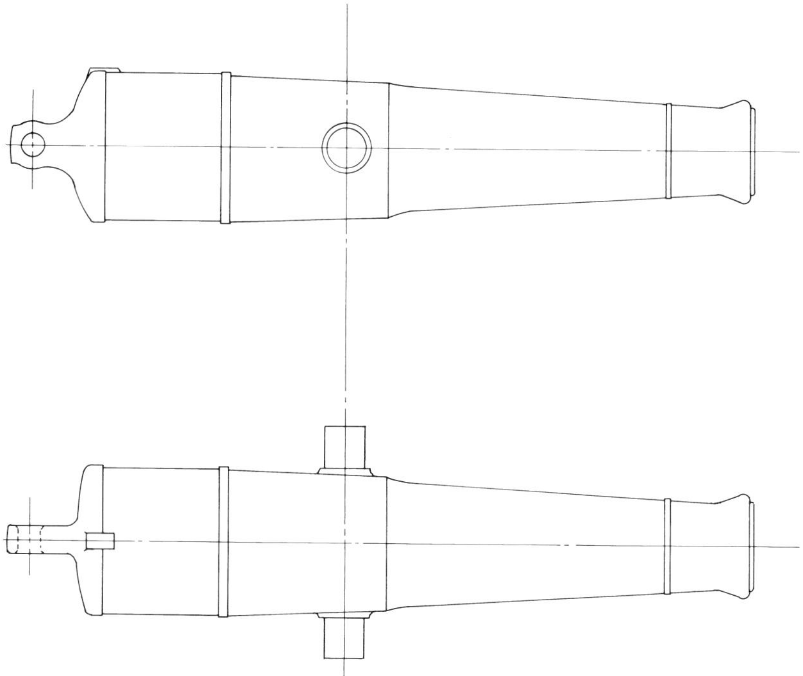

Carriage for 32pdr Gun (reconstruction) (scale = 1:24)

QUOIN
Side elevation
Partial end elevation
QUOIN
Partial plan view

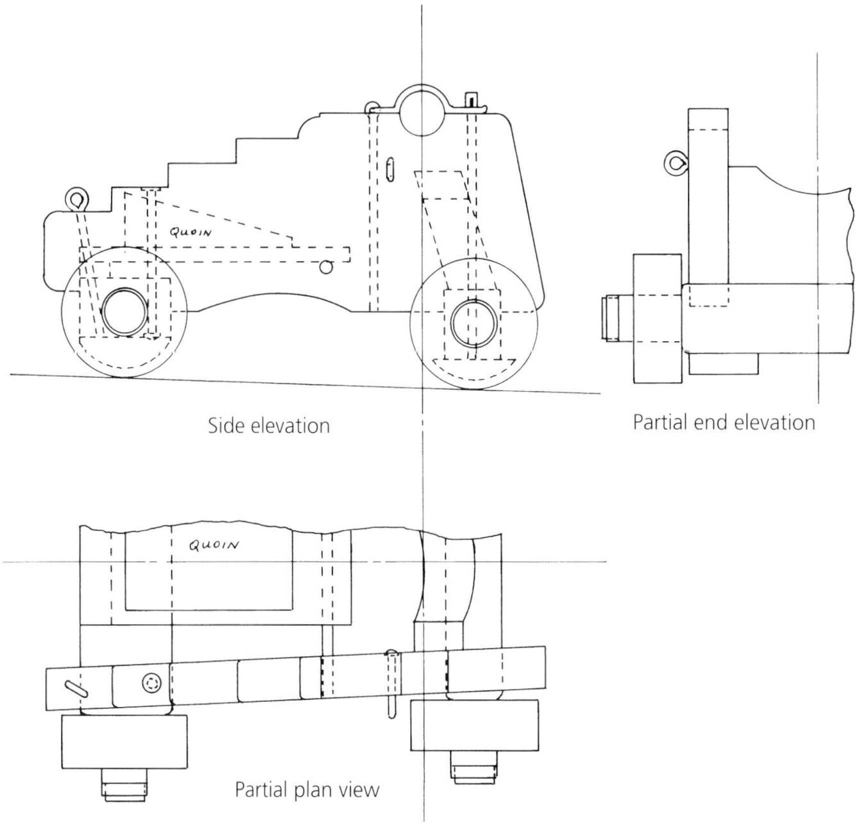

Fore Sight for 32pdr Gun (reconstruction) (scale = 1:3)

After Sight of 32pdr Gun (reconstruction) (scale = 1:3)

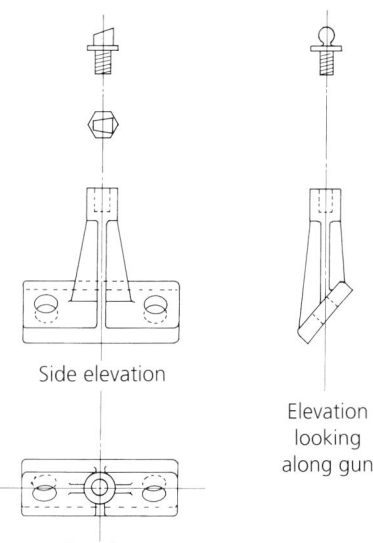
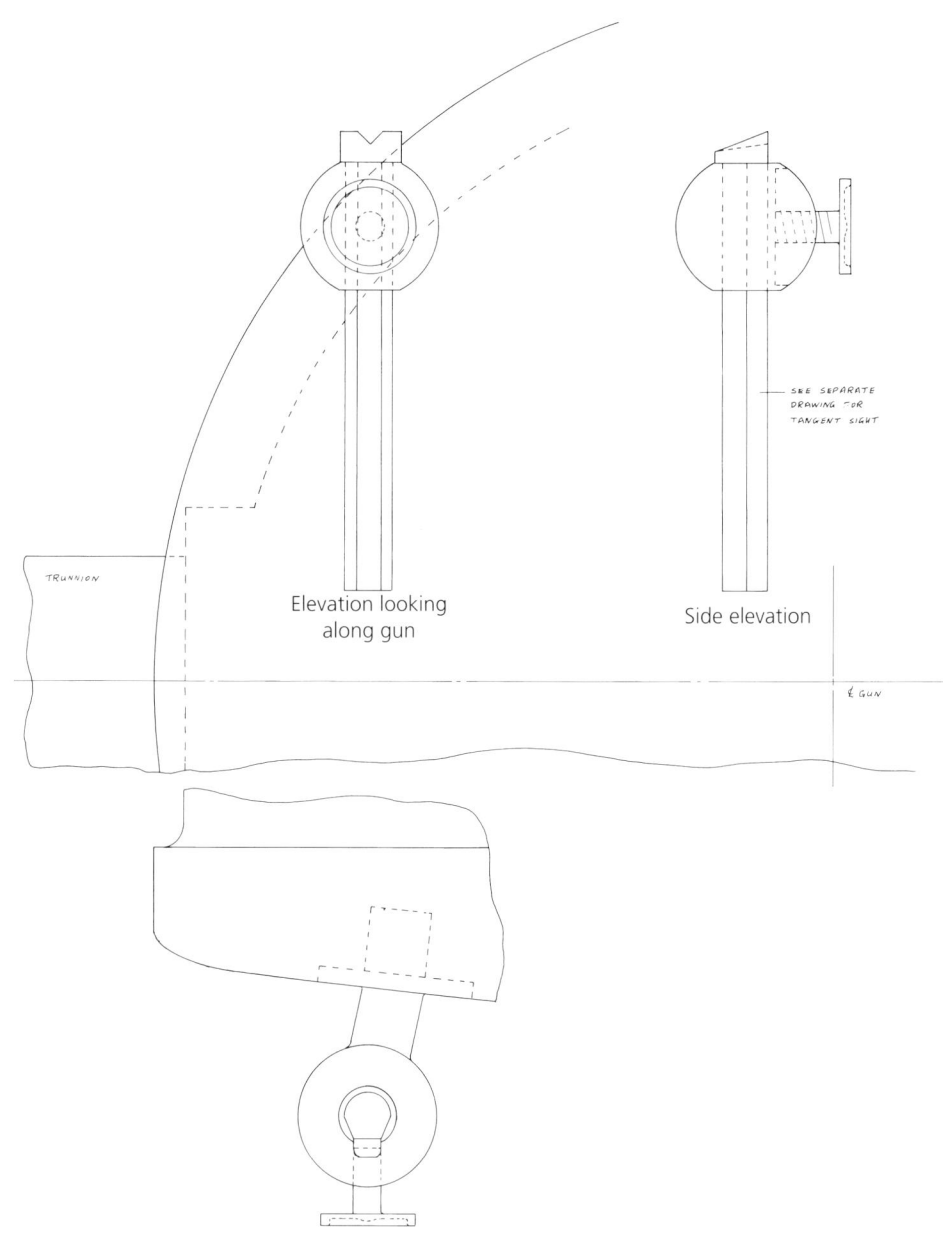

4), which both show the same gun. I think it is reasonable to assume at present that they are both the same, and the reconstructed drawings are based on that assumption. The gun looks to be similar to the type used by the Royal Navy, but it is not known who made it (there might have been different makers for each gun).

The other information about these guns is from the record of the cargo of the *Bahama* going out to the *Alabama* off the Azores. The list is quoted in full in the next section but the following entry refers to the guns, and is the same for both of them.

1 case containing 1 cast-iron gun weighing 49 - 1 - 14 = 5530lbs

The weight of this gun is variously described as 55 cwt (Bulloch), 52 cwt (Semmes, SJ 11/1/63), 5700 lbs (Sinclair, S p7).

The principle difference between the carriage for this gun and those from Fawcett Preston appears to be the quoin, being a wooden wedge rather than an elevating screw which the other guns have.

Based on the photographs it appears that the after sight is of the same form as the other guns (both pivot and broadside). Reconstructions of the fore and after sights are included, based on the assumption that they are similar to those on the other guns.

Other plans

<u>Deck sweeps</u>

As well as showing the position of the deck sweeps the position of various hatches and the bulwarks are also given. The outline given for the hatches will be to the extreme edge, not necessarily the size of the opening in the deck. Sweeps recovered from the wreck off Cherbourg have been marked with the letters shown.

ARMAMENT

Plan of Deck Sweeps for Guns 144 and 145 (scale = 1:48)

The Original (Drawing) of this sent to I.D.B. 8 August 1862

Table showing the manner in which the sweeps are marked

A = 10 pieces
B = 8 "
C = 4 "
D = 6 "
E = 4 "
F = 2 "
G = 2 "
H = 8 "
I = 4 "
J = 8 "
K = 4 "
L = 8 "
M = 2 "
N = 2 "
72 total

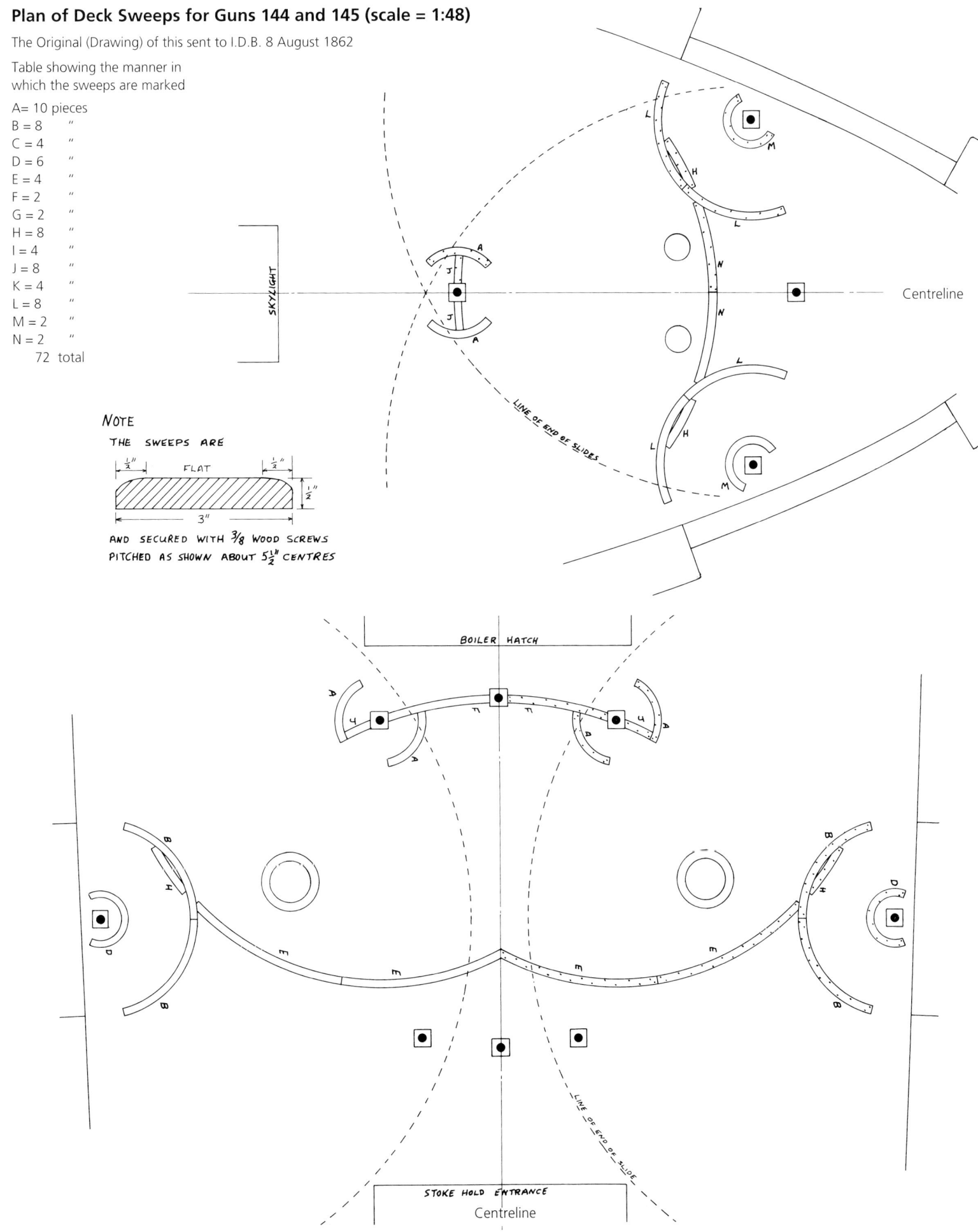

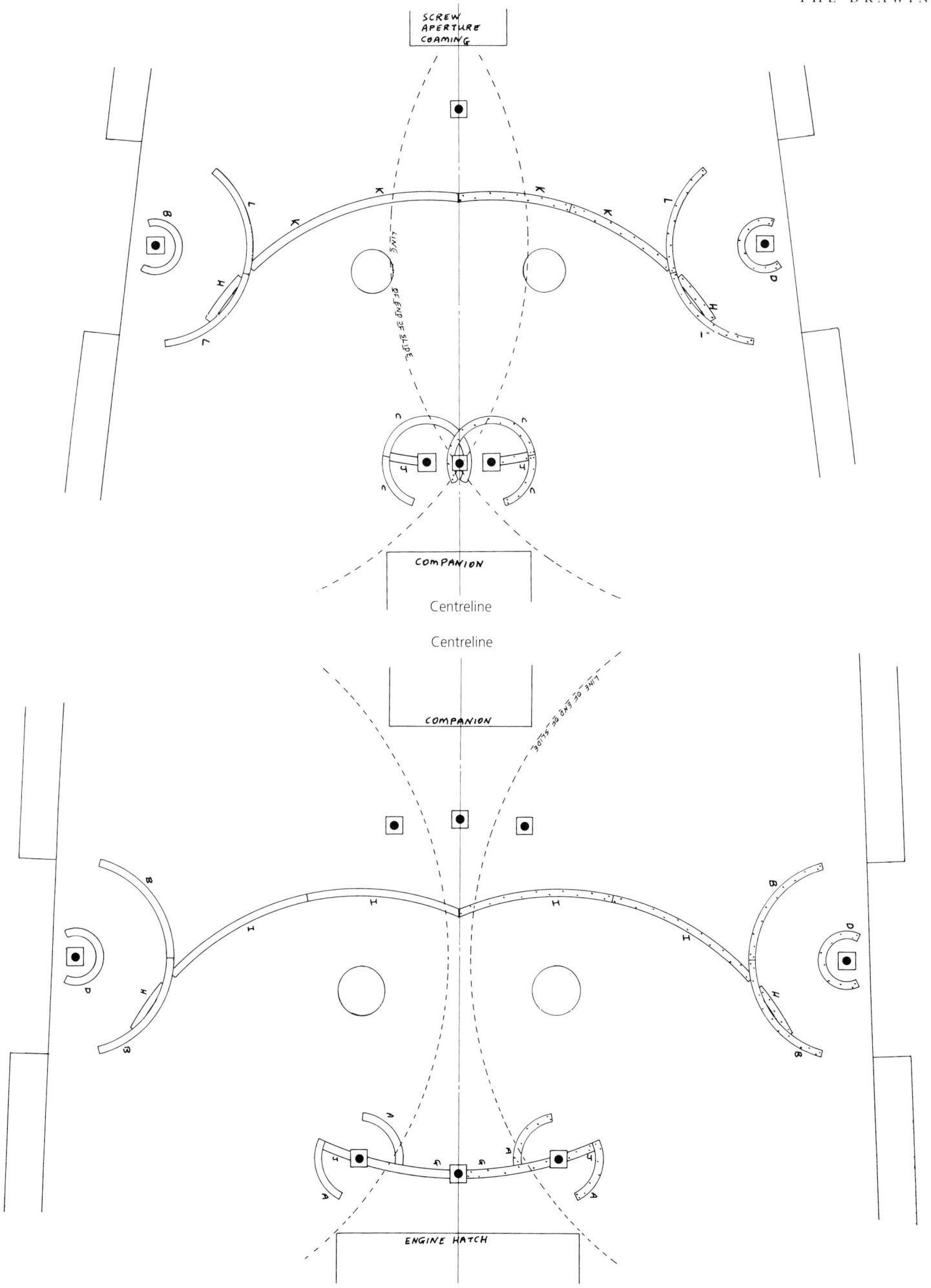

ARMAMENT

Powder canisters

A powder canister made by Fawcett Preston a year or so after the *Alabama* left is used as a basis for this reconstruction. The lid is fastened by a screw, as were the canisters on the ship. Some cartridges went on board ship ready filled. Otherwise the powder came on board the ship in barrels, and could then made up into cartridges, which were then stored in the canisters. As their name suggests powder measures hold a known quantity of powder according to the size. This can then be poured into a cartridge bag or shell using the appropriate funnel. Semmes recorded in his journal (3 September 1862) 'Got up some rifled shell to fill, but were prevented by appearance of rain.' The drawings of the measures and funnels illustrate ones that may have been on board the ship. Further details on the powder are given in the next section.

Powder Canister (reconstruction) (scale = 1:8)

Elevation

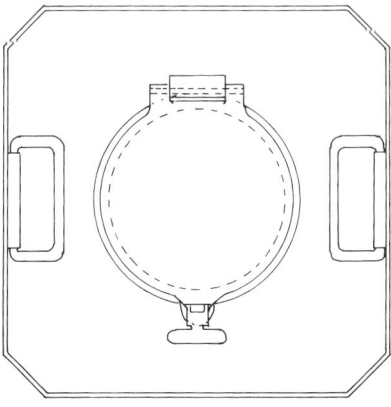

Plan of top

Fuses

There is a drawing of 'fuzes for spherical shells' dated 26 May 1862 which appears to be for the *Alabama*, though it does not specifically say so. The numbers of fuses are:

100 for 15 seconds
250 for 10 seconds
250 for 5 seconds

Powder Measures (reconstruction) (scale = 1:8)

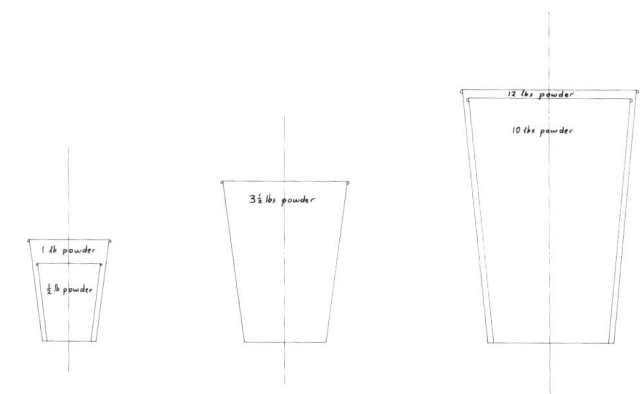

Funnels (reconstruction) (scale = 1:4)

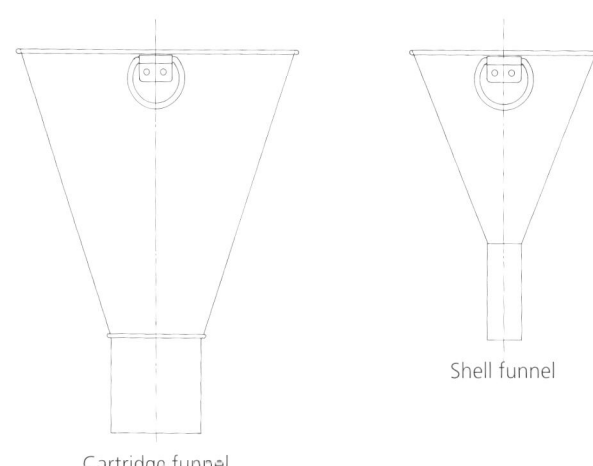

Cartridge funnel

Shell funnel

Fuses for Spherical Shells (26 May 1862) (scale = 1:4)

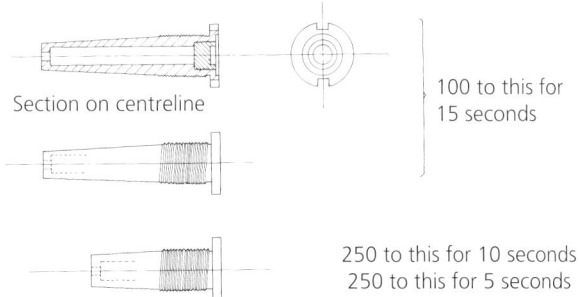

Section on centreline

100 to this for 15 seconds

250 to this for 10 seconds
250 to this for 5 seconds

Fuse Wrench and Spanner (reconstruction) (scale = 1:4)

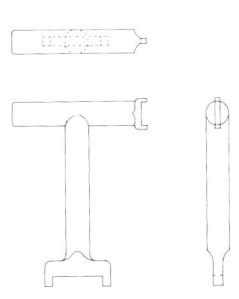

This gives a total of 600 fuses.

The drawing of the fuse wrench is a reconstruction based on the fuses and a drawing for another gun.

AMMUNITION AND STORES

General quantities taken on board

The total quantity of ammunition and powder carried by the *Alabama* is not listed anywhere but it should be possible to estimate it from the known facts.

The *Alabama* left the Mersey without any guns or military stores on board. Therefore everything was taken out to the Azores by the two ships, the *Agrippina* from London and the *Bahama* sailing from Liverpool with Semmes and his officers.

Armaments carried on *Bahama* from ORN II, 2 p392.

	Weight
	(cwt-qrs-lbs)
1 case containing 1 cast-iron gun weighing	49 - 1 - 14
1 case containing 1 broadside carriage weighing	12 - 0 - 14
1 case containing rammers, sponges, handspikes, etc weighing	2 - 1 - 14
1 case containing 1 cast-iron gun weighing	49 - 1 - 14
1 case containing 1 broadside carriage weighing	12 - 0 - 14
1 case containing rammers, sponges, handspikes, etc weighing	2 - 0 - 10
6 cases containing 50 cast shot weighing	13 - 1 - 20
6 cases containing 50 cast shot weighing	17 - 2 - 6
1 case containing brass vent covers weighing	0 - 0 - 5
Total weight	158 - 1 - 27

Total value £220

Additional cargo of *Agrippina* (ORN I, 13 p284)

2 cases pistols
1 case 1¾ leather [*sic*]
6 cases rifles
137 cases (in total) marked cannon
65 casks 6184 pounds powder
15 cases cartridges
1 case percussion caps
39 barrels 3900 pounds powder
1 case cartridges
248 cases iron castings
6 cases signal rockets
1 barrel signal lights
4 packages tubs

Shot and shell

The number of shot and shell carried for some of the guns is given on the drawings or in letters, such as the one quoted below: 'The 8-inch gun is of course provided with shell as well as shot, and I have provided seventy 42-pound spherical shot for the rifled gun in addition to the elongated shell and shot peculiarly adapted to its character' (Bulloch in ORN Series II, 2 p236).

The figures given in italics are estimates. In the case of the non-Fawcett Preston 32pdrs the number has come from the cargo of the *Bahama*. One lot of cases is assumed to be carrying shot and the other shell.

Gun	Shell	Shot
8in smoothbore	70	70
7in Blakely - elongated	70	70
- spherical		70
32pdr Fawcett Preston (40 each)	160	160
32pdr others (25 each)	*50*	*50*
Total - estimated	350	420 = 770 shot & shell

Grapeshot for 32pdr (reconstruction) (scale = 1:4)

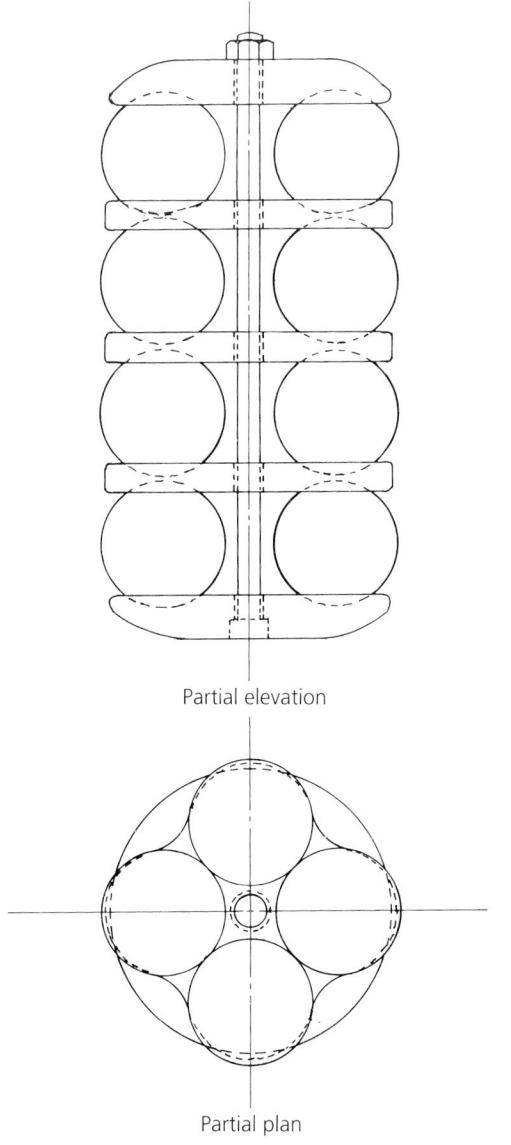

Partial elevation

Partial plan

ARMAMENT

Moving a Pivot Gun

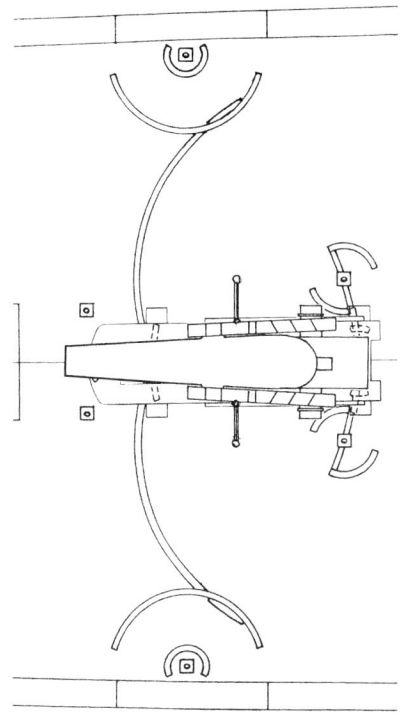

Figure 1 On centreline, slide secured fore and aft by pivots. Carriage secured by means of tackles to brackets (see Photograph 1, page 48).

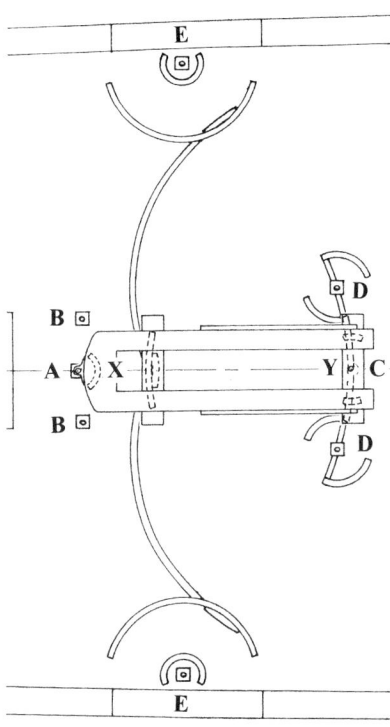

Figure 2 Slide on centreline, pivots at each end. Carriage removed for clarity. X at A, and Y at C.

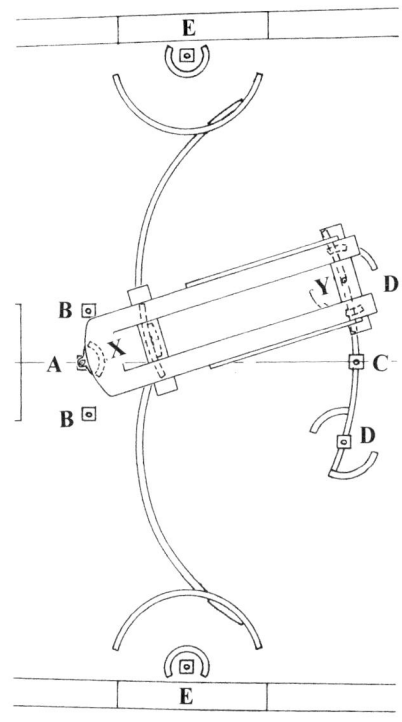

Figure 3 Slide pivots about A, and Y moves along the sweeps to D.

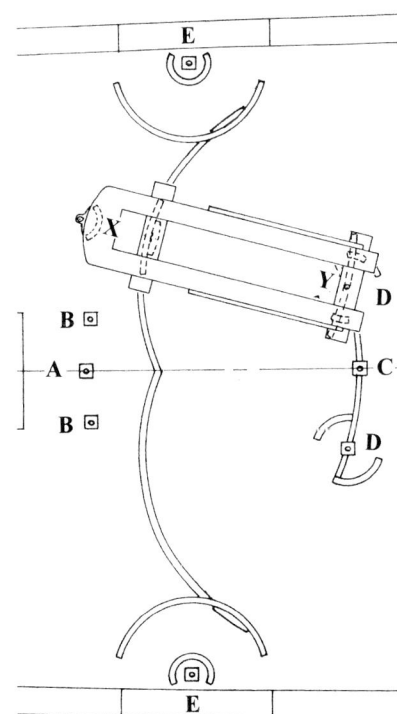

Figure 4 Slide now pivots about point Y, which is at pivot point D. The slide is running on sweeps at each end.

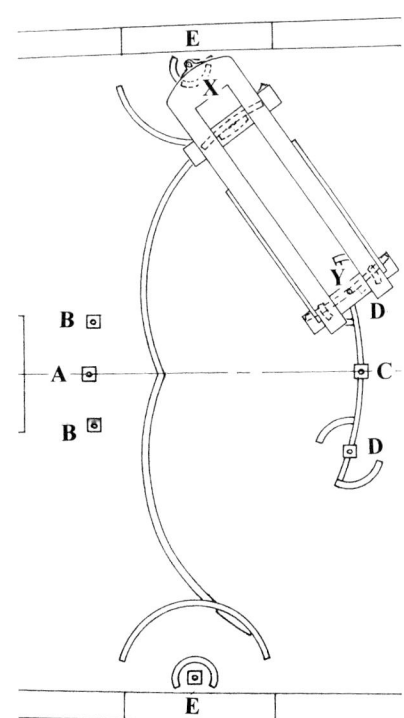

Figure 5 Slide pivots about Y, which is at D, so that X comes to point E. The pivot point then becomes X and the slide pivots about E, running on the two sweeps centred on E.

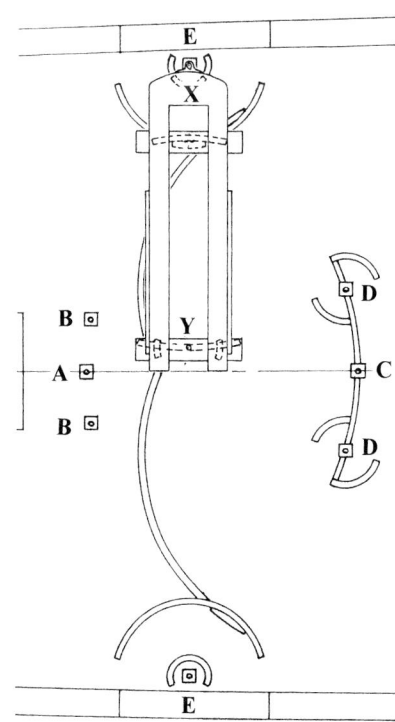

Figure 6 Slide now pivots at X about E, the sweeps under the slide running on the two deck sweeps in front of the gunport. The after end of the slide does not run on any deck sweeps.

There is a reference to grapeshot in Semmes log–'Friday Nov 28, 1862. Getting up grape-shot'. There is no indication as to the quantity carried, or which gun or guns it was for. A round of grapeshot consisted of three or four tiers of cast iron balls, three or four to a tier, between iron discs connected by a central wrought iron pin. The drawing shows grapeshot based on a drawing for a 6.4in gun by Fawcett Preston, that is to say the same size as the 32pdrs.

Powder

The powder carried on the *Agrippina* was:

65 casks	6184lbs
39 barrels	3900lbs

Total of 10,084lbs = 4½ tons powder taken on board.

The powder required for use with the guns comes under the heading of that for filling the shells and then that for firing the guns. Based on the number of shot and shell estimated above the powder for both of these is about 7400 pounds (more details are given in Appendix 4). The amount for charges (firing the guns) is estimated at 6860lbs.

Operating a Pivot Gun

Moving a pivot gun

The 8in pivot gun is used as an example of how the guns were pivoted. The gun was normally on the centreline of the ship when not in use, and therefore able to pivot to either port or starboard as required. This central position is shown in the two photographs of Semmes and Kell standing by the gun (Photographs 1 & 2). They also show how the carriage was lashed to eyebolts in the deck, one each side, by means of tackles.

The movement of the slide is illustrated by the following six diagrams. In all except the first case the carriage and gun have been omitted for clarity. The position of the sweeps on the underside of the carriage are shown by dotted lines and it can be seen how they run on the sweeps on the deck during the movement. The pivot points A, B, C, D and E are on the deck and points X and Y are on the slide (the front and rear respectively).

A pivot bolt would pass through the slide and into the pivot point on the deck. For example in Figure 2 a pivot bolt would go through X and into A, and the slide will rotate about A. The drawing of the carriage and slide for the 8in gun shows pivots which are labelled as FIGHTING (at the front), and HOUSING (at the rear), presumably there were different ones. The slide is moved by means of handspikes from point to point.

The diagrams illustrate how the slide is moved from the centreline to the gunport where it will pivot about E and X. When in this position only the two deck sweeps which are concentric with E are used for pivoting the gun. The sweeps under the other end of the slide (around Y) do not have corresponding deck sweeps to run on. Presumably because when the gun is run out all the weight will be on the front of the slide, and therefore on those deck sweeps.

There does not seem to be any purpose to the pivot at B. From the dimensions it can only be used with C or E (*ie* X at E and Y at A, and X at B and Y at C).

Training a pivot gun

Pivot guns are trained by means of the training tackle which is attached to the rear of the slide. When the slide is on a pivot bolt at the gunport there has to be a means of restraining the rear end of the slide from moving due to the motion of the ship, or the recoil when fired. Therefore there must be an eyebolt at the rear and on the outer side of each rail for one end of the training tackle, even though they are not shown on the plans. There are two loops shown on the plan of the slide for the 8in gun, but on the drawing of the wrought iron work they are marked as not used. The other end of the training tackle must be attached to a ring bolt probably on the deck near to the bulwark. Again there is nothing obvious to be seen on any of the photographs.

Without any further information available the training tackle will be assumed to be similar to that shown in the sketches showing the positions of the crew.

Firing a pivot gun

The crew of the 8in pivot gun was given by Sinclair (p242), as twenty-two men, ten each side and two captains (first and second). However, in an interview given in 1883 (quoted in *Beneath the Stainless Banner*, p216) Kell says 'an eleven-inch shell from the *Kearsarge* entered a port hole and killed eight of the sixteen men serving that gun [eight-inch gun]'. The interview also has the following–'One shell from our eight-inch gun was buried in the stem of the *Kearsarge*'. There are two errors in this last sentence (it was the 7in gun and the shell lodged in the stern) so it is possible that the gun crew of sixteen men could be wrong also.

According to the *Instructions in Relation to the Preparation of Vessels of War* (1852 ed), published by the US Navy, the crew of an 8in pivot gun of 105 cwt was sixteen men and a powder boy (p49). A later edition –1866– gives the crew of an 11in shell gun on a pivot as twenty-five men, including a powder man (p62). The corresponding Royal Navy manual *Instructions for the Exercise and Service of Great Guns*, 1858, has a crew of 17 men and upwards (p34).

The figure of sixteen men plus a powder boy will be assumed to be the crew for each of the pivot guns. The distribution of the men around the gun is assumed to be as in the following drawings.

The gun would be at the inner (rear) end of the slide for loading. With the Blakely there is a rope from the rear end of the left hand rail of the slide which goes round a pulley on the rear of the carriage. The rope then goes through notch at the rear of the right hand rail and then round a small drum, and is presumably used to move the carriage to the rear of the slide for loading. When the

ARMAMENT

Firing a Pivot Gun 1–2

Loading

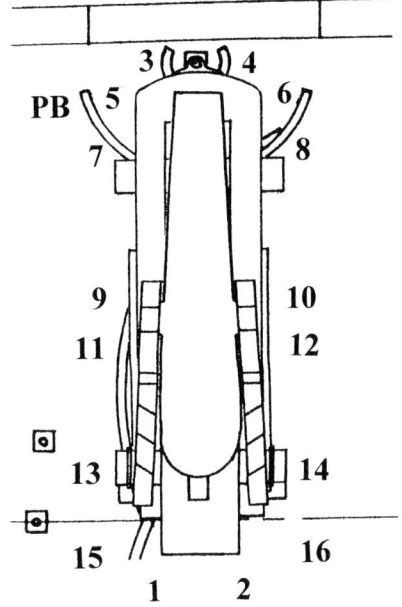

Firing

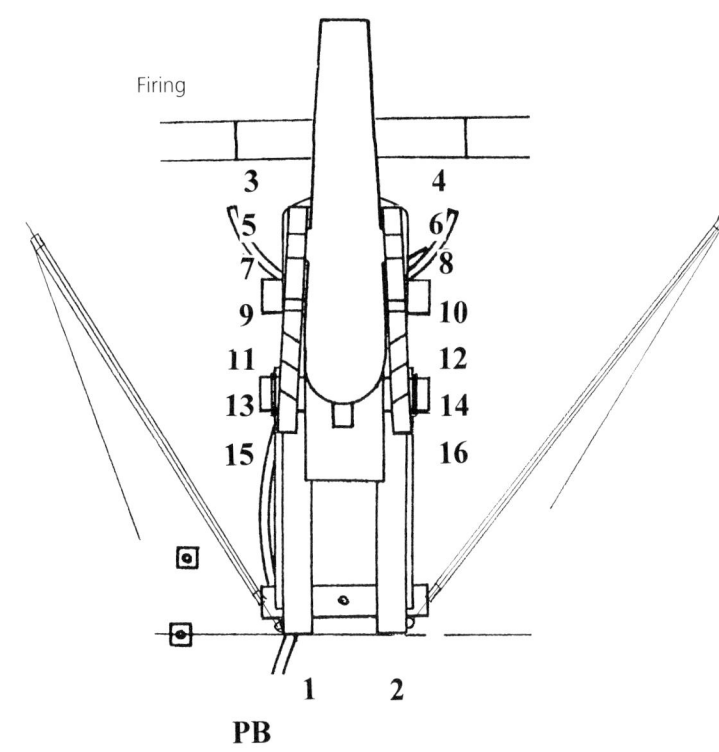

gun was loaded it would be run out along the slide by means of the tackles shown in the diagram, the forward end of which is to an eyebolt on the slide and the aft end attached to the rope levers on the carriage. The rope levers rotate about their top end and force the rear rollers on to the slide, which will tend to raise the carriage on the slide. The tackles will then pull the carriage along the slide, using essentially the four rollers, so that the gun is run out. (This tackle is obviously released before the gun is fired because of the recoil if the rollers were in contact!)

The gun could be trained to bear on the target as necessary, by means of handspikes and the training tackle which is assumed to be there. With the gun working between the two hatchways it would be difficult to achieve a clear line for this tackle.

Before firing the two compressors were tightened down, one on each side. This provides friction between the carriage and slide during the recoil of the gun after it has been fired. The breeching rope will limit the extent of the recoil of the gun. The forward ends of the breeching rope were attached to the breeching shackles at the front end of the slide. It would appear that any movement of the slide during the recoil of the gun was prevented by means of the pivot between the slide and the deck. (The breeching ropes of the 32pdrs were attached to the bulwarks.)

The disposition of the gun crew has been taken as follows. The officers were trained under the US Navy system and the crew under the Royal Navy system. There were slight differences between the two systems, and neither covered drill with a quoin or elevating mechanism such as was fitted to these pivot guns. Therefore the following has been adapted from these and is hopefully similar to the actual drill.

1	Captain
2	Second Captain
3	Loader
4	Sponger
5	Assistant loader
6	Assistant sponger
7	Side tackleman
8	Side tackleman
9	Handspikeman
10	Handspikeman
11	Assistant handspikeman
12	Assistant handspikeman
13	Compressor man
14	Compressor man
15	Train tackle man
16	Train tackle man
PB	Powder boy

The following is an exercise in firing a pivot gun, showing the different commands and actions of the various members of the gun crew.

The gun is pivoted over one of the fighting centres, loaded, cast loose, run out and compressed. All preparatory arrangements are complete and the men in their firing positions.

Prime
The Captain lays back the hammer. Using the priming wire he clears the vent, feels that the cartridge is home and pricks it. He then takes a primer from the box and places it in the vent.

Point

First and second Captains on the slide to the rear of the gun. Others man the training ropes, the Captain directing them to haul to port or starboard as necessary. The compressor men to see that the 'out' tackles falls are clear. If it is necessary to change the elevation two men attend to the pawls, and the second captain to the elevating lever. The correct line of sight and elevation being achieved the next command is

Ready

The men move to their firing positions. The Captain tightens the lockstring.

Fire

The Captain pulls the lock string, and stands clear of the recoil of the gun. If the gun does not recoil far enough for loading the compressor men slacken the compressors and the side tacklemen run the gun in.

Sponge

The crew take their positions for loading. The Captain steps up to the breech, lays back the hammer, and places the lockstring in a loose coil over it. He then clears the vent and stops it. The first sponger and first loader are in place by the muzzle and the second sponger hands over the sponge. The first sponger pushes it down the bore, and with the help of the first loader, pushes it home and turns it several times clockwise. This is so that the worm may clear any remnants of the cartridge bag. The sponge is withdrawn and struck on the muzzle to dislodge anything stuck to it. Any burning fragments are extinguished by the first loader, and then the bore is sponged again. The first captain will try the vent again to ensure that it is clear.

Load with cartidge

The first captain stops the vent. The second loader takes a cartridge, from the box presented by the powder boy, and hands it to the first loader who pushes it well down the bore, seam sideways and bottom first. The sponger puts the rammer in the bore, and with the loader shoves the cartridge home, giving it two smart blows. The Captain unstops the vent and pricks the cartridge if it is home. If not the loader and sponger ram again, and remove the rammer when the cartridge is home.

Load with shot or shell

The second loader passes a SHOT and wad to the first loader, who places them, wad last, in the bore and shoves them well down. The first sponger and first loader then use the rammer to ram them home, and give two smart blows to set the wad into its place.

OR The second loader takes a SHELL out of the box and passes it to the first loader who enters it into the bore, sabot first and fuse upwards. With a heavy shell the first shotman will assist the second loader to bring the shell in its box under the muzzle of the gun. The shell is placed on the shell lifter which is lifted by the first loader and first sponger and entered in to the bore. The first sponger strips the lead patch off the fuze and passes it to the first captain to prove that the priming has been exposed. The first sponger checks the priming and, assisted by the first loader, pushes the shell home without ramming or turning the rammer.

Run out

The compressor men slacken the compressors. All the other men, except the captains, man the out tackles and run the gun out. The compressor men then tighten the compressors and see the out tackles falls clear for running. The next command is

Prime

Firing a Broadside Gun

Crew numbers

'We tried the experiment to day of shifting over another broadside gun to see how the ship would bear her battery, thus all on one side but one gun – giving seven fighting guns – she bore them well and we shall be able to fight them without difficulty. For want of men, however, the crew of the 7th gun will be composed, with one or two exceptions, of officers.' (SJ, 27 October 1863)

'Upon the application of Mr Smith and myself (Fullam), the following officers agreeing and volunteering, viz;- Messrs Howell, Mecaskey, Evans, Mulnier and Schroeder, another guns crew was raised (three men and a powder boy from the other guns also being sent) and one of the after thirty twos was transported to the opposite side of the deck to the after broadside pivot port. Thus making seven guns on a broadside.' (F, p149)

It would appear that ten men were the (minimum) crew of a 32pdr.

1	First Captain
2	Second Captain
3	First Loader
4	Second Loader
5	First Sponger
6	Second Sponger
7	First Shotman
8	Second Shotman
9	Handspikeman
10	Traintackleman
PB	Powder boy

Note: the traintackle runs from the rear of the carriage to a bolt in the deck to the rear of the gun. Looking at the photographs taken

ARMAMENT

Firing a Broadside Gun 1 & 2

Loading

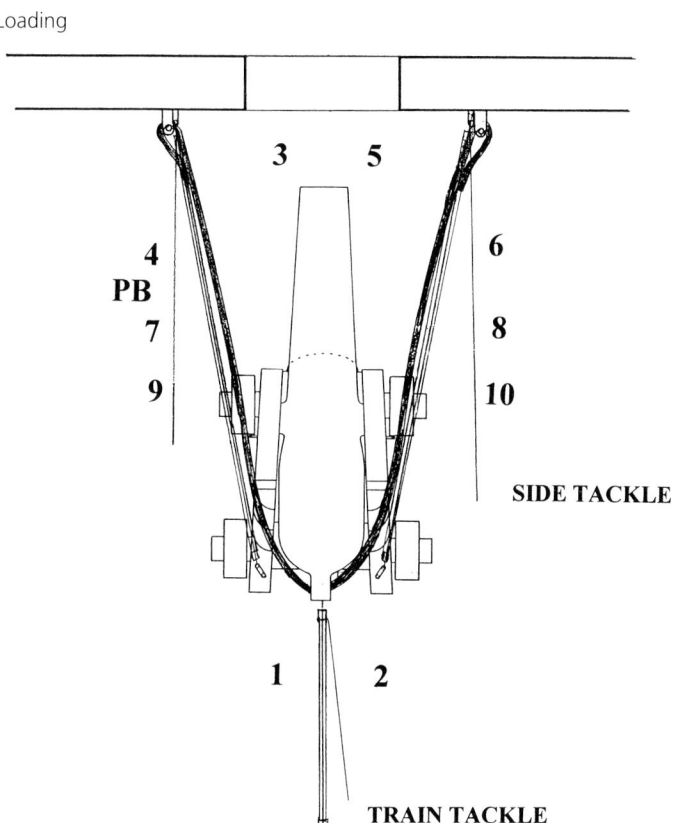

Firing

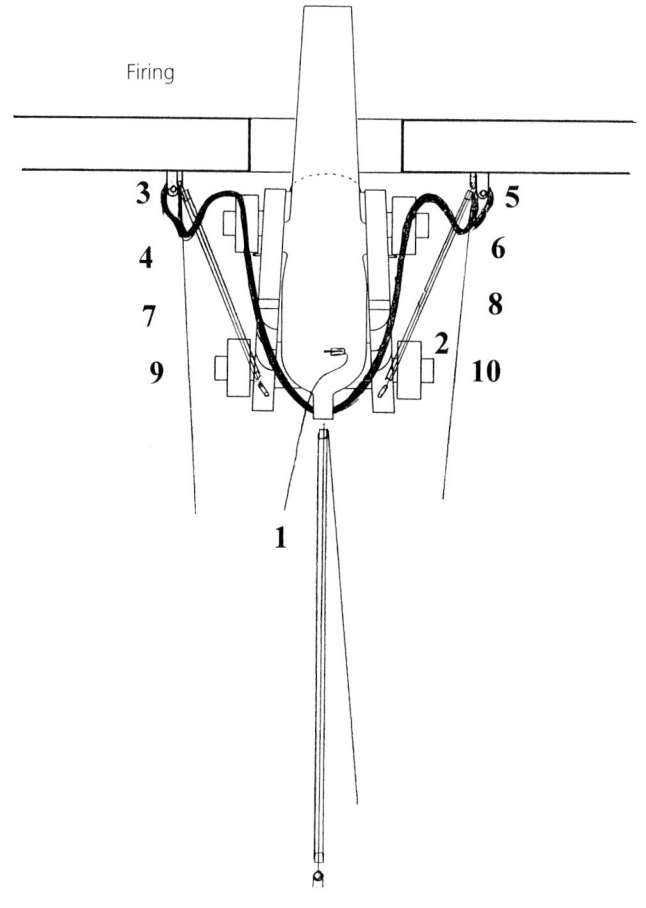

on deck it is not possible to see a ring bolt in the deck in the correct position for any of the broadside guns, however both Semmes and Sinclair state that they were fitted (SM, p625 & S, p9). There is a ring bolt clearly shown on the original plans of the carriage of the Fawcett Preston 32pdrs. As with the pivot guns there must be a means of restraining the guns during loading and bringing them back far enough for loading. Even though there is no ring bolt visible it is assumed that there is one for each 32pdr.

There is very little room on the deck for withdrawing the gun for loading. For example, for the guns level with the steering wheels the grating for the helmsman would have to be removed so that the tip of the muzzle could be completely inside the bulwarks. The run-in of other guns is limited by hatchways and coamings.

Firing the gun

The following gives the orders for loading and firing the gun, and starts with the gun loaded and run out. In this position the next order is:

Prime

The Captain lays back the hammer. Using the priming wire he checks the vent is clear, then he feels that the cartridge is home (fully down in the chamber) and pricks it. He then places a primer in the vent.

Point

The handspikemen use the handspikes to turn the carriage as required. The rest of the men man the side tackle falls, hauling them taut.

The elevation of the gun is changed, by the second captain, either by means of the elevating screw or moving the quoin. To move the quoin the handspikemen use the handspike to raise the breech of the gun, then the second captain moves it. The elevation being changed by the handspikemen, when it is correct the quoin is forced in and the handspikes removed.

Ready

The training men release the side tackle falls. The lock is cocked by the second captain.

Fire

The Captain pulls the lock string with a strong pull, moving to his left clear of the recoil. The traintacklemen then haul on the train tackle ensuring the gun is fully run in, and then secure it for loading.

Sponge

The Captain loosely coils the lock string and places it over the hammer. He then clears the vent and then stops it with a vent plug. The first sponger and first loader step over the breeching rope and stand either side of the muzzle. The sponge is passed by the second to the first sponger who places it in the muzzle and shoves it well down. The sponger and loader then press the sponge against the bottom of the bore and turn it clockwise two or three times so that the worm may clear anything stuck to the bottom of the bore. The vent has been stopped to prevent any air or any burning fragments from lodging in the vent, which could ignite the next charge.

Load

The Captain stops the vent. The second loader takes a cartridge from the passing box carried by the powder boy and passes it to the first loader who places it in the muzzle with the bottom first and the seam sideways - this is to ensure that the seam is not under the vent, and it can be pricked by the priming wire. The rammer is handed to the first sponger who places it in the muzzle and with the help of the first loader rams home the cartridge. The Captain unstops the vent and pricks the cartridge with the priming wire, then the rammer is removed. If the cartridge is not home he will remove the priming wire and the rammer will be used again, until it is home.

The shot and wad are then passed from the second to the first loader, who places them in the bore, wad last. The sponger and loader use the rammer as before to ram the shot and wad home, giving two smart blows to set the wad in place.

If loading with shell instead the second loader takes the shell out of the box and passes it to the first loader, who enters it into the bore, sabot first, and fuse upwards and outwards. The first sponger then strips the leaden patch off the fuze, and passes it to the Captain. The first sponger and loader then push the shell home, without turning or ramming which might upset the fuse (no wad is used).

Run out

The first loader and first sponger lift the breeching rope so that the trucks do not foul it. The rest of the gun crew man the side tackles, uniting to run it out, training it in the required direction.

Then PRIME and continue round again.

General view of engine

General View of Engine
(not to scale)
Numbers refer to all drawings

A   Boiler
B   Stoke hole
C   Coal Bunkers
1   Cylinder
4   Piston rods
7   Slide block
8   Motion bar
9   Connecting rod
10   Crank shaft
11   Main frame
12   Side frame
18   Feed pump
19   Bilge pump
22   Slide valve
31   Steam inlet
32   Steam exhaust
33   Condenser
34   Injection valve
38   Hot well
39   Discharge pipe
43   Expansion valve

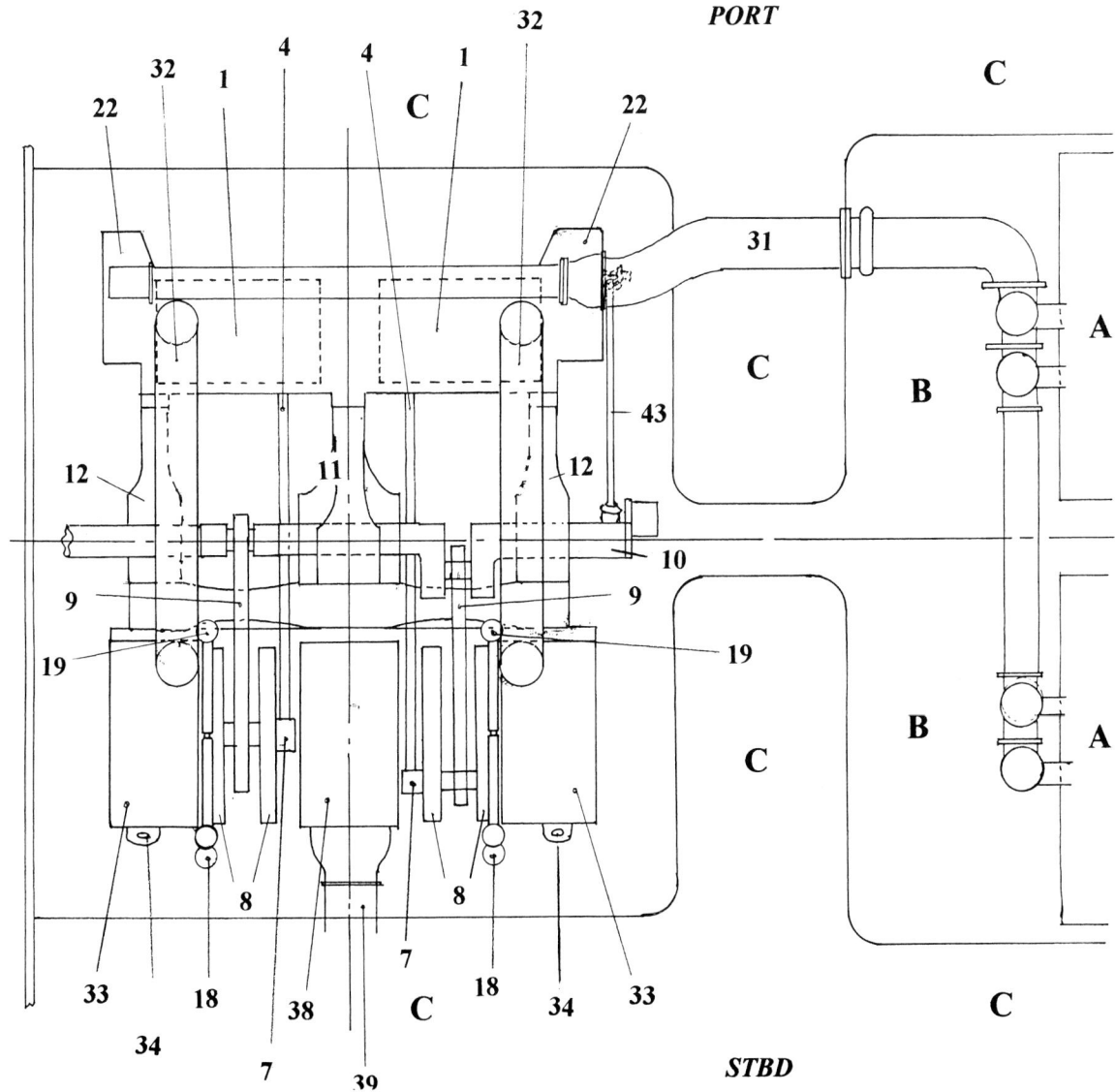

Machinery

Engine

The specification of the machinery was given earlier with the specification of the hull (page 24). The engine was built by the company, but apart from the engine plan, no other information exists. It appears that the engine-building side of the business was run separately from the shipbuilding, and no records remain. There is not even a complete list of all the engines built over the years.

A report in a local newspaper (given in full in Appendix 1) noted, in October 1861, 'one pair of screw-propeller engines of 150 horse-power each, or 300 horse-power collectively' under construction. At that time a cylinder was called an engine; therefore this machinery, which had two cylinders, was called a pair of engines (though it will be referred to here as the engine, without causing too much confusion, I hope).

As noted previously the engine was assembled in the ship after launch. There are no reports of any problems with the engine during construction. During service there is only one major problem described so it appears to have been fairly reliable. However, Sinclair in his book (p19) says that the engineers were able 'to make the frequent and often difficult repairs that usually are intrusted only to machine-shops.'

Shortly after the capture of the *Ariel* in December 1862 the *Alabama* was disabled by an accident. Semmes described this in his Memoirs (p537) as 'the giving way of one of the valve castings. . . . Nothing but the puffing of the bellows, the clinking of the hammer on the anvil, and the rasping of files was heard now for forty-eight hours.' This confirms that the ship was able to carry out significant repairs without the need to return to a dockyard as it carried a forge and anvil.

With respect to the drawings of the engine I think most things are self-explanatory, but brief notes are given for most of the items below. Some have not been drawn, either because they are not

Engine (scale = 1:32)

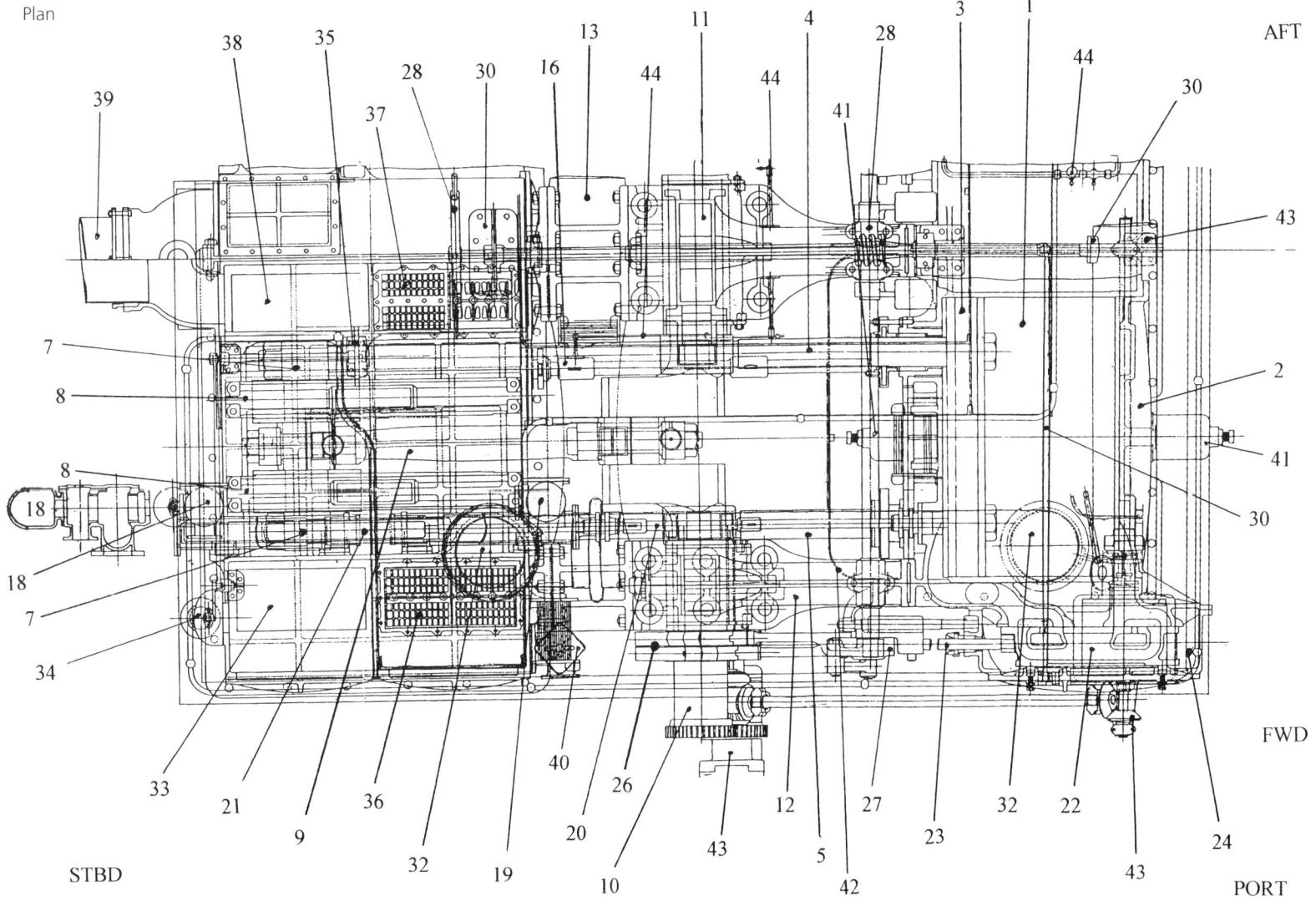

Plan

Elevation

Stbd Port

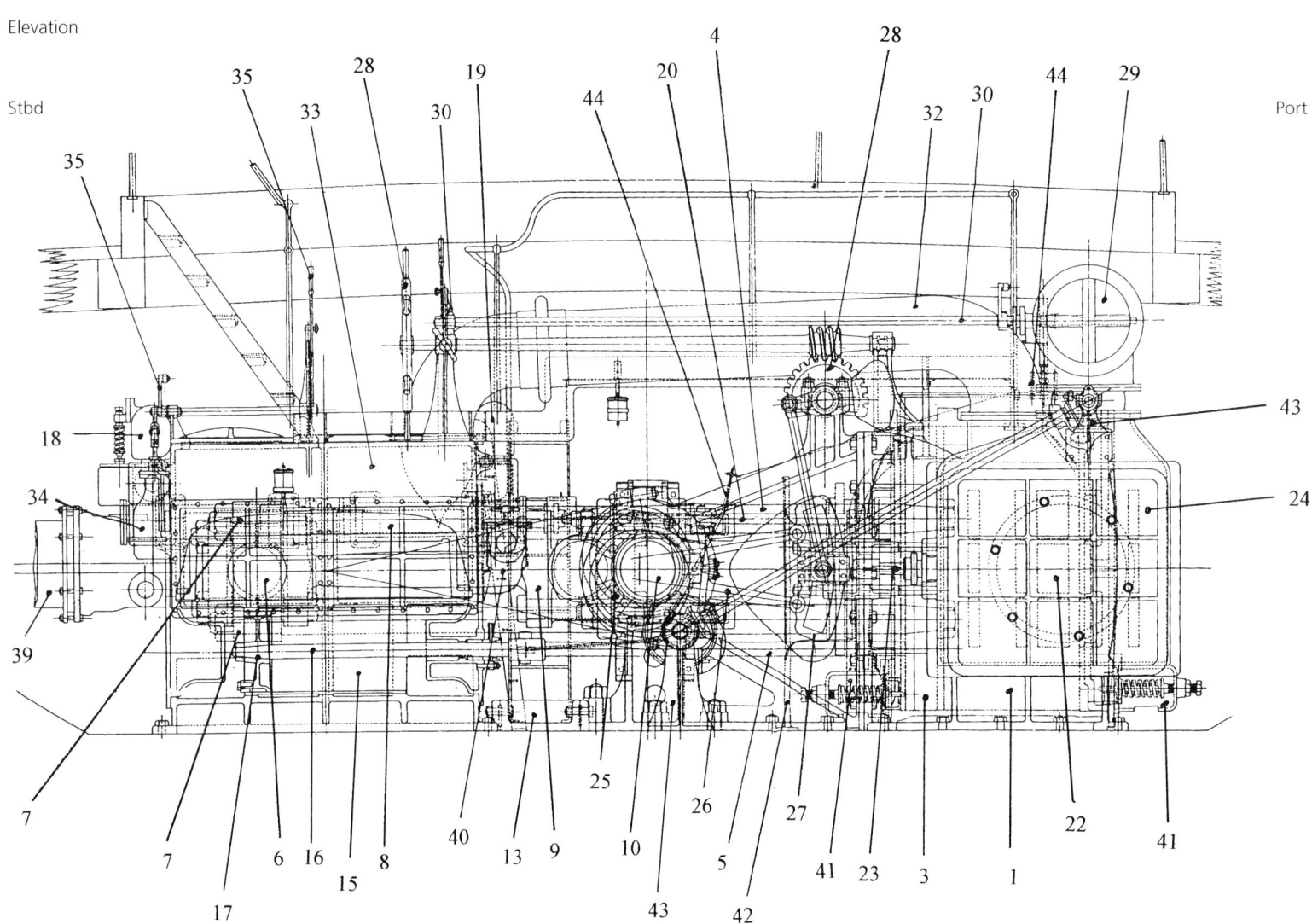

Key
Numbers refer to all 3 views
1 Cylinder
2 Cylinder cover
3 Piston
4 Piston rod
5 Piston rod
6 Crosshead
7 Slide blocks
8 Motion bars
9 Connecting rod
10 Crankshaft
11 Main frame and bearing
12 Side frame and bearing
13 Base plate
14 Structure of hot well and condenser
15 Air pump
16 Air pump rod
17 Air pump piston
18 Feed pump
19 Bilge pump
20 Feed and bilge pump rod
21 Feed and bilge pump plunger
22 Slide valve
23 Slide valve rod and guide
24 Valve chest and cover
25 Eccentric sheave

MACHINERY

Side elevation

Fwd / Aft

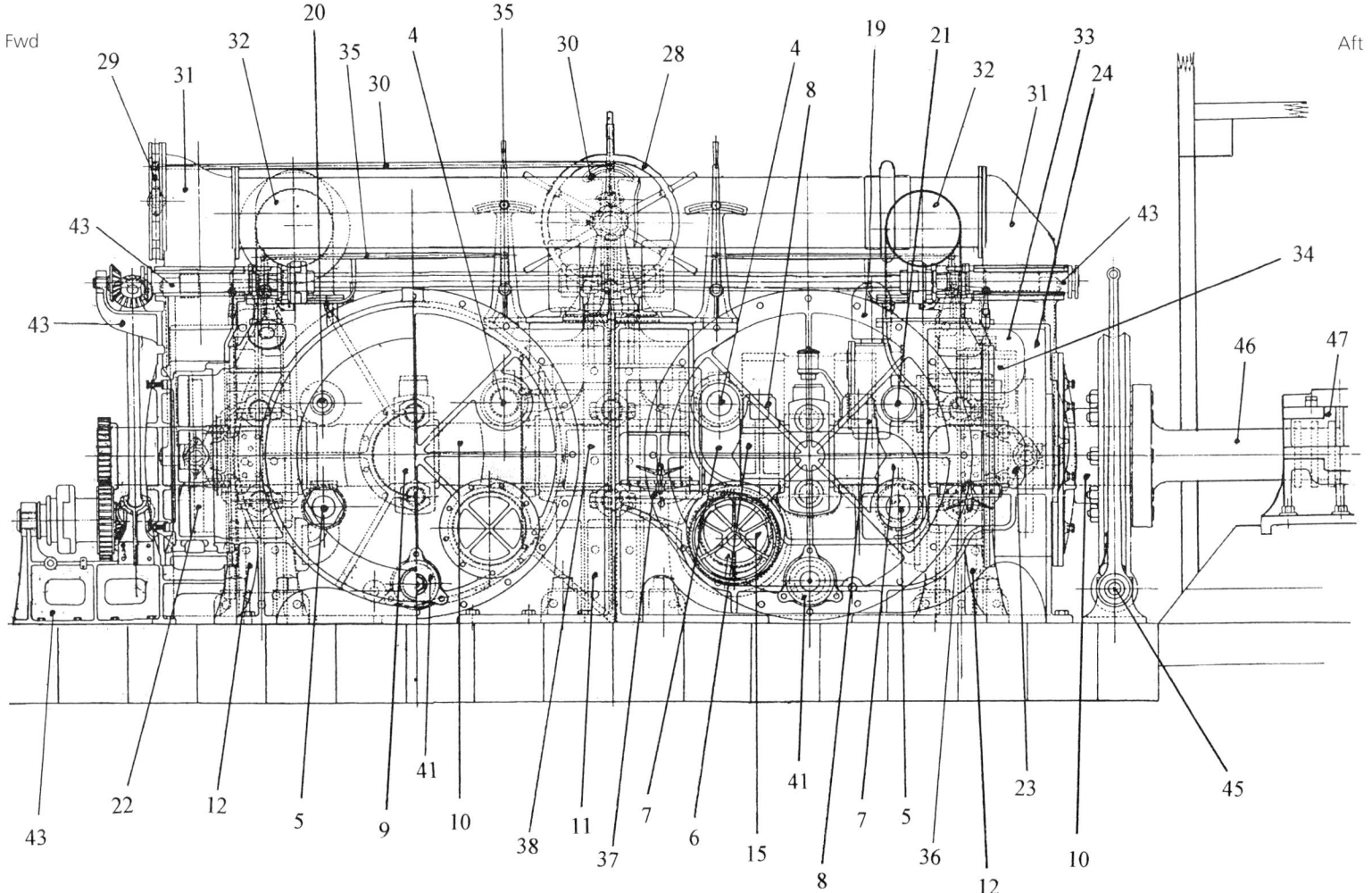

26	Eccentric strap and rod	32	Steam exhaust pipe	38	Hot well	44	Indicator
27	Link	33	Condenser	39	Discharge pipe	45	Turning gear
28	Control for eccentric link	34	Injection valve	40	Blow through valve	46	Propeller shaft
29	Throttle valve	35	Controls for injection valve	41	Relief valve	47	Thrust block
30	Controls for throttle valve	36	Foot valve	42	Barrier/safety guard		
31	Steam inlet pipe	37	Delivery valve	43	Expansion valve		

1. Cylinder (scale = 1:24)

1 and 1 to opposite hand. Mirror image around centreline of engines

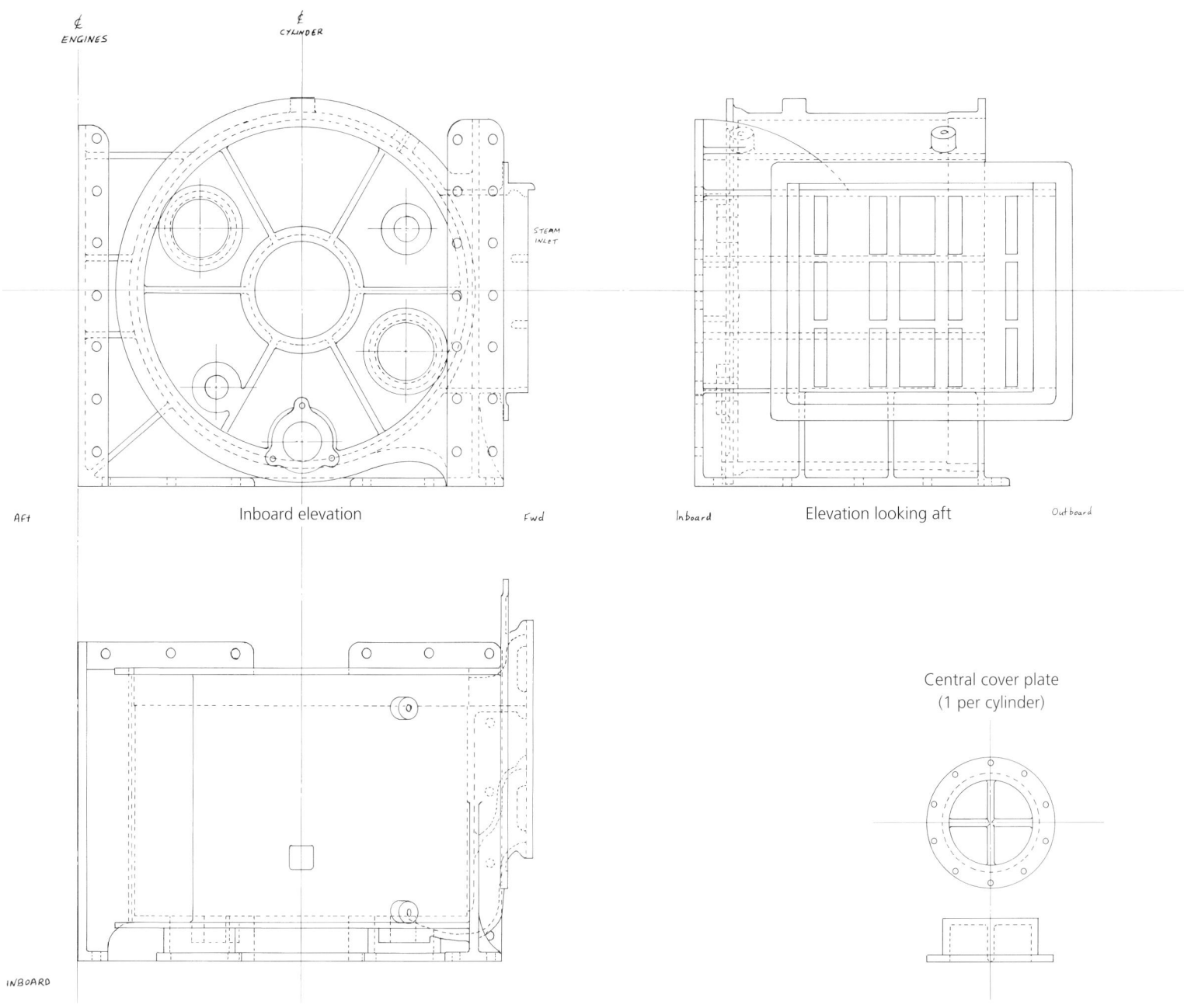

clearly shown or there is not enough information available. Each of these is noted below, or marked on the drawing with the word 'Reconstruction'. The position of the item is also indicated with reference to the centrelines of the ship or engines, as appropriate. The words 'inboard' or 'outboard' refer to whether it is closest to the centreline of the ship or the hull planking respectively. Bolts, nuts and bolt holes are sometimes shown depending on the complexity of the drawing, and if they could obscure other details. Similarly items are not always shown in all views if the drawing would become too complicated.

1. Cylinder
A large casting, which has flanges for bolting to the other cylinder (along the top and outboard side), the side and main frame and vertically down to the wooden bed and the hull. The cylinders are bored after being cast, the boring bar passing through the small

MACHINERY

2. Cylinder cover (scale = 1:24)

1 and 1 to opposite hand

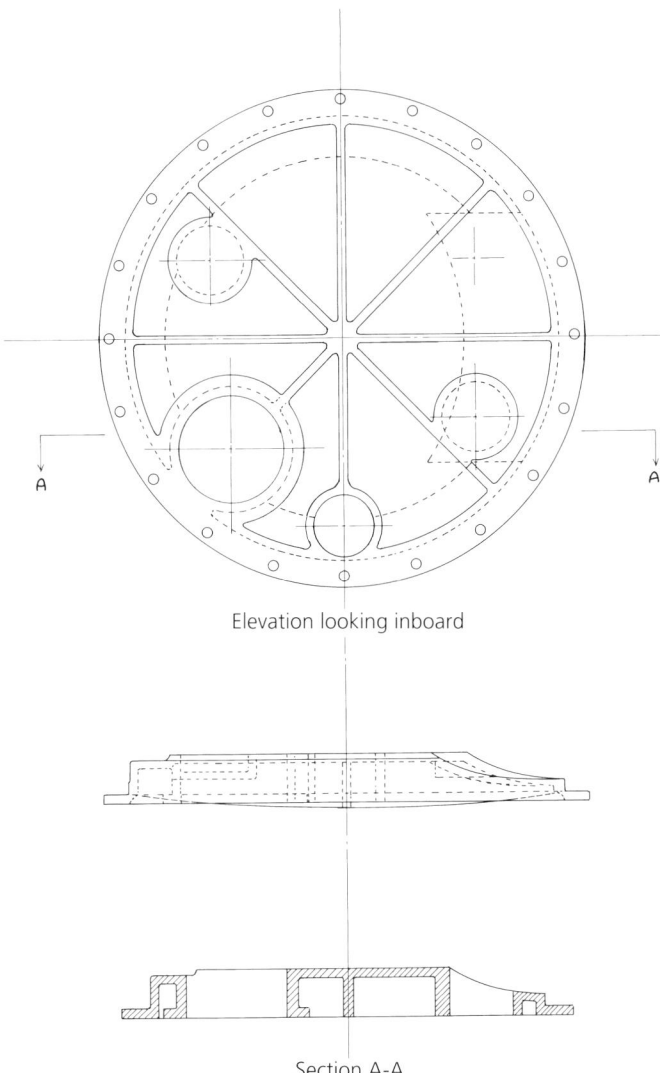

Elevation looking inboard

Section A-A

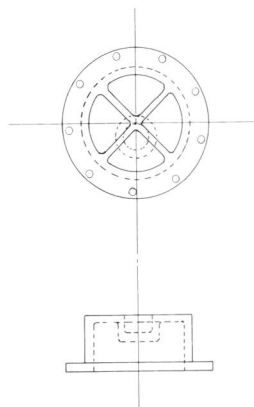

Cover plate over air pump rod

hole in the centre of the inboard face, this hole being covered by the central cover plate. There are a number of holes through the cylinder, the largest and most complicated being the steam inlet on the side. The cylinders would be covered in felt and then cased in wood for insulation.

2. Cylinder cover

The recesses within the cylinder cover are for the nuts on the ends of the piston and air pump rods. The cutout on one side is for the steam inlet.

3. Piston

The piston has been reconstructed, based on similar ones either by Lairds or other builders. Four rods—two piston, air pump and bilge/feed pumps—are attached to the piston by means of nuts on the outboard side. The packing ring goes around the piston and is

3. Piston (reconstruction) (scale = 1:24)

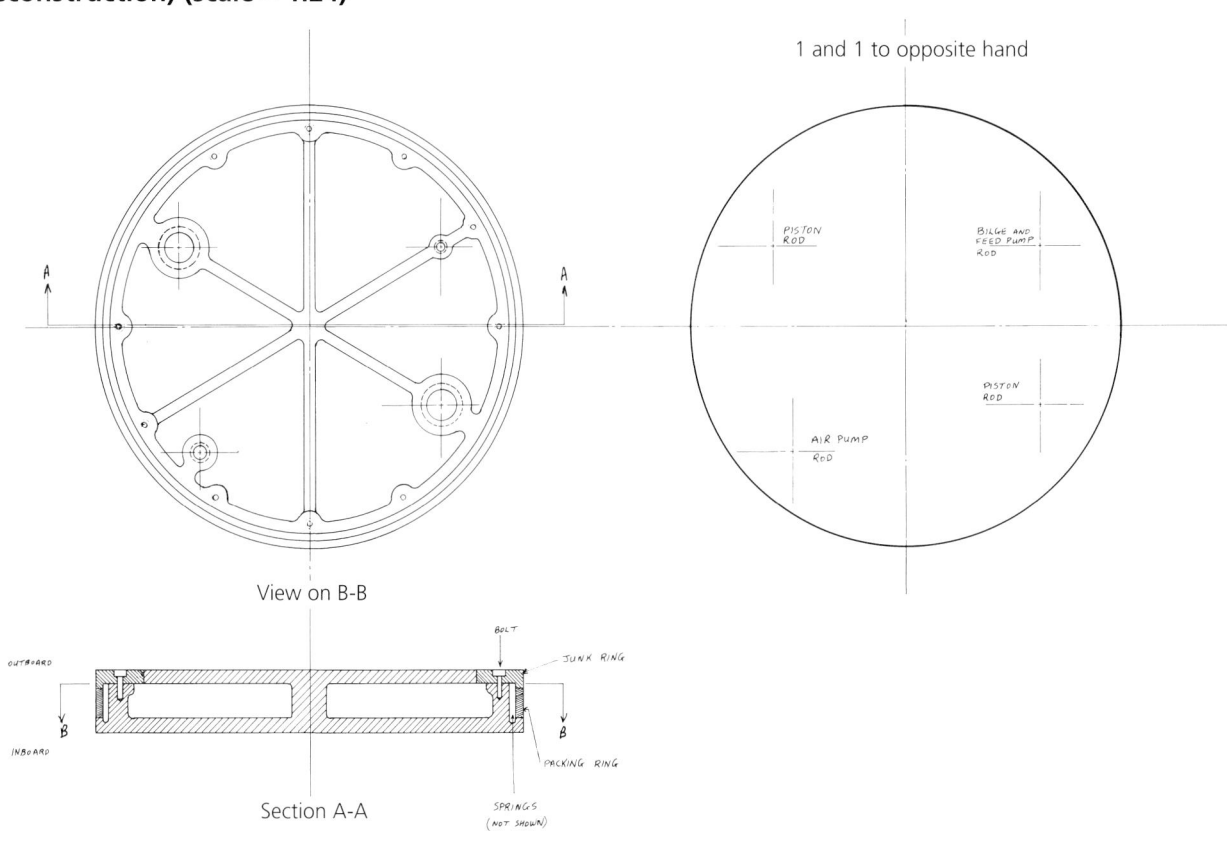

View on B-B

Section A-A

4 & 5. Piston Rod (scale = 1:24)
2 per piston

7. Slide Block (scale = 1:12)

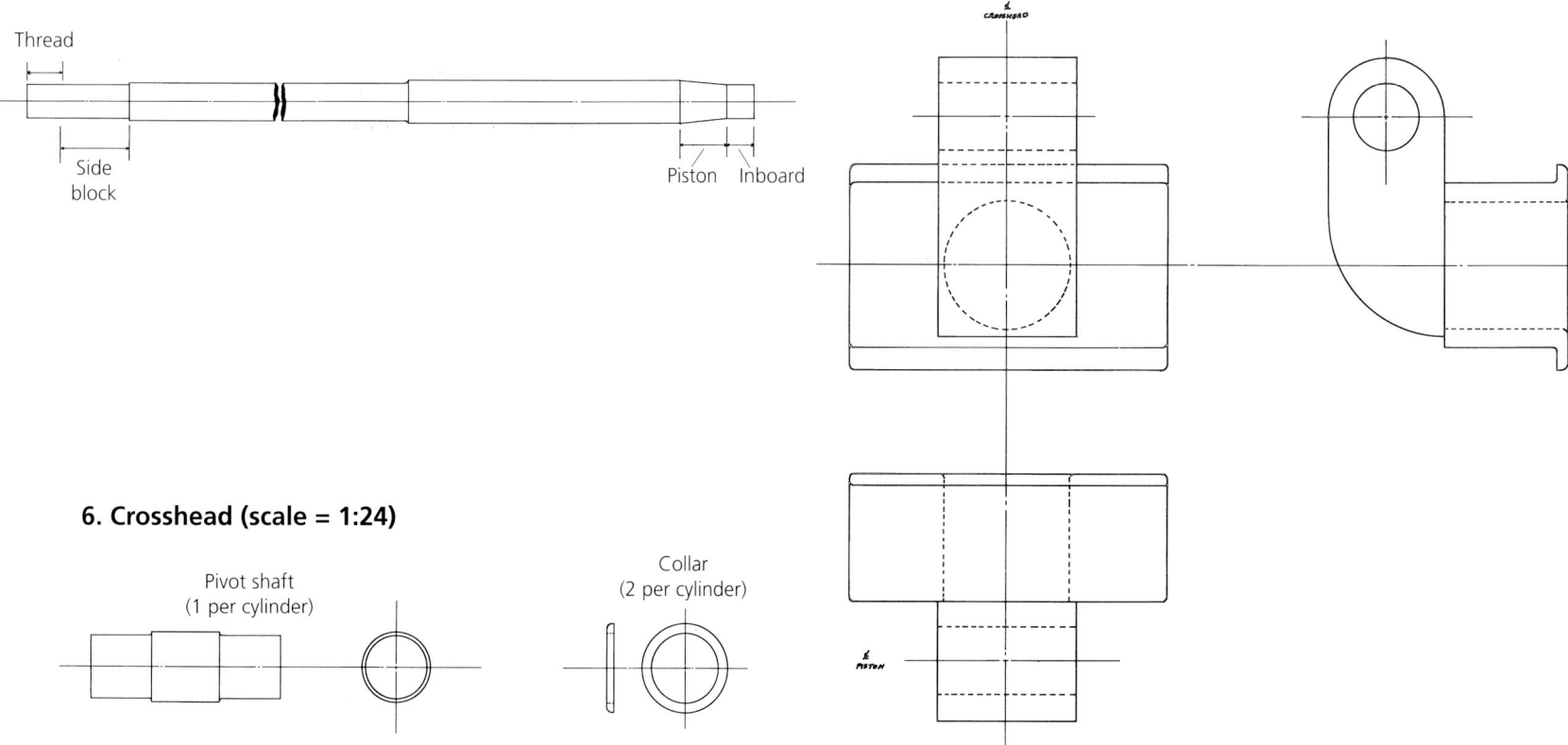

6. Crosshead (scale = 1:24)

8. Motion Bar (scale = 1:12)

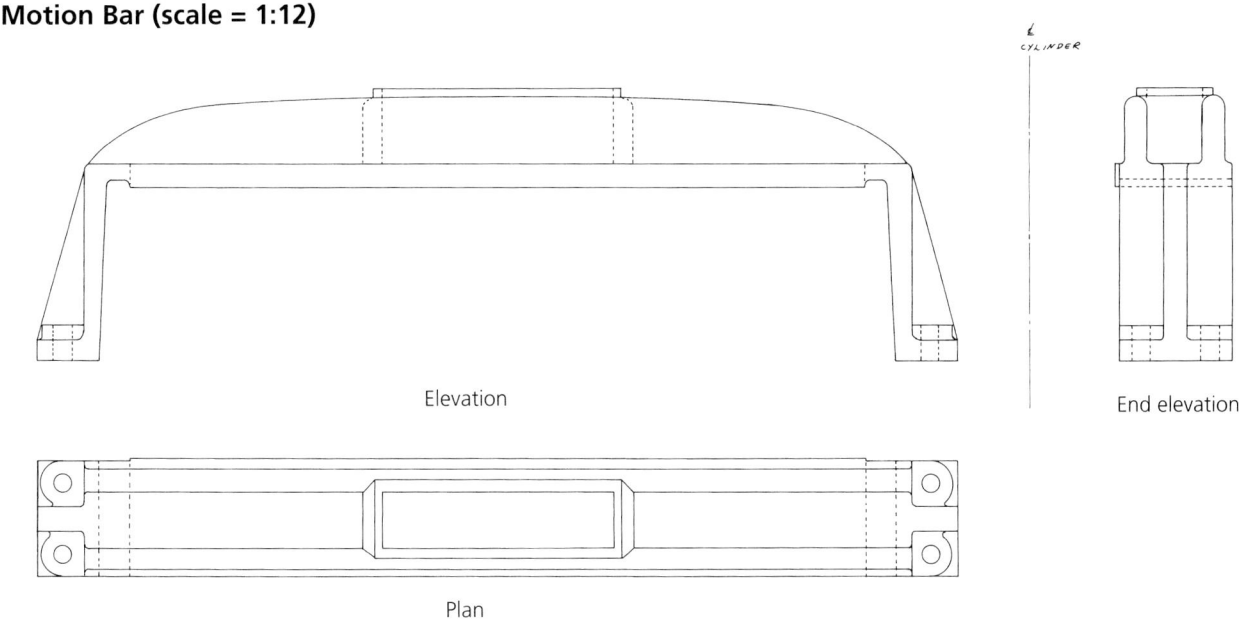

Elevation

Plan

End elevation

9. Connecting Rod (scale = 1:24)
1 per cylinder

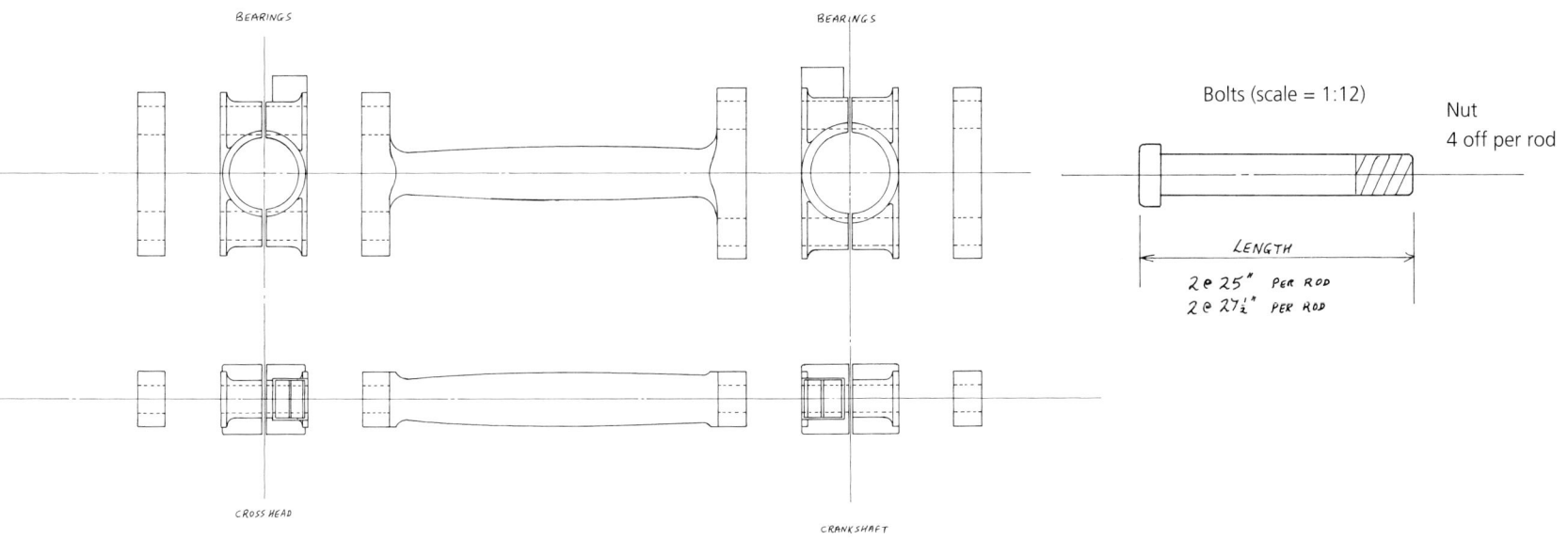

Bolts (scale = 1:12)

Nut
4 off per rod

LENGTH
2 @ 25" PER ROD
2 @ 27½" PER ROD

kept in contact with the cylinder wall by means of springs. The junk ring is a metal ring bolted to the piston which holds the packing ring and springs in place.

4 & 5. Piston rods
Two piston rods per cylinder, attached to the Slide Blocks (7) on the opposite side of the centreline of the ship. One piston rod is above the crankshaft (10) and one below. There is also a support on the centreline, which is attached to either the Side or Main frames (11 or 12) as appropriate.

6. Crosshead
Attached to two Slide Blocks (7) and one end of the Connecting Rod (9).

7. Slide Blocks
Attached to the piston rods and joined by the Crosshead (6). Lubrication is provided by oil from the top of the Motion Bars (8).

8. Motion Bars
There are two motion bars per cylinder which are bolted to the

10. Crankshaft (scale = 1:24)

Fwd
ENGINES
Aft
TURNING GEAR

11. Main Frame (scale = 1:24)

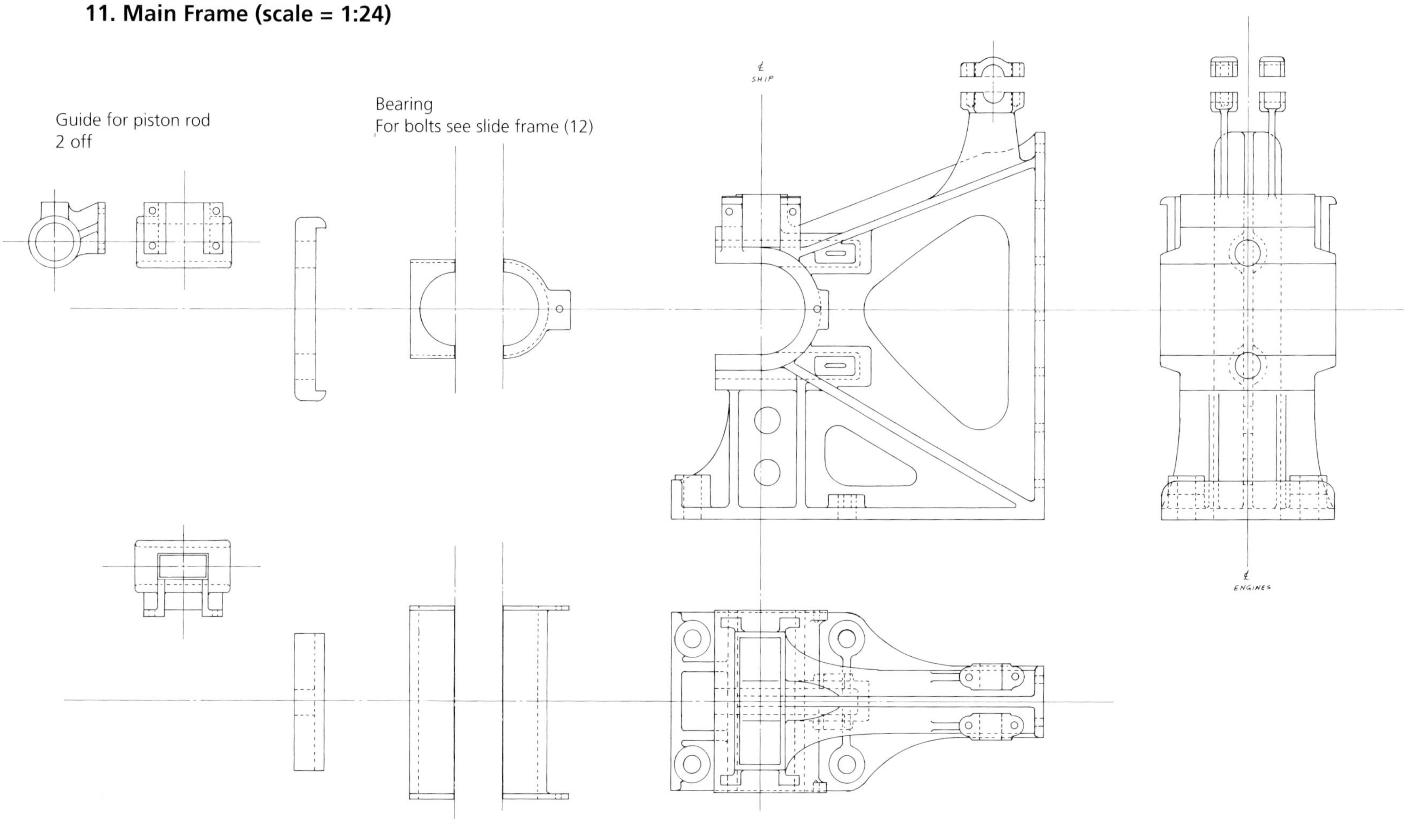

Guide for piston rod
2 off
Bearing
For bolts see slide frame (12)
SHIP
ENGINES

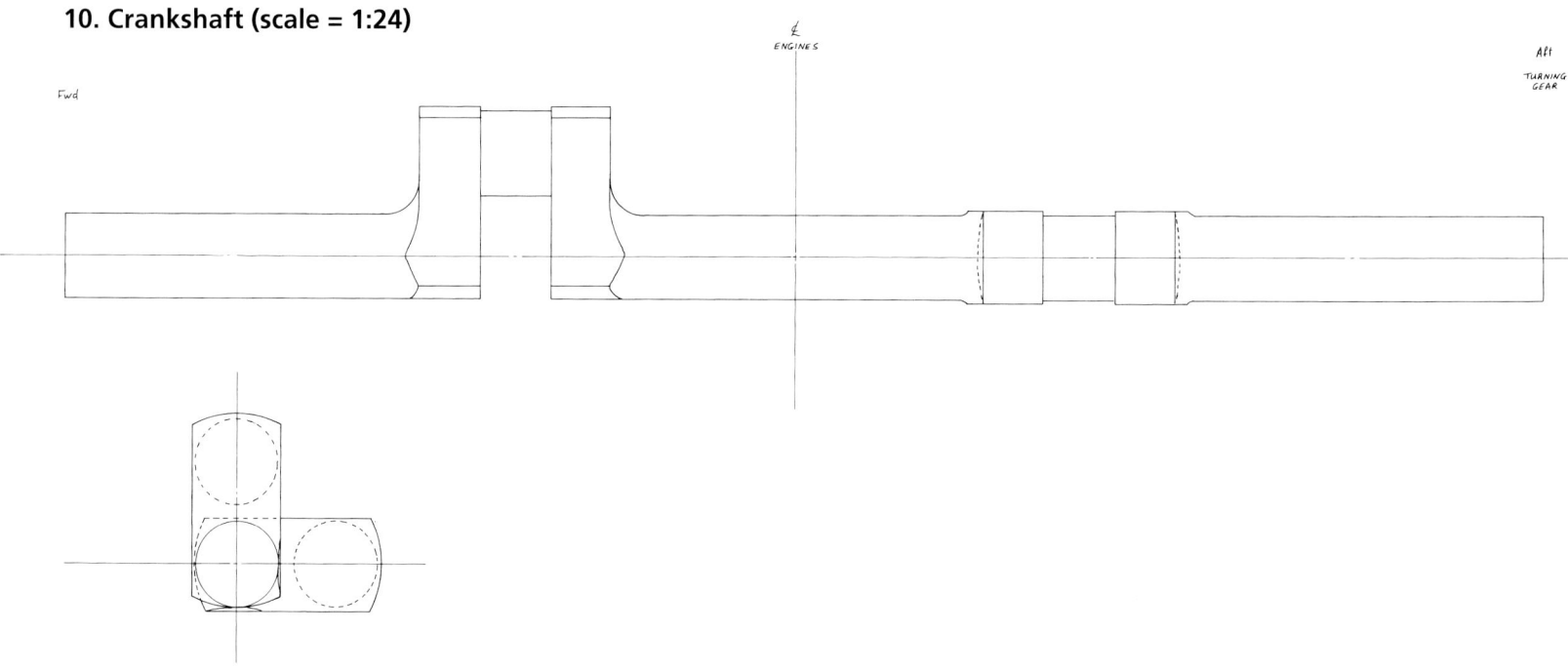

MACHINERY

12. Side Frame (scale = 1:24)

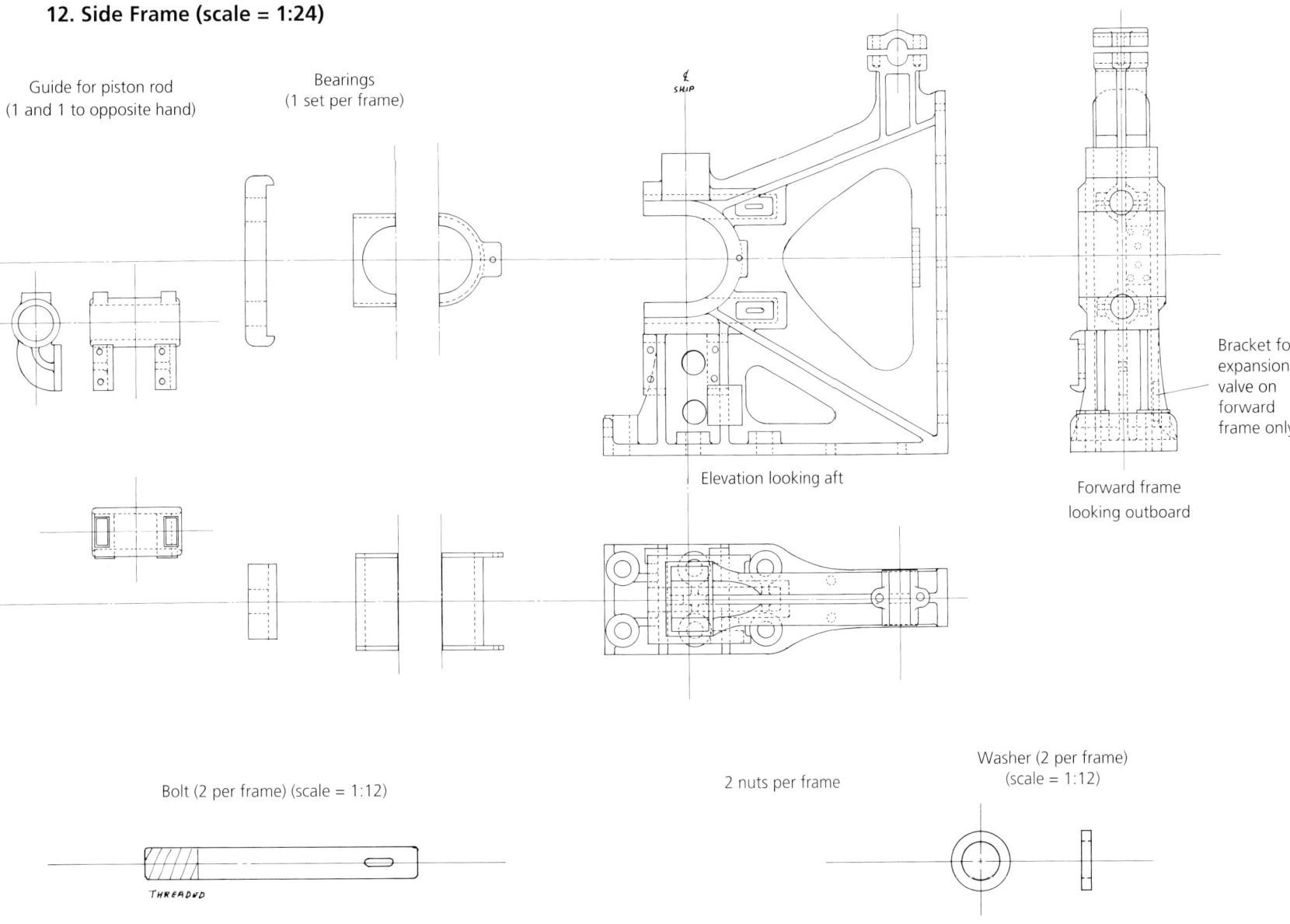

structure between the Hot Well and Condenser (14). The Slide Blocks (7) are held in position by the motion bars which has the Connecting Rod (9) and Crosshead (6) between them. Oil in the top centre part of each bar provides lubrication for the Slide Blocks and Crosshead.

9. Connecting rod
Shown complete with the bearings at each end, one for the Crosshead (6) and the other for the Crankshaft (10). Each bearing has its own oil cup to provide lubrication.

10. Crankshaft
Drawn as a single piece, but it would be made of several individual pieces.

11. Main frame
The Main frame is bolted down to the engine bed by four bolts. It is also bolted to the two Cylinders (1) along the line that is the centreline of the engines. An oil cup provides the lubrication for the crankshaft bearing. On each side of the main frame is a guide (with an oil cup) for a Piston rod (4). On the other side from the cylinders (the starboard side) the frame is bolted the Base plate (13), which is in turn bolted to the structure of the hot well and condenser (14). The bearings on top of the frame are for the control for the eccentric link (28).

12. Side frame
Basically the same as the Main frame (11), except that the guide for the Piston rod (5) has two oil cups.

13. Base Plate (scale = 1:24)

℄ ENGINES

14. Structure of Hot Well and Condenser (scale = 1:24)

1 and 1 to opposite hand

Section A-A

Hot well – top plate
(2 in total)

Condenser side plate
(4 in total)

Hot well – front plate
(2 in total)

Plan view

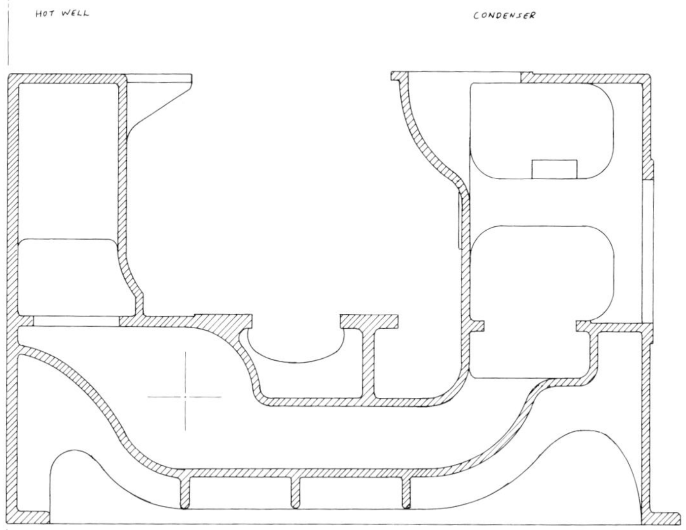

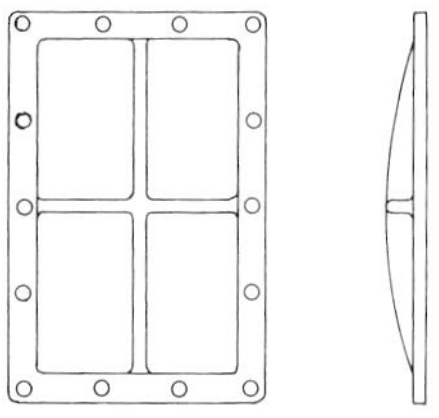

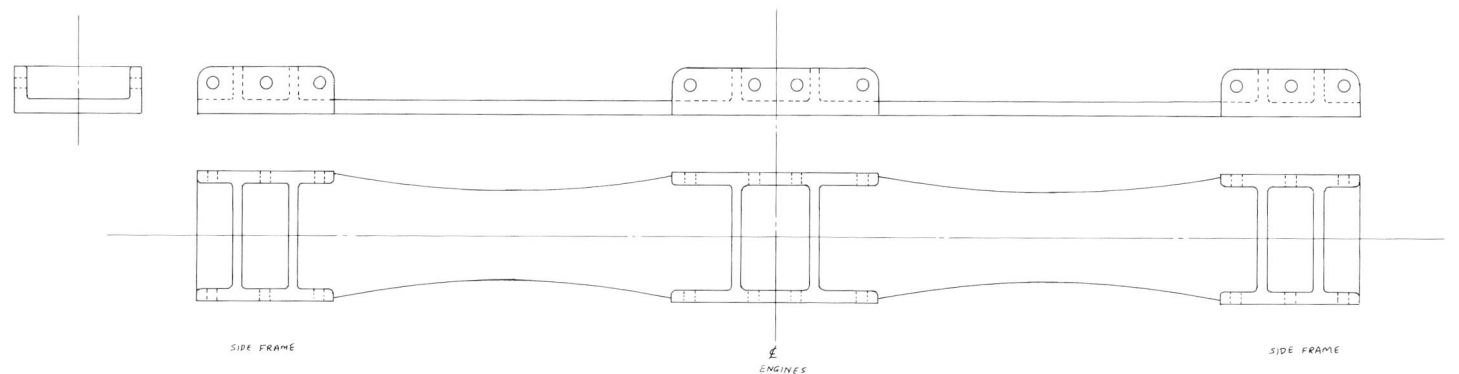

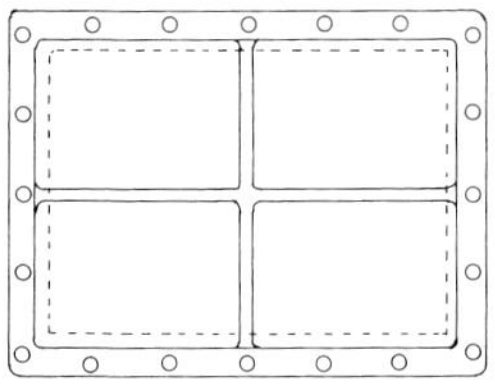

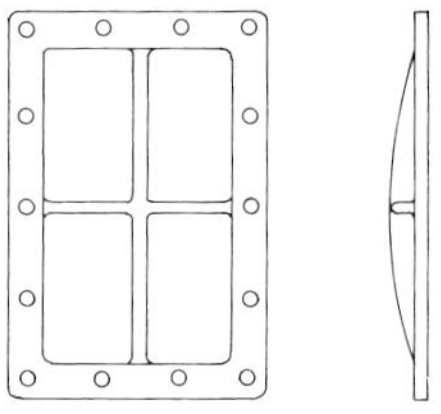

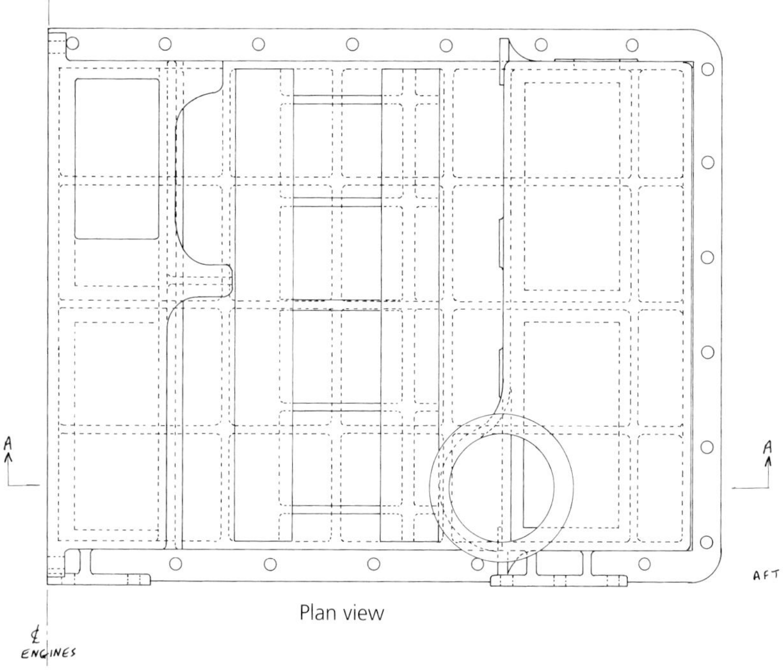

MACHINERY

Air Pump and Hot Well (scale = 1:16)

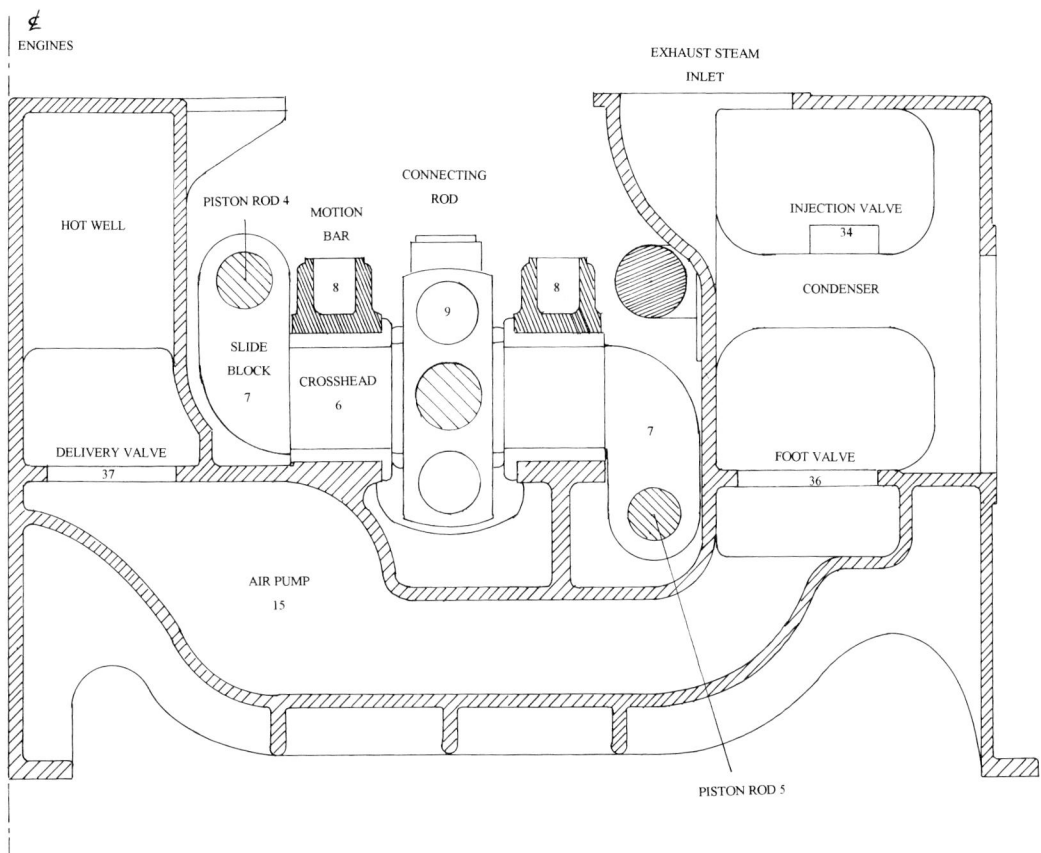

15. Air Pump (scale = 1:24)

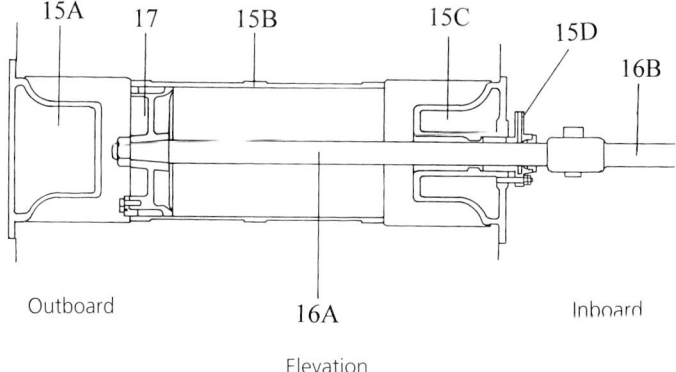

Elevation

13. Base plate
This is bolted to the Main and Side frames (11 and 12) on the port side and the structure of the hot well and condenser (14) on the starboard side.

14. Structure of hotwell and condenser
There are two castings for the complete engine, bolted together along the centreline of the engines and down to the engine bed.

15, 16 & 17. Air pump
The Air pump piston (17) works within a liner (15B) which is in the structure (14). There are covering plates at each end, the inboard one has the stuffing box (15D) that the piston rod (16A) passes through. As the piston moves backwards and forwards the water from the condenser (33) is drawn through the Foot valve (36) into the air pump and then through the Delivery Valve (37) into the hotwell (38). The piston rod is in three separate sections.

15A. Outer End Plate (1 per cylinder) (scale = 1:12)

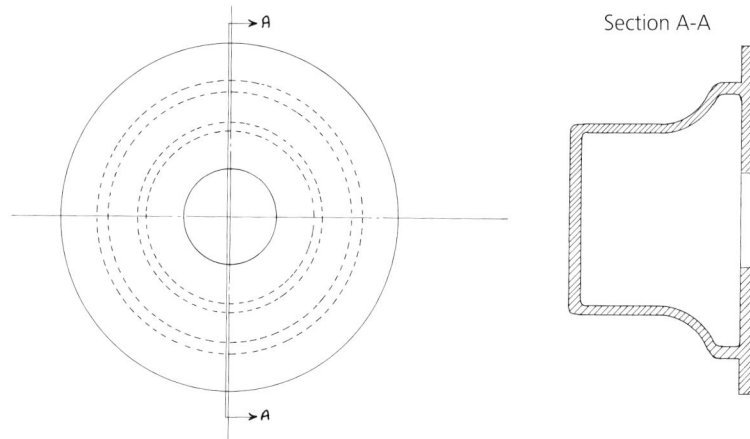

15B. Air pump (1 per cylinder)

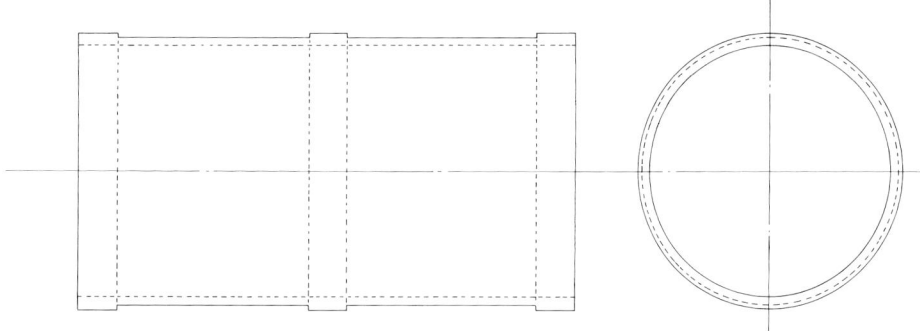

15C & D. Inner Plate and Stuffing Box (1 set per cylinder)

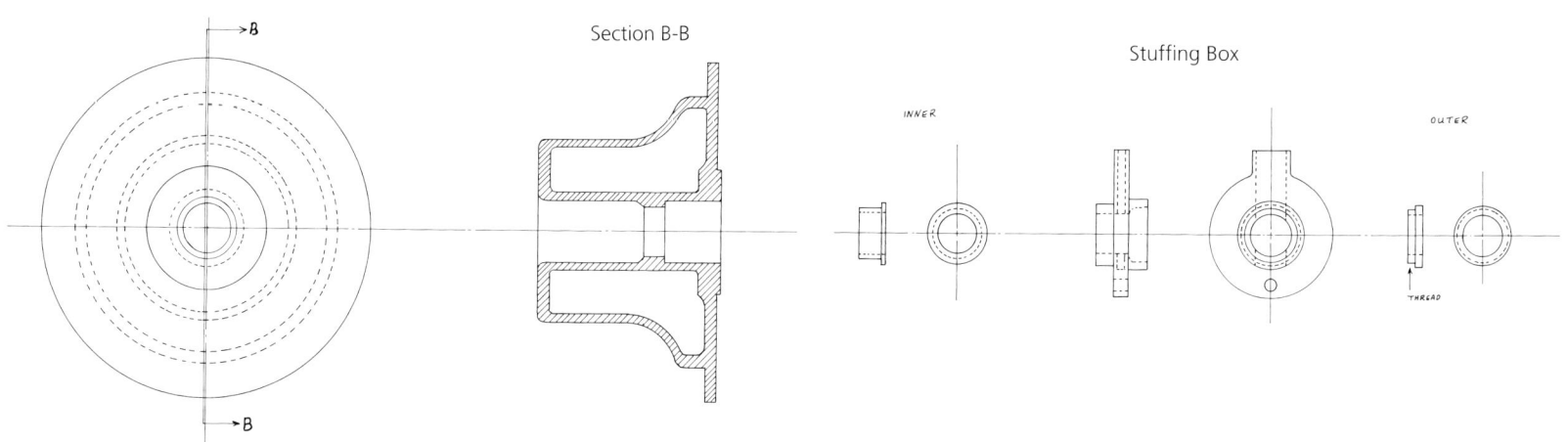

MACHINERY

17. Air Pump – Piston (scale = 1:12)

16. Air Pump – Piston Rod (2 per cylinder) (scale = 1:12)

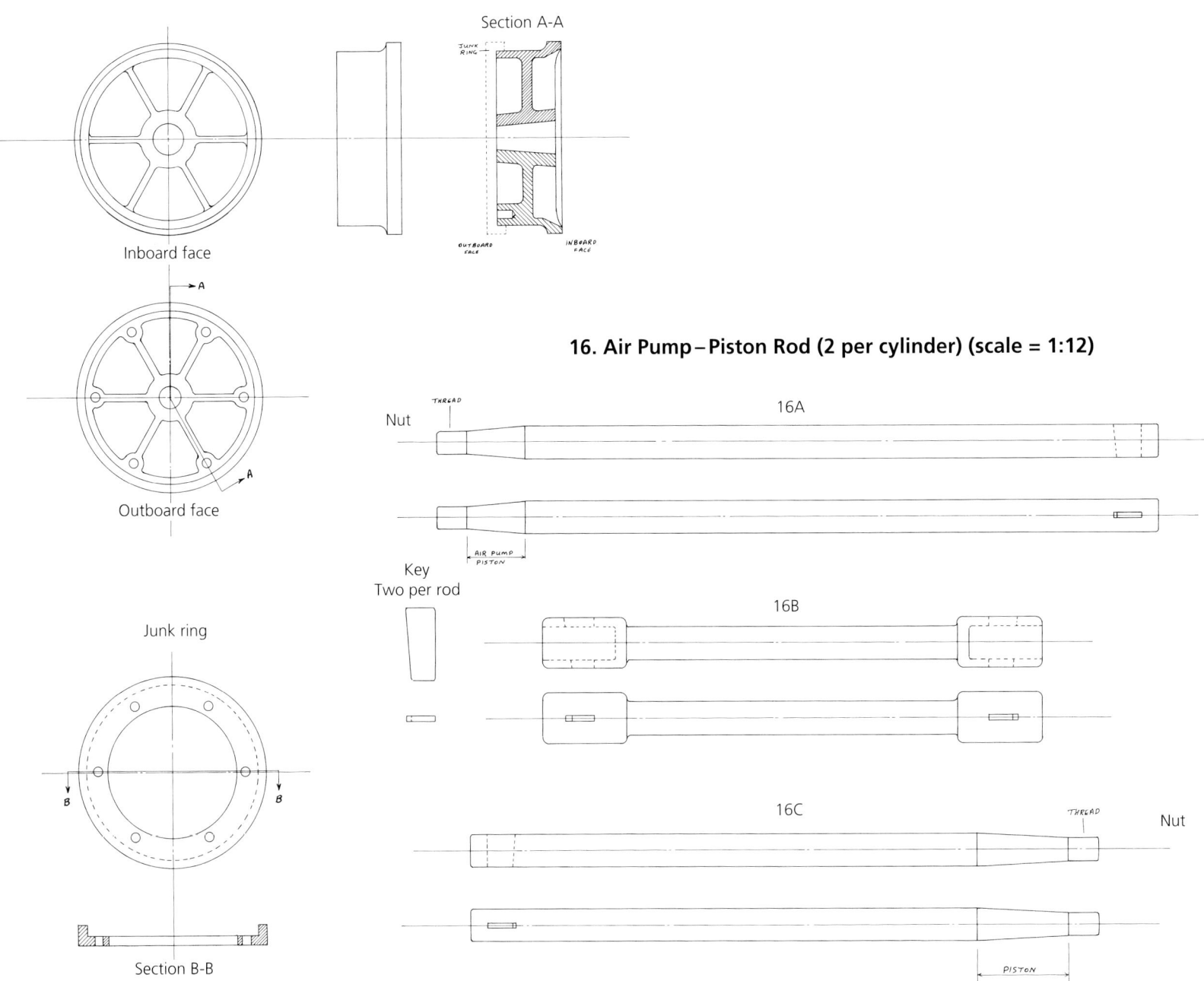

18. Feed Pump (1 and 1 to opposite hand) (scale = 1:12)

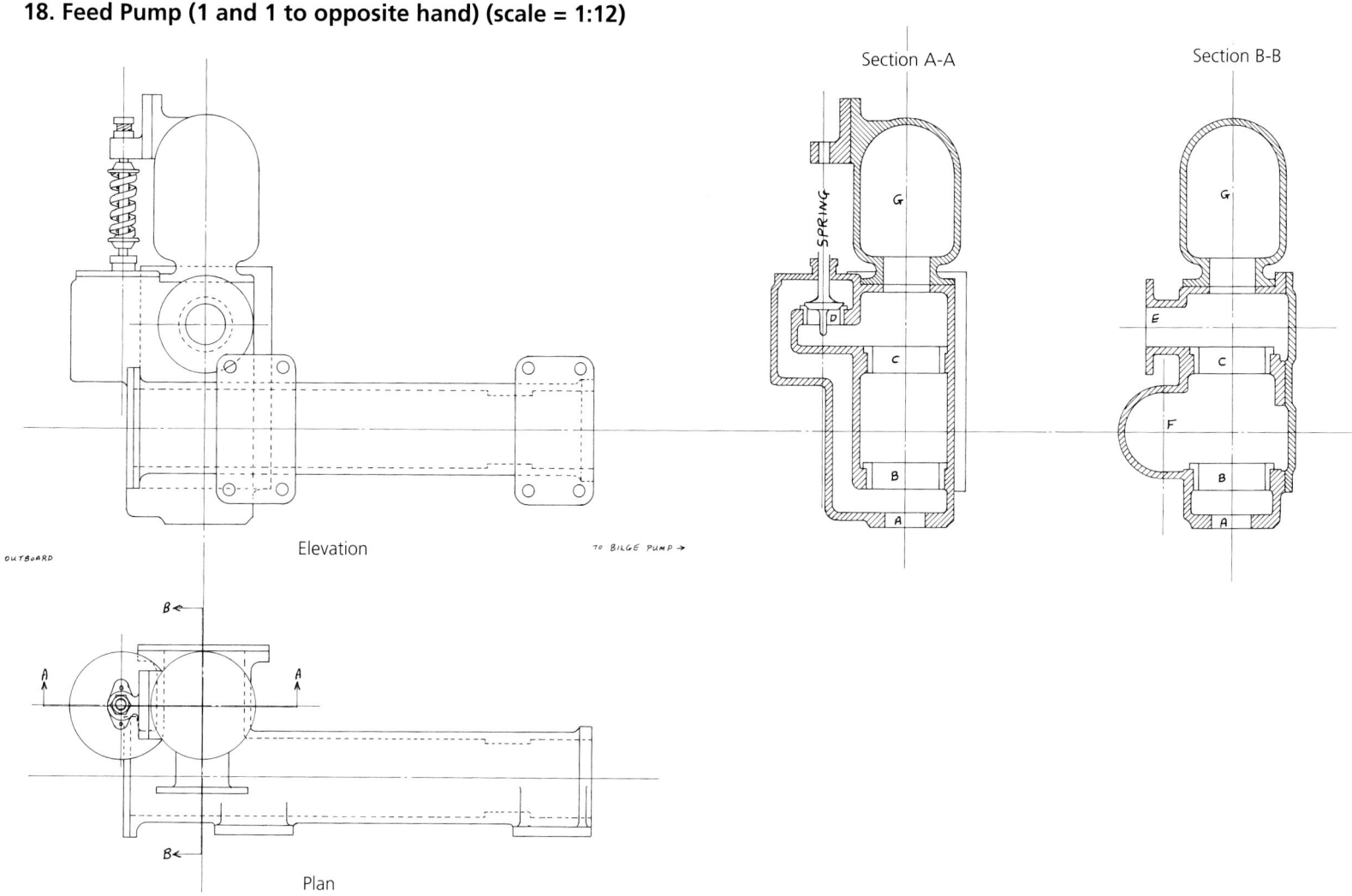

18. Feed pump

This takes condensed water from the hot well (38) back to the boilers. As the water is warm it is quicker, and more economical, to produce steam than if it was cold water. This pump shares a common plunger (21) and rod (20) with the Bilge pump (19), and both are working when the engine is turning.

The various parts of the feed pump are:

A   Inlet from Hot Well
B   Suction valve
C   Delivery valve
D   Relief valve
E   Outlet to boiler
F   Plunger
G   Air vessel

The quantity of water returned to the boilers is controlled by the relief valve (D), which will open if none is required. The water then just circulates within the pump.

19. Bilge Pump (scale = 1:12)

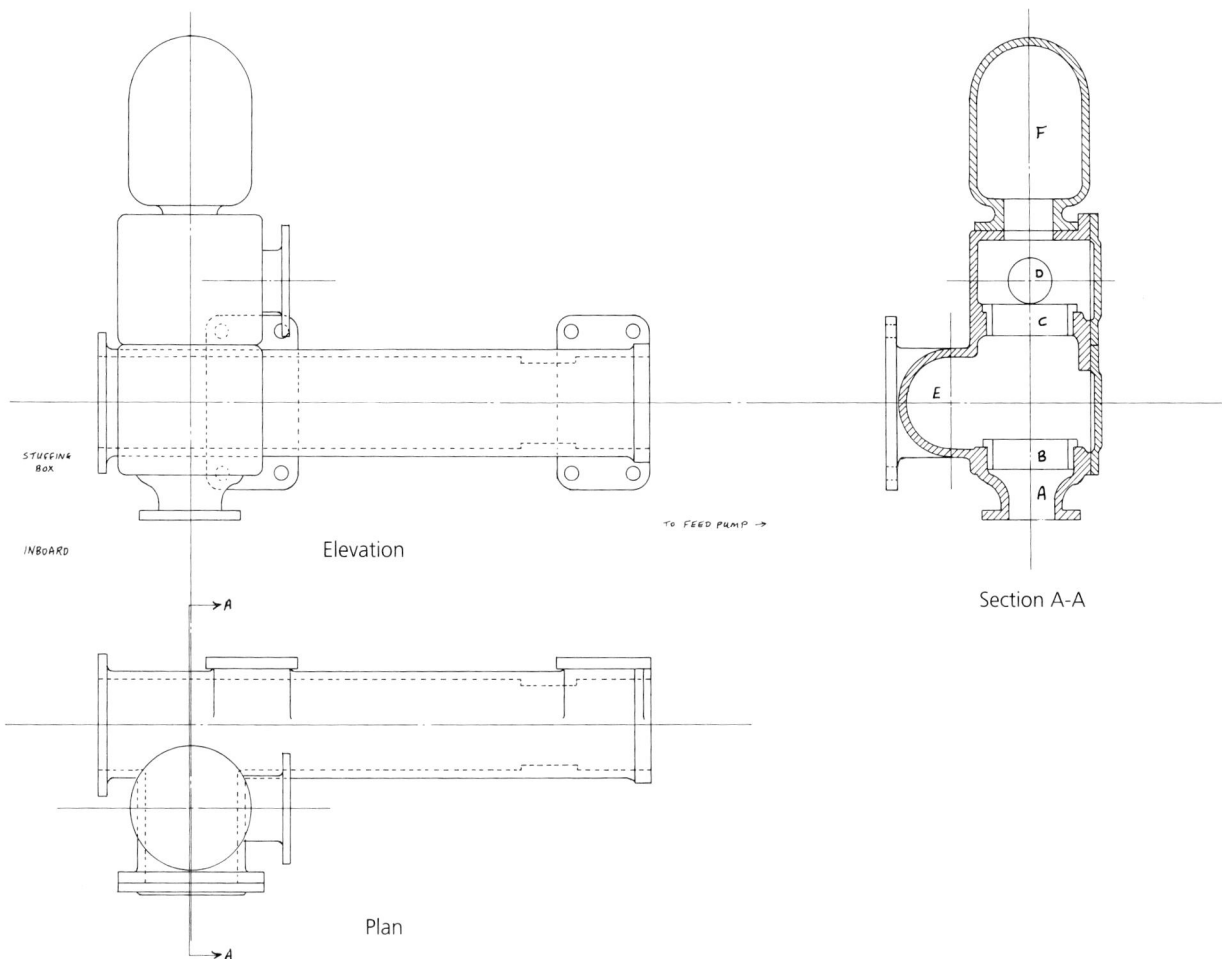

19. Bilge pump

This is basically the same as the Feed pump (18), except that there is no relief valve. The bilge water is discharged into the discharge pipe (39) which is always open, so there is no need for a relief valve.

A   Inlet from bilge
B   Suction valve
C   Delivery valve
D   Outlet to discharge pipe
E   Plunger
F   Air vessel

20. Feed and Bilge Pump – Rod and Stuffing Boxes (scale = 1:12)

Rod 1

Rod 2

Rod 3

Stuffing box

Stuffing box

21. Feed and Bilge Pump – Plunger etc (scale = 1:12)

Plunger

Section A-A

Section between bilge and feed pump bodies

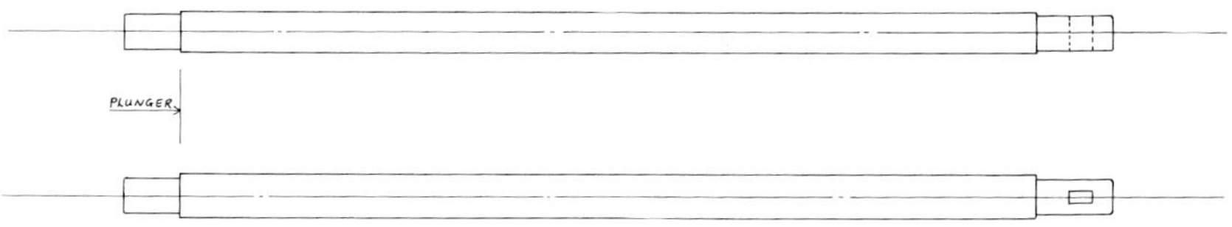

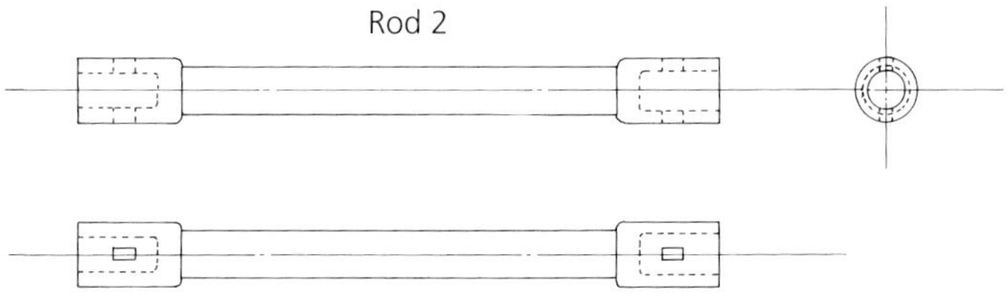

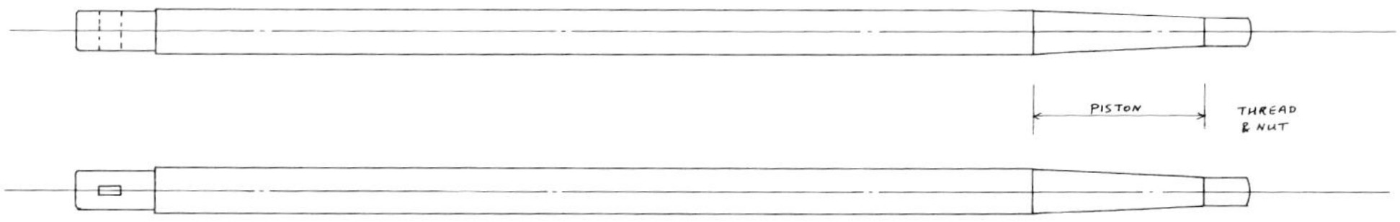

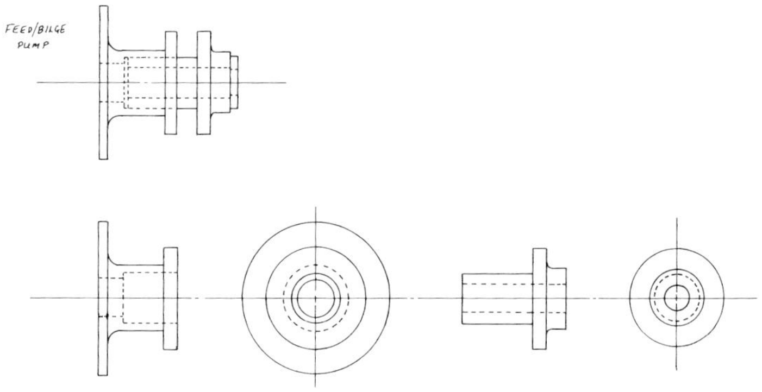

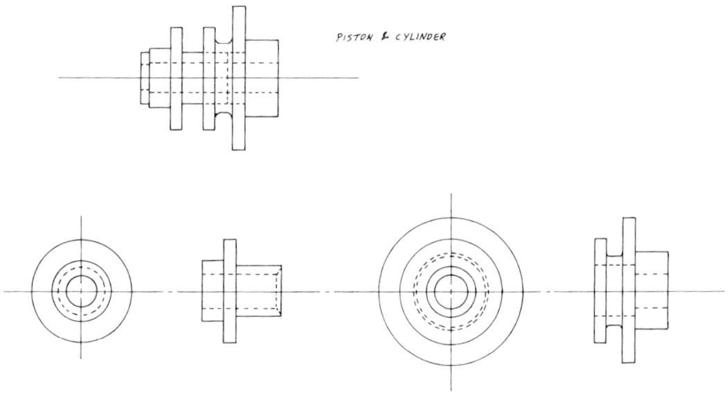

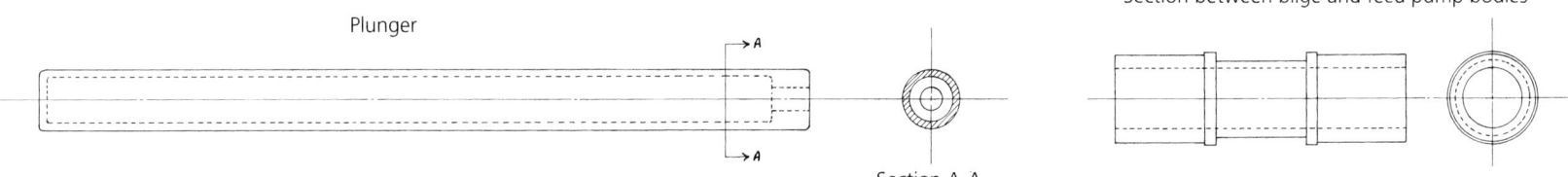

MACHINERY

20. Feed and Bilge pump rod
This is in three sections, similar to the air pump rod (16). The stuffing boxes, one at each end of the rod, are shown complete (above) and separated out.

21. Feed and Bilge pump plunger
There is a common rod for these two pumps, which are joined together by the section shown.

22. Slide valve
The movement of the slide valve is shown in the diagram. The steam enters the valve chest (24) and surrounds the slide valve. A shows the valve in mid position with no steam being admitted to the cylinder, or exhaust steam leaving. B has the valve moved to one end of its range which has uncovered the ports allowing the steam to enter the cylinder on the left and exert pressure on the piston (which is represented by a line). It has also uncovered the exhaust ports allowing the steam to the condenser. The slide valve then moves in the other direction, cutting off steam (as in A). When it has passed the mid point this allows the steam to enter the other side of the cylinder – C, and exert pressure on the opposite side of the piston compared to previously – B.

The slide valve is moved by the rod (23) which is in turn driven by the eccentric (25) on the crankshaft (10).

22. Slide Valve (scale = 1:24)
1 and 1 to opposite hand

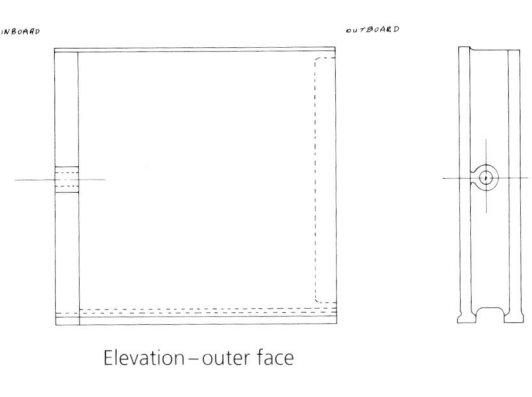

Elevation – outer face

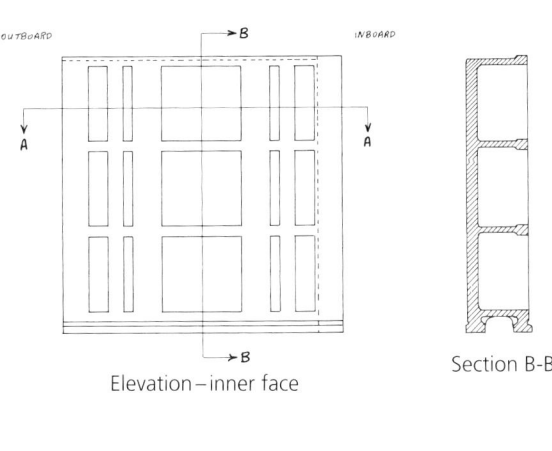

Elevation – inner face

Section B-B

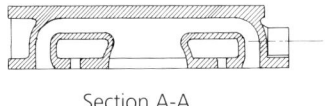

Section A-A

Slide Valve (not to scale)

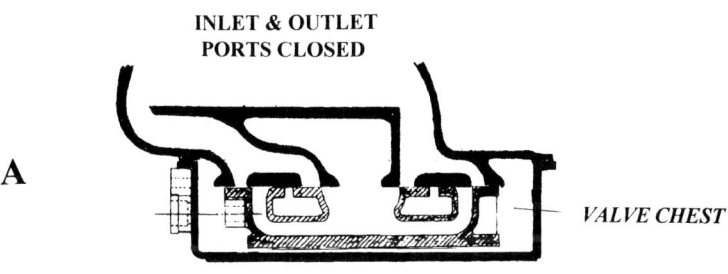

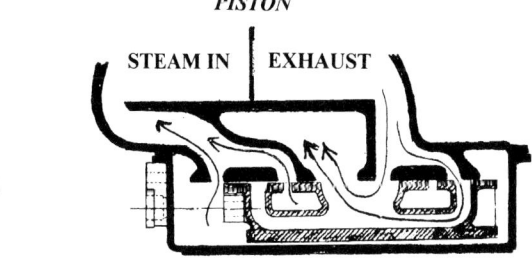

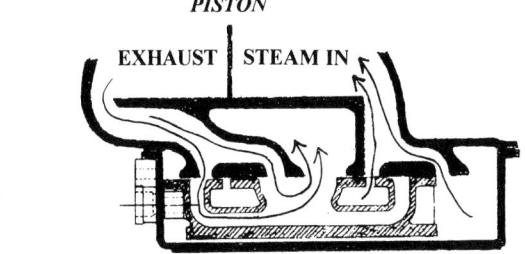

23. Slide Valve Rod and Guide (scale = 1:12)

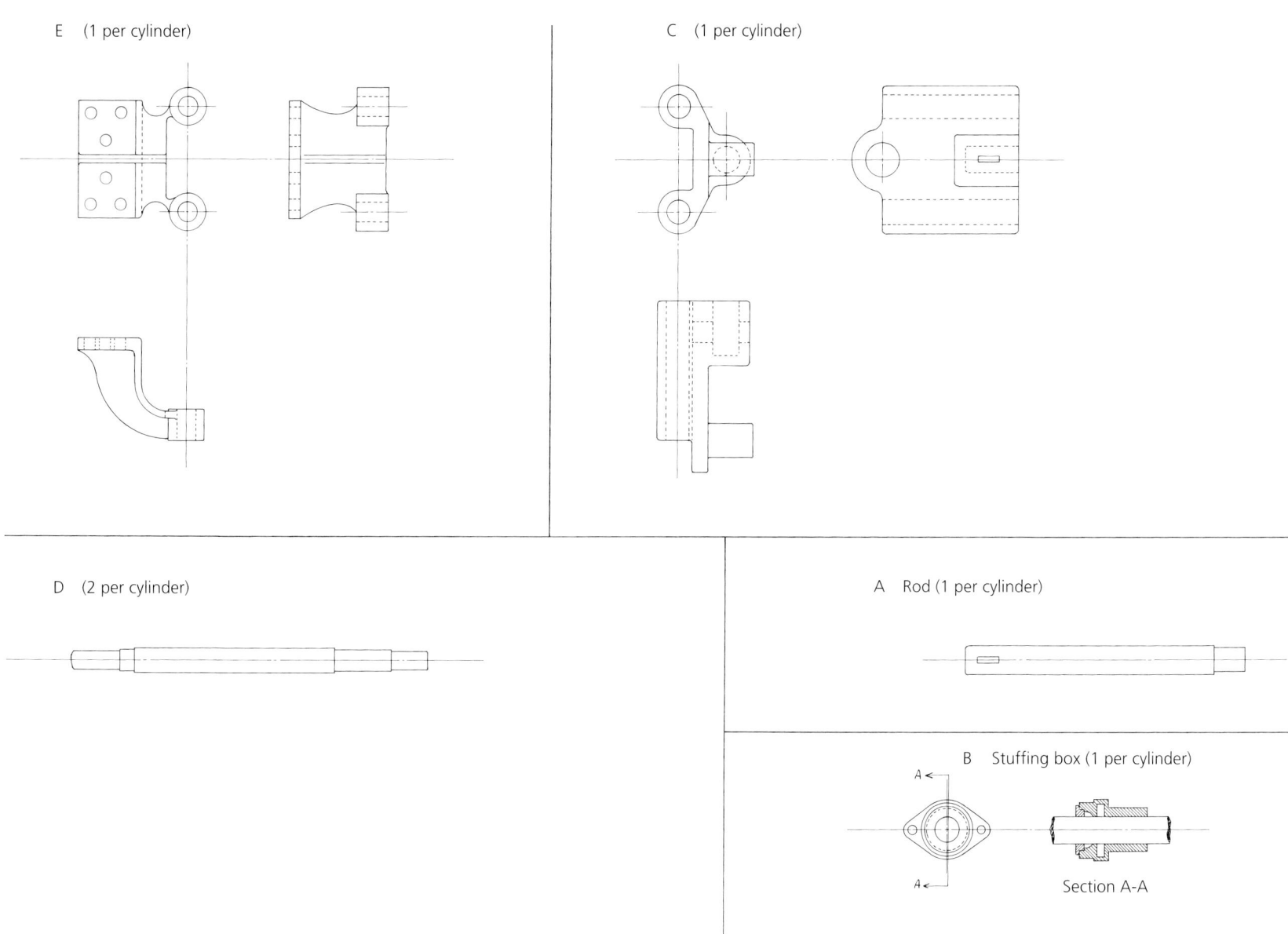

23. *Slide valve rod and guide*

The ends of the guide rods (23D) are attached to the valve chest (24) and at the other end to the bracket (23E), which is in turn fixed to the side frame (12). The slide valve rod is attached to the block (23C) which runs along the guides.

24. *Valve chest*

The valve chest contains the slide valve (22) which runs along the bottom face. The cover has a ring which presses on the back of the slide valve, keeping it in contact with the steam ports. The pressure on the back of the slide valve can be adjusted by means of six bolts through the cover. The steam from the boilers enters the top of the chest, through the expansion valve (43).

MACHINERY

24. Valve Chest and Cover (scale = 1:12)

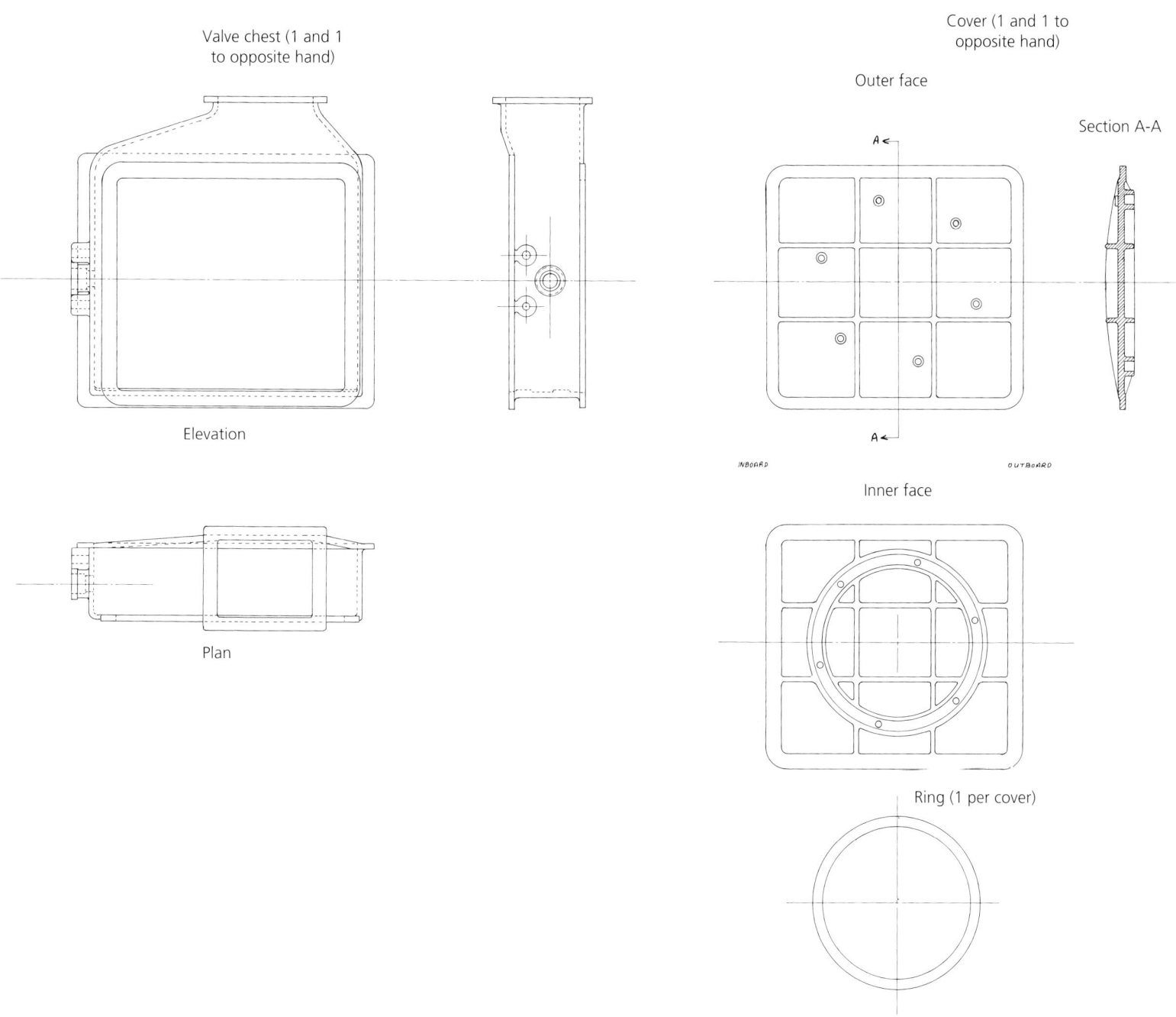

25. Eccentric Sheave (2 per cylinder) (scale = 1:12)

26. Eccentric Strap and Rod (2 per cylinder) (scale = 1:12)

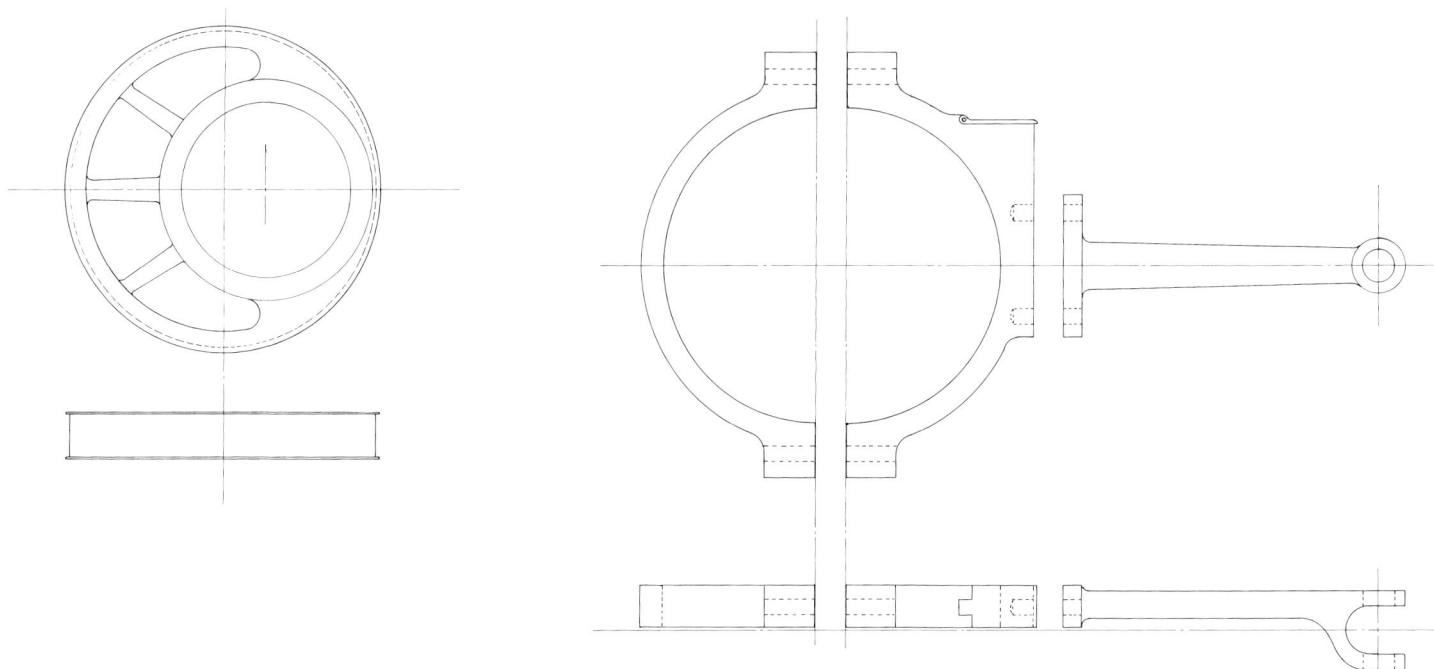

27A. Eccentric Link (1 per cylinder) (scale = 1:12)

27B. Eccentric Link – back lever pin (1 per cylinder) (scale = 1:12)

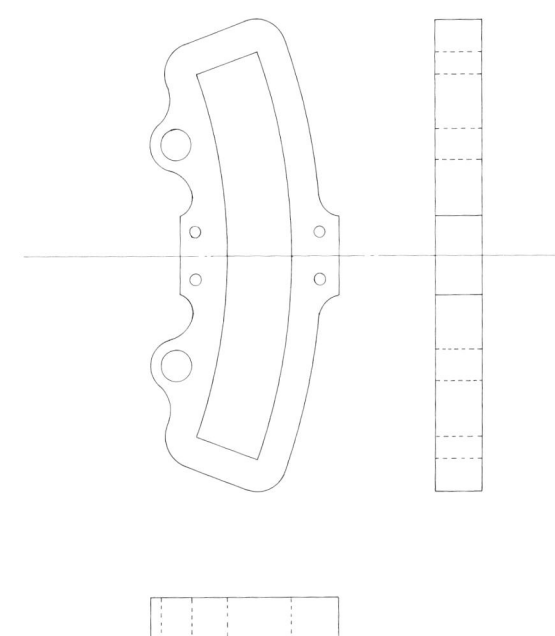

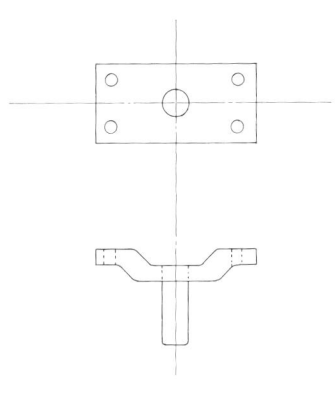

28. Control for Eccentric Link (scale = 1:24)

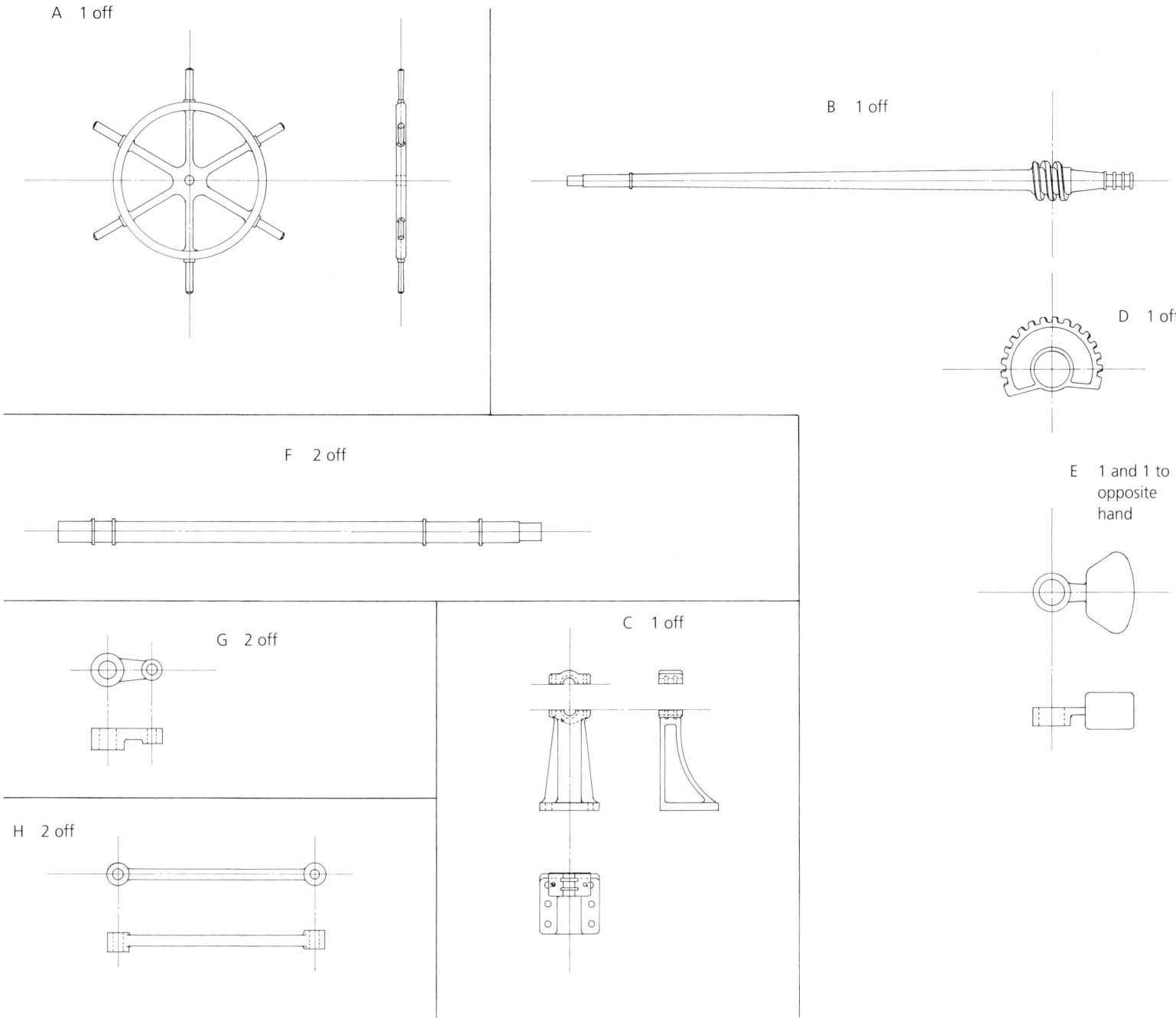

25. Eccentric sheave

There are two eccentric sheaves per cylinder which are fixed to the crankshaft (10). This double eccentric (sometimes called Stephenson's link) motion is used to easily produce the head and back motion *ie* to reverse the direction of the engine.

26 & 27. Eccentric strap and rod & Link

These are driven by the eccentric sheaves (25) and in turn move the slide valve (22).

28. Control for eccentric link

This system is for changing the direction of rotation of the crankshaft (10), altering the motion of the ship from ahead to astern, or vice versa. Turning the wheel (28A) causes the shafts 28B and 28F to rotate, which leads to 28G and 28H moving the link (27A) either up or down. This will happen for both cylinders at the same time. With the link (27A) at the extreme position the motion of the engine will be either ahead or astern. When the link is at the mid point the slide will be stationary.

Eccentric Link and Controls (scale = 1:24)

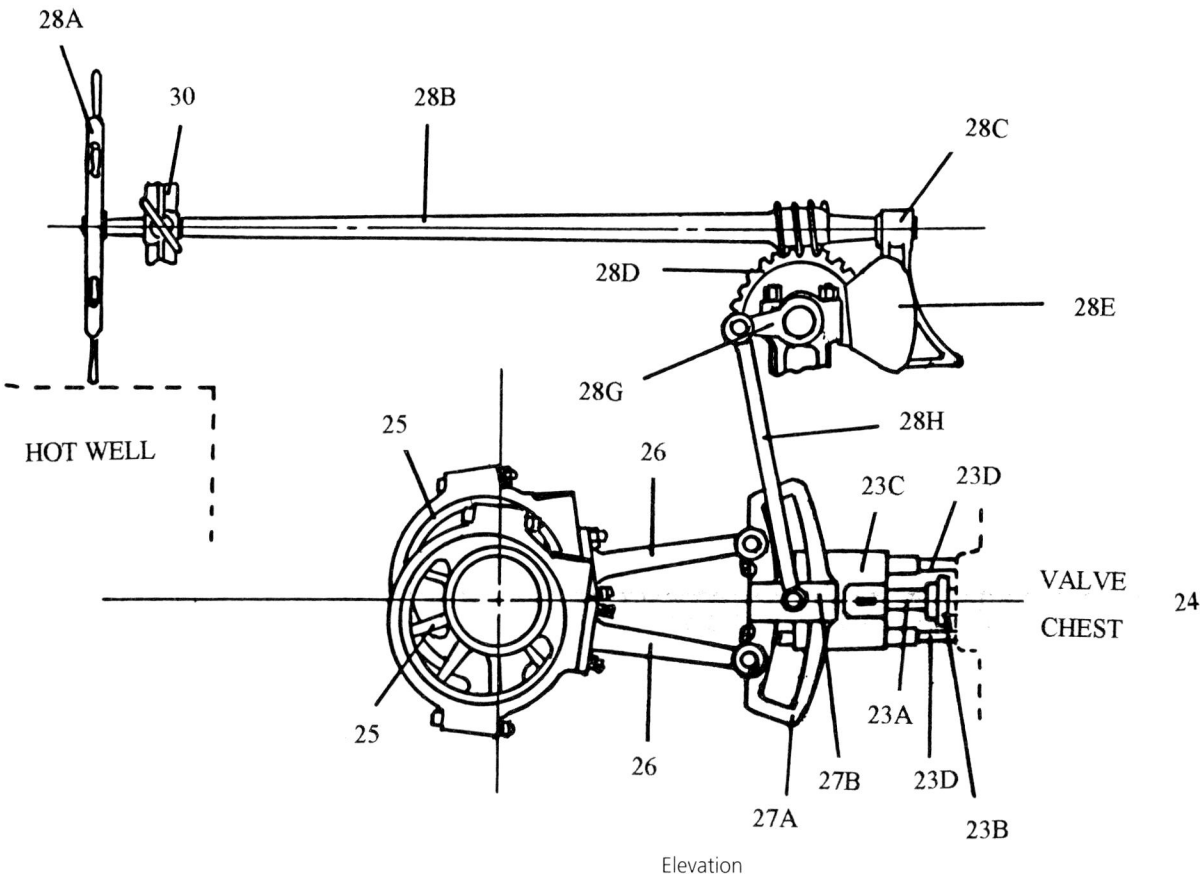

Elevation

29. Throttle Valve (scale = 1:24)

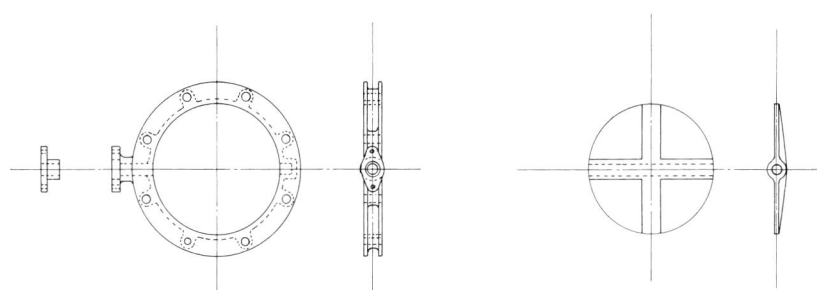

29 & 30. Throttle valve and controls
Through the various linkages this controls the amount of steam from the boiler. There is only one valve for the two cylinders.

31 & 32. Steam inlet and exhaust pipes
These pipes are copper and have a section to allow for expansion. The throttle valve (29) fits immediately before the first section of the inlet pipe (31).

33. Condenser
The structure of this is shown as part of 14.

34 & 35. Injection valve and controls
There is one injection valve per cylinder. Salt water enters through the base of the valve (34A) and then passes to the injection pipe (34B). The injection pipe is a reconstruction of a type that may have been fitted. The pipe is rectangular in section and reduces in area along its length. Saw cuts are made in the pipe which causes the water to form a spray that condenses the steam. The water is admitted to the pipe by means of the sluice valve. The quantity of water entering the pipe is controlled by the valve and will be set at the minimum necessary to condense the steam.

MACHINERY

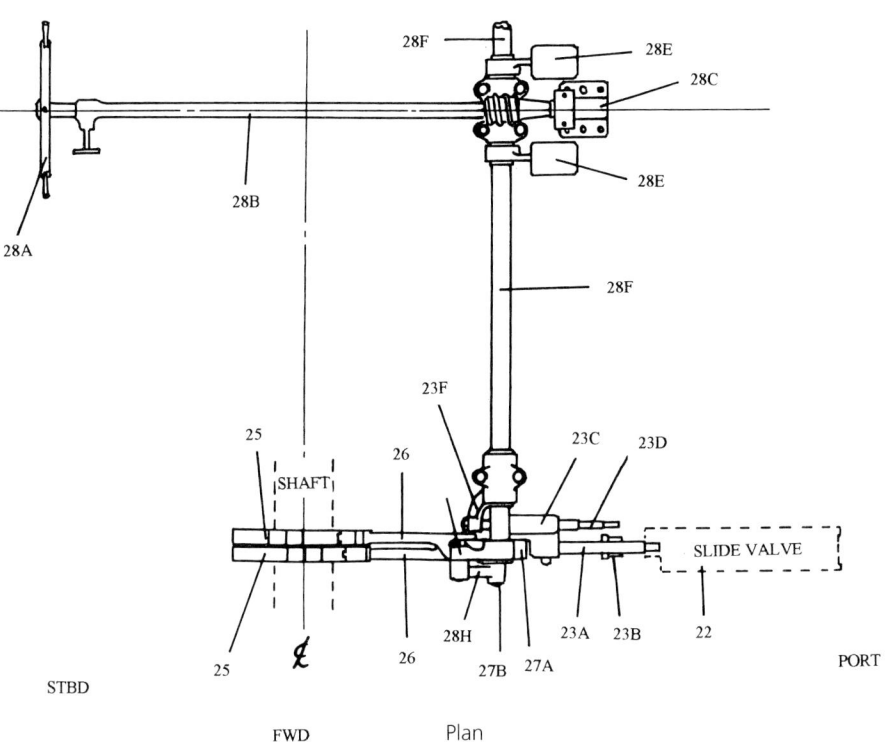

30. Throttle Valve Controls (scale = 1:24)

A 1 of each

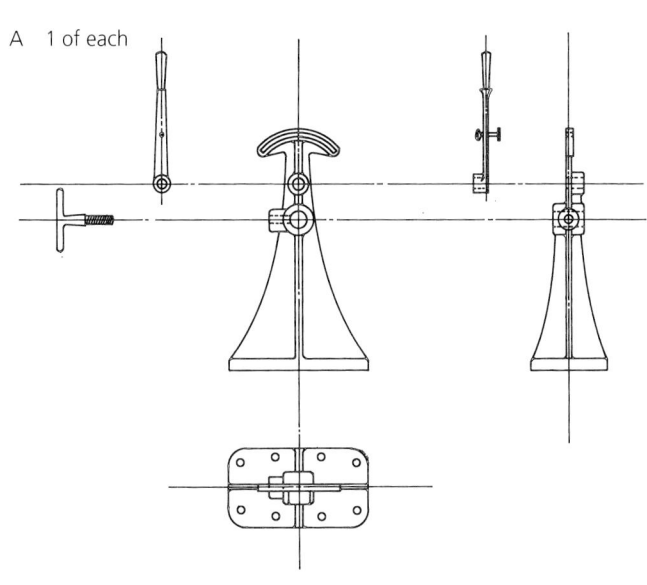

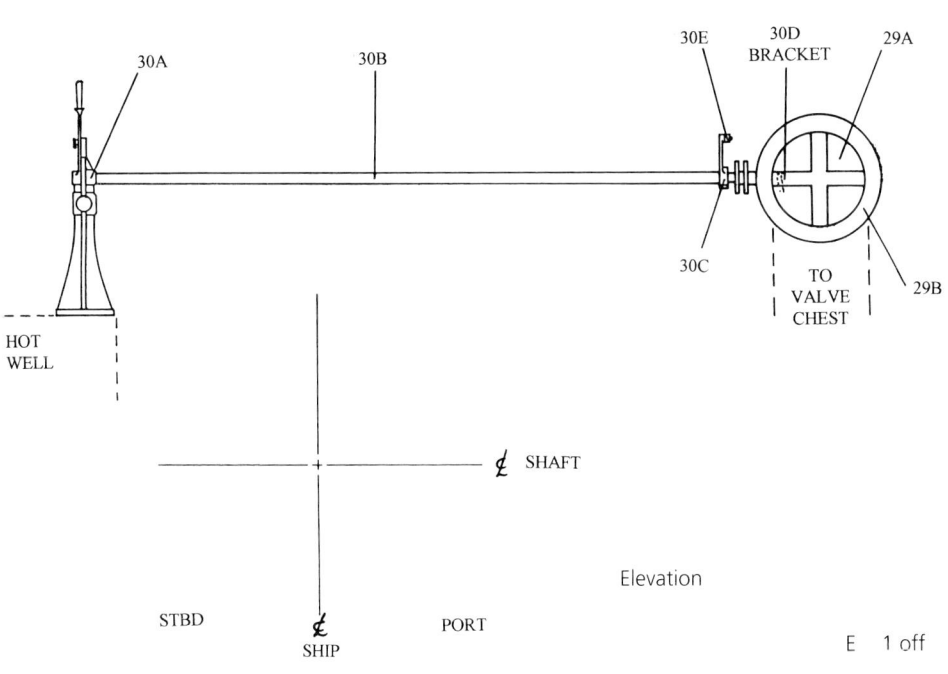

C 2 off

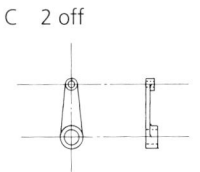

D 1 off

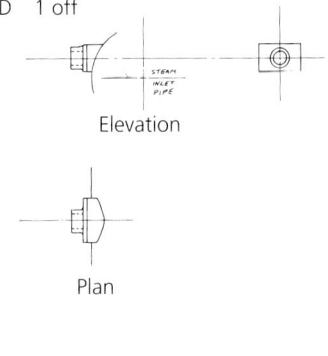

E 1 off

B 1 off

31. Steam Inlet Pipe (scale = 1:24)

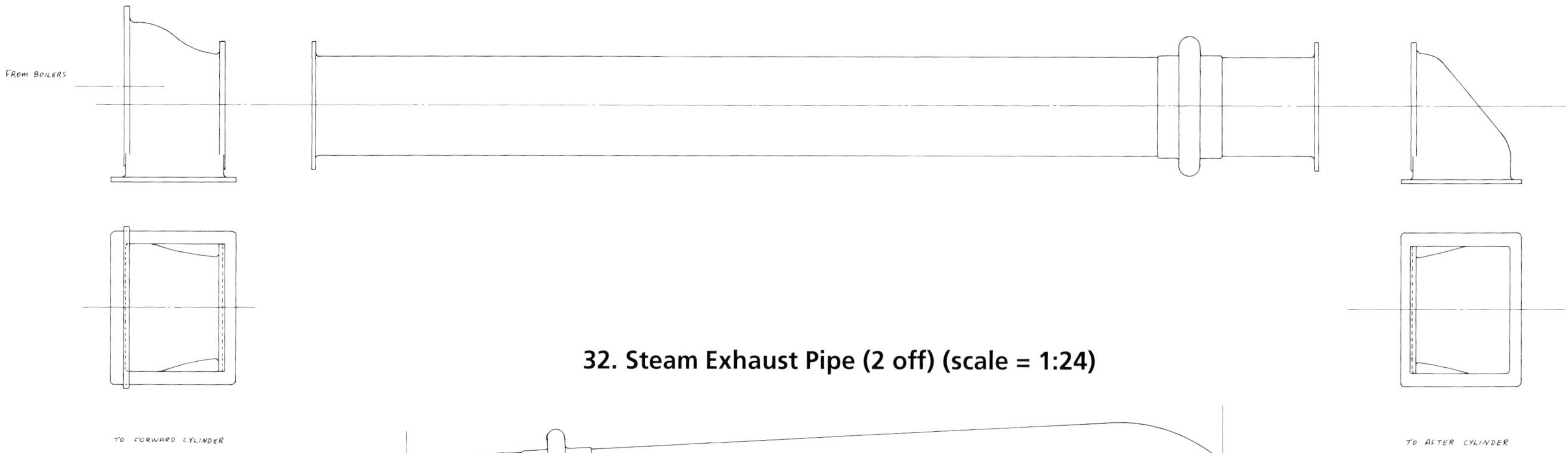

32. Steam Exhaust Pipe (2 off) (scale = 1:24)

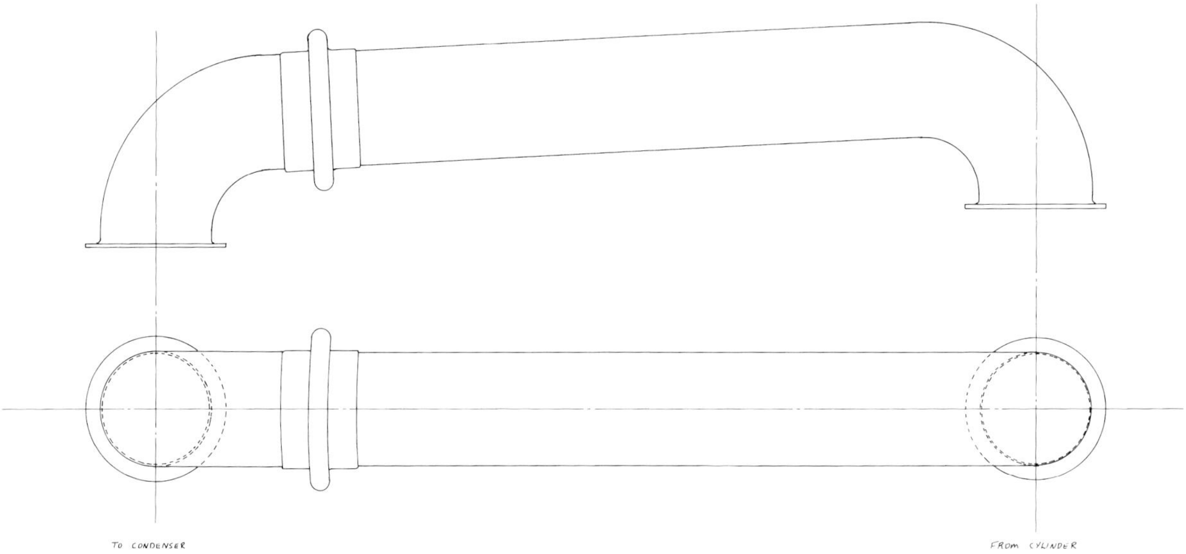

34A. Injection valve (scale = 1:12)

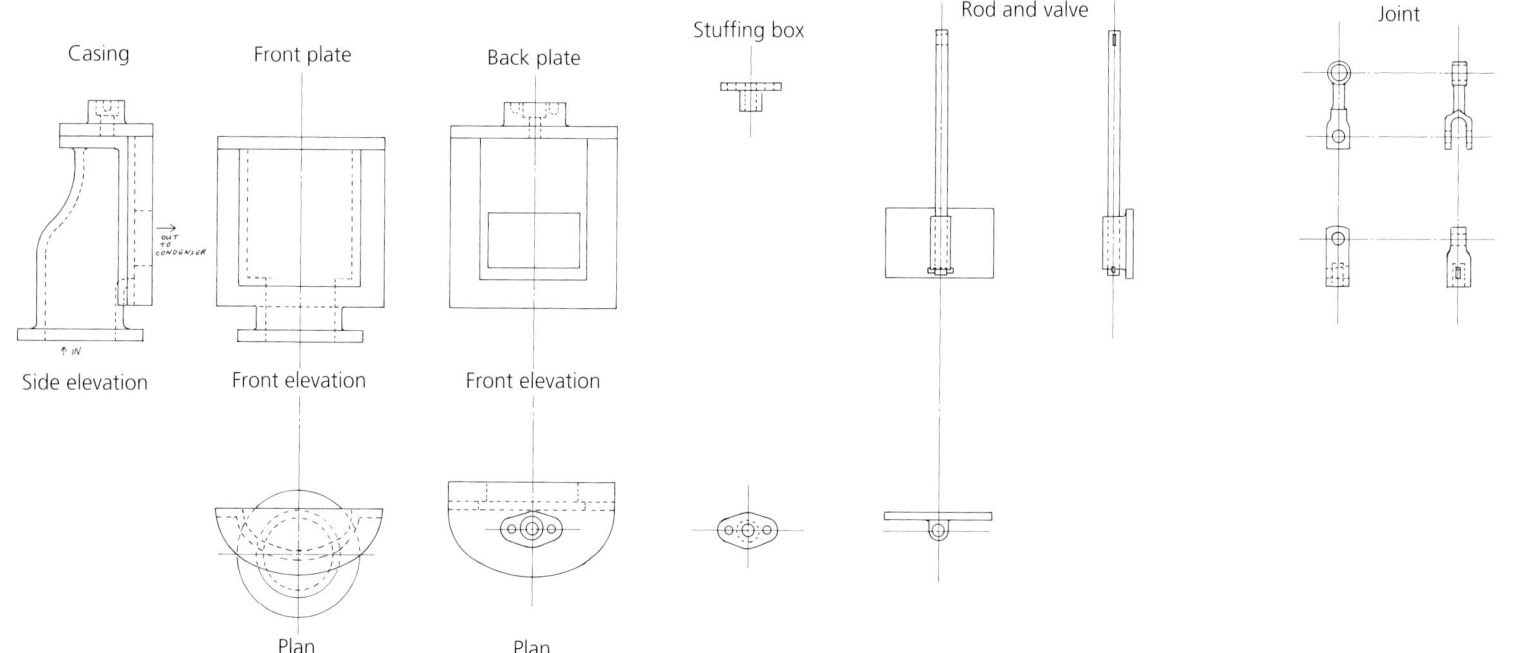

Injection Valve and Controls (scale =1:12)

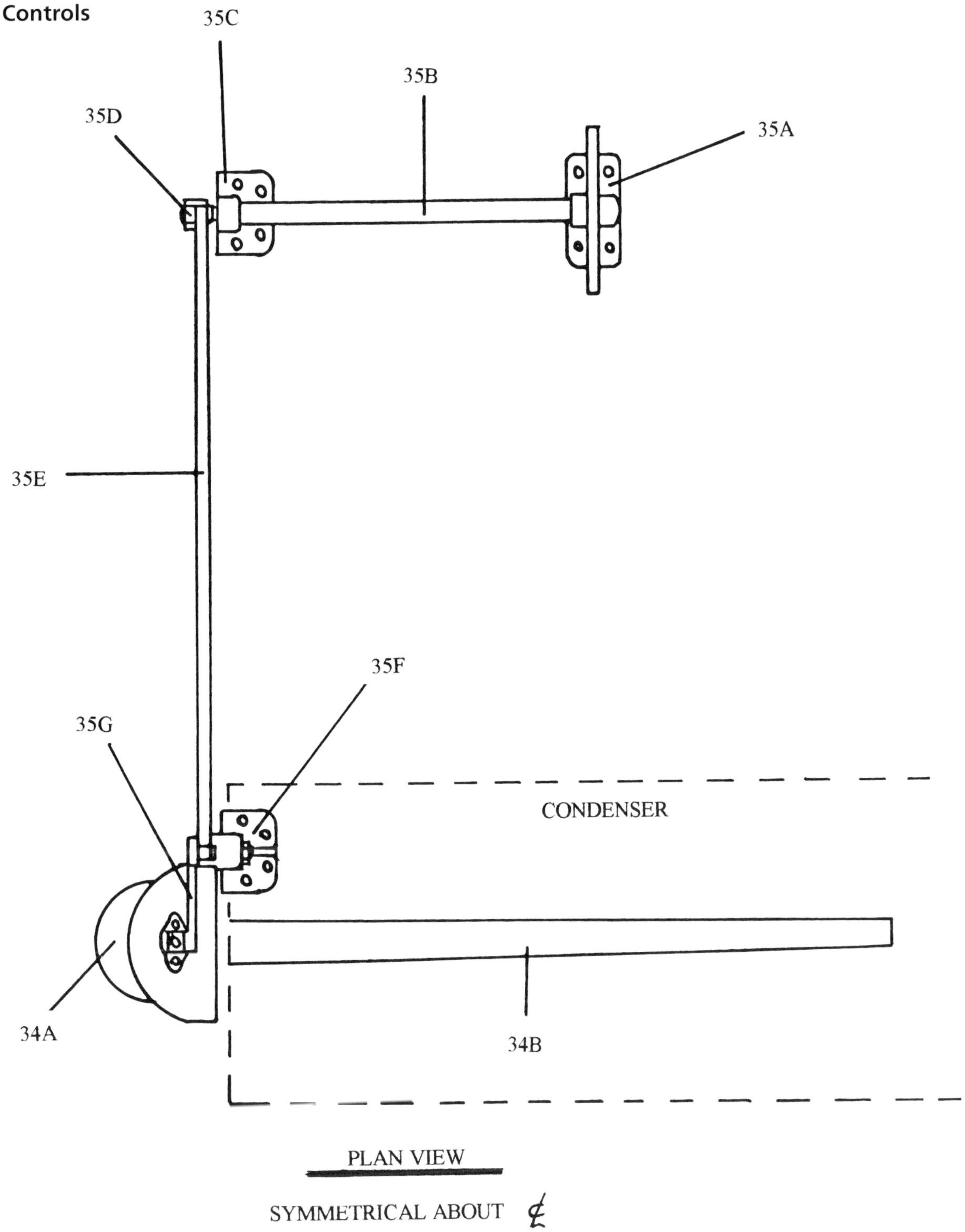

35C
35B
35D
35A
35E
35F
35G
CONDENSER
34A
34B
PLAN VIEW
SYMMETRICAL ABOUT ℄

34B. Inside Injection Pipe (reconstruction) (scale = 1:12)

FROM INJECTION VALVE
SUPPORT

Elevation

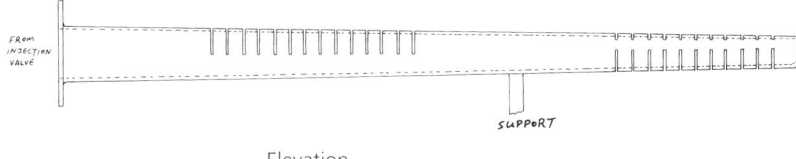

164 THE DRAWINGS

35. Injection Valve Controls
(1 set per cylinder) (scale = 1:12)

A 1 per cylinder

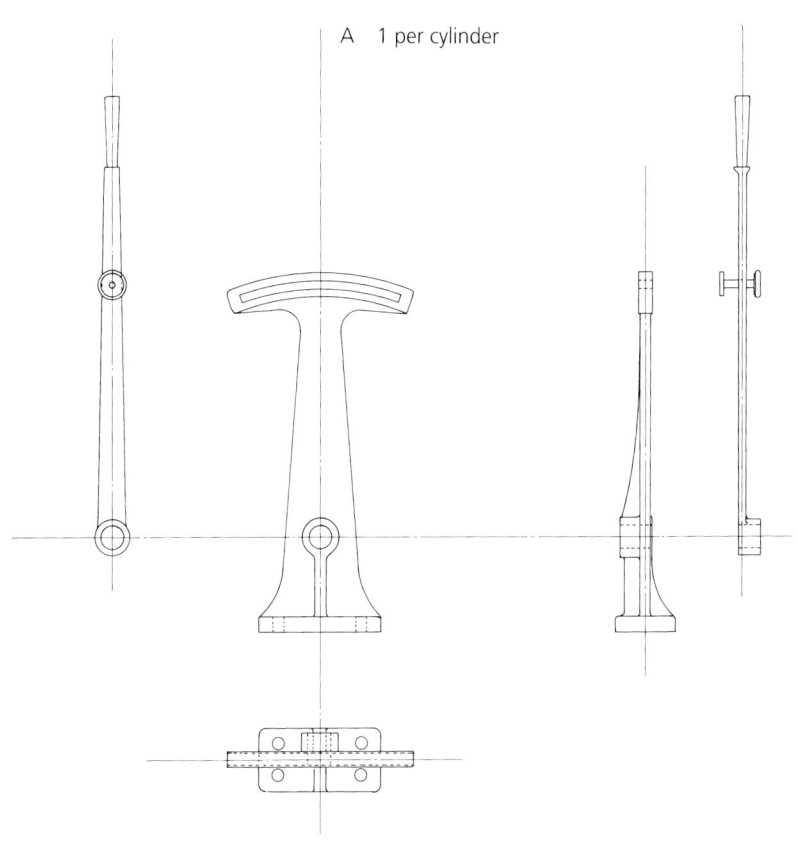

C Central hole 1½in diameter – 1 per cylinder
F Central hole 1¼in diameter – 1 per cylinder

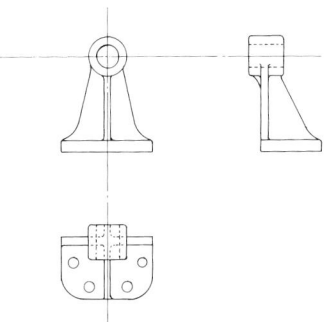

G 1 and 1 to opposite hand

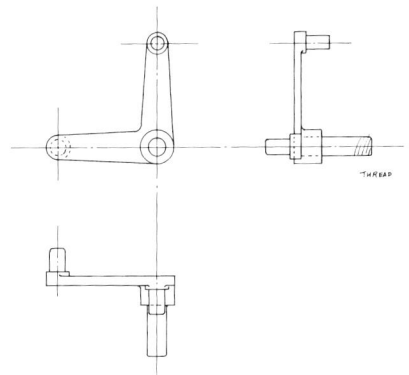

B 1 per cylinder

D 1 per cylinder

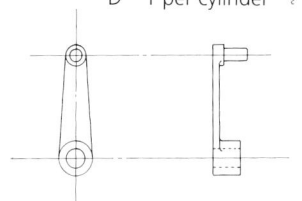

E 1 per cylinder

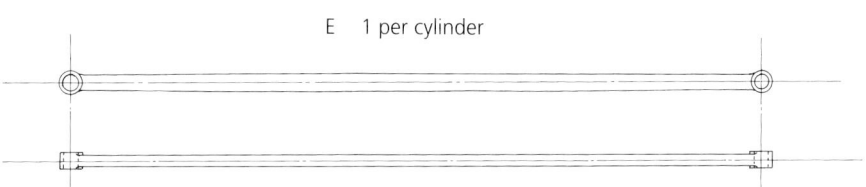

MACHINERY

36 & 37. Foot and Delivery Valves (scale = 1:24)

39. Discharge Pipes (scale = 1:24)

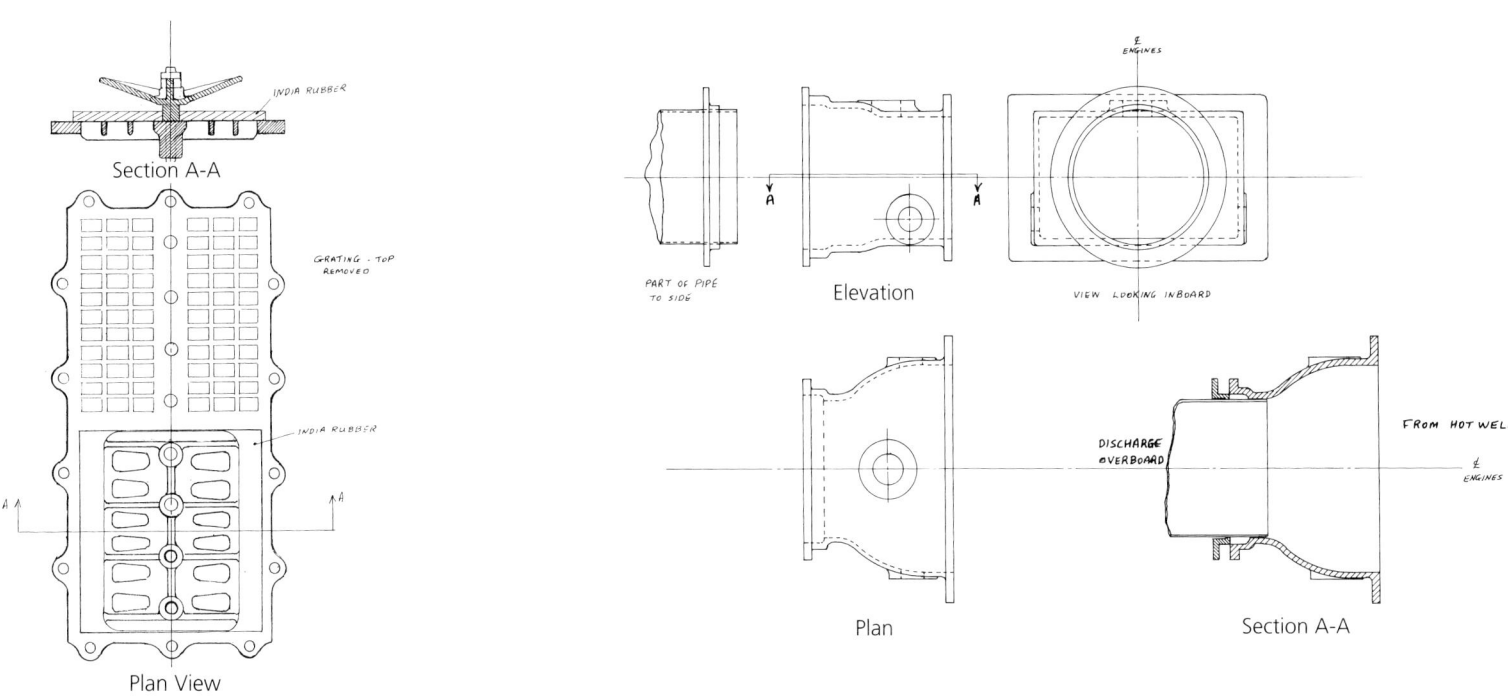

40. Blow through Valve
(1 and 1 to opposite hand) (scale = 1:12)

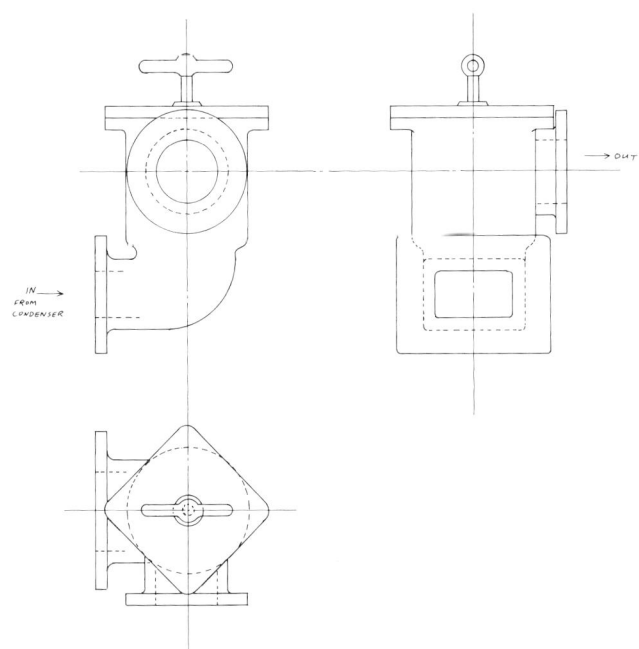

36 & 37. Foot and delivery valves

These are one-way valves of india rubber. The movement of the india rubber is restricted by the angled structure shown. The delivery valve in the hot well is illustrated, the difference with the foot valve is that the india rubber valve is below the grating. These valves are on either sides of the air pump (15) and ensure that the condensed steam is removed from the condenser to the hot well.

38. Hot well

The structure of this is shown as part of 14.

39. Discharge pipe

This discharges the unwanted water from the hot well overboard. The water pumped by the Bilge pump (19) will also be fed into this pipe to be discharged.

40. Blow through valve

Fitted at the lower part of the condenser, to prevent an accumulation of water and air which is driven out of the condenser when 'blowing through'. The interior of the valve has not been drawn, but it should be simple and be operated by turning the spindle.

41. Relief Valve (4 off) (scale = 1:12)

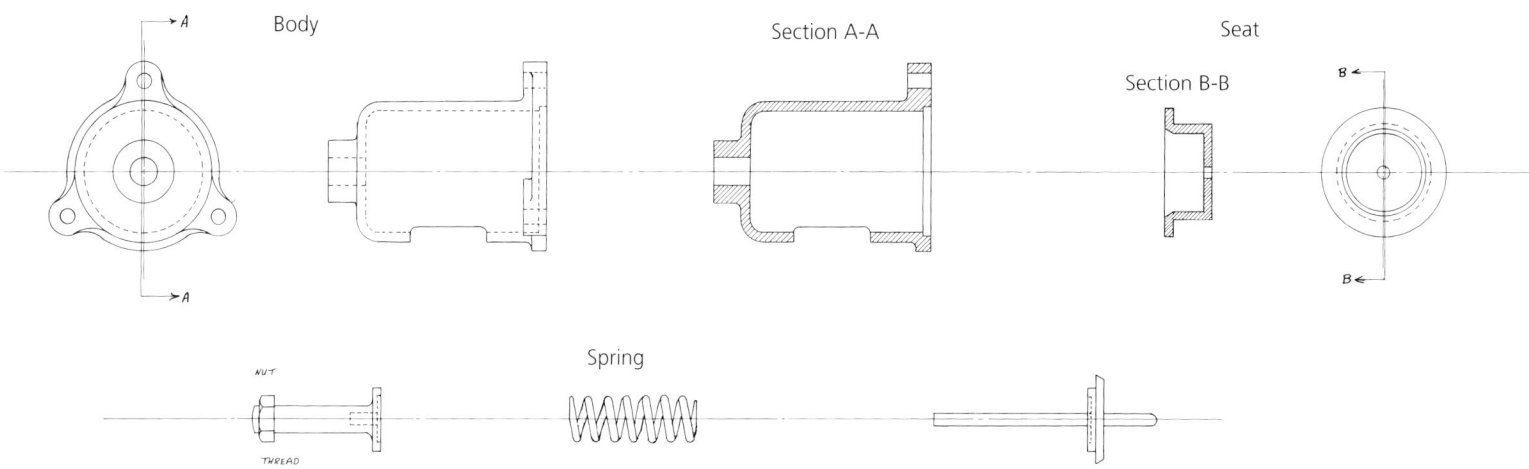

42. Barrier (scale = 1:24)

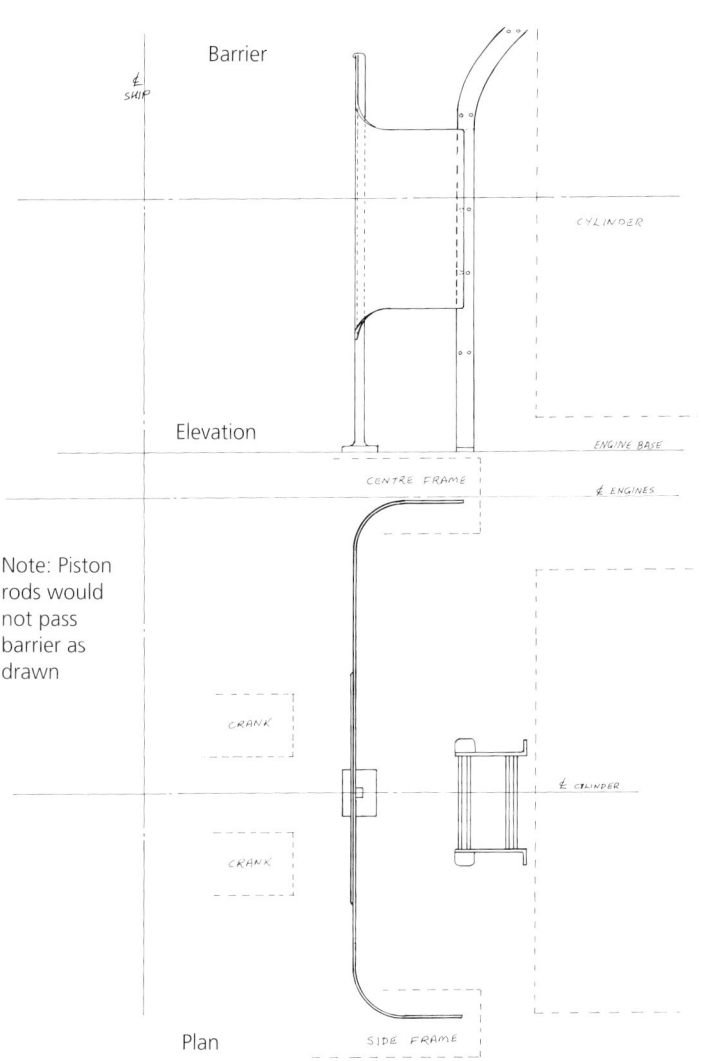

41. Relief valve
One is fitted each side of the piston in each cylinder.

42. Barrier
Between rotating crankshaft and anyone who climbs down the ladder on the front of the cylinder. It is bolted at the sides to either the Side frame (12) or the Main frame (11). This is drawn exactly as on the original drawing but the piston rods (4 & 5) would have to pass through it. Therefore it has holes for the rods or it was modified to fit on the ship.

43. Expansion valve
This shuts off steam to the slide valve, when the piston has travelled a certain distance in the cylinder, leaving the remaining part of the stroke to be performed by the expansion of the steam. Normally the expansion valve is operated by a reciprocal motion. The rotary motion used in this engine was not very common.

The valve is driven from the forward end of the crankshaft (10) and rotates at the same speed as the crankshaft. There appears to be a clutch on the drive shaft (43K), but it is not clear how it works. There are also clutches (43H) which disconnect the valve from the drive shaft (43E). It is assumed that the valve is on a hollow shaft which is moved by the clutch. There is no indication as to the actual shape of the valve but it would probably be square with curved flanges. The drawing (43L) is based on Ravenhill's expansion valve (in N P Burgh, *Modern Marine Engineering* (1869), Figure 158).

MACHINERY

43. Expansion Valve (not to scale)

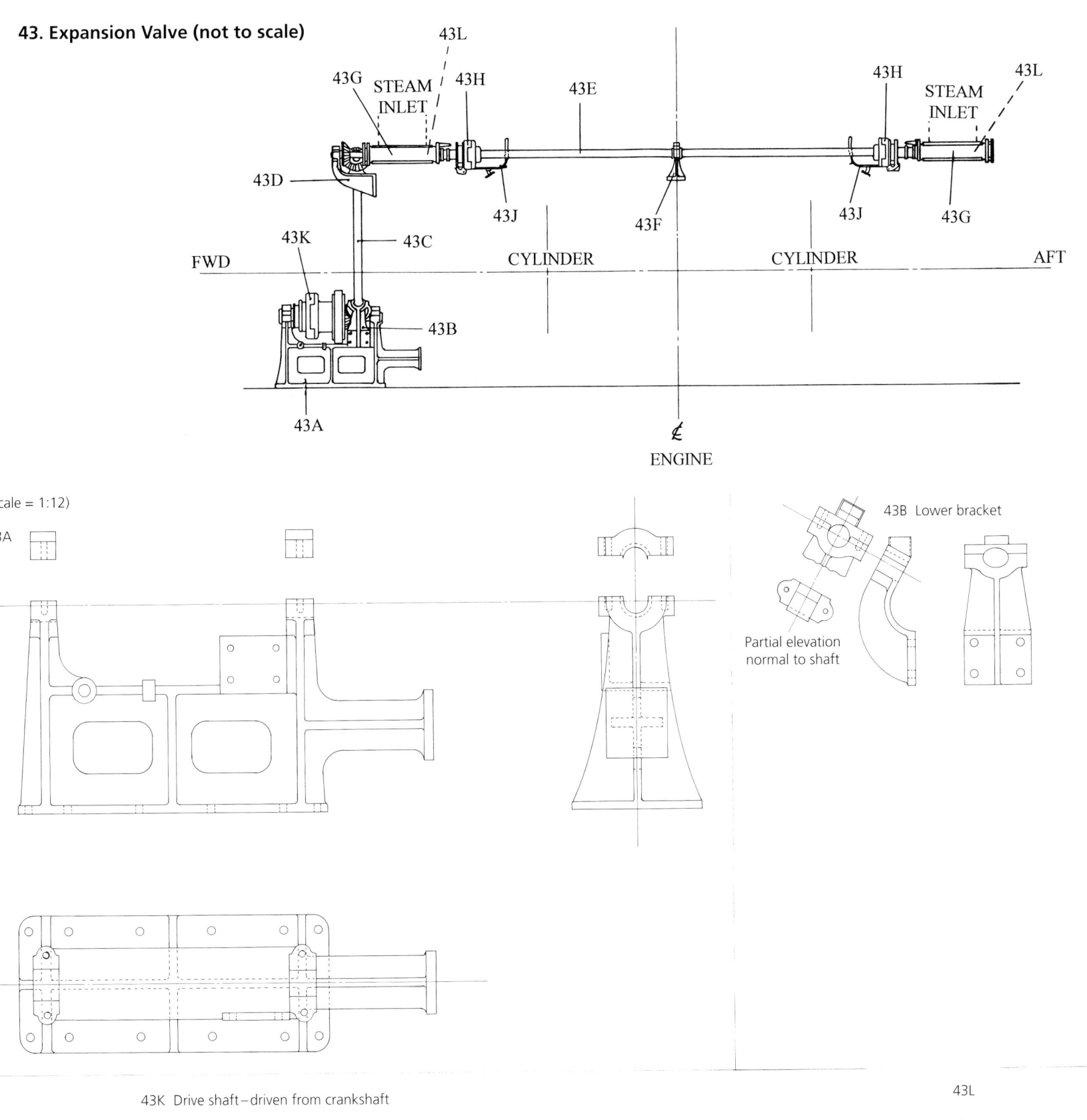

(Scale = 1:12)

43B Lower bracket
Partial elevation normal to shaft

43K Drive shaft – driven from crankshaft
Clutch
Drive shaft

43L
Section through valve (reconstruction)

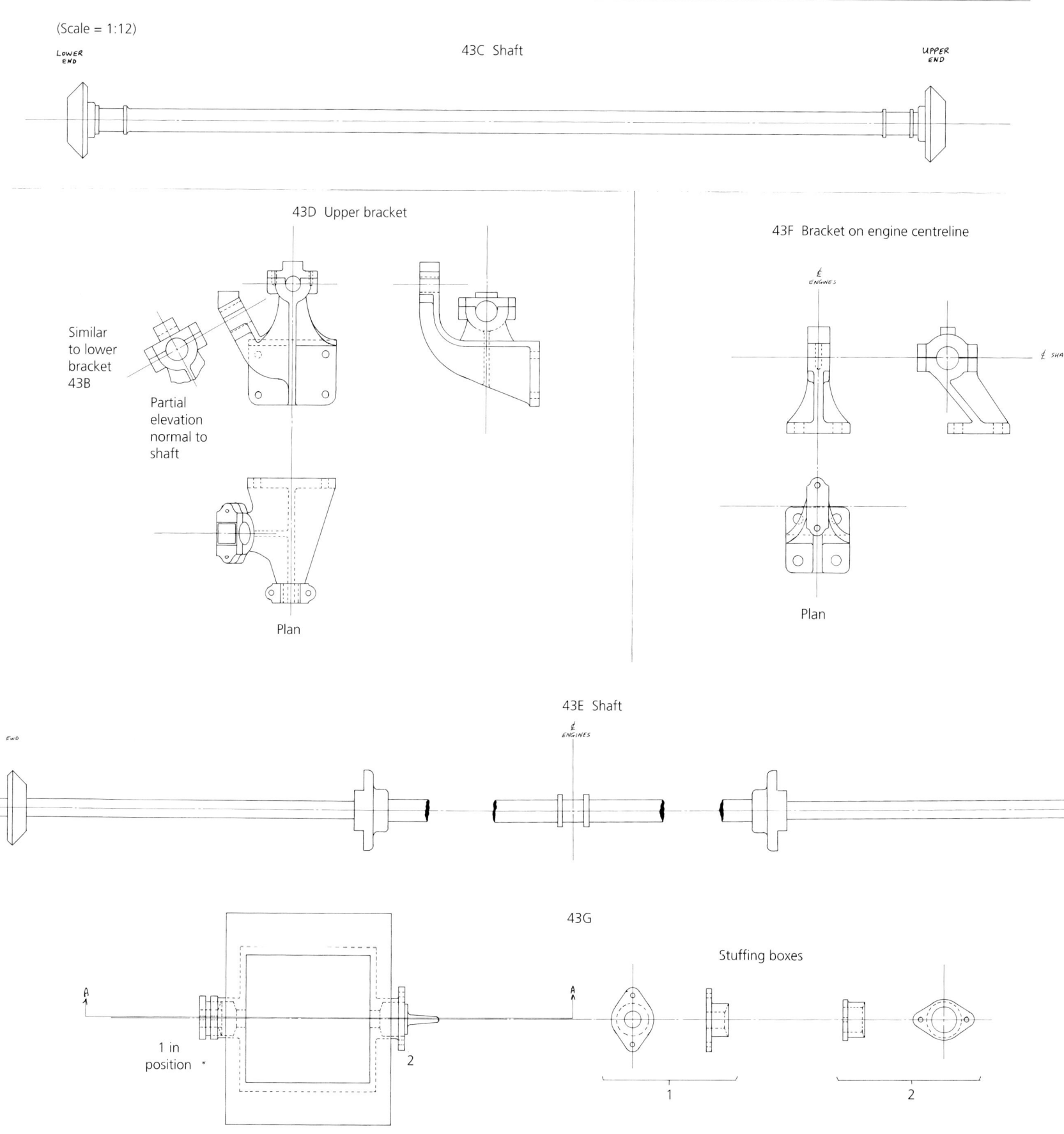

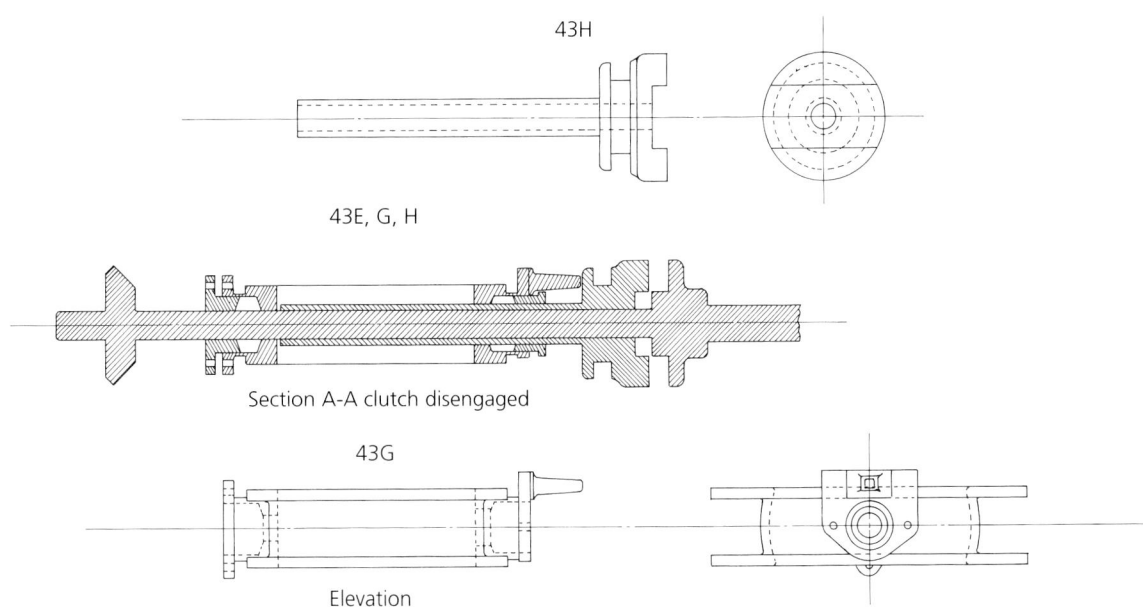

43H

43E, G, H

Section A-A clutch disengaged

43G

Elevation

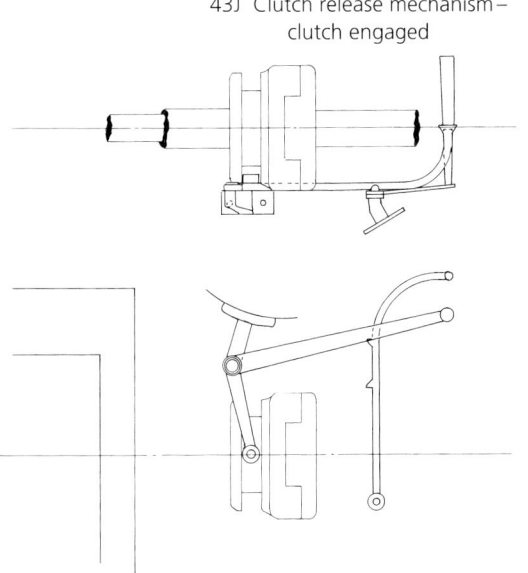

43J Clutch release mechanism – clutch engaged

44. Indicator

An instrument for measuring the pressure of the steam in the cylinder. There is the pipe work fitted so that an Indicator can be used on each cylinder.

The letters below refer to the drawing of a typical indicator.

A Hollow cylinder screwed to pipes from the cylinder.
B Steam inlet from cylinder.
C Piston in cylinder A. The rod is surrounded by a spiral spring fixed to the piston and the upper end of the cylinder. The steam compresses the spring causing the rod to move.
D A pointer attached to the piston rod C, which moves up and down depending in the steam pressure.
E Drum which rotates about a vertical axis. Paper is attached to the drum and a pencil on the end of the pointer D will mark this, showing the change in steam pressure.
F Cord attached to the air pump rod by means of levers. As the air pump rod moves back and forward the cord will turn the drum E marking the variation of the steam pressure during the stroke of the piston. Results showing the indicator diagram taken the day the ship left the River Mersey are given elsewhere (page 38).

44. Indicator and Linkage (scale = 1:24)

Typical Indicator (not to scale)

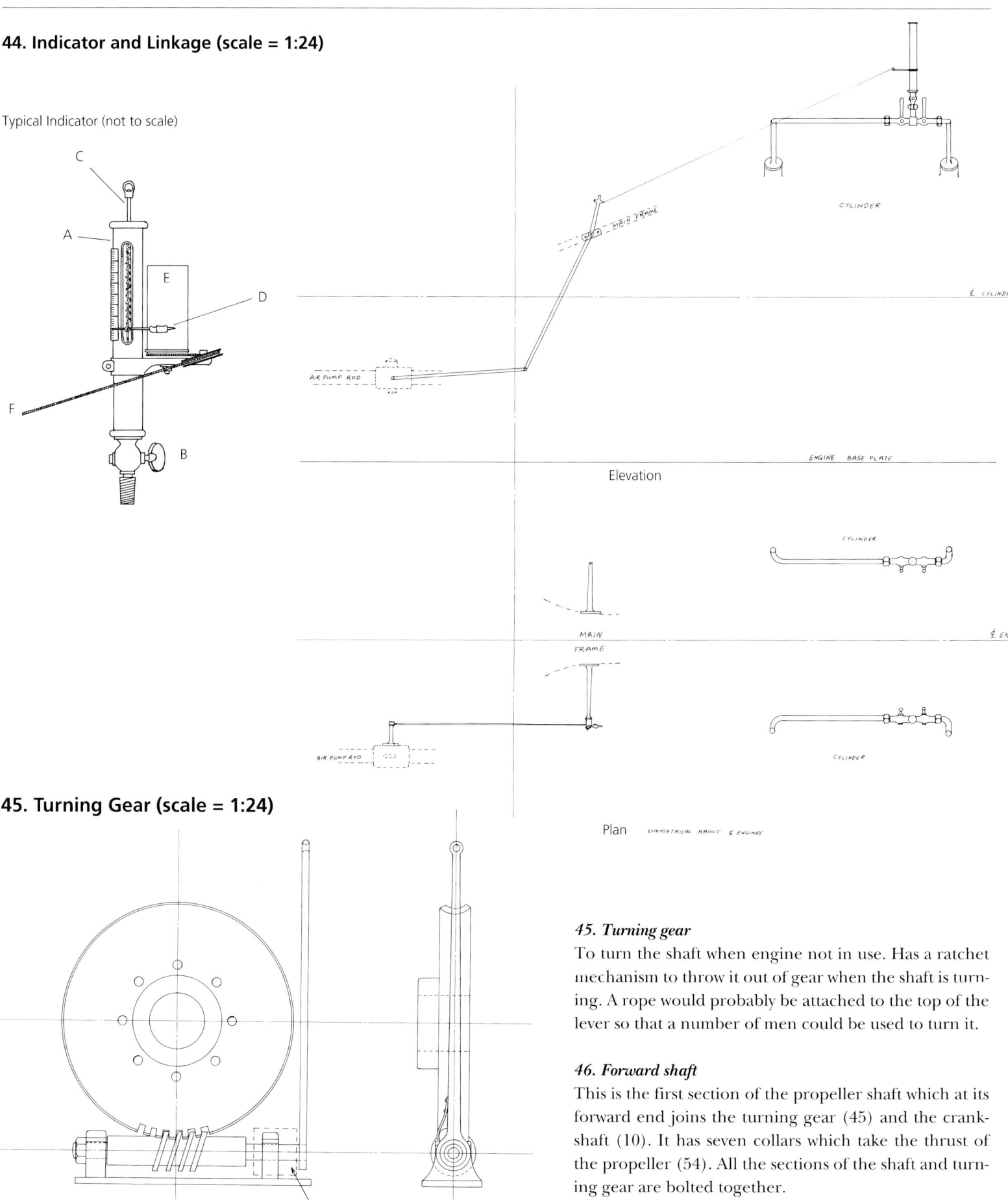

45. Turning Gear (scale = 1:24)

45. Turning gear
To turn the shaft when engine not in use. Has a ratchet mechanism to throw it out of gear when the shaft is turning. A rope would probably be attached to the top of the lever so that a number of men could be used to turn it.

46. Forward shaft
This is the first section of the propeller shaft which at its forward end joins the turning gear (45) and the crankshaft (10). It has seven collars which take the thrust of the propeller (54). All the sections of the shaft and turning gear are bolted together.

MACHINERY

Propeller Shaft (not to scale)

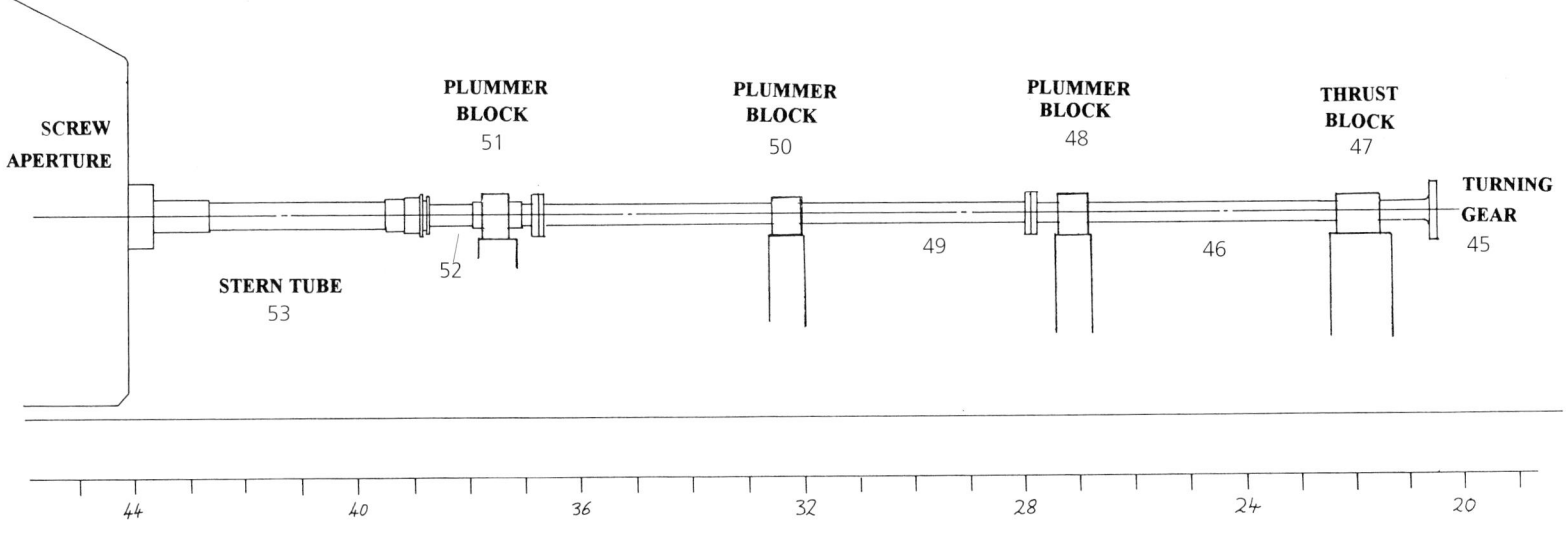

46. Shaft (scale = 1:24)

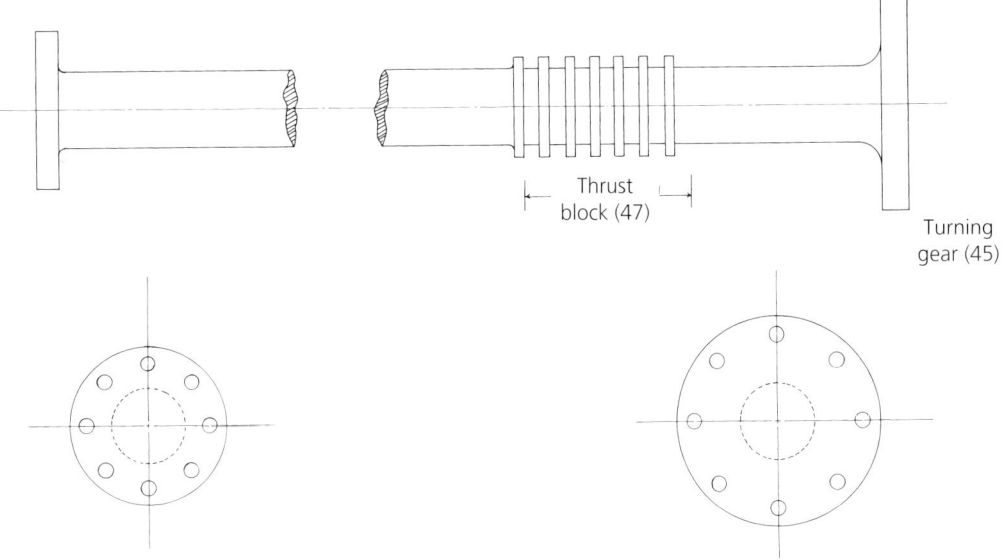

47. Thrust block
The thrust produced by the Propeller (54) is transmitted to the hull of the ship by means of this block. The block is in two parts and held together by bolts. Inside the block will be a white metal bearing, also in two parts. The bearing surfaces are lubricated by means of an oil tank on the top half of the bearing casing.

48, 50 & 51. Plummer blocks
These are basically the same, with the block in two parts, and having a white metal lining. Lubricated by an oil tank on top of the bearing.

52. Stern shaft
The shaft is iron which is covered in two places by brass. At the forward end it is bolted to the intermediate shaft (49) and at the aft end is fitted the propeller driver.

53. Stern tube
This tube carries the propeller shaft through the deadwood at the stern of the ship. It also has the stern bearings which are of wood - lignum vitae. The fillets of wood are fixed in grooves in the stern tube and their surface rubs on the brass which is on the stern shaft (52). The shaft is lubricated by water, the wood being far enough apart to allow a free flow of water around them.

47. Thrust Block (scale = 1:24)

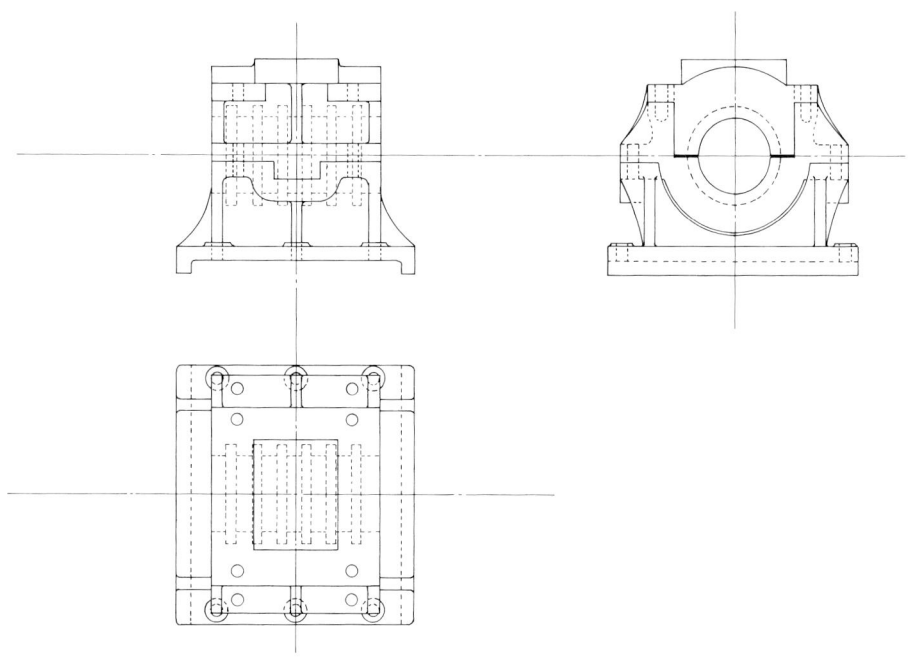

48 & 50. Plummer Block (scale = 1:24)

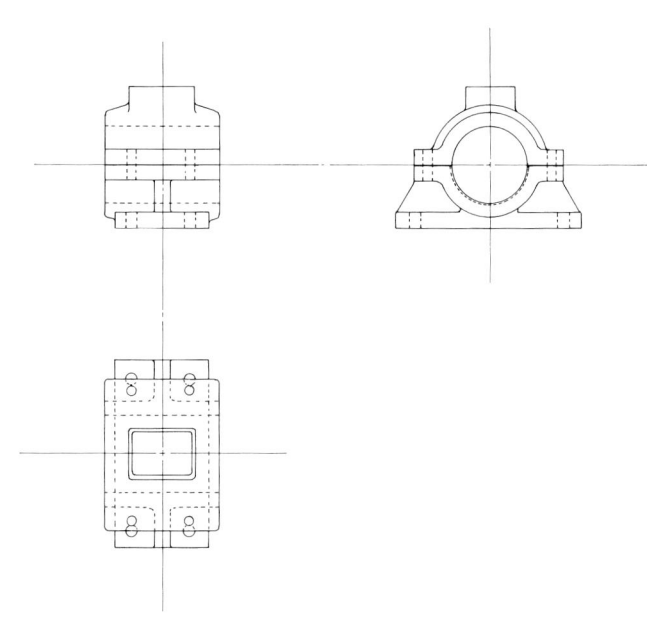

49. Intermediate Shaft (scale = 1:24)

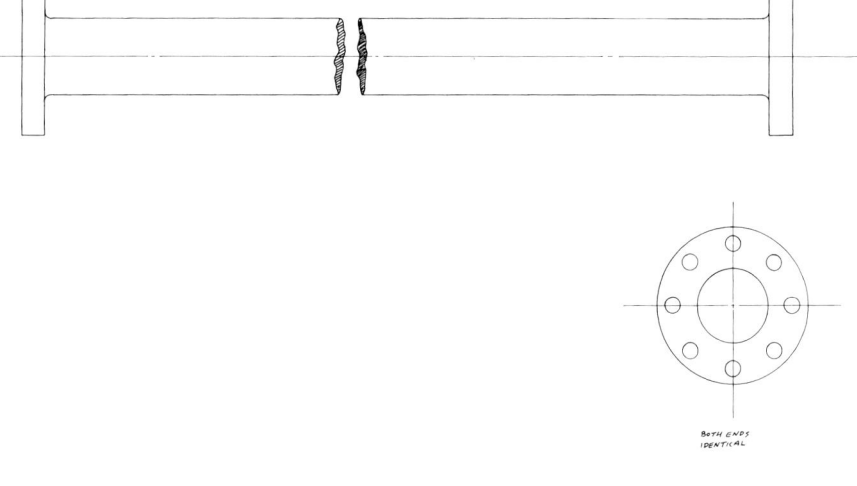

51. Plummer Block (scale = 1:24)

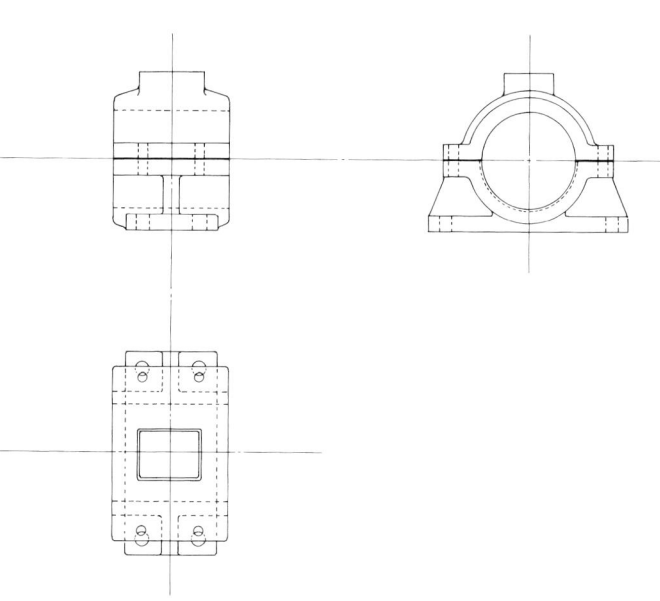

52. Stern Shaft (scale = 1:24)

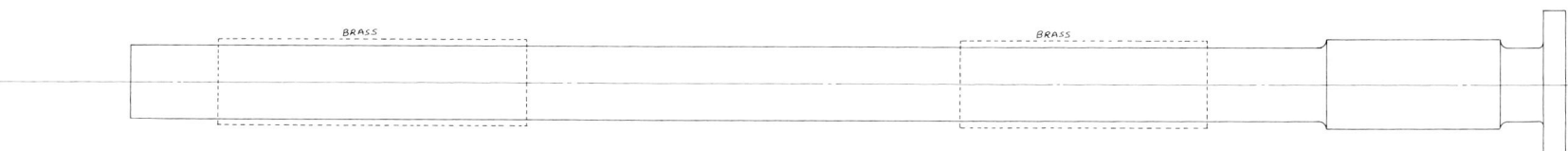

MACHINERY

53. Stern Tube (scale = 1:24)

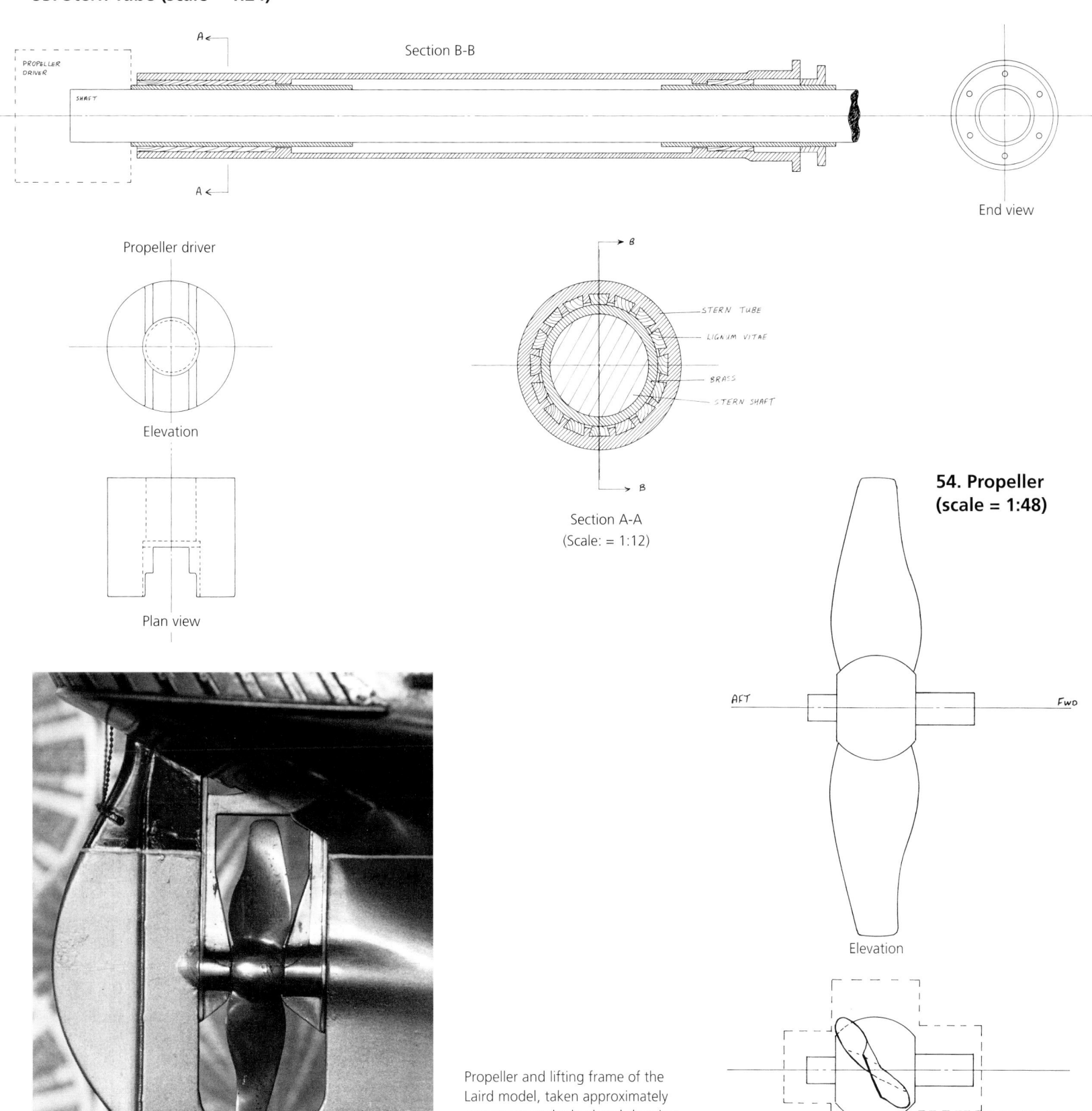

Section A-A (Scale: = 1:12)

54. Propeller (scale = 1:48)

Propeller and lifting frame of the Laird model, taken approximately square-on to the keel and showing the shape of the blades. Note that the propeller has been fitted back to front.

Propeller and lifting frame of the Laird model taken looking along the lower blade. Note that the propeller has been fitted back to front.

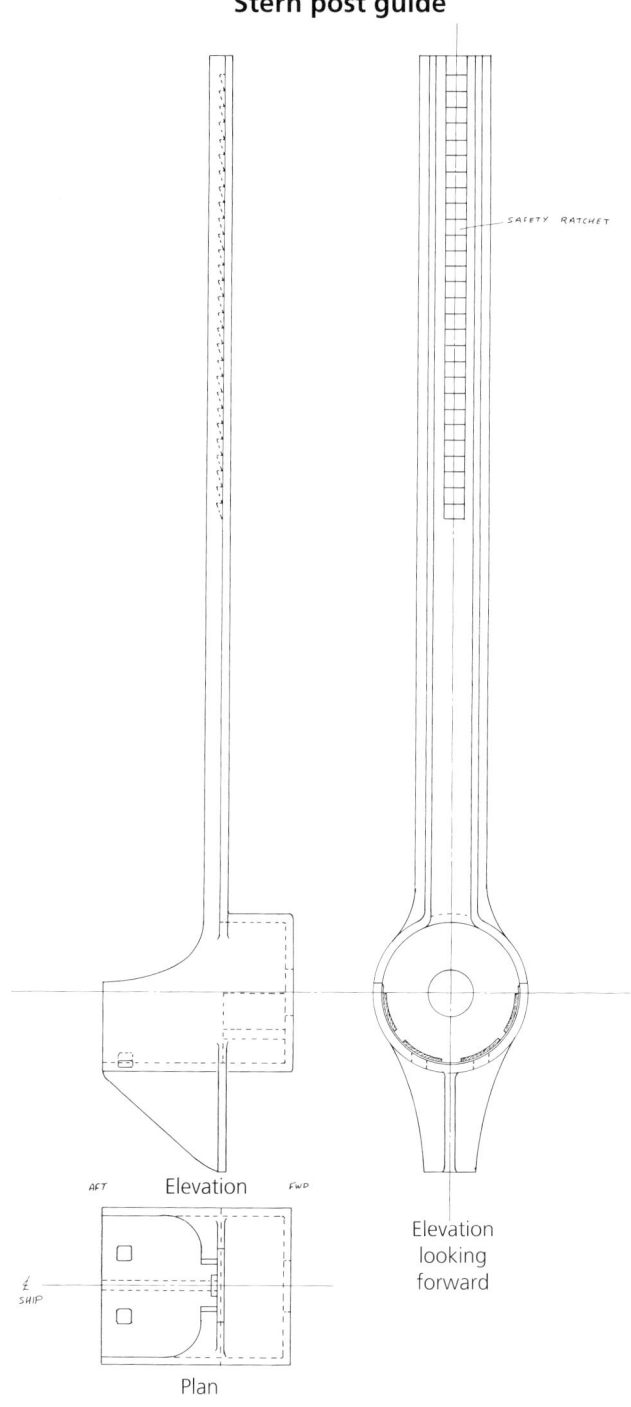

54. Propeller

The propeller drawn is based on the one on the Laird model. Each blade is separately bolted to the boss and it is possible to alter the pitch angle by bolting in a different position. The gudgeons are cast as part of the boss, each running inside the bearing on the lifting frame (55). Two photographs of the model propeller are shown, because I think these show the shape much better than the drawing (even if the propeller is fitted the wrong way round).

55. Lifting frame

This is a reconstruction based on the Laird model and contemporary plans. The bearings for the gudgeons are made in two parts, which are held together by two bolts on each side. The bearings are wood like the stern tube (53) and are lubricated by water. The projections on the bottom of the lower bearings fit into holes in the guides attached to the stern and rudder posts. The front end of the forward gudgeon fits into the propeller driver (52) which, as the names suggests, turns the propeller. It is only possible to raise

55. Lifting Frame and Guides (reconstruction) (scale = 1:36)

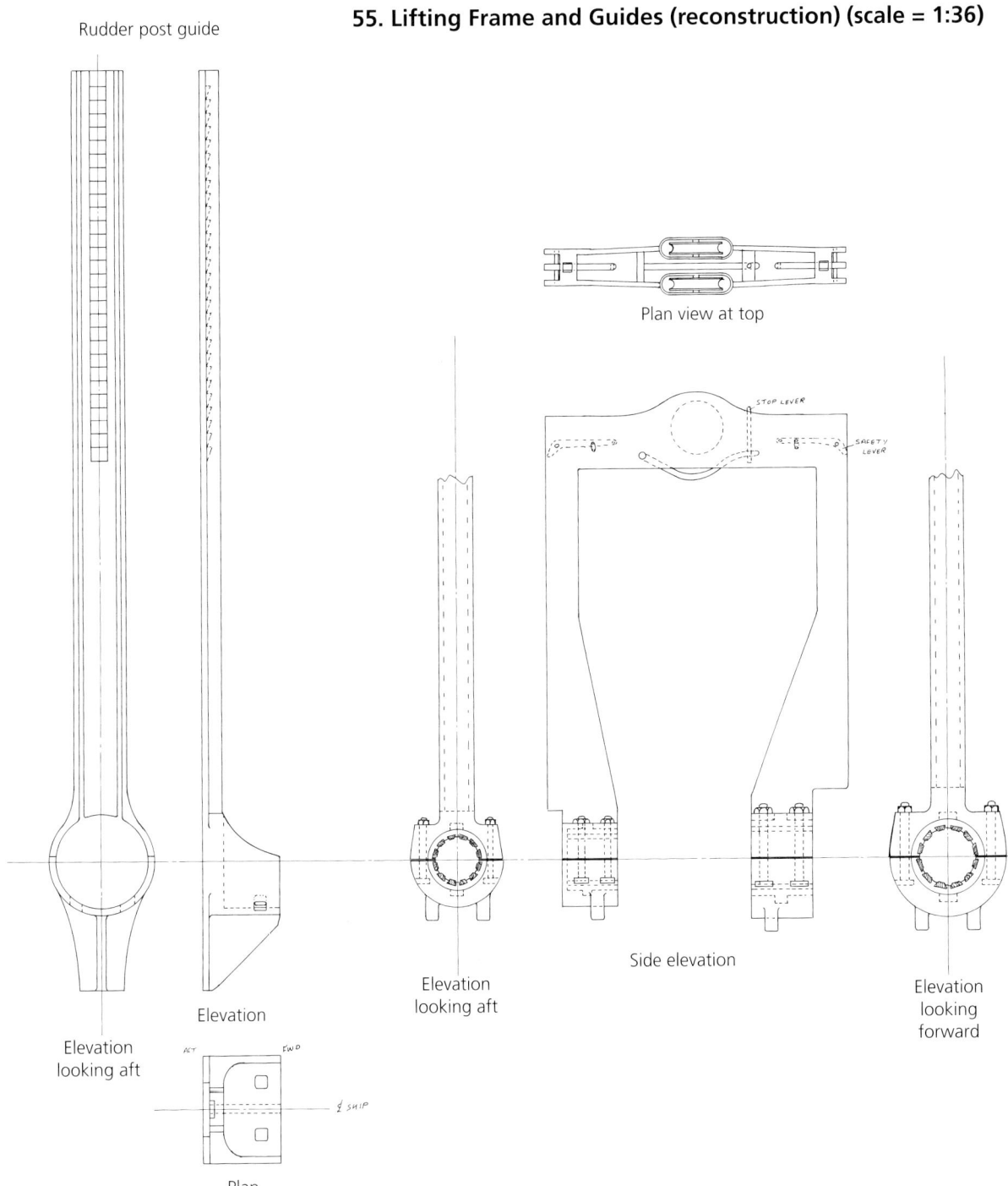

the propeller when the driver is in the vertical position. The blade is held in this position by a stop-lever which is screwed down till it is in contact with the tip of the blade. From what I have been told about the wreck it appears that the *Alabama* has a small square cut out at the top of the blade that the lever fits into, but I have never seen this shown on any drawing of a blade. The lifting frame and propeller are raised by means of rope round the two pulley wheels, and two others above the deck. There is a lever in the top of the frame at each end which will engage with the safety ratchet and is to ensure that the lifting frame does not drop if a problem occurs whilst it is being hoisted. The inner end of the safety lever is probably held down by an india rubber band to ensure it engages with the ratchet. These levers are disengaged, to lower the propeller and lifting frame, by means of a rope attached to eyes at the end of the levers. There are two square holes in the top of the lifting frame which are for the ends of the fixing stays that are to hold the lifting frame down in position when in use.

Boilers (simplified) (scale = 1:96)

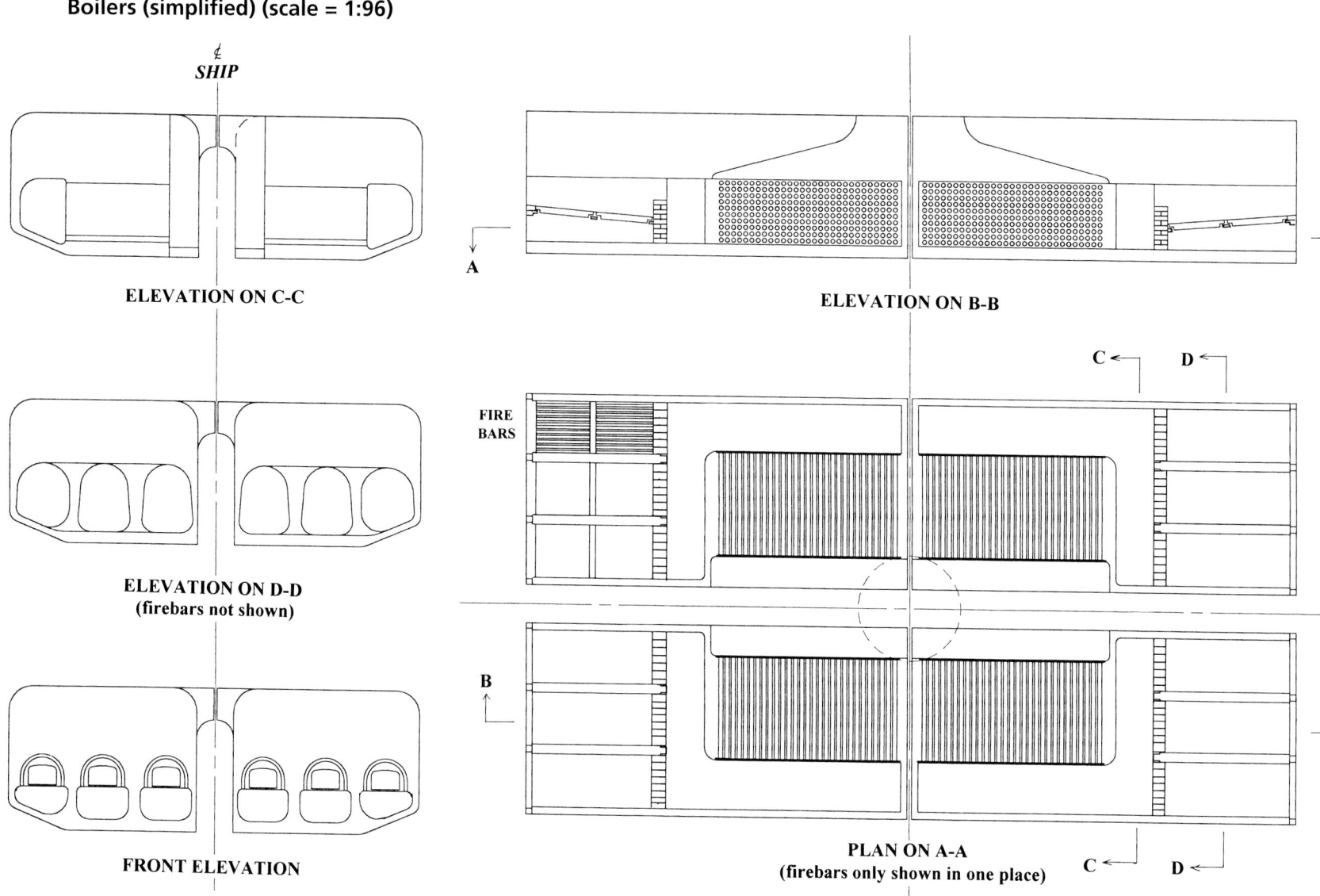

BOILERS & FUNNEL

Boilers

The boilers, along with their coal, were a very substantial part of the ship and occupied a large space. They were also a very important part, as they required constant attention. Rarely were the fires allowed to go out, they were usually banked so that steam could be provided at short notice. At one point Semmes notes in the log (7 December 1862) 'I immediately ordered the propeller lowered, & the fires spread, and in 15 minutes, we had cleared up every thing, & were under steam, with the crew at quarters.'

The boilers burnt about 16 tons of coal per day, which meant that the coal bunkers carried less than 20 days' supply. When the fires were banked they burnt only a ton of coal per day. Starting from cold the boilers could take two to three hours to raise sufficient steam to work the engines. Overall there are very few references to the engines and boilers made in any of the literature by the crew.

The simplified drawing of the boilers show how the four would be arranged in the ship. The actual transverse distance between them has to be sufficient to enable a tube to be changed. There would be doors on the inboard sides of the boilers and by removing them there would be enough room to replace a tube.

The steam from each individual boiler was fed into the main pipe to the engine. It would be possible to shut off each boiler so that any combination of boilers could be used to provide steam. The approximate position of the pipes and the valves are shown on the general drawing of the engine (page 138). The steam pipes from the two forward boilers would have to pass through the two aftermost ones. The usual situation was that these steam pipes passed over the top of the boilers, but with the *Alabama* this was not possible because of the lack of headroom. Nor was there enough room for the pipes between the boilers, on the centreline of the ship, especially around the foot of the main mast.

The main parts of the boiler are given in the sketch, and further

MACHINERY

Boilers (scale = 1:96)

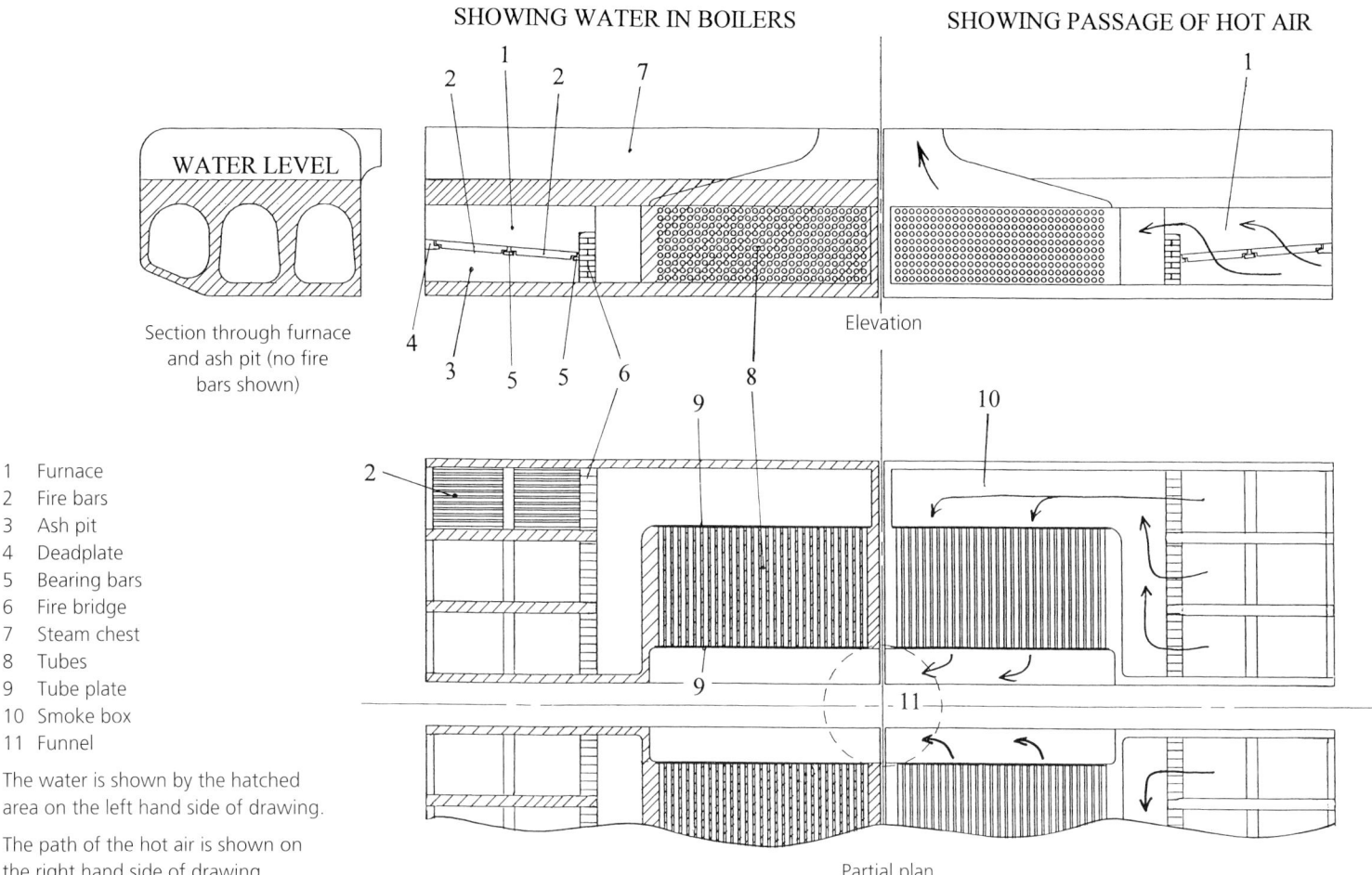

1 Furnace
2 Fire bars
3 Ash pit
4 Deadplate
5 Bearing bars
6 Fire bridge
7 Steam chest
8 Tubes
9 Tube plate
10 Smoke box
11 Funnel

The water is shown by the hatched area on the left hand side of drawing.

The path of the hot air is shown on the right hand side of drawing.

notes are given below. The sketch also shows the water in the boilers and the path of the hot air from the furnace through to the funnel.

There are doors (one above the other) to each Furnace (1) and Ash pit (3).

The fire bars (2), which the coal is burnt on, have a downward slope away from the door. They are supported on the Deadplate (4) just inside the door, and two Bearing bars (5) one at the centre and the other on the Fire bridge (6). The fire bars rest on these supports and are free to expand. The fire bridge is built of brick.

The Tubes (8) are supported at each end by the Tube plates (9) and are held in place by the ferrules. There are also eight stay tubes per boiler which help to hold the plates in position as they were fastened in place with nuts (probably one on each side of the tube plate).

The faces of the boilers have not been drawn as there is not sufficient information available at present. The exact position of the various fittings is not know at present, but should become clear as the excavation of the ship progresses.

On the faces of the boilers there would have been sight tubes. These are glass tubes to show the water level in the boiler and enable the engineers to check on the level. There are gauge cocks fitted at the top and bottom of the sight glass (which could be closed to change the glass tube). There will be a gauge cock for the pressure gauge.

There would also be a relief valve on each boiler, in case the internal steam pressure became too high. Again the position of these is not known.

Other fittings on the boilers would include the steam pipes to the engine, the feed water return from the engine and the blow-down valves.

The cylinders, boilers and pipes were felted and lagged. The usual procedure was to wrap the pipes in felt, around which stout canvas was then sewn, giving a plain exterior which could be painted. Cylinders were covered by felt and then by pieces of wood. Lagging a boiler consisted of covering all exterior surfaces (except the bottom) with felt and wood. The felt was held down by battens and the whole covered with wood, except for the top. The top was

Funnel: Uptake, Casing, Lifting Gear and Chimney (scale = 1:96)

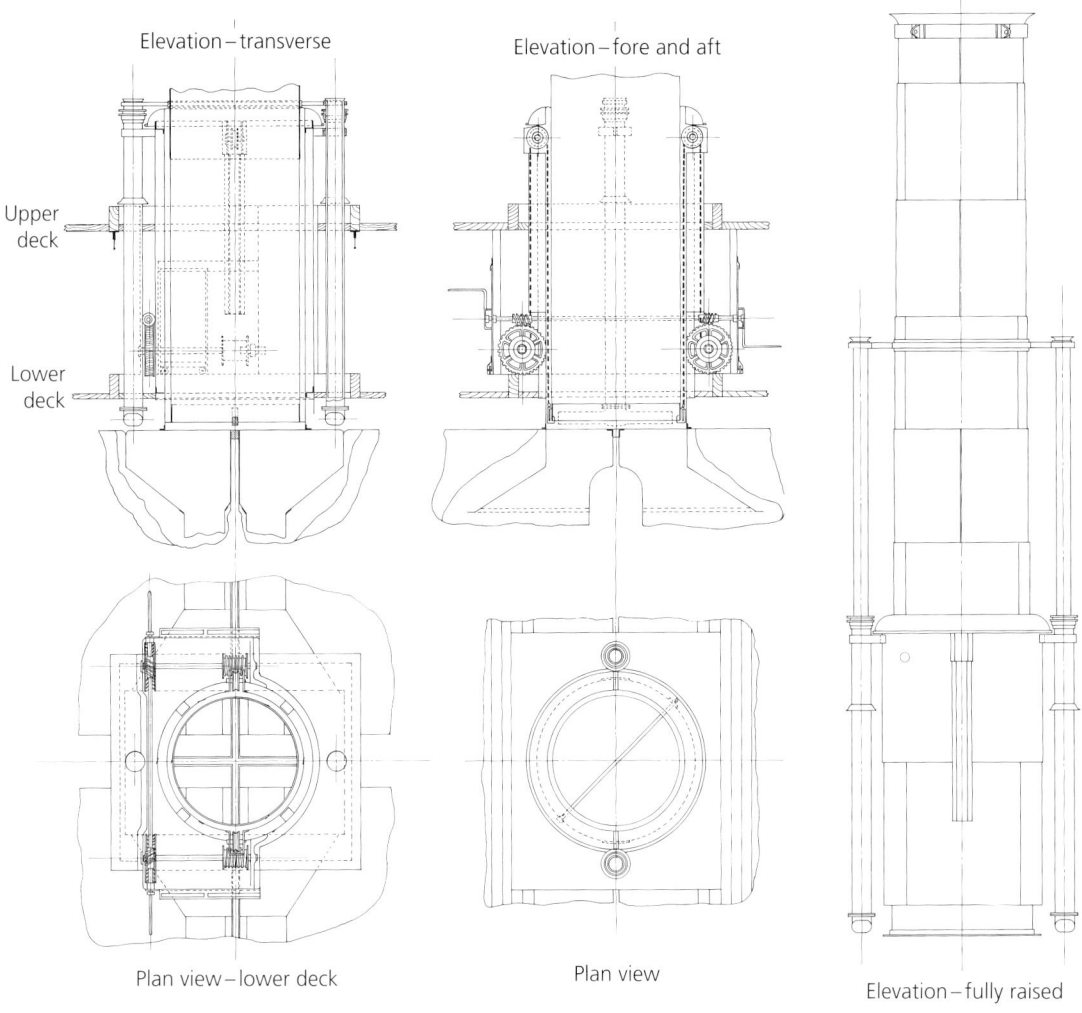

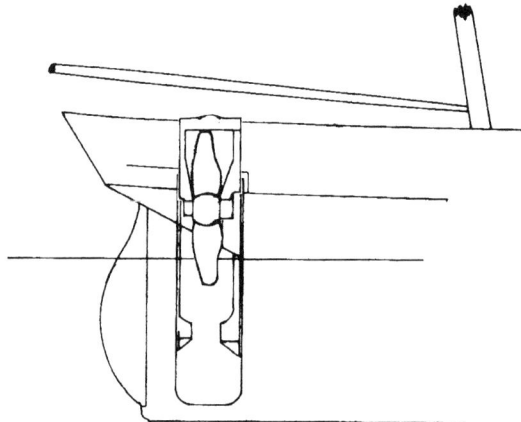

The propeller at its highest position, without the lifting frame leaving the guides. It can be seen that the lower tip is still in the water.

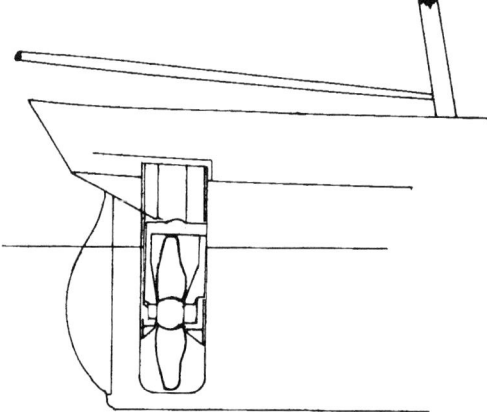

Section in way of propeller well showing propeller in position. Before being raised it would be turned to the vertical position.

covered with lead, instead of wood, so that any water that accumulated did not cause corrosion. The bottom of the boilers sit on a composition of cement on top of wooden boards on the platform, and therefore do not need any lagging.

Funnel

It was possible to lower (or raise) the funnel by means of chains. The mechanism was on the lower deck where handles turned gear wheels attached to two separate drums, one on each side of the funnel. The chains ran up from the drums and over a pulley, then down to the bottom of the sliding section of the funnel.

PROPELLER

The drawings of the propeller shaft are based on the original drawing or on items, such as plummer blocks, that were used by Lairds at that time on other, similar ships. The biggest problem is that there is no drawing of the propeller.

The specification says 'Screw Propeller & lifting frame, to be of Brass, & fitted on the same plan as adopted in H.M. Service'. Sinclair describes it (p7). 'Her screw, which was a two-bladed one, hoisted in a propeller-well, and when triced up was quite clear of the water, hence no drag or impediment to her speed under sail-power alone.' The propeller on each of the models appears to be the same (except that the one on the Laird model is the wrong way round). They are both a Griffiths type screw, named after the man who patented the shape of the blade, a type that was common in the Royal Navy at that time. The drawings are based on the propeller on the Laird model. For more details see Appendix 3.

I do not think Sinclair's description is quite right because if the propeller was completely clear of the water the tip would be so high above the deck as

MACHINERY

to be above the level of the mizzen boom. This would put the boom at risk if the ship were to tack or wear.

To raise the screw it had to be turned so that the blades were vertical. The lifting frame contained two pulley wheels, and a top pulley block would be attached to a pair of sheer legs. The propeller and lifting frame were then hauled up by manpower until sufficient height had been achieved – see sketch.

MISCELLANEOUS: PUMPS, VALVES ETC

There are certain items in the Engine Room for which there is no information available. In these cases general details or drawings are given of typical fittings.

Kingston Valves

These control the flow of water to pipes passing through the hull - both in and out. The boilers are fed with salt water and as the steam is generated the remaining water becomes saturated with salt. A part of this water is 'blown-off' to reduce the concentration of solid matter in the water. For this there would probably be one Kingston Valve for each pair of boilers, making it possible to blow each boiler separately.

There would also be a Kingston Valve on the inlet to the injection valve for the condenser, as salt water was used to condense the steam.

Donkey Engine

Nothing is know about this except what is in the contract– 'Donkey Engine Pump, double acting, of suitable size'. The donkey engine, based on other ships would probably be positioned at the forward end of the boiler room.

Hand Pumps

A widely-used type of hand pump was the Downton Pump, the two Laird Rams each having two of them. It is likely that the *Alabama* would also be fitted with this make of pump. Based on this assumption, there would be two pumps on the lower deck, probably placed one at the aft end of the crew quarters, and the other at the forward end of the ward room or the after end of the gun room.

The drawing shows a typical Downton Pump for pumping out the bilges etc. These pipes come up to the suction plate adjacent to the pump. The pipe to the pump is in the centre of the suction plate, and is connected to any one of the other pipes around the edge of the suction plate by means of the gooseneck. This gooseneck can be moved to provide the suction to the pump from any

Typical Kingston Valve (not to scale)

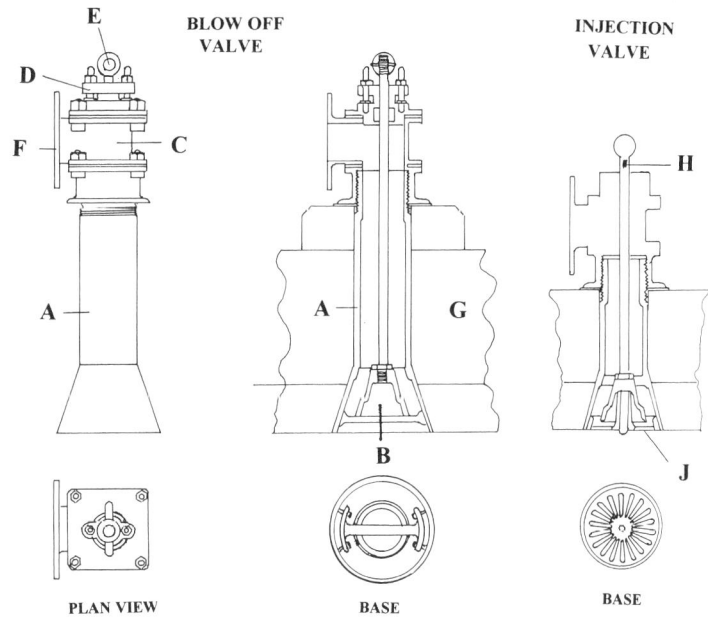

Blow off valve
- A Gunmetal pipe with conical base
- B Valve – opens outwards
- C Cover – screws on A
- D Stuffing box
- E Handle for lifting the valve
- F Nozzle
- G Bottom timbers and planking

Injection valve – similar to above except for
- H Copper standards, with keyway used to keep valve completely open
- J Grating – to prevent weeds etc from being sucked in.

Downton Pump (not to scale)

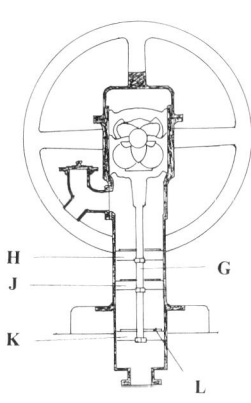 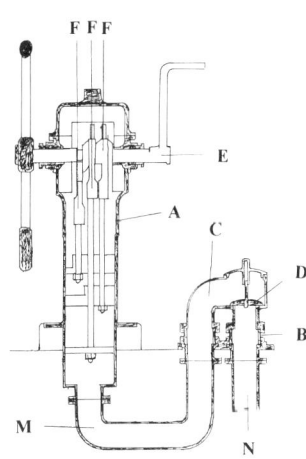

- A Cylinder
- B Suction plate
- C Goose neck
- D Foot valve
- E Crankshaft
- F Cam
- G Rod
- H Upper bucket
- J Middle bucket
- K Lower bucket
- L Valve
- M Pipe from suction plate
- N Suction pipe

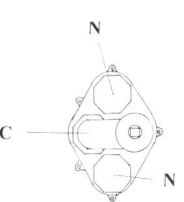

Suction plate

particular pipe, therefore only one pipe can be connected to the pump at any time.

There may be four or five separate pipes (from different places) coming to the suction plate. The water is sucked through the pump and discharged through the delivery nozzle into, for example, a flexible hose for fire fighting or onto the main deck. A ship built by Lairds a few years after the *Alabama* had '240 feet of copper riveted leather hose in 40 feet lengths with brass couplings'. The pumps can probably be used as a syphon (not shown), for example to flood the magazines.

Condenser – Fresh Water
The ship was fitted with a fresh water condenser (probably a Normandy condenser, like the Laird Rams) which is likely to have been fitted below the lower deck, forward of the boiler room. Fresh water was condensed from steam, from the boilers, by means of salt water circulating around the pipes. The fresh water, which was still very hot, was then piped to the water tanks placed around the magazine. This fresh water, when cooled, was the drinking water for the crew.

Water Closets
The Specification (page 23) says that there were a number of water closets fitted. There would be one in the deck houses fitted each side under the bridge. One has been recovered from the wreck and is pictured in the *National Geographic* magazine.

Pipework
There is a large amount of pipework associated with the engine and boilers but unfortunately there do not appear to be any drawings for it. Below is a list which should cover the range of the fixed pipes.

1. Engine
Steam from Boilers to Engine
Water to Injection valve from overboard
Water from Hot well to Boilers via Feed Pump
Water from Hot well to Discharge overboard
Bilge water via Bilge pump to Discharge overboard

2. Boilers
Steam from Boilers to Engine
Steam from Boilers to Fresh Water Condenser
Steam from Boilers to Donkey engine
Water blow-down to overboard

3. Fresh Water Condenser
Steam from Boilers
Water to tanks
Cooling circulating water from and to overboard

4. Downton Pumps
Water from bilges to discharge overboard

5. Magazine
Flood with water from overboard
Drain to Bilges

There were problems with the pipes as Semmes notes in the log (19 April 1863): 'Our steam tubes are leaking badly, and I am afraid the leaks will increase so as to give us trouble. Every time we get up steam, even a few pounds for condensing water, we find that large quantities of hot water flow into the hold; 8 inches escaped in about twelve hours yesterday. Unfortunately, too, this tubing is laid so low in the bottom of the ship as to be out of reach for examination or repairs without being taken up.' The problem must have been solved as there does not appear to be a further reference to it.

Speed
The question of the speed of the *Alabama* is not an easy one to answer. There are quite a variety of figures in the contemporary literature, and the same person can give different figures at different times. The various figures and conditions given by different crew members are listed below.

Semmes
(those marked SC could be by other officers, especially Fullam)

'— sometimes at a speed of upwards of 13 knots' (SC I, p279).
'The guns were now run in and secured, the word passed to the engineers to fire up and give her a full head of steam; the men were piped below, and the *Alabama*, throwing off the silence in which for the last hour she had been wrapped fore and aft, darted off merrily over the rippling waves, in the direction of the island of Blanquilla, at the rate of 14 knots an hour' (SC I, p386).
'— we were scudding at the rate of very little less than 15 knots' (SC II, p204 & SJ 16 October 1863).
'— driving her along 12 & 13 knots per hour, under topgallant sails & a topmast studding sail' (SJ 11 October 1863).
'The speed of the *Alabama* was always greatly over-rated by the enemy. She was ordinarily about a ten-knot ship. She was said to have made 11½ knots on her trial trip, but we never afterward got it out of her. Under steam and sail both, we logged on one occasion, 13¼ knots, which was her utmost speed' (SM, p403 – writing in 1868).

Bulloch
'The day (July 29) was fine and the trials were very satisfactory. We ran several times between the Bell Buoy and the north-west lightship. The average speed was 12.8, the sea being quite smooth, and

the wind light from northwest' (B I, p239).

'We set all sail to a middling fresh breeze, and bowled along 13½ knots, good' (B I, p242)

'— I made the average speed of the *Enrica* to have been 12.89 from Moelfra to the Giants' Causeway' (B I p243).

Fullam
'— at a rate of 13½ knots an hour' (F p6; voyage out to the Azores)
'Got up steam and lowered propeller, with 8lbs. of steam going 9 knots (F p44, 29 October 1862).
Martinique – 'After the pilot had left us, the engines were set agoing, and away we steamed at the rate of 14 knots an hour' (F p53, 19 November 1862).
'Made sail on her, keeping the screw turning with 2 lbs. of steam, and going a comfortable 14 knots' (F p79, 16 January 1863).

Kell
'Her speed, independent, was from 10 to 12 knots; combined, and under favorable circumstances, she could make 15 knots' (CMK p911).
'She had never the very great speed accredited to her, though when under both sail and steam she could be made to run 15 knots an hour' (K p186)'

Sinclair
'Her speed under the most favorable conditions was 13-4 to 13-6 knots by actual observation, or fifteen and three-quarters statute miles' (S p7).

Anderson
'At the time we overhauled her [E Dunbar] we were making 13 knots under sail alone' (A p.419).

I have only found the following references to speed under power. The first is by Fullam in his journal on 29 October 1862: 'Got up steam and lowered propellor, with 8 lbs. of steam going 9 knots'.

The second is in a letter written by E M Anderson: 'The night that we ran the Blockade from Martinique we made twelve knots, with only 11 pounds of steam on.' However, referring to the same time Semmes in his Memoirs (p516) says 'giving my ship a full head of steam, we passed out'.

The last reference is also by Fullam (16 January 1863): 'Made sail on her, keeping the screw turning with 2 lbs of steam, and going a comfortable 14 knots'.

Further details are given in Appendix 2.

DISTANCE RUN – all from Semmes's Log

Sat Oct 17. Distance run 230 miles
Tues Oct 20. Distance run 178 miles
Wed Oct 21. Having made this run in twenty four days & ¾; the distance run being 4410 miles, & the average run per day, 178 miles. I presume this run has seldom been beat.

Conclusion
It would appear that the ship was capable of nearly 15kts under full sail and about 14kts under steam. Under combined sail and steam the speed appears to have been 15kts. For some reason the speeds given by Semmes in his Memoirs are less than those he recorded in his daily log. It would appear that the figures in the log are the more accurate, being compiled at the time, and used for the navigation and safe running of the ship.

A released prisoner, Captain Julius, of the *Tonawanda*, says she is the fastest ship under canvas he has ever been on board of (ORN II, 2 p294).

The *Alabama* was undoubtedly a fast ship.

Departure from Liverpool
'I made the average speed of the *Enrica* to have been 12.89 from Moelfra to the Giants' Causeway' (B I p.243).

The following times are taken from Bulloch and Low for the voyage from Moelfre to the Giants Causeway. The approximate distances between each point are given below, and are in nautical miles. Fullam also has the departure from Moelfre Bay in his journal, saying 'Passing successively the Isle of Man, Ailsa Craig, &c, we hove to off the Giants Causeway'. Apart from the departure time of 2am no other times are given. Looking at the map (page 12) it is unlikely they will have actually passed Ailsa Craig because it is so far off their track.

	Bulloch	*Low*	*Distance*
Under weigh	2.30am	2.30am	Start
Point Lynas	–	3.30am	6
Calf of Man (Chicken Rock)	8.00am	–	42
South Rock	Noon	–	29
The Maidens	–	2.00pm	34
Fairhead	–	4.30pm	} 27
Between Rathlin Island and Fairhead	5pm	–	
Giants Causeway	6pm	5.40pm	17
			155

The time spent sailing is about 15 hours, therefore the average speed is just over 10¼kts, or about 12mph. Bulloch gives the speed as 12.89, no units given. How does he arrive at this figure? All the distances from the pilot would be in nautical miles, and so the speed Bulloch gives should be in knots.

Appendices

APPENDIX 1: IRON-WORK CAPABILITIES OF LIVERPOOL

THIRD NOTICE
MESSRS. LAIRD, SONS, AND CO.'S
BIRKENHEAD IRON WORKS

In offering a few additional illustrations of the vast iron-work capabilities of Liverpool, it cannot be deemed anomalous in our seeking those illustrations on the Cheshire bank of the noble river Mersey. The local proximity of Birkenhead to Liverpool would, under any circumstances, suggest that the conjoined energies of the two towns are essentially necessary to the welfare of each, and this accidental ground of amity is greatly strengthened by the nuptial bond which, a few years ago, linked the two communities together by those indissoluble ties which have made them one for better or worse. Cemented by such a union, they can incalculably benefit each other; and even if it could ever unfortunately have become otherwise, the broad and nursing bosom of the Mersey must, in the eyes of all the rest of the world, have continued to unite them inseperably in the friendly regards of mankind. Such being the case, the propriety of seeking on the western margin of the estuary our third and probably most striking illustration of what knowledge and perseverance, combined with enterprise and adaptive skill, can effect in the way of forwarding the beneficial industry of the community cannot be doubted, far less disputed. This will probably become more distinctly self-evident when it is borne in recollection that probably the most important use to which iron has been applied in modern times is to be found in its adaptation to the numerous and interesting purposes of shipbuilding. Many years ago the intuitive sagacity of the late Mr. Wm. Laird manifested itself in various ways. Conspicuous among these was his early perception and advocacy of the propriety of applying iron as the principal material in the art of shipbuilding. This opinion he entertained and boldly advocated long before such a view obtained the concurrence of popular conviction. Another indication of his prescience consisted in his rooted belief that Birkenhead, then, to common eyes presenting no very direct evidence of the fact, possessed many, if not all, the natural elements of a great and prosperous commercial emporium. Both of these advanced and frequently disputed views have within a comparatively brief period been incontrovertibly realized. Iron, as the best material for shipbuilding is now all but universally admitted; the rapid increase of Birkenhead, and above all, the extraordinary development of the capacious and admirably adapted works established at Birkenhead by his son, the present head of the firm, and carried on by him and his sons, afford additional and irrefragable proof of the sound judgement which foresaw and advocated both.

Somewhat better than three years ago we felt pride in giving a detailed account of those extensive works, which were originated by Mr. John Laird—who still continues their able conductor—and under his approval carried out by Mr. James Abernethy, C.E., of London. In the description to which we now refer the works were properly pointed out as in all respects complete, and they had even provided themselves admirably suited to all the purposes of iron shipbuilding on the most extensive scale. Since then, however, so efficiently have the capabilities of these works been made demonstrably available that even the most formidable operations connected with the construction or repair of iron ships, of whatever class, have been entrusted to the executive skill and intrepidity which pervades every department of this vast establishment. If evidence of this were demanded, Messrs. Laird might with safety take the incredulous into their premises, and desiring him to 'look around,' leave the issue of his inquiry to his own conviction; but as we do not possess such a privilege, and are unacquainted with the sceptic, we may be permitted in our own homely way to give passing allusion to a few of the more striking indications which have been afforded as to the skill and integrity with which these admirably contrived appliances have been used in forwarding the objects for which they were contrived and brought together.

Up to the present time the total number of ships built and in progress of being built at this establishment amounts to 300 sailing vessels and steamers; of these the total aggregate tonnage is about 130,000 tons, and the aggregate impelling power of the steamers alone is 23,000 horse power. Besides the vessels constructed by them, Messrs. Laird have had a most extensive experience in repairing and strengthening steam vessels of the largest class. Indeed, at the present moment, their largest graving-dock is occupied by the Atlantic paddle-steamship *Hibernia*, of 800 horse-power. This large vessel, it may be remembered, broke down on her first attempted voyage across the Atlantic, and was sent round here to be repaired. A thorough overhaul at once evinced the necessity for giving her such a complete repair as, in the caustic parlance of our Scottish brethren is said to have been required by the 'Hielanman's gun,' which needed a new stock, a new lock,

APPENDIX 1

and a new barrel. The *Hibernia*, if not requiring to be entirely rebuilt, was found to call for additional strength in every part. The whole of her rivets had to be cut out and her construction had to be altered in many important particulars. This large vessel was admitted into Messrs. Laird's large graving-dock in April, and it is not expected that she can be got out again, fully repaired, in less than two or three months; yet such are the vast resources and capabilities of their works that those gentlemen have never had occasion to interrupt their business, or to hesitate in undertaking even the largest contracts. So true is this, that they are at present building a large wooden steam vessel of 1,100 tons. Convinced of the propriety of building under cover, from the experience they had in building thirty gun and mortar boats for Government, Messrs. Laird have constructed a shed under which they are building the vessel now spoken of. In incurring this apparently unnecessary outlay, they are fortified in adhering to their own judgement by the report of a select committee of the House of Commons. The gun and mortar boats built by Mr. Laird, then the only party interested in the establishment, were launched early in 1856, and the committee, in their report dated 13th April 1860, say :- 'Your committee have to report, that in general the gun and mortar boats were not built under cover, and that they were much exposed to the weather, so as to aggravate any original defect in the timber. Mr. Laird constructed roofs on purpose to protect the materials and workmen, and as yet no complaint whatever has been made against the vessels supplied by him; it would, therefore, seem desirable that, on any future case of emergency of the like character, a preference should be given to those builders prepared to construct the vessels under cover.' Apart from this commendation, the accurate observation of Mr. Laird, and his desire to give the benefit of the knowledge which flowed upon him from experience, to those who might employ him, he has not forgotten the advantage to be derived from 'building under cover,' but has applied that experience to assist in making his work the best that can be turned out.

This digression has somewhat mislead us from the purpose of pointing out the capabilities of Messrs. Laird's establishment by reference to the magnitude of their operations and contracts. In continuation of that purpose, let us refer to the fact, that upon the blocks from which, so lately as Saturday last, they launched a new and elegant ship, iron-built, named the *Orient*, 950 tons, constructed for Messrs. Clint and Co., of Liverpool, they will immediately proceed to lay down the new iron troop ship *Orontes*, of about 3,000 tons and 500 horse-power, for the construction of which Messrs. Laird were commissioned by the Lords of the Admiralty in July last. It should be added, however, that considerable progress has already been made in forming and bending the framing of this large vessel. The last process is an exceedingly formidable one, as well as one of great nicety, the ultimate form and strength of the vessel being altogether dependent on the successful manipulation of these large and durable masses of iron which must be moulded with the most scrupulous accuracy. Besides the new vessels already specified, they are also busied in the completion of an exceedingly elegant steamer of light draft of water, intended for river navigation in South America. This beautiful yacht-like steam-clipper is named the *Beelam*, and is propelled by oscillating engines of 180 horse-power. She is to draw only about six feet of water, and is expected to be a very swift sailer. Messrs. Laird are also busy in fitting out a number of river barges, intended to be taken to pieces and shipped to their destination on rivers in South America; and they have also nearly ready for delivery a steam tug-boat of great power. In addition to all these, and another important commission to which allusion will presently be made, they are busily employed in conferring on the *Columbia*, another of the Atlantic Steam Navigation Company's vessels, a series of repairs and improvements similar to those on the *Hibernia*. It is true that having at present only one graving dock large enough to contain this last class of paddle steamers, they have agreed to rent for a few months the graving dock of Messrs. Clover and Royle, in which the repairs of the *Columbia* are being carried out; notwithstanding which, the accommodation of their own graving docks and yard seem almost equal to any emergency.

In short the capabilities of this important establishment are altogether unequalled in the building yard or graving docks of any private individual or firm in the kingdom. This important fact is fully, although only incidentally, borne out by the evidence given by Admiral Robinson, Comptroller of the Navy, in his examination before a Parliamentary commission relative to the extension of the Chatham Dock Yard. The evidence was presented to both houses on the 16th July, 1860. In his evidence the gallant Admiral says, in general terms, that in the private dock yards of the kingdom, all of which he says he has inspected, there are no docks available for the present large class of war ships. The great deficiency he admits being mostly in draught of water; some of them are too narrow; and a great many of them are too short. He then continues, 'The new dock now under alteration at Birkenhead by Mr. Laird, will take in ships of the *Warrior* class; indeed a ship which we are now going to build, 400 feet in length. On comparing it with the dimensions of the ship, I saw that it would hold her: but that is the only dock in the kingdom that will do it.' In continuance of his evidence upon this point, he says, 'I do not hesitate to say that, after a naval engagement, the country that can first repair its ships damaged in action will thereby double its force. In such a case one ship with proper dock and basin accommodation is equivalent to two.' Here then we find incontrovertible evidence of the gigantic and unequalled capacity of this noble dock and building yard, not merely as a local advantage, but as a matter of national importance, by which we are told on the highest authority, one ship can be made 'equivalent to two.' Surely this will be admitted as a conclusive proof of the vast 'iron-working capabilities of Liverpool,' for the kind of ships referred to, are all iron ships.

The testimony alluded to, however, complimentary although it undoubtedly is, is not the only, or even the most practical illustration of the value of such an establishment. The Lords of the Admiralty, convinced alike of the capabilities of the building yard, and by the experience of the thorough integrity of its owners, have commissioned the Messrs. Laird to build an iron-clad vessel larger than the *Warrior*, indeed 400 feet long, the kind of vessel Admiral Robinson referred to in his evidence as one which could be accommodated in the graving dock of Messrs. Laird, although he said there was no other dock in the kingdom, except the Government docks, into which she could be taken. Indeed, further than that, he believed, but was not sure, that there 'is a dock at Southampton which will possibly take ships of the *Warrior*'s class,' but for such a purpose, says he, 'There is nothing whatever in the Thames; there is nothing in the Humber, and nothing in the Tyne.' Not content with having graving docks large enough to repair vessels of the size referred to, Messrs. Laird have struck out the bold as well as novel idea of building the gigantic iron-cased frigate *Captain* [later *Agincourt*] in a graving dock instead of on blocks and a slip, as has hitherto been the practice. This ship, which has been recently ordered by the Lords of the Admiralty, is to be a screw propeller, of about 7,000 tons and 1,250 horse-power, and will be built in their graving dock No. 3. To extend the efficiency of this already very large and commodious dock, it is to be deepened and otherwise altered, not merely with a view to give more facility for constructing the *Captain* with ease and rapidity, but also for the purpose of making it a deep water graving dock, capable of taking in vessels of this class for repair, a want which is now being greatly felt by the Government of this country. That no time may be lost in the construction of this vast iron cased floating castle, the iron framing, the woodwork, and the plates will be in rapid and steady preparation while the requisite alterations are being made to the dock in which she is to be built.

The alterations of such docks, as these will constitute a permanent addition to the shipbuilding capacity of Liverpool, and become in themselves even more important than the ship for the accommodation of which they are to be effected. The entrance gates will be widened to eighty feet, and the dock itself deepened so much that at highest spring tides there will be twenty-five feet of water on the blocks. While the *Captain* is in course of construction, the entire area of the dock will be roofed over by a shed 420 feet long and eighty feet wide, lighted by side windows and skylights. Under this immense shed a steam travelling crane is to be erected, so that all the heavy portions of the work and material can be lifted off the quay and lowered into its place, instead of being raised fifty or sixty feet, as would be the case were the vessel built in the ordinary way upon a slip. Besides the immense shed under which the *Captain* is to be built, there will also be constructed along side of it a shed 300 feet long and forty feet wide, for the purpose of making the beams and other large forgings required for this immense ship.

In proceeding in this unusual way with the construction of the great ship referred to, Messrs. Laird contemplate that it will afford many advantages over the ordinary mode. The most conspicuous among these will be found in the absence of risk in launching, which with vessels of such a class must always be great. When completed, the *Captain* will not be launched from the ways, but floated off the blocks on which she was built. From the great depth of water in the dock she will not require to be floated till she is in every respect complete, thus avoiding the inconvenience hitherto experienced with similar ships, although of an inferior class as to size, of having to launch them in a very incomplete state, and having to get a large portion of the armour plates fitted on with very great inconvenience afterwards. To the men employed the advantages will be very great, as by working under a roof, protected at all times, they can proceed without interruption, and will be enabled to pursue their avocations early and late, as the whole will be efficiently lighted with gas. This latter circumstance will also aid materially in ensuring a speedy termination of the work; while, as has already been shown, the work itself will be of a superior character, the whole of the materials being protected from the vicissitudes of weather.

An established axiom in social economics assures us that to stand still is retrograde; and this important fact is fully appreciated and acted on by Messrs. Laird. They seem evidently resolved to keep pace with the times, and to evade no demands which the requirements of their immense trade makes upon them, and also upon their resources. Thus the vast, and as it not long ago appeared gigantic and complete series of premises, works, and implements which they possessed; and which, in point of fact, appeared to simple-minded spectators almost too large and too comprehensive to be fully occupied, or to have their innumerable appliances called into useful occupation have been overstepped; within a year or two, not only have these extraordinary 'means and appliances to boot' been called into full requisition – more than this, they have been taxed to the full extent of their productive power, and been found in some measure inadequate to the strain. In obedience to the calls of a still growing necessity, one department or branch of a department was made to encroach, by little and little, on the spare space, – the elbow room as it were, – of another, till the whole of the working space has become as thickly studded with productive occupants that they more resemble the clusterings of a beehive than the working halls of the Titans, whose fabulous labours are successfully emulated here, or, to speak with greater accuracy, immeasurably excelled, in magnitude and usefulness. While thus speaking of the encroachments made by one department on the convenience of another, it must not be imagined that we mean to insinuate, far less to state, that the heavy portions of the working departments, are made to jostle each other. On the contrary, these leading features of the establishment remain exactly in the relative positions which they originally occupied; but some spare room has been taken now from one squeezable branch, now from another, to make room for the expansion of some equally elastic and more fortunate one; while on the whole the general demands of the business have become more expansive.

To meet these growing requirements, Messrs. Laird have taken on lease, from the Corporation of Liverpool, a space of about 20,000 square yards of land immediately contiguous to the southern boundary of their original premises, and on this land they are already busy in constructing the large wood steamship previously referred to. Here, also, they have erected suitable apparatus and cover for the construction and shelter of large paddle-wheels for steamships; and here also, in the course of a week or two, will be put up large sheds for additional smithies, intended to facilitate the construction of the great ironclad ship. Among the improvements immediately about to be made in these works is the erection of a new mould-room, 150 feet long by 60 feet wide, in addition to the one already in use, which is 120 feet long by 60 feet wide. In the extended space thus obtained there will be ample room for laying down on the full scale the different lines of the great *Captain*. New punching presses and rolls of the largest size and best design are also in course of construction; and, in short, every appliance which can be desired for more efficiently carrying on the operations of these works is in course of being practically carried out.

The engine and boiler departments of these works have also been greatly extended, while their previously simple resources have been enormously augmented. The engine shops are full of tools of the best construction, made by the best makers in the kingdom, and some of them are of sufficient size and power to execute the work required for engines of the largest size and highest class. As an illustration of this the steam cylinders of the *Persia* and *Scotia* are each about 100 inches in diameter, and these are deservedly looked on as of immense – indeed, as of extraordinary – size; but the machinery in the boring mills of this establishment is capable of turning out steam cylinders of 120 inches in diameter. Besides the machinery already referred to, there are planing machines and lathes of the largest size and best construction; and among the additional facilities about to be afforded to the working of the splendid machinery alluded to, is a new erecting shop, which is to be 120 feet long, 60 feet wide, and 35 feet high.

In the present erecting shops there are now in course of construction several pairs of marine engines. Among them are two pairs of screw-propeller engines for the Admiralty; one pair of screw-propeller engines of 150 horse-power each, or 300 horse-power collectively; one pair of diagonal engines of 400 horse-power, on the plan which has been found to work most successfully in several vessels which have been already built by Messrs. Laird. Several other diagonal engines of the same construction are in different stages of advancement, together with a pair of oscillators of 180 horse-power. In short, there are now in these works, in course of active preparation, a number of steam-engines having an aggregate about 1,500 horse-power. From these few facts, hurriedly put together, some idea of the capabilities of the engine department of this establishment may easily be formed; and extensive as these already are, they will be increased to an extraordinary extent when the new erecting shop has been completed.

Before taking leave of this most important and most interesting establishment, we cannot resist allusion to the enormous crane which is erected on the north quay of the large paddle-steamer graving dock. This important implement of labour is of large dimensions and vast power, a condensed idea of both of which may probably be formed from the simple statement that it is capable of lifting fifty tons, and is most complete in all its machinery and particulars. It is placed on a traverse, and so admirably constructed that it can be worked all round a horizontal circle. This enormous implement confers many advantages on the establishment, conspicuous among which is the advantage it offers in connexion with the graving dock for putting boilers and machinery of the largest size on board the vessels they are meant to impel, without the trouble, expense, and risk of carting them to a distance.

From the preceding notes it will be readily obvious that in possessing such an establishment, so employed, and so managed, Liverpool is entitled to claim a very high place as to her iron-work capabilities, as applied to shipbuilding, and the supply of steamships and engines of the highest class. Indeed, from the concurrent testimony of the facts stated, and of the competent witnesses cited, there is just reason to claim for the Birkenhead Ironworks a status and a consideration second to none in the kingdom, or the world.

(From the Liverpool *Albion*, 7 October 1861)

APPENDIX 2: SPEED AND POWER

Speed – Calculations

The results of the two trial trips are:

Trial Date	12 June	29 July
Engine RPM	65	60
Indicated Horse Power (IHP)	1001	914
Steam Pressure (lbs)	–	20
Ship displacement (tons)	1067	1421

Unfortunately the speed is not noted for either of the trials in the (Laird) book. The figures given by other people are not clear.

Bulloch says (Vol 1, p239) the average speed was 12.8 (over several runs on 29 July). Semmes (*Memoirs*, p403) says 11½kts on her trial trip (but not which one). Bulloch does not state the units of speed - knots or miles per hour (1 knot = 1 nautical mile per hour =1.15 miles per hour) but it is reasonable to assume it is knots.

Power Losses

The Indicated Horse Power is the power produced in the cylinders of the engines. The power actually used by the propeller is less because of losses due to friction in the engine (cylinders, air pump etc), in the bearings of the propeller shaft and the slip of the propeller. The power to overcome the ship's resistance is called the Effective Horse Power (EHP). For wooden ships it is generally regarded that the EHP is only about 40 per cent of the IHP, a figure that will vary from ship to ship. Therefore less than half the power produced by the engine is actually used to drive the ship.

Nominal Horse Power

The Nominal Horse Power is a means of comparing different engines which is based on a steam pressure of 7lbs per square inch. In reality the IHP will be from three to four times the NHP.

From White, *Manual of Naval Architecture* (1894), p537.

Nominal Horse Power = (7 x area of piston x piston speed)/33,000

Where area of piston = $2463in^2$

piston speed = 2 x stroke x RPM
= 2 x 2.25ft x 65
= 292.5ft per minute

Therefore NHP = 153

For both cylinders NHP is approximately 300

APPENDIX 3: PROPELLER

The propeller on the Laird model has a diameter of 14ft 3in and a pitch angle of 35°. The pitch of a propeller is the distance the propeller would advance during one complete revolution. Therefore, using these two numbers the pitch of the propeller on the Laird model is equal to 31ft. It can be seen that this distance will depend on the pitch angle: the greater the angle the greater the distance. However, a propeller is working in water and the advance of the propeller is less than it would be if it were, for example, a screw going into a solid such as wood. This is a condition known as slip, which is the ratio of the actual advance through the water divided by the theoretical advance.

Unfortunately the trials results of the *Alabama* do not appear to have survived, but there are figures available for other Laird-built ships. The following figures for slip are from the Dimensions and Particulars Books (Book 2, p114).

Scorpion	21 per cent
Wivern	25 per cent
Huascar	10 per cent
Minerva	19 per cent

Speed

From Indicator diagrams.

June 12	65 RPM	1001 ihp
July 29	60 RPM	914 ihp

—— trials (July 29) —— average speed was 12.8 (should be knots) (Bulloch I p239), but unfortunately there is no guarantee that this was the speed when they did the indicator diagram.

According to Semmes (SM, p403) the speed on trial trip was 11½kts. This is 13.2mph and is probably not the trial figure quoted by Bulloch of 12.8 – units assumed to be knots.

It is possible the 11½kts refers to the first trial trip, on 12 June, but this is unlikely based on the simple assumption that a higher propeller RPM gives a higher ship speed.

A calculation for the size of the propeller using contemporary practice is given below and is based on 'A Treatise on the Screw Propeller' by John Bourne, 1867 – Scientific principles, p.252

Screw disc generally has about $1ft^2$ of area for every 2½ to $3ft^2$ of immersed transverse section

Alabama - immersed section 362.2ft² (from Book of Elements)

Therefore using the figure of 1ft² for every 2¾ft² of immersed surface gives the following:

Disc area = 366.2/2.75 = 133
Diameter of screw = sqrt (disc area* 4/pi) = 13.0ft
Pitch of screw = diameter* 1.25 = 16.25ft
Length of screw = pitch/6 = 2 ft 9in

Therefore the ideal size would appear to be 13.0ft diameter.

The water above the centre of propeller shaft at 14ft draught is 6.0ft. Therefore the tip of the blade will break the surface of the water at normal draught conditions. I have only found one set of draughts in the log (25 November 1862) which were 15ft 4in aft and 14ft 10in fwd. Even with this trim of 6in by the stern the tip of the propeller is still clear of the water.

This situation seems unlikely, but trials with the *Flying Fish* in 1856 with a Griffiths screw had the tip of the blade from 11¼in to 1ft 5¼in above the water.

(1) Using the figures calculated for this propeller, and the design RPM, gives;

Speed = (pitch* RPM* 60)/6080
= 16.25* 65* 60/6080kts
= 10.4kts – with no slip

Assuming a slip of 15 per cent give a speed of 10.4* 0.85 = 8.8kts Both speeds are lower than anything quoted by Bulloch or Semmes.

(2) Using the figures from the Laird model propeller, and the design RPM, gives;

Speed = (pitch* RPM* 60)/6080
= 31* 65* 60/6080kts
= 19.9kts – with no slip

Again assuming a slip of 15 per cent give a speed of 19.9* 0.85 = 16.9kts. This time both speeds are higher than anything quoted by Bulloch or Semmes.

Therefore it would appear that the pitch of the propeller is between the figures from the model and that calculated from contemporary practice. It is hoped that excavation of the wreck will provide the answer of the diameter and pitch of the propeller.

APPENDIX 4: POWDER

Shells

The powder in the rifled shell recovered from the stern frame of the *Kearsarge* is quoted as 2.44lbs. Books give varying figures for the other shells but the following seem to be average.

Shell	Powder	Number carried
8in	2¼lbs	70
7in	2.44lbs	70
32pdr	1lb	210

The total weight of powder to fill all the shells is approximately 540lbs (loose powder, shells to be filled as required).

Charges for Ordinary Firing

According to Bulloch, 'The powder on board the *Alabama* was manufactured and put up into cartridges especially for her by Messrs Curtiss and Harvey' (B I p286).

Taking average figures for each gun gives, for both shot and shell:

Gun	Powder	Number
8in	10lbs	140
7in	10lbs	210
32pdr	8lbs	420

The total weight of powder for firing is approximately 6860lbs – in cartridges

Totals

For shells	540lbs	loose
For charges	6860lbs	in cartridges
Total	7400lbs	

The amount of powder carried in casks from the *Agrippina* was 6184lbs and 3900lbs in barrels, a total of 10,084lbs.

Canisters

Maguire reported 'Messrs Sidderley & Co of William St. have got the order to make the copper powder cans which are of a new patent. . . . There are 200 powder cases for her, 60 of which are delivered and the remainder to be delivered by the end of the week. The screws of them cost £2 each'. (see page 40) That the tanks were made of copper is confirmed by Semmes (ORN I, 3 p663). The magazine tanks cost £616 (see page 29) – this must be the cost of the powder canisters.

A full-size powder case contained 200lbs of loose powder, but less than that if the powder was in cartridges (depending on the size of the cartridge). The cases were also usually in half (100lbs) and quarter (50lbs) sizes, but unfortunately Maguire does not say what size they were.

If there were 200 cases at £616 this means each one cost approximately £3/1/7, and if the screws cost £2 the actual canister was only just over £1. In a letter dated 9 May 1863 (ORN II, 2 p420) Fawcett Preston offered to make powder tanks of 200lbs size for the following costs:

Copper, tinned	£ 7/10/–
Zinc	c£4
Block tin	£10

It would therefore seem unlikely that Messrs Sidderley & Co could produce a 200lb powder canister for just over £3, especially if it was of a new patent. Therefore it would appear that either the canisters were smaller than 200lbs capacity or there were not 200 in total. Maguire claimed sixty had been delivered but if this was the total number, and there were to be no more, the cost of each canister would be £10/5/4. If the canisters were of 200lbs capacity and there were 200 of them, they would hold up to 40,000lbs of powder (about 17½ tons). This total is about four times the quantity carried in casks and barrels from the *Agrippina*. However, if there were only sixty canisters they would hold about 12,000lbs compared with the 10,084lbs on the *Agrippina*.

The canisters were made to a new patent, according to Maguire. It is not clear which patent is being referred to, but one which could fit was granted to Emile Peltier of Paris, France. This was dated 27 August 1861 (No. 2132) and called 'Metallic Boxes', and was sealed 14 February 1862. It was for an improvement in the way of manufacturing metallic boxes and the machinery to be used. The method was claimed to be particularly suitable for boxes which are for gunpowder or other similar articles. The boxes are formed by folding the edges together and a hole left in the top can be closed by means of a moveable lid. From the drawings in the Fawcett Preston Archive it does not appear that their canisters were made by this means. I think this is another situation where the answer can only come from the exploration of the wreck. However, I think it reasonable to assume that there were not 200 powder cases (of 200lbs capacity) on board as suggested by Maguire, only the sixty he saw.

APPENDIX 5: MASTS, SAILS AND SAIL AREAS

Original Information

The information on sail plans falls into two main areas. Firstly there are the plans from the US National Archives and the University of Alabama, both of which contain tables of spar sizes. These plans have the same date – 9 October 1861 – a few months after the contract was signed and refer to the ship as proposed. Only the first plan will be considered because the second one has been both copied and reduced, thereby introducing the possibility of unknown errors. Secondly there is the information concerning the ship as actually built. This consists of the Laird sail plan and the entries in the data books, the main one being in the Book of Elements. There is also the undated sail plan in the Merseyside Maritime Museum (called the MMM plan for convenience here), which will also be considered thereby making three different plans.

The details from the Book of Elements are repeated below.

Area of sails	14661ft^2
Centre of effort of sail	
1. Before middle of Load Water Line	17.4ft
2. Above Load Water Line	51.3ft
Moment of Sails above Load Water line	748,356ft^3

Plans

The origin for the plans is the point where the AP (aft perpendicular) crosses the LWL (Load Water Line).

The Laird sail plan is assumed to be based on the ship as built rather than as planned. The plan appears at first glance to be the same as the two earlier ones except for the omission of one sail from each mast. Measurements show that the spars agree with the figures given in the tables of the earlier two plans (there are slight differences, but they are not significant). However, there are changes to the length of a number of masts. The increase is variable and is given below. There appears to be no change in the length of the royal masts or the poles.

Lower Mizzen mast	18in
Lower Main mast	15in
Lower Main mast head	3in
Lower Fore mast	15in
Mizzen Topmast	12in
Main Topmast	6in
Fore Topmast	6in
Main Topgallant	6in
Fore Topgallant	6in

Overlaying the US National Archives plan on the Laird plan shows the differences (page 40).

The Laird sail plan has one error that came to light when measuring the length of the spars to check against the figures in the tables. The foresail is not symmetrical on the fore yard but one side is set in by the equivalent of 12in when compared to the other at the head of the sail. The sail plan as drawn is the one used in the following work, *ie* with the error.

CENTRE OF EFFORT

The centre of effort of the sail plan is found by first finding the centroid of each sail and then taking horizontal and vertical moments and summing them to find the centroid for the whole plan. Detailed calculations have been done for the sail plans and the results are given in the table below.

For comparison the calculation has also been tried on the MMM sail plan. As only the three gaffs are shown on the drawing the square sails from the Lairds plan have been used. Therefore the areas will be the same but they obviously have a different centre. This will not be very accurate but should give an indication of the position of the centre of effort.

Source	Area (ft^2)	VCG above LWL	LCG fwd mid LWL
Book of Elements	14,661	51.3	17.4
US National Archives	14,473	48.9	16.4
Laird	14,377	50.7	17.3
MMM	14,192	50.3	18.2

The details from the Book of Elements were given earlier, but there is a mistake with one of the numbers, because when the Area is multiplied by the Centre of Effort the result is not the value given for the Moment. To repeat the numbers:

Area of sails	14661ft^2
Centre of effort above LWL	51.3ft
Moment of sails above LWL	748,356ft^3

The moment of sails is the product of the area and the lever = 14,661 x 51.3 = 752,109ft^3.

At least one of the numbers in the Book of Elements must be wrong as can be seen by the difference in the two resultant moments.

The calculation is done by summing the areas and moments of each individual sail and then dividing the total moment by the sum of the areas to give the resultant lever. The error could be in calculating any one of the numbers or simply in wrongly copying them into the Book of Elements and subsequently other data books.

The figures worked from the plans (from the table above) show some interesting variations (if we ignore the MMM plan because of its unknown origin). The most noticeable differences occur in the VCG (Vertical Centre of Gravity or Centre of Effort above LWL) of the sail area which vary by more than 2ft between the early plan and the later data. From the Laird plan it appears that the length of the lower and top masts was increased over the values proposed and this is reflected in the increase of VCG. It also appears from the Inboard Profile plan that the deck height on the lower deck was increased and when combined with the longer masts leads to an increase in vertical height for the centre of the sail area.

In light of the confusing data from the Book of Elements it is considered that the masts were increased in length, as noted above, and that the Laird Sail plan is a better representation of the ship as built.

APPENDIX 6: HULL FORM

About ten years ago (1990) an investigation was carried out into the shape of the hull of the *Alabama*. The basis for this investigation was the receipt of a body plan of the *Alabama* based on the model in the Mariners' Museum. This plan was significantly different to an existing plan which had been modified from lines taken originally from the Cammell Laird model. This latter plan was drawn by W E Geoghegan. The lines of the Cammell Laird model were taken off by George Campbell in 1936. He produced a body plan of nine unequally-spaced sections and no waterlines or bow or buttock lines. This plan was passed to the Smithsonian Institution where it was redrawn in the late 1950s by Geoghegan following the discovery of the plans in the US National Archives. When the Mariners' Museum body plan had been received it was compared with Geoghegan's and considerable differences were noted which seemed to run contrary to visual observations of the two models.

The opportunity was taken to compare Geoghegan's sections with the Cammell Laird model and there were noticeable differences. These were to be expected bearing in mind the changes made to Campbell's lines so it was decided to take-off the lines of the Cammell Laird model again, there being no point in re-drawing Campbell's lines as there were not enough sections. Consequently sections were taken at 16 stations along the hull and the lines drawn to produce a 23-station body plan.

Therefore there have been three lines plans developed from the two models (the first two from the Laird model), which are listed below.

1. Geoghegan (Geog)
2. Cammell Laird (CLS)
3. Mariners' Museum (MM)

All three lines plan have been drawn or redrawn on computer with a body plan of 23 standard displacement stations which makes it very easy to overlay one on top of another. From this it was seen that the three sets of lines are similar in the fore body but that Geoghegan's lines varied considerably from the other two in the middle and after bodies. The stem and stern profiles were plotted together for comparison along with those from the plans in the US National Archives and gave very good correlation.

Hydrostatic Data

Two books contain valuable details with respect to draughts and displacements. The Dimensions and Particulars of Vessels gives nine draughts and their corresponding displacements. There is also some information in the Book of Elements.

A set of hydrostatics was run for each of the three hull forms using a commercial program for each of the known draughts and trims. One problem was that each model hull form has a different length and beam (see below) so it was decided to change them all to the dimensions given in the Book of Elements (213ft 8in length and 32ft beam) using a computer program.

Hull Lines	Length	Beam
Geoghegan	214ft 0in	32ft 0in
Cammell Laird	214ft 0in	31.678ft
Mariners' Museum	207ft 3in	31.292ft

These results are summarised in Tables 1 and 2 at the end. These show that all the displacements (Table 1) are lower than the original but in each case the Cammell Laird model is closest to the original. Table 2 gives the comparison between the hull lines and the data from the Book of Elements. For the modified lines each model has some values close to the original.

Conclusion

The three lines plans are constructed from dimensions lifted off the models and raise the question of accuracy. We do not know what plans were used originally to make the models, how accurately the models were built or if they have been subject to any distortion, warping etc over the years.

There will be slight errors in lifting the figures from the hulls as they are at a scale of 1:48. However, the lines plan of the Cammell Laird model appears to be reasonably fair as lifted, the same for the Mariners' Museum model. Geoghegan's lines plan has been modified to an unknown degree over Campbell's original drawing.

Comparisons of the displacements of the three plans, calculated by computer program, with the original figures imply that the new lines from the Cammell Laird model are the closest to the ship. However, there is very little difference really between the two models.

Table 1
Displacements (Tons)

Mean Draught	Original	Geog.	CLS (modified to 213.8ft)	MM
9ft 8in	690	678	687	670
10ft 8⅞in	832	813	828	809
11ft 9½in	978	950	971	950
12ft 0in	1007	977	998	976
12ft 1in	1016	989	1011	989
12ft 5in	1067	1033	1057	1035
13ft 0in	1149	1113	1139	1116
14ft 0in	1294	1252	1284	1259
15ft 0in	1438	1395	1432	1406

Table 2

All at 15ft LWL	Original	Geog.	CLS (modified to 213.8ft)	MM
LCB rel. to ⊗	-0.75	1.17	0.42	-0.17
LCF rel. to ⊗	-2.37	-1.673	-2.007	-2.167
Midship Section	362.2	364.4	356.0	353.7
Waterplane Area	5185.3	5055.4	5234.2	5217.7
TPI	12.35	12.04	12.46	12.42
KMT	15.85	15.49	15.83	16.03
VCB	8.52	8.47	8.54	8.58
Centroid of Midship Section	8.15	8.07	8.19	8.22

Index

Page numbers in *italics* refer to illustrations.

Adams, Charles Francis 7, 11, 29
Agrippina 11, 12, 43, 44, 104, 132, 134, 187, 188
Alabama, CSS
  battle with USS *Hatteras* 12-13, *45*
  Boiler Book 28, 37, 38
  Book of Elements 28, 34, 35, 46, 56, 68, 187, 188, 189, 190
  Contract 18, 19, 20
  description (newspaper) 44-6
  Estimate of Building Costs 28, 32-4
  First Cost Accounts 28, 29-31
  Indicator Diagrams 28, 38
  launch 9
  Masts and Spars
    original dimensions 27
    revised dimensions 37
  models of 60-5
  paintings of 57-60
  photographs of 48-57
  propeller Appendix 3
  sea trials 10-11, *11*
  sinking 13
  speed Appendix 2
  Specification 20-5
  Specification, Copy 25-7
  wreck, discovery of 13, *13*
  see also under Drawings
Anderson, Midshipman Edward *50*
Armstrong, Lieutenant *52*

Bahama 7, 11, 12, 43, 128, 132
Birkenhead Iron Works 8, 10, *10*, Appendix 1
Blakely, Captain 106, 115
Books by crew 46

Bulloch, James Dunwoody 7, 8, 9, 10, 11, 12, 13, 15, 16, 17, 18, 28, 40, 41, 42, 46, 60, 61, 81, 104, 116, 128, 180, 181, 186, 187
Burgoyne, General Sir John 7, 9
Butcher, Mathew 10, 11, 12, 41, 42, 43
Byrne, A E & Co 7, 31, 40

Campbell, George 189, 190
Cherbourg 13, 46, 49, 57, 79, 113, 128
Cuddy, Gunner Thomas C *50*

Davenport pottery 10, *12*
de Lôme, Dupuy 28, 36
Description (newspaper) 44-46
Dimensions & Particulars of Vessels 28, 29, 35-7, 186, 190
Drawings
  ammunition *113, 120, 125, 131-2*
  below lower deck *82-3*
  boilers *176-7*
  engine *139-75*
  funnel *178*
  guns *104-29*
  hull *66-77*
  lower deck *81-3*
  masts and yards *84-9*
  propeller *173-5, 178*
  sails and rigging *90-103*
  upper deck *77-81*
Dudley, Thomas Haines 7, 10, 29, 57

Fawcett Preston & Co 7, 8, 11, 17, 28, 106, 107, 128, 131, 134, 188
Florida (*Oreto*), CSS 7, 8, 9, 10, 11, 13, 17, 39, 40, 41, 106, 107
Fraser Trenholm & Co 7, 8, 40

Geoghegan, W E 189, 190
Great Float, Birkenhead Docks 10, 11, 42

Hatteras, USS 12, 44, 45
Hoole, William Stanley 15, 16, 17

Kearsarge, USS 7, 13, 113, 115, 134, 187
Kell, Lieutenant 45, *48, 49, 50*

Laird Rams 7, 10, 181, 182
Lairds 7, 8, 10, 11, 15, 16, 18, 38, 39, 40, 41, 42, 44, 46, 60, 143, 178, 181, Appendix 1
Liverpool *9*

Maguire, Mathew 7, 9, 10, 11, 29, 74, 78, 81, 187, 188
  report 38-44
Mallory, Stephen 7, 8, 13, 18
Miller, W C (shipbuilders) 7, 8, 41

Nassau 9, 11, 12, 42, 43
North, James 13, 18

Oreto see *Florida*

Praya Bay, Terceira 10, 12, 45

Russell, Lord 7, 29

Semmes, Raphael 7, 11-3, 28, 43, 44-5, 47, *48, 53, 54*, 57, 60, 81, 82-3, 85, 88, 94, 104, 128, 131-3, 136, 139, 176, 181, 182, 186-7
Sinclair, Lieutenant *52*
Singapore 13, 44, 54, 55, 56, 60, 65, 81, 87, 94
South Africa 44, 48, 60, 94

Tuscarora, USS 11

Walters, Samuel 56-8, 60, 65, 94